Sources on Polish Jewry
at the
Central Archives for the History
of the Jewish People

Compiled and edited by
Hanna Volovici, Witold Medykowski,
Hadassah Assouline and Benyamin Lukin

(Based on the 1988 edition edited by Adam Teller)

Avotaynu Foundation
2004

Requests for permission to make copies of any part of this publication should be addressed to:

Avotaynu Foundation, Inc.
155 N. Washington Ave
Bergenfield, NJ 07621

Published in the United States of America

Library of Congress Cataloging-in-Publication Data

Volovici, H.
 Sources on Polish Jewry at the Central Archives for the History of the Jewish People / compiled and edited by Hanna Volovici ... [et al.].
    p. cm.
 "Based on the 1988 edition edited by Adam Teller."
 ISBN 0-9668021-4-4
 1. Jews—Poland—Sources—Bibliography—Catalogs. 2. Jews—Poland—History—Sources—Bibliography—Catalogs. 3. Poland—Ethnic relations—Sources—Bibliography—Catalogs. 4. Arkhiyon ha-merkazi le-toldot ha-'am ha-Yehudi—Catalogs. I. Title.

 Z6373.P7V65 2004
 [DS135.P6]
 016.9438'004924—dc22

                                                           2004010593

Contents

Introduction

In 1988 the Central Archives for the History of the Jewish People published a guide to sources on Polish Jewry, in the original and in microfilm, held at the Central Archives. Great pride was taken in the 300 cities, towns and villages for which the Central Archives had succeeded in collecting material, ranging from the 15th to the 20th century.

A number of years passed. Archives in the former Soviet Union opened their doors, making a wealth of material available to the public. The Archives has succeeded since then in gathering millions of pages in "Soviet", Polish, Austrian and German government archives. It was therefore decided to issue a revised and much broadened edition of the first guide, relating to approximately 1000 cities, towns and villages and ranging from the 14th to the 20th centuries.

The vast majority of the material consists of documentation created by the non-Jewish authorities under whose rule the Jews lived. Of the material created by Jewish communities and organizations, little has survived. (Some of this material found its way into government archives such as in Kraków, Łódź and Lwów and parts of these collections were microfilmed for the Central Archives).

The present guide, in spite of its size, is really only a sample of the kinds of material relating to the Jews of Poland that can be found in archives. In the first place, the Central Archives has, as yet, (for financial reasons) been able to conduct surveys in only a relatively small number of archives (15 in Poland and several more in Austria and the former Soviet Union).

Even in these archives, many record groups still await examination. Indeed, the only archives to date in which all of the material was examined for Jewish content, is the state archives at Radom, Poland. (a guide to this archives is available in print, as noted on the Central Archives' web site).

Thousands of pages, listing the millions of files and documents identified in these survey activities, are available on the Central Archives' premises in Jerusalem. Of this material, only a small selection has been microfilmed, and of the material microfilmed, only those files and documents catalogued up to the end of the year 2000 were entered in the present guide. The remainder warrants an additional guide or an extended visit to Jerusalem.

Finally, the genealogists perusing this guide will note an almost total absence of birth, marriage and death registers. Indeed, it has generally not been the policy of the Central Archives to microfilm these sources, which are relatively easy to access. The emphasis was rather on material less accessible to the layman or even the trained historian. A glance through the guide will reveal sources found in highly unexpected places, such as lists of Grodno Zionist organizations, found at the State Archives in Uzbekistan!

This Guide

This guide is arranged in the same fashion as the first guide (and in accordance with the principle by which all the Archives' material is arranged)—geographically, beginning with material relating to the Jews of Poland as a whole, followed by regional entries and then by individual entries for each community, in alphabetical order.

Each town name is accompanied by the district (*powiat*) and province (*województwo*) to which it belongs. When a particular town is itself the seat of its district, only the province name is noted.

The material consists of originals, photocopies and microfilms. Virtually all of the originals are of Jewish provenance, while the photocopies and microfilms are generally of non-Jewish provenance. Some Jewish material was located and microfilmed in official repositories, (such as the Centrum Judaicum in Berlin and state archives in Lwów, Kraków and Łódź).

The descriptions are arranged by record groups, in chronological order. The material within each record group is described in chronological order as well.

The borders of Poland by which material is arranged in the Central Archives and in the guide are those which were in effect between the two World Wars. Thus prominent contemporary Polish cities such as Wrocław (Breslau), Szczecin (Stettin) and Gdańsk (Danzig), which were not in Poland between the Wars, are absent from the guide, while Lwów and Wilno, today in the Ukraine and Lithuania, respectively, do appear.

Poland was partitioned three times (in 1772, 1792 and 1795) between Austria, Prussia and Russia, and disappeared as a political entity until after World War I. Material on Polish Jews can therefore be found in, Austrian, German, Russian, Ukrainian and Belarussian as well as in Polish archives. Many documents are accordingly in German, Russian and Ukrainian.

The names of the archives and of the cities in which they are located are cited as they are today. Lwów, for instance, is written L'viv and the archives in this city bear Ukrainian names. The names of the archival record groups, on the other hand, remain in their original languages. The names of the entries, however, are given in their Polish form. German equivalents of Polish names are provided in an appendix.

The languages of the files are given in square brackets. Most of the files are entirely in Polish, in which case, no language is cited.

Hadassah Assouline, Director
The Central Archives for the History of the Jewish People
Jerusalem, Nisan 5764
April 2004

Acknowledgments

Thanks are due to Ms. Rachel Manekin and Ms. Olga Shraberman of the Central Archives' staff for their assistance in editing the guide.

Finally, great thanks are due to the various archives and their staffs, who graciously and patiently enabled the conduct of the survey and microfilming activities, which made this guide possible.

May this guide serve as a memorial to the Jews and communities which once flourished on Polish soil and are no more.

We are grateful for the support received for this project from:

Conference on Jewish Material Claims Against Germany

Hanadiv Foundation

Mr. Danek Gertner of Vienna.

Center for Research on the History and Culture of Polish Jews at the Hebrew University

Abbreviations

Arch.	Archiwum
Bibl.	Biblioteka
Castr.	Castrensia
EKOPO	Evreiskii komitet Obshchestva pomoshchi zhertvam voiny
HIAS	Hebrew Immigrant Aid Society
IKG	Israelitische Kultusgmeinde
Inscr.	Inscriptiones
JDC	Joint Distribution Committee
JTS	Jewish Theological Seminary, New York
Kgl.Reg.	Koenigliche Regierung
m.	Miasto
Man.	Manualia
n.d.	no date
Obl.	Oblata, oblatarum
Oddz.	Oddział
OPE	Obshchestvo rasprostraneniia prosveshcheniia sredi evreev Rossii
OSE	Oeuvre de Secours aux Enfants
OŻPP	Ogólno-Żydowska Partia Pracy
Pow.	Powiat
Prow.	Prowincja
Rel.	Relationes
Woj.	Województwo
Zb.	Zbiór, zbiory

Languages

[E] English
[F] French
[G] German
[H] Hebrew
[L] Latin
[P] Polish
[R] Russian
[Rt] Ruthenian
[U] Ukrainian
[Y] Yiddish

Abbreviations of Archives and Record Groups

Archives in Poland

Archives and Record Groups	Full Name
AGAD	Archiwum Główne Akt Dawnych
AGWAO	Archiwum Gospodarcze Wilanowskie Administracji Opatowskiej
AP	Archiwum Państwowe
ASK	Archiwum Skarbu Koronnego
CWW	Centralne Władze Wyznaniowe
DP	Dokumenty Papierowe i Pergaminowe
GUW	Gubernialny Urząd Włościański
GZŻ	Gubernialny Zarząd Żandarmerii
IT	Inwentarz Tymczasowy
KCWWK	Komisja Cywilno-Wojskowa Województwa Krakowskiego
KP	Kancelaria Prezesa
KrzPiS	Komisja Rządowa Przychodów I Skarbu
KRzSW	Komisja Rządowa Spraw Wewnętrznych
MK	Metryka Koronna
ML	Metryka Litewska
MSW	Ministerstwo Spraw Wewnętrznych
NP	Naczelnik Powiatu
OKŻ	Okręgowy Komitet Żydowski
PAN	Polska Akademia Nauk
PP	Policja Państwowa
RO	Rada Opiekuńcza
ROGK	Rada Opiekuńcza Guberni Kaliskiej
ROPK	Rada Opiekuńcza Powiatu Kaliskiego
RsiRMKW	Rada Stanu i Rada Ministrów Księstwa Warszawskiego
RSKP	Rada Stanu Królestwa Polskiego
SSKP	Sekretariat Stanu Królestwa Polskiego
UW	Urząd Wojewódzki
WA	Wydział Administracyjny
WCPL	Władze Centralne Powstania Listopadowego
WKNZNP	Wyższe Kursy Nauczycielskie Związku Nauczycielstwa Polskiego we Lwowie
WP	Wydział Prawny
ŻIH	Żydowski Instytut Historyczny

Archives in France

Archives	Full Name
AIU	Alliance Israélite Universelle [F]

Archives in Belorussia

Archives	Record Groups	Full Name
NARB		Natsional'nyi Arkhiv Respubliki Belarus' [R]
NIAB		Natsional'nyi Istoricheskii Arkhiv Belarusi [R]
"	Direktsiia narodnykh uchilishch…	Direktsiia narodnykh uchilishch Minskoi gubernii [R]
"	Kantseliariia minskogo gubernatora	Kantseliariia minskogo grazhdanskogo gubernatora [R]

Archives in Lithuania

Archives	Full Name
LCVIA	Lietuvos Centrinis Valstybinis Istorijos Archyvas [Lithuanian]

Archives in Russia

Archives	Record Groups	Full Name
GAOmO		Gosudarstvennyi arkhiv Omskoi oblasti [R]
GARF		Gosudarstvennyi arkhiv Rossiiskoi Federatsii [R]
"	Bomash	Lichnyi arkhiv Meira Bomasha, chlena Gosudarstvennoi Dumy [R]
	Departament politsii…	Departament politsii Ministerstva vnutrennikh del [R]
"	Katsenel'son	Lichnyi arkhiv Aleksandra Katsenel'sona, evreiskogo obshchestvennogo deiatelia [R]
"	Kollektsiia nelegal'nykh izdanii…	Kollektsiia nelegal'nykh izdanii (listovok I broshur), otlozhivshikhsia v materialakh politseiskikh I sudebnykh organov dorevoliutsionnoi Rossii [R]
"	Marek	Lichnyi arkhiv Petra Mareka, evreiskogo istorika [R]
"	Moskovskoe okhrannoe otdelenie	Otdelenie po okhraneniiu obshchestvennoi bezopasnosti i poriadka v Moskve pri Moskovskom gradonachal'nike [R]
"	Tret'e otdelenie…	Tret'e otdelenie Sobstvennoi Ego Imperatorskogo Velichestva kantseliarii [R]
"	TSEVAAD	Tsentral'noe upravlenie evreiskikh obshchin v Rossii ("TSEVAAD") [R]
"	Val'	Lichnyi arkhiv Viktora fon Valia, general-leitenanta [R]
"	Vsesoiuznoe obshchestvo…	Vsesoiuznoe obshchestvo politkatorzhan i ssyl'noposelentsev [R]
RGADA		Rossiiskii gosudarstvennyi arkhiv drevnikh aktov [R]
"	KFE	Komisja Funduszu Edukacijnego [P]
"	ML	Metryka Litewska [P]
"	Vorontsovy	Rodovoi arkhiv grafov i kniazei Vorontsovykh [R]
RGAVMF		Rossiskii gosudarstvennyi arkhiv voenno-morskogo flota
"	Dubasov	Semeinyi arkhiv Fedora Dubasova, admirala [R]
RGIA		Rossiiskii gosudarstvennyi istoricheskii arkhiv [R]
"	Departament dukhovnykh del…	Departament dukhovnykh del inostrannykh ispovedanii Ministerstva vnutrennikh del [R]
"	Dokumenty iz unichtozhennykh del…	Dokumenty iz unichtozhennykh del Senata i Ministerstva iustitsii (kollektsiia) [R]
"	Glavnoe upravlenie neokladnylh sborov…	Glavnoe upravlenie neokladnylh sborov I kazennoi prodazhi pitei Ministerstva finansov [R]
"	Khoziaistvennyi departament MVD	Khoziaistvennyi departament Ministerstva vnutrennikh del [R]
"	Obshchestvo polnopraviia…	Obshchestvo polnopraviia evreiskogo naroda v Rossii [R]
"	OPE	Obshchestvo rasprostraneniia prosveshcheniia sredi evreev Rossii [R]
"	Rimsko-katolicheskaia kollegiia…	Rimsko-katolicheskaia dukhovnaia kollegiia Ministerstva vnutrennikh del [R]
RGVIA		Rossiiskii gosudarstvennyi voenno-istoricheskii arkhiv [R]
"	Kantseliariia glavnogo nachal'nika snabzheniia…	Kantseliariia glavnogo nachal'nika snabzheniia Zapadnogo fronta [R]
"	Kantseliariia nachal'nika shtaba…	Kantseliariia nachal'nika shtaba Zapadnogo fronta [R]
"	Shtab…	Shtab Verkhovnogo glavnokomanduiushchego [R]
"	Voenno-uchenyi arkhiv…	Voenno-uchenyi arkhiv Glavnogo shtaba Voennogo ministerstva [R]
RNB		Rossiiskaia natsional'naia biblioteka [R]
"	Gintsburg	Lichnyi arkhiv barona Davida Gintsburga, vostokoveda i evreiskogo obshchestvennogo deiatelia [R]
"	Kamenskii	Lichnyi arkhiv Abrama Kamenetskogo, filologa i evreiskogo obshchestvennogo deiatelia [R]
TsGIASP		Tsentral'nyi gosudarstvennyi istoricheskii arkhiv Sankt-

Archives	Record Groups	Full Name
		Peterburga [R]
"	"Evreiskaia Starina"	Arkhiv redaktsii zhurnala "Evreiskaia Starina" [R]
TsKhIDK		Tsentr Khraneniia Istoriko-Dokumental'nykh Kollektsii [R]

Archives in Ukraine

Archives	Record Group	Full Name
DAIFO		Derzhavnyi arkhiv Ivano-Frankivs'koi oblasti [U]
"	Komenda Powiatowa PP, Stanisławów	Komenda Powiatowa Policji Państwowej w Stanisławowie [P]
"	Komenda Wojewódzka PP, Stanisławów	Komenda Wojewódzka Policji Państwowej w Stanisławowie [P]
"	Posterunek PP, Śniatyn	Posterunek Policji Państwowej w Śniatyniu [P]
"	Upolnomochennyi Soveta…	Upolnomochennyi Soveta po delam religioznykh kul'tov pri Sovete ministrov SSSR po Stanislavskoi oblasti [R]
"	UW, Stanisławów	Urząd Województwa Stanisławowskiego [P]
DAKhO		Derzhavnyi arkhiv Khmel'nyts'koi oblasti [U]
"	Direktsiia narodnykh uchilishch…	Direktsiia narodnykh uchilishch Podol'skoi gubernii [R]
DALO		Derzhavnyi arkhiv L'vivs'koi oblasti [U]
"	Drogobychskii obkom…	Drogobychskii obkom kommunisticheskoi partii Ukrainy [R]
"	Prokuror…	Prokuror L'vovskoi oblasti [R]
"	L'vovskii obkom…	L'vovskii obkom kommunisticheskoi partii Ukrainy [R]
"	UW, Lwów	Urząd Województwa Lwowskiego [P]
DAOdO		Derzhavnyi arkhiv Odes'koi oblasti [U]
"	Kantseliariia popechitelia…	Kantseliariia popechitelia Odesskogo uchebnogo okruga [R]
"	Popechitel'skii komitet…	Popechitel'skii komitet inostrannykh poselentsev Iuzhnogo kraia Rossii (Evreiskii stol) [R]
DARO		Derzhavnyi arkhiv Rivnens'koi oblasti [U]
DATO		Derzhavnyi arkhiv Ternopil'skoi oblasti [U]
"	Komenda Powiatowa PP	Komenda Powiatowa Policji Państwowej [P]
"	Komitet pomoshchi…	Komitet pomoshchi evreiskomu naseleniiu, postradavshemu v voennykh deistviiakh, otdelenie v Kopychintsakh [R]
"	UW, Tarnopol	Urząd Województwa Tarnopolskiego [P]
DAVO		Derzhavnyi arkhiv Vinnyts'koi oblasti [U]
DAZhO		Derzhavnyi arkhiv Zhytomyrs'koi oblasti [U]
NBANU		Naukova biblioteka Akademii nauk Ukrainy im. Stefanyka, L'viv [U]
TsDIAU, Kyiv		Tsentralnyi derzhavnyi istorychnyi arkhiv Ukrainy, Kyiv [U]
"	Dokumenty, sobrannye…	Dokumenty, sobrannye Evreiskoi istoriko-arkheograficheskoi komissiei pri Vseukrainskoi Akademii nauk (Kollektsiia) [R]
"	Fridman	Lichnyi arkhiv Naftali Fridmana, chlena Gosudarstvennoi Dumy [R]
"	Kantseliariia…general-gubernatora	Kantseliariia kievskogo, podol'skogo i volynskogo general-gubernatora [R]
TsDIAU, L'viv		Tsentralnyi derzhavnyi istorychnyi arkhiv Ukrainy, L'viv [U]
"	Kolektsiia dokumentiv…	Kolektsiia dokumentiv pro finansovo-mainovi spravy evreis'koho naselennia na teritorii Rechi Pospolytoi ta Halychyny [U]
"	Kolektsiia dokumentiv pro katolyts'ki monastyri…	Kolektsiia dokumentiv pro katolyts'ki monastyri, kostely ta okremi parafii na teritorii Pol'shchi, Ukrainy, Bilorusii ta Lytvy [U]

Archives	Record Group	Full Name
"	Kolektsiia lystiv…	Kolektsiia lystiv derzhavnykh, gromads'kikh ta tserkovnykh diiachiv Ukrainy, Pol'shchi, ta inshykh krain [U]
"	Rada Rus'ka	Golovna Rus'ka Rada [U]

Archives in Uzbekistan

Archives	Full Name
TsGAU	Tsentral'nyi gosudarstvennyi arkhiv Uzbekistana [R]

German Equivalents of Polish Place Names

Polish	German	Polish	German
Brodnica	Strasburg	Nowy Tomyśl	Neutomischel
Bydgoszcz	Bromberg	Oborniki	Obornik
Chodzież	Chodziesen/Kolmar	Obrzycko	Obersitzko
Cieszyn	Tessin	Odolanów	Adelnau
Czarnków	Czarnikau	Opatów	Opatow
Czempiń	Czempin	Ostrów Wielkopolski	Ostrowo
Czerniejewo	Schwarzenau	Ostrzeszów	Schildberg
Dobrzyca	Dobberschuetz	Piaski	Sandberg
Donaborów	Louisenhof	Piotrków Kujawski	Kujawien
Fordon	Fordon	Pleszew	Pleschen
Gniezno	Gnesen	Pniewy	Pinne
Gostyń	Gostyn	Pobiedziska	Pudewitz
Grodzisk	Graetz	Połajewo	Polajewo
Grudziądz	Graudenz	Poznań	Posen
Inowrocław	Hohensalza	Pszczyna	Pless
Jaraczew	Jaratschewo	Rakoniewice	Rakwitz
Jarocin	Jarotschin	Raszków	Raschkow
Jastrzębie Zdrój	Koenigsdorff	Rawicz	Rawitsch
Jutrosin	Jutroschin	Rogoźno	Rogasen
Kamienna Góra	Landshut	Rybnik	Rybnik
Katowice	Kattowitz	Ryczywół	Ryczywol
Kępno	Kempen	Rydzyna	Reisen
Kobylin	Kobylin	Sarnowa	Sarne
Konarzewo	Kniephof	Sępolno	Zempelburg
Kórnik	Kurnik	Siemianowice	Siemianowitz
Kościan	Kostschin	Sieraków	Zirke
Kostrzyn	Kostschin	Starogard Gdański	Preussische Stargard
Koźmin	Koschmin	Strzewo	Dirschau
Krobia	Kroeben	Sulmierzyce	Sulmirschuetz
Królewka Huta	Königshütte	Swarzędz	Schwersenz
Krotoszyn	Krotoschin	Szamocin	Samotschin
Książ	Xions	Szamotuły	Samter
Lądek	Landau	Śrem	Schrimm
Leszno	Lissa	Środa	Schroda
Lwów	Lemberg	Toruń	Thorn
Lwówek	Neustadt bei Pinne	Trzemeszno	Tremessin
Łabiszyn	Labischin	Wągrowiec	Wongrowitz
Margonin	Margonin	Wieleń	Filehne
Międzyrzecz Wielkopolski	Meseritz	Wolsztyn	Wollstein
		Wronki	Wronke
Miłosław	Miloslaw	Września	Wreschen
Mosina	Moschin	Wyszanów	Wyszanow
Murowana Goślina	Murowana Goslin	Zaniemyśl	Santomischel
Mysłowice	Myslowitz	Zduny	Zduny
Nakło	Nakel	Zerków	Zerkow
Nowe Miasto nad Wartą	Neustadt a. d. Warthe	Żory	Sohrau

Glossary

Aliyot la Tora [H, plural] Invitations to the reading of the Torah in the synagogue.

Arenda [P] Concession, granted by a noble family.

Arendar [P] Leaseholder.

Asygnacja/e [P] A payment order.

Bikur cholim [H] Visiting the sick.

Chasidim [H] Adherents of the Chasidic movement which evolved in 18th century Eastern Europe.

Chaver [H] Title bestowed on a learned layman.

Cheder/chadorim [H] Traditional elementary school/s.

Cherem [H] Excommunication.

Chevra Kadisha [H] Burial society.

Choshen Mishpat [H] Fourth part of the *Shulchan Aruch*, the code of Jewish law assembled by Rabbi Joseph Caro.

Dayan/im [H] Rabbinical court judge/s.

De non tolerandis Judaeis [L] A royal privilege allowing the exclusion of Jews.

Duma [R] State Duma. The Russian parliament existed in 1906-1917.

Ekonomia [P] Royal estate in Poland .

Eruv/im [H] Border/s within which it is permitted to carry objects on the Sabbath.

Etrog [H] Citron. Fruit associated with the Feast of Tabernacles (Sukkot).

Gabbai/im [H] Trustee/s of a synagogue.

General Gubernator [R] Governor-General, a chief of the military and civil authorities for the region, which includes corresponding guberniias.

Gmilus Chasodim [H] Charitable society.

Grod [P] Castle court which judged civil and criminal cases.

Guberniia [P] Province in czarist Russia .

Hajdamak [Turkish] Designation for robber by Ukrainians .

Jurydyka/i [P] Populated locality under the jurisdiction of its owner.

Kahal [H] The governing body of a Jewish community.

Kapturowy court Court at period of interregnum in the Kingdom of Poland.

Karaites Jewish sect that rejected the Oral Law.

Ketubot [H] Jewish marriage contracts.

Kloiz [Y] Prayer and study house

Klucz [P] Feudal estate, consisting of several towns, villages and manors.

Kollel [H] Community in Eretz Yisroel of people from the same geographic area or affiliation.

Komitet Starozakonnych [P] Committee of Jews (in Czarist times).

Korobka/krupka [R/P] Tax on kosher meat and other consumer items.

Laissez-passer [F] Travel document.

Landesgubernium [G] Provincial government.

Landsmannschaft [Y] Organization of people from the same town.

Lulav [H] Palm branch used on the Feast of Tabernacles (Sukkot).

Lustracja/e [P] Inspection documents of estates and taxes.

Maskil [H] A Jew influenced by the Enlightenment.

Matzot [H] Unleavened bread eaten on Passover.

Melamed/melamdim [H] Teacher/s in traditional elementary schools.
Memorbuch [G] Jewish community register, listing names of the deceased.
Mikve/mikvaot [H] Ritual bath/s.
Mishna [H] Collection of Oral Laws.
Misnagdim [H] Opponents of Chasidim.
Mohel/mohalim [H] Ritual circumciser/s.
Morenu [H] Honorary rabbinic title.
Oberlandrabbiner [G] Chief rabbi.
Pinkas/sim [H] Minute book/s.
Pinkas hakahal [H] Community minute book.
Powiat [P] Polish district, subdivision of województwo.
Propinacja [P] A monopoly to produce and trade in alcoholic beverages.
Revizskie skazki [R] A list of inhabitants
Sejm [P] Polish legislative assembly.
Sejmik [P] Regional legislative assembly of Polish noblemen .
Shechita [H] Ritual slaughter of animals.
Shochet/shochatim [H] Ritual slaughterer/s.
Shtadlan [H] Community representative before the authorities.
Starosta [P] A holder of a starostwo .
Starostwo/a [P] Polish royal land grant limited in time; local administration in Galicia
             and in interwar Poland
Summariusz [P] A compendium of annual incomes.
Suplika/i [P] Petition/s.
Talmud [H] Commentary on the Mishna.
Talmud Tora [H] Society for the study of the Talmud.
Tzadikim [H] Chasidic rabbis.
Uezd [R] Tsarist Russian district, subdivision of a guberniia.
Ukase [R] Tsarist edict.
Uniwersał/y [P] Edict/s.
Wojewoda [P] Governor of a województwo.
Województwo/a [P] Voivodship/s, Polish province .
Wójt [P] Head of local administration.
Yeshiva [H] Talmudical academy.

Poland, General

Originals:

An order by King Zygmunt III permitting Jews to buy food at fairs, 1588; a royal decree on the poll tax, 1715; handwritten copies from documents of the Four Years *Sejm*, 1790 and a royal decree on the status of the Jews, 1792.

Letters and pamphlets written by Polish rabbis [H], 19th–20th cent.; stamps and seals of Jewish organizations and official institutions dealing with Jewish affairs, 19th cent.; a government permit for a Jew to raise funds in Polish cities for the Jews of Palestine (*Eretz Yisroel)* , 1837; a proclamation by the Polish Socialist party against conscription into the Russian army [Y], 1905; a proclamation by the German army to the Jews of Poland [H, Y], 1914; a proclamation on the hosting of Jewish soldiers during holidays [H], 1914–18; a petition to assist Ukrainian Jews [H], 1918.

An antisemitic proclamation issued by an anti-Communist political party, 1919; a typewritten article containing statistics and copies of documents on the 1918 pogroms in Poland [H], 1919; a proclamation urging Galician Jews to declare Hebrew or Yiddish as their first language in censuses [Y], 1920–30's; ten diaries of young Polish Jews [G, H, P, Y], 1930s; a questionnaire on health matters issued by *OSE* [P, Y], 1920; newsletters of Jewish cooperatives in Poland [P, Y], 1927; instructions issued by the Jewish representatives in the minorities bloc [H, P, Y], 1930s; a proclamation by the *Bund* on elections to the Printers' Union [Y], 1931; a proclamation urging the boycott of German products [P, Y], 1933; statutes of the Jewish Artisans' Association [Y], 1935; a copy of a speech at a World Jewish Congress meeting on pogroms in Poland [Y], 1936; minutes of a JDC meeting , Warsaw [E], 1937; a special issue of the newspaper of the Jewish veterans of Piłsudski's Polish Legion, 1938.

A declaration by the organization of Jews from Wilno in Poland [Y], 1946; petition of rabbis and *chasidic* leaders in Poland, requesting help in emigrating to *Eretz Yisroel* (Palestine) [H], 1946; a proclamation to Polish Jews by the Committee of Jewish Communities [Y], 1948.

Private collections

1.Gelber, Natan Michael, historian – Copies of documents, notes and correspondence relating to his research activity on the history of Zionism and Polish Jewry, especially Galicia, 17th–20th centuries.

2. Halperin, Israel, historian – Notes, photocopies and copies of documents, manuscripts and correspondence relating to his studies of Eastern European Jewry, 13th–20th centuries.

3. Posner, Akiva, Rabbi and historian – Notes and manuscripts on Jewish communities in Poznań under Prussian rule.

4. Tugendhold, Jacob, censor, - Personal papers and docuements relating to his public activity in Warsaw, 1828–50.

5. Weinryb, Bernard, historian – Notes and papers relating to his historical research on Polish Jewry, 18th–20th centuries.

Photocopies, 1655–1940:

Copies of decrees by King Carl X of Sweden concerning the Jews of various communities in Poland [G], 1655–57.

(Riksarkivet and Kammararkivet, Stockholm)

The German translation of a decree by the Bishop of Kraków against the Jews [G], 1751; documents on activities of the Jewish Scouts in Poland, 1916–36; files from the Ministry of the Interior in Poland on pogroms in 1918–19; government documents on minorities in Poland, 1923–37; correspondence and reports by the Polish Embassy in Berlin on the situation of Polish Jewish citizens in Germany, and on antisemitism in Poland, 1925–38; correspondence and minutes of government bodies and the International

Emigration Commission on emigration of Jews to *Eretz Yisroel* (Palestine), 1925–39; letters and reports on the *Mizrachi* party [G,H], 1927–35; 2 documents on changing the law on *shechita* in Poland, 1938; correspondence on the expulsion of Polish Jews from Germany to Poland, 1939–40.

Microfilms:

1. A list of books written by *Karaites* [H], n.d.; a collection of legal documents and charters granted to Jews [L, P], 14th–16th cent.; chronicles (mostly on *Shabbetai Tzvi*), 17th cent.; documents about Jews on the Sieniawski and Czartoryski estates, 1691–1746; records of the poll tax paid by Jews, 1734–55; apportioning by the Council of the Four Lands of taxes due from each region, 1753; documents on the Bar Confederation (including material on the Jews), 1768–72; references to Jews in the records of deputations to the *Sejm* on the peasants' revolts, 1783–92; project for the reform of Polish Jews (including Polish translations of documents on the reform of French Jewry during the French Revolution), 1792.
(Bibl. Czartoryskich, Kraków)

2. *Laisser-passer* for a journey to Jerusalem [L, P], 1467–69; a *lustracja* of Lithuania containing details on Jews in Wilno, 18th cent; pamphlets on the Jewish religion and conversion of Jews to Christianity [L, F], 1759; a letter by Jewish converts to Christianity to senators, ministers and noblemen, 1764; a bibliography of Hebrew books printed in Poland and Lithuania [P, H], 19th cent.; letters on Jewish matters, by Eliza Orzeszkowa, Ferdynand Hoesick, Zenon Przesmycki, Aleksander Kraushar and other writers, 1867–1909.
(Biblioteka Narodowa, Warszawa)

3. Copies of documents from the Vatican archives on blood libel accusations in Poland [L], 1540, 1754–75.
(Archivio Segreto Vaticano)

4. Regulations regarding the Jewish poll tax, 1590–1787.
(AGAD, Warszawa, Księgi Grodzkie Bobrownickie, Ciechanowskie, Kowalskie; Łęczyckie, Płockie; Ziemia Nurska Rel. Obl.; Castr. Obl., Wieluń)

5. Lists of Jewish traders and innkeepers, contracts for various *arendas* and the lease of the right to *propinacja* on the Radziwiłł estates, 1596–1839; letters to Jews by Radziwiłł family members, 1648–1820; documents on trading activities of the Ickowicz family in Prussia, 1728–47; charters granted by Prussian authorities to Polish Jews, 1729–43; *supliki* made by Jews, 1768–78.
(AGAD, Warszawa, Arch. Radziwiłłów)

6. Royal decrees on taxes due from Jews [P, L], 1600–1738; records regarding *arenda* and Jewish rights to deal in property on the Zamoyski estates, 1603–1785, as well as complaints against Jewish subjects of the Zamoyski family, 17th cent.; verdict of a rabbinical court [P,H], 1756; supplication to the archbishop of Lwów by Jewish converts to Christianity, 1759; regulations on the Jewish oath, 1761.
(AGAD, Warszawa, Arch. Zamoyskich)

7. Documents containing references to Jewish rights [P, L], 17th-18th cent.; documents on the social and economic life of Jews on the Ostrogski estates, 1620; *uniwersał* issued by the Bar Confederation concerning taxes, 1769.
(AP Wrocław, Ossolineum)

8. Charters and financial records on Jews, 1654–1790.
(AP Poznań; AP Lublin)

9. Confirmation of a charter to the Polish Jews by King Michał Korybut Wiśniowiecki, 1669.
(AGAD, Warszawa)

10. A royal letter of protection for the Jewish population, 1684.
(AP Poznań, Księgi Grodzkie Kaliskie)

11. Decrees of a Royal Court on relations between Jews and peasants on royal estates, 1698–1750.
(AGAD, Warszawa, Księgi Referendarskie)

12. *Lustracje* and inventories of various districts and their inhabitants, 18th cent.
(AGAD, Warszawa, ASK)
13. Records of litigation between Jews and the Tyzenhaus family [P, Byelorussian], 18th cent.
(AGAD, Warszawa, Arch. Tyzenhausów)
14. The assessment of the poll tax and other taxes due from Jews, 1726–90.
(AP Lublin, Księgi Grodzkie Chełmskie)
15. Report of damage caused by the *hajdamaks;* files on the ennoblement of converts to Christianity 1751–71.
(AGAD, Warszawa, MK)
16. Instructions on the liquidation of Jewish debts, 1756.
(AGAD, Warszawa, Castr. Obl., Łęczyca)
17. A supplication by Jews converting to Christianity, 1756.
(Bibl. Kórnicka, Kórnik)
18. Letters by a priest, accusing the Jews of ritual murder; documents on the punishment of a Jew and the intervention of other Jews on his behalf, 1761–95.
(AGAD, Warszawa, Arch. Roskie)
19. Instructions on the registration of the Jewish population; files on taxes to be paid by Jews for the army and other purposes, 1762–1806.
(AP Lublin, Księgi Miasta, Modliborzyce)
20. Files on the Jews and their economic activity in Prussian Poland [G], 1772–1808.
(Deutsches Zentralarchiv Merseburg, Geheimes Staatsarchiv)
21. Letters of protection and moratoria granted by King Stanisław August Poniatowski to various Jews [L], 1775.
(AGAD, Warszawa, Księgi Kanclerskie)
22. *Lustracja* of the poll tax paid by Jews on the Czartoryski estates, 1766; memoranda on the Jewish question during the period of the Four Year *Sejm*, 1788–92.
(AGAD, Warszawa, Arch. Potockich)
23. Decrees issued by the Crown Treasury Commission on the poll tax, a stamp tax on Jewish books, and other "Jewish" taxes, 1775–90.
(AP Lublin, Księgi Grodzkie Lubelskie, Krasnostawskie)
24. Legal records of an attack on a Jew; an order by the Crown Treasury Commission to report on markets in towns and villages, 1780–89.
(Bibl. PAN, Kraków)
25. Documents from the period of the Four Year *Sejm* on a project for Jewish reform; correspondence between Tadeusz Czacki and Hugo Kołłątaj on the Jewish question and the project for Jewish reform, 1788–1811.
(Bibl. Jagiellońska, Kraków)
26. A memorandum by Jews to Prince Ivan Paskiewicz on improving their situation, 19th cent.
(AP Kraków, Zb. Rusieckich)
27. Files on the administration of Jewish communities in Poland; records on Jewish settlement and purchase of property in towns (including regulations, restrictions and charters of *de non tolerandis Judaeis*) [P, L]; files on the *krupka*; prohibitions on the production and sale of alcohol by Jews; records on blood libel; files on the adoption of family names by Jews; records on the travels of English missionaries among Jews; files on the order forbidding Jews to live within three miles of the Prussian, Austrian or Russian borders; documents on granting citizenship to Jews (incl. proposals by Sir Moses Montefiore); records on

payment of "protection tax" by Jews; restrictions on Jewish emigration; records on Jewish dress; files on the expulsion of foreign Jews from Austria and Prussia; records on aid granted to Jews after the 1831 uprising; files on *propinacja* in towns, 1807–68.
(AGAD, Warszawa, KRzSW)

28. Files on Jewish matters; cancellation of restrictions on Jewish residence and purchase of property; prohibition of Jewish trade in alcohol; records on taxes paid by Jews; files on litigation involving Jews, 1808–12.
(AGAD, Warszawa, RSiRMKW)

29. Reports and correspondence concerning collection of taxes, register of the recruitment tax and its division in the Polish Kingdom, 1812–45; documents on the administration of Jewish communities, 1816–66.
(AGAD, Warszawa, KRzPiS)

30. Proposals to expel Jews from villages; reports of the Committee for the Reform of the Jewish People; records on taxes paid by Jews; details of a projected law for the Jews, 1816–62.
(AGAD, Warszawa, RSKP)

31. Instructions, minutes and correspondence about religious celebrations in the Polish Kingdom; participation in prayers, a prohibition of marriage in other communities, payment to the burial society, 1821–71.
(AGAD, Warszawa, CWW)

32. A register of decrees concerning the Jews in the Polish Kingdom between the years 1821–73 [R], 1870–73.
(AP Lublin, Rząd Gubernialny, Lublin)

33. Records concerning the abolition of the *kahal* by Tsar Alexander I, 1822.
(AGAD, Warszawa, Komisja Wojewódzwa Kaliskiego)

34. Requests by Jews to acquire land, attain citizenship, build schools, return after expulsion etc. [R], 1826–61.
(AGAD, Warszawa, SSKP)

35. Records on payment of the recruiting tax by Jews; Jewish participation in the city guard and in the Kraków district militia; records on the separation of Jewish districts; files on Jews living near the border; a list of Jews who received passports to leave Poland; permission for Jews to lease taverns and the right of *propinacja;* files on the kosher meat tax, 1831.
(AGAD, Warszawa, WCPL)

36. A file on the municipal status of settlements in the *guberniias* of Kiev, Podolia and Volhynia, including a list of charters granted to the settlements by the kings of Poland and decrees of the Russian authorities [R], 1849–52
(TsDIAU, Kyiv, Kantseliariia... general-gubernatora)

37. A report following an inspection by Leon Mandelshtam of Jewish schools in the Western *guberniias* of the Russian empire and the Polish Kingdom, including information about schools, teaching staff, rabbis, patrons and Jewish communities [F, H, P, R], 1856–62.
(RGIA, St. Petersburg, Departament narodnogo prosveshcheniia)

38. File concerning a secret circular of the Ministry of Internal Affaires about remarks on "Jewish capitalists" entering the "international Jewish *kahal*," 1880.
(AP Lublin, Kancelaria Gubernatora Lubelskiego)

39. Records on Jewish dress; regulations of the Jewish Colonization Association (JCA); files on Jews sent into and released from exile [R], 1882–1911.

(AP Łódź, Kancelaria Gubernatora Kaliskiego)

40. Instructions of a director of the Health Dept. about employing Jews with medical or veterinary education in the civil service; reports and correspondence about changes in laws relating to Jews in the Russian Empire: qualifications and regulations for the elections of rabbis, economic supervision of synagogues and a statistical report about Jews, synagogues and prayer houses in various *guberniias* of Russia [R], 1883–1903; a file about synagogues constructed on peasants' lands in Western *guberniias* of Russia [R], 1895–1906; a file on the conduct of civil registers for the Jewish population, a list of rabbis and *dayanim* in Western *guberniias* [R], 1903.

(RGIA, St. Petersburg, Departament dukhovnykh del…)

41. Correspondence and articles by Eliza Orzeszkowa on the "Jewish question" and other topics, 1900–10.

(PAN, Warszawa, Arch. Orzeszkowej)

42. Reports on Jews [R], 1906–10.

(AP Łódź, Rząd Gubernialny, RO, Piotrków)

43. Files on Jewish societies [R], 1907–09.

(AP Łódź, Rząd Gubernialny, KP, Piotrków)

44. Proposals of a rabbinical commission to the Ministry of the Interior on a meeting of rabbis in St. Petersburg regarding the religious problems of Russian Jews [R], 1908–13.

(AP Łódź, Kancelaria Gubernatora Piotrkowskiego)

45. Report by *Achduth-Bnai Brith* in Kraków concerning activity of the local branches in Poland, and a list of them, 1928.

(DAIFO, Ivano-Frankivs'k, Towarzystwo *Achaduth-Bnai Brith,* Stanisławów)

Regions

GALICJA (Galicia), 18th–20th cent.

Originals:

An order by the Austrian Emperor Franz I, on the Jewish candle tax [G, P], 1810; Jewish manifesto calling for the preservation of the Jewish middle class in Galicia [G], 1913; a Russian military order expelling the Jews from Galicia [R], 1915; a file on the election districts of Jewish institutions in Galicia, 1931.

Photocopy:

Letter from the Ministry of Religious Affairs to the government representative in Lwów requesting information about Jewish communities in different areas, 1920–23.

(DALO, L'viv, UW, Lwów)

Microfilms:

1. Copies of official documents on the history of Galicia and its Jews [P, L], 18th cent.

(AP Wrocław, Ossolineum)

2. Files on tax, agricultural, religious, matrimonial and other matters of Galician Jewry [G, P], 18th–19th cent; the "Toleranz Patent" of Emperor Joseph II, 1789; a detailed report on the "harmful influence" of the Jews on different areas of public life, memoranda on regulations on Jews, brochures about the "Jewish question" [G], 1791–1856; orders of the authorities regarding the entry of foreign Jews to Galicia [G], 1804–07.

(AP Kraków, Teki Schneidra)

3. Correspondence about the economic situation of the Jews in Galicia [G, H, L, P], 1775–80; correspondence with the authorities on the deportation of foreign Jews from Bukovina, [G], 1805; official announcements and communal reports regarding ritual taxes [G], 1810; correspondence on the civil rights of the Jews in Galicia [G], 1829–43; correspondence and tax tables from various localities in Galicia [G], 1842–1859; files on the confirmation of Galician Jewish community statutes and on the reorganization of communities, 1846–96; proposal of a Jewish merchant to improve the situation of Galician Jews [G], 1848; an appeal by Hungarian Jews to the Jews of Galicia to take part in the 1848 uprising, [G, Y–D], 1849; correspondence between Jewish communities and government authorities on collecting money in Galicia for Jews in Palestine (*Eretz Yisroel)* [G], 1851–53; correspondence about reorganization of Jewish communities in Galicia and problems of education, a file on *chasidim* [G], 1852; correspondence about censoring articles from Galicia to foreign newspapers [G], 1858; files on propaganda for army service among Jewish youth in various localities of Galicia, 1870; correspondence with various *starostwa* on registration of vital statistics, 1891–92; a statute of a political society for Galician Jews, 1894; documents on kosher butchers in various localities, 1894–97; correspondence on the positions of rabbis in various Galician localities, 1895–96.

(TsDIAU, L'viv, Namiestnictwo Galicyjskie)

4. Instructions issued at Lwów by the Governor of Galicia on recording Jewish births [G, P]; two treasury orders canceling the Jews' oath on certain financial matters [G], 1816–46.

(Bundesarchiv, Koblenz)

5. Correspondence regarding the collecting of taxes and the responsibility of the Jewish communities for foreign Jews in their midst [G], 1827–28.

(DALO, L'viv, Magistrat, Lwów)

6. A prohibition for Jews to trade in paintings in Galicia and penalties for its violation [G, P], 1831.

(NBANU, L'viv, Zb. Goldsteina)

7. Correspondence regarding public schools in Galicia [G, P] 1878–80; correspondence with authorities on Jewish communities and the confirmation of their statutes, on taxes and on other payments, 1895–1905; reports on religious education of Jewish children in various Galician towns [G, P], 1882–89.

(TsDIAU, L'viv, Krajowa Rada Szkolna)

8. Discussions concerning statutes for the Jewish communities in Galicja [G, P], 1882.

(ŻIH, Warszawa, Gmina Żydowska, Kraków)

9. Files on Galician Jewish matters [G], 1885–1920.

(Bundesarchiv, Koblenz, Auswaertiges Amt)

10. Correspondence with the governor of Kiev concerning prohibition for Jews from Galicia to move towards eastern areas of Russia, 1915

(RGIVA, Moscow, Shtab Kievskogo voennogo okruga)

11. A report of the Conjoint Committee in London on the Jews of Galicia [E], 1916.

(Central Zionist Archives, Jerusalem, Movshovicz Collection)

12. Statutes of the *Mizrachi* in Galicia [G, P], 1919–21.

(DAIFO, Ivano-Frankivs'k, UW, Stanisławów)

MAŁOPOLSKA (Little Poland), 1633–1931

1. Confirmation by King Jan Kazimierz of a charter given to the Jews of Małopolska by King Kazimierz Wielki in 1367 and confirmed by King Zygmunt August in 1559 [L], 1633.

(AP Przemyśl, DP)

2. A file on a meeting of the *Związek Rabinów Małopolski* [Union of Rabbis in Little Poland], 1927; Reports about a conference of the presidents of the local comittees and members of the party council of the Zionist Organization in Lwów, a list of members ot the *Organizacja Syjonistyczna Małopolski Wschodniej*, 1931; a report on a conference of Jewish cooperatives from Małopolska in Lwów, 1932.

(DAIFO, Ivano-Frankivs'k, UW, Stanisławów)

3. Reports and correspondence concerning activity of the *Komisja Organizacyjna Zjazdu Gmin Wyznaniowych Izraelickich Małopolski* in Lwów, the statutes of *Związek Żydowskich Gmin Wyznaniowych Małopolski*, 1926.

(DAIFO, Ivano-Frankivs'k, Gmina Żydowska, Stanisławów)

4. Reports by elementary school principals on social, economic, ethnic, and cultural characteristics of their localities [P, U], 1930.

(DAIFO, Ivano-Frankivs'k, Inspektorat Szkolny, Stanisławów)

5. Monographs containing demographic and economic data on localities, 1936.

(AP Wrocław, Ossolineum, WKNZNP, Lwów)

MAZOWSZE, 1570–1871
Microfilms:
1. A *lustracja* of the mazowieckie *województwo*, 1570.

(AGAD, Warszawa, ASK)

2. Files on the setting up of *eruvim* in various towns of the *województwo* and the ensuing conflicts between Jews and Christians, including a list of towns where *eruvim* were set up, 1818–71; files on Jewish burial societies, 1822–50; files on irregularities in the kosher meat trade [P, R], 1846–56.

(AGAD, Warszawa, CWW)

WIELKOPOLSKA (Great Poland), 1744–1783
Microfilms:

1. Files concerning debts of Wielkopolska Jews, 1744–83.
(AP Lublin, Kolegiata w Zamościu)
2. Confirmation of a charter for the Jews of Wielkopolska by King Stanisław August Poniatowski, 1766.
(AP Kraków, DP)

WOŁYŃ (Volhynia), 1632–1936
Photocopy:
File about Jewish transgressions in matters of military conscription [R], 1839–40.
(GARF, Moscow, Tret'e otdelenie…)
Microfilms:
1. Minutes of the Volhynian *kapturowy* court [R], 1632.
(TsDIAU, Kyiv, Glavnyi Kapturovyi Sud Volynskogo Voevodstva)
2. Descriptions of various communities, 17th–18th.
(AGAD, Warszawa, Zb. Czołowskiego)
3. Register of Jewish inhabitants and taxes, 1705–08.
(Bibl. Czartoryskich, Kraków)
4. Documents of the Catholic Church in Zamość regarding debts of Jews from Volhynia, 1744–82.
(AP Lublin, Kolegiata, Zamość)
5. Regesta from court records regarding debts of Volhynian Jews to Prince Sanguszko, 1749.
(AP Kraków, Archiwum Sanguszków)
6. Reports about the oppression of Jews [R], 1804–21.
(RGIA, St. Petersburg, Dokumenty iz unichtozhennykh del…)
7. Statistical data on communities, synagogues, charitable institutions, schools and Jewish inhabitants [R], 1834, 1837, 1838; a report on *propinacja* rights for the Jewish inhabitants of several towns [R], a list of Polish royal charters and Russian decrees [R], 1849–52; reports on the use of *krupka* tax income for the benefit of communities [R], 1905–06; reports, minutes and correspondence on pogroms in various towns and on measures to prevent them [R], 1905; reports of the secret police on political activities [R], 1911.
(TsDIAU, Kyiv, Kantseliariia…)
8. Files on communities, synagogues, Jewish schools and debtors in the Volhynia *guberniia* [R], 1834–50; a report about laws concerning settlement in towns and permission of *propinacja* granted the Jews in the regions of Kiev and Volhynia, [R], 1849–52; files on pogroms in the regions of Podolia, Volhynia and Kiev, including investigations of participants and lists of victims [R], 1881; reports and correspondence on calls for anti-goverment and anti-Jewish disorders and pogroms in towns and villages and preventive measures [R], 1905–07;
(TsDIAU, Kyiv, Kantseliariia... general-gubernatora)
9. Decrees and correspondence of various authorities regarding competence of rabbinical and non Jewish courts [R], 1856.
(DATO, Ternopil', Magistrat, Krzemieniec)
10. Statistical data on towns and a report on Jewish charitable institutions [R], 1871, 1886.
(RGIA, St. Petersburg, Khoziaistvennyi departament MVD)
11. Decrees and correspondence on the appointment of Jews to special tasks in the offices of the governor-generals [R], 1858–70; laws on the Jews in Russia, information about conscription of Jews and their employment [R], 1880–81; material on the opening and maintenance of Jewish and professional schools, on allowances paid to rabbis and their widows from the *krupka* tax income, community accounts [R], 1881–95; decrees, reports and correspondence on the rules governing the election of rabbis and community

board members [R], 1883–89; reports and correspondence on the election of rabbis, on their duties, on charitable societies and prayer houses, economic supervision of synagogues; statistical data on the number of Jews and synagogues in various Russian regions [R], 1888–92; instructions on registering vital statistics of the Jewish population, a list of rabbis and *dayanim* in Volhynia [R], 1903; a report on rabbis and synagogues [R], 1908.

(RGIA, St. Petersburg, Departament dukhovnykh del...)

12. Lists and addresses of Zionist groups and organizations in Volhynia [R], 1907–16.

(TsGAU, Tashkent, Turkestanskoe okhrannoe otdelenie)

13. Materials of the *EKOPO* association on relations between Jews and Christians, on antisemitism and on the expulsion of Jews from front line areas. Materials on permission to publish Jewish newspapers [R], 1915–16.

(GARF, Moscow, Bomash)

14. Monographs on various towns in Volhynia, 1936.

(AP Wrocław, Ossolineum, WKNZNP, Lwów)

Communities

ALEKSANDRIA (pow. Równe, woj. wołyńskie) 1706–1785
Microfilms:
Contracts, decrees, payments and other documents about the Sieniawski-Czartoryski estates in the town and its inhabitants, 1706–85.
(Biblioteka Narodowa, Warszawa)

ALEKSANDRÓW (pow. Łódź, woj. łódzkie) 1822–1914
Microfilms:
1. Records on community accounts and elections; files on tax payments, 1822–65.
(AP Łódź, Anterioria Rządu Gubernialnego, Piotrków)
2. Correspondence and financial records on the community, 1826–59.
(AGAD, Warszawa, CWW)
3. Ratification of community elections and accounts; files on the building of new synagogues; the leasing of the *mikve;* appointment of a new rabbi; sales of seats in the synagogue [R], 1889–1911.
(AP Łódź, Rząd Gubernialny, WA, Piotrków)
4. Fines for evading conscription [R], 1896–1900.
(AP Łódź, Rząd Gubernialny, WP, Piotrków)
5. Two requests to register charitable societies [R], 1910–14.
(AP Łódz, Rząd Gubernialny, KP, Piotrków)

ANNOPOL (pow. Janów, woj. lubelskie) 1853–1867
Microfilms:
1. Correspondence of *guberniia* authorities with community authorities on appointments of rabbis, a list of rabbis, reports on activities of the community board, 1853–56.
(AGAD, Warszawa, CWW)
2. Correspondence on election of community authorities [R], 1867.
(AP Lublin, Rząd Gubernialny, Lublin)

AUGUSTÓW (woj. białostockie) 1807–1913
Originals:
Records of four marriages [R], 1872; sale of a synagogue seat [H], 1913.
Photocopies:
Orders and announcements of the authorities on conscription of Jews, including a list of Jewish conscripts, 1850–52.
(AP Suwałki, Akta m. Suwałki)
Microfilms:
1. Lawsuit of a Jew against the town regarding provisions to the French army in 1807, 1817–23.
(AGAD, Warszawa, KRzSW)
2. Reports, correspondence on the appointment of rabbis, 1856–64; records on the burial society (*Chevra Kadisha*), correspondence, minutes, complaints, 1822–50.
(AGAD, Warszawa, CWW)
3. Requests for release from fines and taxes, 1858–59.
(AGAD, Warszawa, SSKP)
4. Documents on the prohibition of religious services in private homes [R], 1858–83; private documents of candidates for the rabbinate [R], 1886–1913.

(AP Białystok, Rząd Gubernialny, Łomża)

AUGUSTÓW, suroundings, 1823–1856
Microfilms:
Files on the appointment of rabbis, on taxes and on aid for poor and sick Jews [P, R], 1823–56.
(AGAD, Warszawa, CWW)

BAKAŁARZEWO (pow. Suwałki, woj. białostockie) 1826–1864
Microfilms:
Marriage register, 1826; birth and death registers, 1826–64.
(AP Suwałki)

BALIGRÓD (pow. Lesko, woj. lwowskie) 1853–1935
Microfilms:
1. Correspondence about inns leased by Jews from Christians [G], 1853.
(TsDIAU, L'viv, Namiestnictwo Galicyjskie)
2. Correspondence about community affairs (budget, etc.), 1930–35.
(DALO L'viv, UW, Lwów)

BARANÓW (pow. Kępno, woj. poznańskie) 1807–1812
Microfilms:
Files on *propinacja*, 1807–12.
(AGAD, Warszawa, Komisja Wojewódzwa Kaliskiego)

BARANÓW (pow. Puławy, woj. lubelskie) 1571–1810
Microfilms:
Charter granted to the Jews by King Zygmunt II, 1571–72; municipal records, 1797–1810.
(AP Lublin, Księgi Miejskie, Baranów)

BEŁCHATÓW (pow. Piotrków, woj. łódzkie) 1822–1911
Microfilms:
1. Records and accounts of the community, 1822–66.
(AP Łódź, Anterioria Rządu Gubernialnego, Piotrków)
2. Records on taxes and loans, 1843–66.
(AP Łódź, Komisja Województwa Kaliskiego)
3. Correspondence on *chadorim* in Bełchatów and Rozprza, 1890–99.
(AP Łódź, Dyrekcja Szkolna, Łódź)
4. Ratification of community elections and accounts; appointment of a new rabbi; building a new synagogue; renovation of the *mikve* and of synagogue pews [R], 1890–1911.
(AP Łódź, Rząd Gubernialny, WA, Piotrków)
5. Complaint of two Jewish estate managers; fines for evading conscription [R], 1898–1902.
(AP Łódź, Rząd Gubernialny, WP, Piotrków)
6. Copies of inscriptions from cemeteries and synagogues, 1910.
(RGIA, St. Petersburg , Departament dukhovnykh del…)
7. Request to register the *bikur cholim* (sick care) society [R], 1910–11.
(AP Łódź, Rząd Gubernialny, KP, Piotrków)

BEŁZ (pow. Sokal, woj. lwowskie) 1669–1929
Microfilms:
1. Confirmation by King Michał Korybut of various contracts between town authorities and the Jewish community (on *arendas* and purchasing real estate), signed by King Jan Kazimierz, 1669.
(AP Kraków, Teki Schneidra, DP)
2. Records on community debts, mainly to monasteries and the nobility [P, L], 1727–58.
(TsDIAU, L'viv, Kolektsiia dokumentiv…)
3. Documents, including promissory notes [P, H], 1730–96.
(TsDIAU, Kyiv, Arch. Tarło)
4. Settlement of a dispute between the communities of Bełz and Chełm and that of Zamość on the allocation of the poll tax, 1745.
(AP Lublin, Księgi Grodzkie Krasnostawskie)
5. Poll tax records from Bełz and Chełm, 1769.
(AP Lublin, Księgi Grodzkie Chełmskie)
6. Statutes of the *Yishrei Lev* society, 1909–10.
(TsDIAU, L'viv, Namiestnictwo Galicyjskie)
7. Reports and correspondence on community elections, 1928–29.
(DALO, L'viv, UW, Lwów)

BEŁŻYCE (pow. Lublin, woj. lubelskie) 1570–1869
Microfilms:
1. Municipal, village and other local records (fragmentary), 1570–1820.
(AP Lublin, Księgi Miasta, Bełżyce)
2. An investigation of the town's owner regarding a Jew's imprisonment, 1843–59.
(AGAD, Warszawa, KRzSW)
3. Statistical description of Bełżyce, 1861; a complaint against *chasidim* for conducting prayer services in a private home, 1869.
(AP Lublin, Rząd Gubernialny, Lublin)

BERESTECZKO (pow. Dubno, woj. wołyńskie) 1619–1817
Microfilms:
1. Excerpts from the books of the Łuck, Krzemieniec and Włodzimierz Castle Courts, on judicial matters and copies of charters to the Jews of Beresteczko, 1619–1774.
(TsDIAU Kyiv, Arch. Zamojskich)
2. Excerpts from the court books of Beresteczko on judicial matters, 1676–80.
(TsDIAU, Kyiv, Magistrat, Beresteczko)
3. Inventories, contracts, and other documents on the *Berestecki* estate, 1811–17.
(NBANU, L'viv, Arch. Sapiehów)

BEREŹNICA (pow. Sarny, woj. wołyńskie) 1755–1876
Microfilms:
1. Contract of an *arenda*, 1755–61.
(NBAN, L'viv, Arch. Sapiehów)
2. Copies of documents on *tzadikim* from Bereźnica and other localities, 1834–76.
(TsDIAU, Kyiv, Dokumenty, sobrannye…)

BĘDKÓW (pow. Brzeziny, woj. łódzkie) 1849–1906
Microfilms:
1. A concession to deal in alcohol; financial records, 1849–64.
(AP Łódź, Komisja Województwa Kaliskiego)
2. Request to found a new community [R], 1901.
(AP Łódź, Rząd Gubernialny, WA, Piotrków)
3. Fine for evading conscription [R], 1899.
(AP Łódź, Rząd Gubernialny, WP, Piotrków)
4. Case of a Jew found guilty of a misdemeanor [R], 1906.
(AP Łódź, GZŻ, Piotrków)

BĘDZIN (woj. kieleckie) 1669–1915
Original records:
Pinkas hakahal (community record book) [H], 1770–1912.
Photocopies:
Confirmation by King Michał Korybut Wiśniowiecki of a charter issued by King Władysław IV in 1614, confirming rights of the Jews, 1669.
(AP Kraków, DP)
Microfilms:
1. Confirmations by Kings Michał Korybut and Stanisław August Poniatowski of the charter granted to the Jews [P, L], 1669, 1766.
(AGAD, Warszawa, Księgi Kanclerskie)
2. Confirmation by King Stanisław August Poniatowski of an agreement between the Jews and the municipality [P, L], 1767.
(AP Kraków, DP)
3. Reports on the community; files on financial aid granted to individuals, 1841–66.
(AP Łódź, Anterioria Rządu Gubernialnego, Piotrków)
4. Ratification of community accounts and elections; a file on corruption in the community; records on the *mikve*; appointment of a rabbi; charitable payments for medical treatment [R], 1885–1915.
(AP Łódź, Rząd Gubernialny, WA, Piotrków)
5. Correspondence on Jewish doctors and medical aid, [R], 1899–1912.
(AP Łódź, Rząd Gubernialny, RO, Piotrków)
6. Files on *chadorim* and elementary schools for boys and girls [R], 1871–1914.
(AP Łódź, Dyrekcja Szkolna, Łódź)
7. Requests to establish philanthropic societies; licenses to found Jewish journals [R], 1908–13.
(AP Łódź, Rząd Gubernialny, KP, Piotrków)
8. Investigations against individuals suspected of illegal activities [R], 1905–12.
(AP Łódź, GZŻ, Piotrków)
9. Fines for evading conscription; records of illegal activities of Jews; request by two Jewish traders to register as agents of the "Portland Cement Company" [R], 1891–1904.
(AP Łódź, Rząd Gubernialny, WP, Piotrków)
10. Correspondence on steps taken by the government to stop pogroms [R], 1906.
(GARF, Moscow, Departament politsii...)
11. Record of a Jew sent into exile [R], 1908.
(AP Łódź, Kancelaria Gubernatora Kaliskiego)

ה ו ד ע ה

היער מיט ווירד בעקאַננט געמאכט , דאַס געגען מיטען מאָנאַט אווגוסט ווערד

אנפֿאַנגען דיא בעשאַפֿטיגונגען אין דער ביאליסטאָקער רעמעסליענא

אוטשיליטשטשע , און דיעזער רעמעסליענאַיע אוטשיליטשטשע

ווערדען אנגענאָממען יודישע קינדער פון ביאליסטאָק און פון דעו

פּראָווינץ אום עלטער פון 13 ביז 16 . דיא יעניגע וועלכע בעזיטצ

איין אַטעסטאַט דאַס זייא האבען גע'ענדיגט איין יעוורייסקאַיע'

נאטשאַלנאַיע אוטשיליטשטשע אָדער איין 2 קלאַססיגע נאראָדנאָ

אוטשיליטשטשע ווערדען אנגענאָממען אהנע פּרופֿונג . דיא יעניג

אבער וועלכע בעזיטצען ניט איין זאָלכען אַטעסטאַט מוסס

זייא בייא דעם אַריינטרעטען אין דער ר עמעסליענאַיי

אוטשיליטשטשע . אום אנגענאַממען צו ווערען . איין עקזאַם

אין דעם קורס פון איין 2 קלאַססיגע נאראָדנאַיע אוטשילישי

בעלייגען . און דער רעמעסליענניע אוטשיליטשטשע ווירד

אבטהיילונגען געעפֿנעט : איין ווערבער - אבטהיילונג . א

איין סלוועסאַר - מעכאַנישע , און דעם יעצטיגען לעהר - יא

ווערדען ניט מעהר וויא 40 שיללער אנגענאָממען , אי

שרייבין זיך קען מען קומען אללע טאג פֿאָן 10 ביז 12 א

ליפּאָווע שטראַססע אין דער נייער הויז פֿאָן ד ער

ת ל מ ו ד ת ו ר ה

Białystok: Opening of a Jewish vocational school, 1905 (Yiddish)

BĘDZIN, surroundings, 1892–1911
Microfilms:
1. A request to establish a cemetery in a village [R], 1905–11.
(AP Łódź, Rząd Gubernialny, WA, Piotrków)
2. Files on *chadorim*, 1895–1900.
(AP Łódź, Dyrekcja Szkolna, Łódź)
3. Investigations of Jews suspected of misdemeanors [R], 1905–11.
(AP Łódz, GZŻ, Piotrków)
4. Fines for evading conscription [R], 1892–1901.
(AP Łódź, Rząd Gubernialny, WP, Piotrków)

BIAŁA (woj. krakowskie) 1766–1920
Microfilms:
1. Reprieve from a death sentence, granted by King Stanisław August Poniatowski, 1766.
(AGAD, Warszawa, Księgi Kanclerskie)
2. Correspondence and minutes on reorganization of schools attended by Jewish pupils [P, G], 1878;
correspondence on the position of rabbi [G], 1896; statistical accounts and lists of pupils in a trade school
[P, G], 1915–20.
(TsDIAU, L'viv, Krajowa Rada Szkolna)

BIAŁA (pow. Rawa Mazowiecka, woj. warszawskie) 1822–1913
Microfilms:
1. The establishment, records and accounts of the community; Jewish purchase of houses, 1822–64.
(AP Łódź, Anterioria Rządu Gubernialnego, Piotrków)
2. Ratification of community elections and accounts; the appointment of a new rabbi [R], 1899–1913.
(AP Łódź, Rząd Gubernialny, WA, Piotrków)
3. Fines for evading conscription [R], 1898–1901.
(AP Łódź, Rząd Gubernialny, WP, Piotrków)

BIAŁA PODLASKA (woj. lubelskie) 1645–1872
Microfilms:
1. Records of an *arenda*, 1645; files on the community; *arendars* and their financial accounts, 1728–1811.
(AGAD, Warszawa, Arch. Radziwiłłów)
2. Files on permission for a Jew to wear traditional dress, 1871–72
(AP Lublin, Rząd Gubernialny, Lublin)

BIAŁOZÓRKA (pow. Krzemieniec, woj. wołyńskie) 1928–1935
Microfilms:
1. List of local children under the care of *Towarzystwo Opieki nad Żydowskimi Sierotami i Opuszczonemi
Dziećmi na Wołyniu* [Society for Care for Jewish Orphans and Abandoned Children in Volhynia] and
budget of the society, 1928–30.
(DATO, Ternopil', Starostwo Powiatowe, Krzemieniec)
2. Files on *chadorim*, 1931–35.
(DATO, Ternopil', Inspektorat Szkolny, Krzemieniec)

BIAŁY KAMIEŃ (pow. Złoczów, woj. Tarnopolskie) 1752–19th cent.
Microfilms:

1. Charter for the town, 1752.
(AGAD, Warszawa, Arch. Radziwiłłów)
2. Instructions on payment of taxes by the Jewish community [P, L], 1784, 1793.
(TsDIAU, L'viv, Kolektsiia dokumentiv…)
3. Inventory, containing lists of inhabitants, 19th cent.
(NBANU, L'viv, Zb. Czołowskiego)

BIAŁYSTOK (woj. białostockie) 1742–1938
Originals:
Copy of the "Psalm-Readers' Society" record book [H], 1766; proclamations, documents and accounts of philanthropic societies [H, R], 1900–10; official proclamations and press cuttings on the pogroms of 1906; telegrams on a conference in Białystok on June 17, [G], 1906; proclamations and manifestos for the State *Duma* elections, 1906–10; birth, marriage and death registers (fragmentary), 1896–1939, [H, P, R, Y]; various invitations [H, R], 1931.
Photocopies:
1. Report on the acquisition of weapon parts by a Jewish merchant from Białystok [R], 1831.
(GARF Moscow, Tret'e otdelenie…)
2. Photographs and inscriptions of tombstones from the Jewish cemetery, 1850–1929.
(Urząd Miejski, Białystok)
Microfilms:
1. *Uniwersał* by Jan Klemens Branicki to the Jews and burghers of the town, 1742; letters on Jews, the community and the *arendas* in Białystok and Tykocin, 1750–1789.
(AGAD, Warszawa, Arch. Roskie)
2. Prussian records on butchers, midwives, and leasing of taverns [G], 1797–1807.
(Staatsarchiv Koenigsberg)
3. Files on the leasing of land belonging to the Catholic Church [R], 1839.
(RGIA, St. Petersburg, Rimsko-katolicheskaia kollegiia…)
4. Birth, marriage and death registers, 1835–77; divorce records, 1846.
(AP Białystok)
5. Files on Jewish smugglers from Białystok [R], 1861.
(GARF, Moscow, Tret'e otdelenie…)
6. Files on Jewish hospitals and homes for the aged [R], 1861–63.
(RGIA, St. Petersburg, Khoziaistvennyi departament MVD)
7. Files on rabbis' salaries, paid from the *krupka* tax [R], 1877–81.
(RGIA, St. Petersburg, Departament dukhovnykh del…)
8. Correspondence of the community with the Alliance Israelite Universelle in Paris [F, H], 1880–1911.
(AIU, Paris)
9. Files on illegal Jewish political organizations [R], 1899–1902.
(GARF, Moscow, Departament politsii…)
10. Order of exile [R], 1907.
(AP Łódź, Kancelaria Gubernatora Kaliskiego)
11. Materials on organization of elections to the State Duma, on the *Bund*'s call to boycott the elections; on the pogrom in Białystok [R], 1905–06.
(RGIA, St. Petersburg, Obshchestvo polnopraviia…)
12. Copies of inscriptions from cemeteries and synagogues, 1910.

(RGIA, St. Petersburg, Departament dukhovnykh del…)
13. Account books of a Jewish hospital, petition of a Jew to exempt him from the community tax [R], 1913.
(AP Białystok, Rząd Gubernialny, Łomża)

BIAŁYSTOK, surroundings, 1566, 1850–1939
Photocopies:
Orders and announcements of the authorities on conscription of Jews, a list of Jewish conscripts from the Białystok *guberniia*, 1850–1852; decrees and circulars by the local authorities requiring information on *Hechalutz* centers, 1938–39.
(AP Suwałki, Akta m. Suwałki)
Microfilms:
Lustracja of the Białystok region, 1566.
(AGAD, Warszawa, ASK)

BIECZ (pow. Gorlice, woj. krakowskie) 1766
Microfilms:
Confirmation by King Stanisław August Poniatowski of the charter, *De non tolerandis Judaeis,* granted to the town [L], 1766.
(AGAD, Warszawa, MK)

BIELSK PODLASKI (woj. białostockie) 1507–1914
Microfilms:
1. Charters and decrees [P, L], 1507–1778.
(TsDIAU, L'viv, Arch. Lubomirskich)
2. *Lustracja* of the town, 1566.
(AGAD, Warszawa, ASK)
3. *Arenda* records [Rt], 1558–61.
(RGADA, Moscow, ML)
4. Files on requests for tax exemptions [R], 1914.
(AP Białystok, Rząd Gubernialny, Łomża)
5. Birth, marriage and death records [R], 1835.
(AP Białystok)
6. Materials on elections to the State *Duma* [R], 1906–07.
(RGIA, St. Petersburg, Obshchestvo polnopraviia…)

BIEŻUŃ (pow. Sierpc, woj. warszawskie), 1856–1864
Microfilms:
Reports and correspondence on the position of rabbi, 1856–64.
(AGAD, Warszawa, CWW)

BIŁGORAJ (woj. lubelskie) 1776–1868
Originals:
Account book of the Orthodox Church in Luchów, containing information on purchases from Jewish merchants from Biłgoraj [R], 1852–68.

Microfilms:
1. Court case on a Jew from Biłgoraj, 1776.
(AP Kraków, Arch. Potockich)

2. Statistical data on the town, 1820–59.
(AP Lublin, Rząd Gubernialny, Lublin)

BIRCZA (pow. Dobromil, woj. lwowskie) 1846–1936
Photocopies:
Community budget and a list of tax payers, 1933–35.
(DALO, L'viv, UW, Lwów)
Microfilms:
1. Documents on confirmation of the Jewish community statutes, 1846–96.
(TsDIAU, L'viv, Namiestnictwo Galicyjskie)
2. Correspondence on community elections, 1869–89.
(TsDIAU, L'viv, Ministerium fuer Kultus und Unterricht, Wien)
3. Correspondence on community matters e.g. budget and elections to the community board, 1925–36; a list of donors from Bircza for a *kollel* from Galicia in *Eretz Yisroel*, 1928–30.
(DALO, L'viv, UW, Lwów)
4. Correspondence about the registration of *Agudas Yisroel*, 1935.
(DALO, L'viv, Magistrat, Lwów)

BISKUPICE (pow. Bochnia, woj. krakowskie) 1786
Microfilms:
Arenda contract, 1786.
(TsDIAU–L'viv, Arch. Lanckorońskich)

BŁASZKI (pow. Kalisz, woj. łódzkie) 1851–1912
Microfilms:
1. Records of the Jewish shelter, 1851–59.
(AP Łódź, ROPK)
2. Reports of police investigations; order of exile; confirmation of the appointment of a new rabbi [R], 1904–12.
(AP Łódź, Kancelaria Gubernatora Kaliskiego)
3. Files on the appointment of a rabbi, 1856–64.
(AGAD, Warszawa, CWW)
4. Copies of inscriptions from cemeteries and synagogues, 1910.
(RGIA, St. Petersburg, Departament dukhovnykh del...)

BŁAŻOWA (pow. Rzeszów, woj. lwowskie) 1846–1937
Microfilms:
1. Documents on confirmation of community statutes, 1846–96.
(TsDIAU, L'viv, Namiestnictwo Galicyjskie)
2. Correspondence about the registration of the *Mizrachi* organization, including statutes and a list of board members, 1930–37.
(DALO, L'viv, Magistrat, Lwów)
3. Correspondence on the community budget, 1933–35.
(DALO, L'viv, UW, Lwów)

BŁONIE (woj. warszawskie) and its surroundings, 1566
Microfilms:

Lustracja, 1566.
(AGAD, Warszawa, ASK)

BOBOWA (pow. Grybów, woj. krakowskie) 1767–1896
Microfilms:
1. *Propinacja, arenda,* taxes and other financial matters between town authorities and the Jewish community [G], 1767–84; a document on a conflict between Jews and Christians in the town, 1784.
(AP Kraków, Teki Schneidra)
2. Documents on confirmation of community statutes, 1846–96.
(TsDIAU, L'viv, Namiestnictwo Galicyjskie)

BOBROWNIKI (pow. Puławy, woj. lubelskie) 1860
Microfilms:
Statistics on the town, 1860.
(AP Lublin, Rząd Gubernialny, Lublin)

BOCHNIA (woj. krakowskie) 1633–1892
Microfilms:
1. Confirmation by King Władysław IV of the royal statute granted to the tailors' guild by King Stefan Batory, with references to Jewish tailors, 1633.
(AGAD, Warszawa, Akta Cechowe m. Bochni)
2. Records of the *starostwo; supliki* by *arendars* of taverns, 1717, 1757.
(AP Kraków, IT)
3. Correspondence with *guberniia* authorities on taxes, 1820–41; correspondence on the leasing of taxes and permission to settle in Bochnia, [G], 1820–59; correspondence with the *starostwo* on recording vital statistics, 1891–92.
(TsDIAU, L'viv, Namiestnictwo Galicyjskie)

BOĆKI (pow. Bielsk, woj. białostockie) 1721–1835
Microfilms:
1. *Pinkas hakahal* (community record book) [H, P], 1721–1808.
(AGAD, Warszawa, Arch. Roskie)
2. Court records relating to the case of a Jew in Boćki [R], 1835.
(AP Białystok, Rząd Gubernialny, Łomża)

BODZENTYN (pow. Kielce, woj. kieleckie) 1850
Microfilms:
Records of a suit against a Jewish *arendar,* 1850.
(AGAD, Warszawa, KRzSW)

BOHORODCZANY (woj. stanisławowskie) 1842–1939
Microfilms:
1. Files on taxes [G], 1842–59; files on Jewish youth and the army [P,G], 1870; correspondence with the district authorities regarding *chadorim,* including lists of children and teachers, 1877–1908; correspondence on communal matters, e.g. elections, community statutes, communal taxes, reorganization of the community, appointment of a rabbi [P,G], 1891–1906.
(TsDIAU, L'viv, Namiestnictwo Galicyjskie)

2. Correspondence on *chadorim* and other private schools, 1878–81, [P,G]; reports on the teaching of the Jewish religion [P,G],1882–89.
(TsDIAU, L'viv, Krajowa Rada Szkolna)
3. Files on the foundation of the *Gmilas Chesed* society, 1928; statutes and correspondence on Zionist and other organizations, including *Hashomer Hatzair,* 1920–37; complaints of cemetery employees; files on the election of a rabbi and a list of community members, 1925–39; files on collecting money for *Eretz Yisroel,* 1926; files on activities of the *Bund, Poalei Zion,* Revisionist Zionists and other political parties, 1923–27; community elections, statutes draft, budget, taxes, statistical reports*,* 1926–38; lists of Jewish organizations and societies, 1930–37.
(DAIFO, Ivano-Frankivs'k, UW, Stanisławów)
4. Statistics on the district, 1920; files on the foundation of the *Hatchiya* society, 1920; files on confirmation of the community budget, 1922–23.
(DAIFO, Ivano-Frankivs'k, Wydział Powiatowy Samorządu, Bohorodczany)

BOJANOWO (pow. Rawicz, woj. poznańskie) 1857–1950
Originals:
A letter from community officials in Leszno, Rawicz and Bojanowo requesting aid for Jewish fire victims [G], 1857; the leaflet of an institute for Jewish deaf, dumb and blind children, requesting donations [G], 1934; *Zur Geschichte der jüdischen Gemeinde und der jüdischen Familien in Bojanowo, Prov. Posen (*a history of the Jewish community and Jewish families in Bojanowo), 1851–1950, by Akiva Posner, 1953.

BOLECHÓW (pow. Dolina, woj. stanisławowskie) 1612–1960
Originals:
Letter of safe conduct, 1794; letter on an individual's debt, 1832; authorization to sell tobacco [G], 1844.
Photocopies:
Photographs of synagogues in Bolechów [R], 1946–60.
(DAIFO, Ivano-Frankivs'k, Upolnomochennyi Soveta…)
Microfilms:
1. Municipal records (fragmentary), 1612–1730.
(AGAD, Warszawa, Zb. Czołowskiego)
2. A protest against an official decision regarding building matters [G], 1813.
(AP Kraków, Teki Schneidra)
3. Correspondence with the Ministry of Religion and Education on a German Jewish school [G], 1844–60; correspondence on elections to the community board and confirmation of community statutes [P, G], 1895–98.
(TsDIAU, L'viv, Namiestnictwo Galicyjskie)
4. Reports on the inspection of Jewish schools and the closing of *chadorim* [P, G], 1861–1909.
(TsDIAU, L'viv, Krajowa Rada Szkolna)
5. Files on elections to the community board, a list of community members, protests regarding the elections and the dissolution of the Jewish community, [P,G], 1905–13.
(TsDIAU, L'viv, Ministerium fuer Kultus und Unterricht, Wien)
6. Files on the *Agudas Achim, Merkaz Ruchani* and *Talmud Tora* societies, 1920–30; records on Zionist organizations, 1921–30; list of boards members of the *Achva* and *Hatzofim Brit Trumpeldor* societies, 1930–37; files on elections to the community board, files on rabbis, 1932–35; records on activities of the All Jewish Labour Party (OŻPP), 1933.
(DAIFO, Ivano-Frankivs'k, UW, Stanisławów)

BOLESŁAWIEC (pow. Wieluń, woj. łódzkie), surroundings, 1534–1615
Microfilms:
Inventories and accounts of the *Starostwo Bolesławskie*, 1534–1615.
(AGAD, Warszawa, ASK)

BOLIMÓW (pow. Łowicz, woj. warszawskie), 1570–1765
Microfilms:
Lustracja, 1570; inventory of *arendas*, 1765.
(AGAD, Warszawa, ASK)

BOŁSZOWCE (pow. Rohatyń, woj. stanisławowskie) 1921–1936
Microfilms:
Files on various organizations, 1921–30; elections to the community board, 1933–36; files on activities of the *Poalei Zion* party, 1935.
(DAIFO, Ivano-Frankivs'k, UW, Stanisławów)

BOREK (pow. Koźmin, woj. poznańskie) 1833–1905
Originals:
Community records: minutes, details of educational and philanthropic activities [G], 1833–1903; correspondence on police matters [G], 1834–44; complaints against the community and individual members [G], 1834–44; community real estate [G], 1834–51; religious matters, divorces [G], 1834–1835; complaints against the burial society [G], 1838–44; tax reports [G], 1838–1900; files on administration of the synagogue [G], 1839–48 legal proceedings against a Jew [G], 1845–46; correspondence on colonization of Jews in the province of Poznań [G], 1846; complaints [G], 1848; community finances [G], 1849, 1904–05; complaints by representatives of the community of Gostyń against the community of Borek regarding burial costs [G], 1861; documents on the foundation of the "*Centralverband für israel. Krankenpfleger in der Provinz Posen* (general organization of Jewish medical personnel in the Posen province) [G], 1893–94; a file on upkeep of the cemetery [G], 1896.
Microfilms:
Litigation between the Catholic Church and the community over interest payments [G], 1828–41; instructions to the community in the wake of the Constitution of 1848 [G], 1848–72; documents relating to religious practices [G], 1849–51; construction of a new synagogue [G], 1855–59; composition and publication of community statutes [G], 1858–94; decisions of the community board [G], 1897–1901.
(Centrum Judaicum, Berlin)

BORSZCZÓW (woj. tarnopolskie) 16th cent.–1930
Originals:
Documents and letters of the Mercantile and Industrial Bank [G, P, Y], 1901–14; correspondence and speeches of Zvi Heller [G, H, P, Y], 1920–30.

Microfilms:
1. List of inhabitants, 16th cent.
(TsDIAU, L'viv, Arch. Lanckorońskich)
2. Correspondence on *chadorim* in the area, including lists of teachers, 1877–1908; correspondence with the district authorities of Tłuste regarding complaints against the community of Borszczów; files on community matters, among them statutes, taxes and the election of a rabbi, [G, P], 1882–1905;

correspondence between the community and district authorities regarding complaints about the community elections, 1904–06; correspondence on reorganization of the community, 1903–06.
(TsDIAU, L'viv, Namiestnictwo Galicyjskie)

BORYNIA (pow. Turka, woj. lwowskie) 1737–1763
Microfilms:
Arenda contracts, 1737–63.
(TsDIAU, L'viv, Arch. Lanckorońskich)

BORYSŁAW (pow. Drohobycz, woj. lwowskie) 1895–1955
Photocopies:
Records of the Ministry of Interior on pogroms in Eastern Poland, 1918–19; reports about the situation and activities of the Jewish community [R], 1949, 1951, 1955.
(DALO, L'viv, Drogobychskii obkom…)
Microfilms:
1. Statutes and correspondence of the *Gmilos Chesed, Osei Tsedek* and other societies [P,G] 1895–1912.
(TsDIAU, L'viv, Namiestnictwo Galicyjskie)
2. Correspondence on founding a separate community, 1909–24; a list of community members, statutes of the community, lists of tax payers, files on elections and budget matters, 1920–39; membership list of a Zionist organization, 1931; reports to the Ministry of Interior on activities of the *Poalei Zion Lewica* party, 1930–32.
(DALO, L'viv, UW, Lwów)
3. Correspondence on registration of the *Machzikei Hadas* society, 1932.
(DALO, L'viv, Magistrat, Lwów)
4. A monograph on the demography and economics of the town and its Jews, 1936.
(AP Wrocław, Ossolineum, WKNZNP, Lwów)

BOŻEJEWO (pow. Łomża, woj. białostockie) 1915
Microfilms:
Reports by the gendarmerie on Jews arrested for political disloyalty [R], 1915.
(AP Białystok, Rząd Gubernialny, Łomża)

BÓBRKA (woj. lwowskie) 1738–1939
Photocopies:
1. Letter by the Ministry of Religious Affairs to the governor of Lwów requiring data on Jewish communities and reports from various cities, including Bóbrka, 1920–23.
(DALO L'viv, UW, Lwów)
2. Lists of merchants, entrepreneurs and homeowners [R], 1939.
(DALO L'viv, L'vovskii obkom…)
Microfilms:
1. A receipt from the Jewish community to the priest of Wołków, 1738.
(TsDIAU, L'viv, Kolektsiia dokumentiv pro katolyts'ki monastyri…)
2. Correspondence with the district authorities regarding *chadorim,* including lists of *melamdim,* 1877–1908; correspondence with the *Ahavas Zion* colonization society about emigration to Palestine, 1898; correspondence with the district authorities about a candidate for the rabbinate, 1899–1904.
(TsDIAU, L'viv, Namiestnictwo Galicyjskie)
3. Reports on teaching Jewish religion in elementary schools, [G, P], 1882–89.

(TsDIAU, L'viv, Krajowa Rada Szkolna)
4. Statistical data on churches, cemeteries and synagogues over 50 years old, 1924.
(DALO, L'viv, Starostwo Powiatowe, Bóbrka)
5. Correspondence and reports on community elections and budgets; statistics on political parties in the region; correspondence about Zionist organizations including names of active members; correspondence about *Poalei Zion* and *Kultur Liga*; statistics of community board members and rabbis; permission to solicit funds for the Galician *kollel* in *Eretz Yisroel*, 1926–39.
(DALO, L'viv, UW, Lwów)
6. Correspondence on the registration of *Agudas Yisroel* and *Machzikei Hadas*, 1932, 1934.
(DALO, L'viv, Magistrat, Lwów)
7. Lists of traders from the region of Bóbrka with enterprises in other regions, [U], 1939.
(DALO, L'viv, L'vovskii obkom…)

BRATKOWCE (pow. Stanisławów, woj. stanisławowskie) 1930
Microfilms:
Reports of elementary school principals in the Stanisławów region [P, U], 1930.
(DAIFO, Ivano-Frankivs'k, Inspektorat Szkolny, Stanisławów)

BRDÓW (pow. Koło, woj. łódzkie) 1891
Microfilms:
Request by the community to join the Kalisz religious district [R], 1891.
(AP Łódź, Rząd Gubernialny, WA, Kalisz)

BRODNICA (pow. Śrem, woj. poznańskie) 1924
Originals:
Three letters on synagogue maintenance [G], 1924.

BRODY (woj. tarnopolskie) 1651–1919
Originals:
Conferral of the title of *chaver* [H], 1695; testimony before the rabbinical court at the Brody fair [Y], 1750; a letter from the municipality to a Jew, 1759, confirmation of Jewish ownership of property in villages [H], 1799; a marriage agreement and its German translation [G, H], 1801; a report on the Mayer Kallir foundation [G], 1879;.
Microfilms:
1. *Suplika* of the Brody town council to the council of Lwów on raising taxes from Jewish traders of Brody, 1651.
(TsDIAU, L'viv, Kolektsiia lystiv…)
2. Contracts, *supliki*, and other materials [P, L, G], 1686–1805.
(AP Lublin, Zb. Czołowskiego)
3. Promissory notes, rabbinical court testimonies, letters etc. [H, Y], 1711–1845.
(TsDIAU, Kyiv, Arch. Potockich z Tulczyna)
4. *Suplika* of the Jews, 1730; a letter from the bishop of Łuck to the community of Brody [P,L], 1744; Jewish and Christian population statistics for army conscription, 1778, 1783; a list of Jewish and Christian tradesmen, 1783.
(NBANU, L'viv, Arch. Ossolińskich)
5. Requests of Jewish traders to enter Russia with merchandise [R], 1739.
(TsDIAU, Kyiv, Kievskaia gubernskaia kantseliariia)

6. Confirmation of an agreement between the communities of Brody and Żółkiew [P, L], 1752.
(AGAD, Warszawa, Arch. Radziwiłłów)
7. Records of the repayment of a debt to a Jew, 1772.
(AP Kraków, Arch. Podhoreckie Andrzeja hr. Potockiego)
8. Files on *arenda* and *propinacja*, 1774–76; commerce matters, 1775–76, 1783; complaints against the *Oberlandrabbiner*, 1785–86; complaints of Jewish merchants regarding customs taxes, 1786–1805; a letter of a Jew on his debt to the Dominican convent in Tarnopol, 1787; files on Jewish service in the army, 1788–89; establishment of a private synagogue, 1794; files on Jewish agricultural settlements, 1794, 1802, 1880; files on the Jewish hospital, 1800, 1808, 1829; building of a Jewish school, 1808; elections to the Jewish community, 1802, 1827, 1830; a list of eligible voters to the *Sejm* [G, P], 1870.
(AP Kraków, Teki Schneidra)
9. Correspondence between the community and the Alliance Israélite Universelle, Paris [F, H], 1870–91.
(AIU, Paris)
10. Report on a Jewish school, 1878 [P, G]; files on opening a trade school, 1888.
(TsDIAU, L'viv, Krajowa Rada Szkolna)
11. Correspondence on the opening of a Jewish school, 1784; correspondence on the Jewish school (*Realschule*), 1817–19; correspondence with the Jewish election committee in Brody about the voting rights of Jews in different cities in Galicia, 1829–35; correspondence on moving Jews 50 km from the border, 1843; correspondence with regional authorities on the *Henrietta von Wertheimstein* foundation, 1830–1916 and the *Majer Kallir* foundation for a Jewish school, 1854–60 [G]; reports about Jewish communities in the Brody district [G, P], 1890; correspondence on the *Postęp* society, including statutes, 1894–95; correspondence with the *starostwo* on taxes and confirmation of the Jewish community statutes, 1895–1905; correspondence on election of a rabbi, 1904–05; correspondence regarding the *Bursa Żydowska* for elementary and high school pupils, 1904–07 [G]; statutes of the *Safa Berura* society, 1910.
(TsDIAU, L'viv, Namiestnictwo Galicyjskie)
12. Documents on Jewish community taxes, 1913–19 [P, G]; a report of a fund for Jewish schools in Lwów, Brody and Tarnopol [G], 1915–18.
(TsDIAU, L'viv, Ministerium fuer Kultus und Unterricht, Wien)

BROK (pow. Ostrów Mazowiecki, woj. białostockie) 1912–1915
Microfilms:
Files on the arrest of Jews accused of assisting other Jews to leave Russia illegally [R], 1912–15.
(AP Białystok, Rząd Gubernialny, Łomża)

BRONOWO (pow. Łomża, woj. białostockie) 1912–15
Microfilms:
Files on the arrest of Jews accused of assisting other Jews to leave Russia illegally [R], 1912–15.
(AP Białystok, Rząd Gubernialny, Łomża)

BROSZNIÓW (pow. Dolina, woj. stanisławowskie) 1930–1960
Photocopies:
Report on synagogues and prayer houses, photographs of synagogues [R], 1946,1957, 1960.
(DAIFO, Ivano-Frankivs'k, Upolnomochennyi Soveta…)
Microfilms:
List of members of the *Herzliah* society, 1930; file on a candidate for the rabbinate, 1936; files on *WIZO*, 1937–38.

(DAIFO, Ivano-Frankivs'k, UW, Stanisławów)

BRUŻYCA (pow. Łódź, woj. łódzkie) 1871–1914
Microfilms:
Records on the seal tax and local taxes; records of district meetings; foreign citizens; records of food stocks and prices; requests for the return of transport costs; reports on synagogue and community affairs; Jewish educational, medical, philanthropic and financial matters [R], 1871–1914.
(AP Łódź, Urząd Gminy, Brużyca)

BRZESKO (woj. krakowskie) 1708–1904
Microfilms
1. An inventory of the town, 1708.
(AP Wrocław, Ossolineum)
2. Correspondence on Jewish merchants [G], 1784; a report on the Jewish community [G], 1785.
(AP Kraków, Teki Schneidra)
3. Correspondence on *propinacja,* 1850–58; files on an inn's *arenda,* 1852–67.
(AGAD, Warszawa, KRzPiS)
4. Reports on inspection of Baron Hirsch Foundation (JCA) schools [P, G], 1896–1904.
(TsDIAU, L'viv, Krajowa Rada Szkolna)

BRZEŚĆ KUJAWSKI (pow. Włocławek, woj. warszawskie) 1775–1877
Originals:
Copies of marriage records (fragmentary) [P, R], 1839–77.
Microfilms:
Letter from King Stanisław August Poniatowski granting the Jews one year's protection from the local judge, 1775.
(AGAD, Warszawa, Księgi Kanclerskie)

BRZEŚĆ LITEWSKI (woj. poleskie) 15th–20th cent.
Originals:
Letter from the community on Jewish captives [H], 1741; copy of King Zygmunt August's 1562
charter to the Jews, 1766; two printed proclamations issued by the *Chevras Tohoras Banos* [Y], 20th cent.
Photocopies:
Excerpts from municipal records on Jews [Rt], 1589–1679; decree by Kazimierz Pac releasing Jews from payment of taxes after the Cossack incursion [Rt], 1674.
(NIAB, Minsk, Brestskii zemskii sud)
Microfilms:
1. Municipal records [L], 15th cent.
(Bibl. Uniwersytecka, Warszawa)
2. Charter to the Jewish community on tax exemptions after a fire, 1613; confirmation by King Jan III Sobieski of a charter to the Jewish community, 1669.
(AGAD, Warszawa, Archiwum Radziwiłłów)
3. A court verdict in Lublin on litigation between a Jew from Brześć Litewski and furriers from Przemyśl [L], 1655.
(AP Przemysl, Akta m. Przemyśla)
4. Files on *arendas* and taxes, [Rt], 16th cent.
(RGADA, Moscow, ML)

5. Memorandum of the community requesting a prolongation of debt payments, 1785.
(RGADA, Moscow, KFE)
6. File on confiscation of goods brought to Brześć from Gdańsk by a Jewish trader [R], 1803.
(RGADA, Moscow, Kommerts-kollegiia)
7. File on the Jewish hospital and old-age home [R], 1863–64.
(RGIA, St. Petersburg, Khoziaistvennyi departament MVD)
8. Correspondence of the community with the *Alliance Israélite Universelle*, Paris [F, H], 1882–1908.
(AIU, Paris)
9. Correspondence on organization of elections to the State *Duma* [R], 1905–07.
(RGIA, St. Petersburg, Obshchestvo polnopraviia...)
10. Correspondence on steps taken by the government to prevent or stop pogroms [R], 1906.
(GARF, Moscow, Departament politsii...)

BRZEŚCIANY (pow. Sambor, woj. lwowskie) 1936
Microfilms:
Monograph on demographic and economic data, 1936.
(AP Wrocław, Ossolineum, WKNZNP, Lwów)

BRZEZINY (woj. łódzkie) 1822–1915
Microfilms:
1. Records of the community and its debts, 1822–65.
(AP Łódź, Anterioria Rządu Gubernialnego, Piotrków)
2. Ratification of community elections and accounts; reports on the *arenda* of community income and the *mikve*; reports on the construction of a new synagogue and the renovation of the *mikve*; sale of seats in the synagogue; the appointment of a religious official [R], 1885–1915.
(AP Łódź, Rząd Gubernialny, WA, Piotrków)
3. Reports on *chadorim* and other Jewish elementary schools [R], 1912–13.
(AP Łódź, Dyrekcja Szkolna, Łódź)
4. Fines for evading conscription, 1891–1901; investigation of a group of Jews who participated in a demonstration [R], 1906.
(AP Łódź, Rząd Gubernialny, WP, Piotrków)

BRZEZINY, surroundings, 1889–1909
Microfilms:
1. Correspondence on *chadorim,* 1889–98.
(AP Łódź, Dyrekcja Szkolna, Łódź)
2. Fines for evading conscription [R], 1892–99.
(AP Łódź, Rząd Gubernialny, WP, Piotrków)
3. A request to open a kerosene store [R], 1909.
(AP Łódź, Rząd Gubernialny, WA, Piotrków)

BRZEŻANY (woj. tarnopolskie), 1628–1930
Microfilms:
1. Contracts, accounts, inventories, lists of taxes and other materials on Jews on the Sieniawski and Czartoryski estates, 1628–1785.
(Bibl. Czartoryskich, Kraków)
2. *Lustracja* of the poll tax on Czartoryski estates, 1766.

(AGAD, Warszawa, Arch. Potockich w Łańcucie)
3. Lists of Jewish and non-Jewish tax payers, 1772–1826.
(TsDIAU, L'viv, Arch. Lanckorońskich)
4. Reports about Jewish and non-Jewish schools, 1788; correspondence on leases, taxes, sale of wine, residence, marriage permits [G], 1798–1859.
(TsDIAU, L'viv, Namiestnictwo Galicyjskie)
5. Reports andcorrespondence on *chadorim* and Jewish schools, [P,G], 1878–81.
(TsDIAU, L'viv, Krajowa Rada Szkolna)
6. Correspondence on restoration of the 300 years' old cemetery, 1930.
(DALO, L'viv, UW, Lwów)

BRZEŻANY, surroundings, 1666–1698
Microfilms:
1. Excerpt from an inventory of a nearby village, 1666.
(AP Kraków, Teki Schneidra)
2. Inventory of the district, 1698.
(AP Wrocław, Ossolineum)

BRZEŹNICA (pow. Radomsko, woj. łódzkie) 1822–1913
Microfilms:
1. Reports on community accounts, 1822–66.
(AP Łódź, Anterioria Rządu Gubernialnego, Piotrków)
2. Ratification of community elections and accounts; appointment of a new rabbi [R], 1889–1913.
(AP Łódź, Rząd Gubernialny, WA, Piotrków)
3. Fines for evading conscription [R], 1895–1901.
(AP Łódź, Rząd Gubernialny, WP, Piotrków)
4. Files on appointment of rabbis, 1856–64.
(AGAD, Warszawa, CWW)

BRZOSTOWICA WIELKA (pow. Grodno, woj. białostockie) 1629–1841
Microfilms:
Supliki and letters [P, R], 1629–1841.
(TsDIAU, Kyiv, Arch. Potockich z Tulczyna)

BRZOZDOWCE (pow. Bóbrka, woj. lwowskie) 1738–1935
Photocopies:
Community budget and a list of taxpayers, 1933–35.
(DALO, L'viv, UW, Lwów)
Microfilms:
1. *Arenda* contracts, 1738–76.
(TsDIAU, L'viv, Arch. Lanckorońskich)
2. Minutes and inventory on the sale of a Jewish estate in the town for debts, 1819.
(TsDIAU, L'viv, Kolektsiia dokumentiv…)
3. Reports and other materials on community elections; correspondence on budget matters; list of taxpayers, 1929–35.
(DALO, L'viv, UW, Lwów)

BRZOZÓW (woj. lwowskie) 1853–1938
Microfilms:
1. Correspondence on leasing inns on land owned by Christians [G], 1853; correspondence with the district authorities regarding *chadorim*, including lists of *melamdim,* 1877–1908.
(TsDIAU, L'viv, Namiestnictwo Galicyjskie)
2. Files on community board elections, on community matters, budget, rabbinate, list of taxpayers, list of community board members; statistical data on political parties, 1928–38.
(DALO, L'viv, UW, Lwów)

BRZOZÓW, surroundings, 1748
A *lustracja* of the entire district, 1748.
(AP Wrocław, Ossolineum)

BUCZACZ (woj. tarnopolskie) 17[th]cent.–1910
Original:
Receipt of payment for release from military service [G], 1853.
Photocopy:
Suplika on debts, 17th cent.
(AGAD, Warszawa, DP)
Microfilms:
1. Supplication by a Jewish trader to be released from debts to Wallachians, 17th cent.
(AGAD, Warszawa, DP)
2. Files on sale of houses by Jews, and trade contracts, 1664–1709.
(NBANU, L'viv, Zb. Czołowskiego)
3. Contracts, *supliki*, receipts and other materials on Jews [H,Y,L,P], 1686–1805.
(AP Lublin, Zb. Czołowskiego)
4. Files on *shechita,* 1704–21.
(NBANU, L'viv, Arch. Ossolińskich)
5. Description of the town, 1783; propaganda urging young Jews to enlist in the army [P, G], 1870; statutes of various societies, 1873–74; reports, including lists of *chadorim* 1877–78, 1892–1908; correspondence on vital statistics registers, 1891–92; files on *shechita,* 1894–97; correspondence and reports on confirmation of community statutes, 1895–99; correspondence with the *Ahavas Zion* colonization society about emigration to Palestine, 1898; correspondence on community elections, 1901–04; correspondence regarding the *Bursa Żydowska* society for elementary and high school students, 1904–07.
(TsDIAU, L'viv, Namiestnictwo Galicyjskie)
6. Inquiry into a dispute between two Jews [P, G], 1821.
(TsDIAU, L'viv, Arch. Lanckorońskich)
7. Files on citizenship for 29 Jews who evaded military service, 1840–41
(TsDIAU, Kyiv, Kantseliaria…)
8. Reports, including lists of *chadorim* and *melamdim,* 1875–77; files on teaching Jewish religion in a public school for boys, including statistical data on the Jewish pupils of this school, 1902–10.
(TsDIAU, L'viv, Krajowa Rada Szkolna)
9. Files on relations between the community and the landowners, churches, city administration and tailors' association, on taxes, trade in wood and salt; a list of voters (1870), a charter given to the Jews by the Potocki family, 1771–1870; permission to open a Jewish school [G, P], 1877.
(AP Kraków, Teki Schneidra)

BUDZANÓW (pow. Czortków, woj. tarnopolskie) 1753–1786
Microfilms:
1. *Arenda* contract, 1753.
(AP Lublin, Zb. Czołowskiego)
2. Various receipts of the community, [P, G, H] 1738–86.
(NBANU, L'viv, Zb. Goldsteina)

BUK (pow. Grudziądz, woj. pomorskie) 1848–1873
Originals:
An appeal for funds in the wake of attacks on Jews and destruction of the synagogue [G], 1848; printed list of donors for a new synagogue [G], 1872–1873.

BUKACZOWCE (pow. Rohatyń, woj. stanisławowskie) 1910–1936
Microfilms:
1. Reports and correspondence on mistreatment of the local rabbi [P, G], 1910–11.
(TsDIAU, L'viv, Ministerium fuer Kultus und Unterricht, Wien)
2. Reports, lists, statutes and correspondence of various societies, 1921–38; files on community elections, 1932–36.
(DAIFO, Ivano–Frankivs'k, UW, Stanisławów)
3. A list of *chadorim*, 1934–36.
(DAIFO, Ivano–Frankivs'k, Inspektorat Szkolny, Stanisławów)

BUKOWSKO (pow. Sanok, woj. lwowskie) 1846–1938
Microfilms:
1. Files on confirmation of the community statutes, 1846–96.
(TsDIAU, L'viv, Namiestnictwo Galicyjskie)
2. Correspondence with the *starostwo* in Sanok on uniting the Nowotaniec Jewish community with that of Bukowsko, 1921–25; correspondence on election of a rabbi, 1924–31; authorization to collect money for the Galician *kollel* in Palestine (*Eretz Yisroel*), including a list of donors, 1928–30; reports and correspondence on community board elections, 1930–38; correspondence on the community budget; and a list of tax payers, 1932–35.
(DALO, L'viv, UW, Lwów)

BURSZTYN (pow. Rohatyń, woj. stanisławowskie) 1753–1937
Microfilms:
1. Files on payments of military taxes, 1753–67.
(TsDIAU, L'viv, Arch. Lanckorońskich)
2. Statute of the *Żydowski Konsum Ludowy* society, 1920; files on the Jewish public library, 1921–30.
(DAIFO, Ivano-Frankivs'k, Starostwo Powiatowe, Rohatyn)
3. Reports, correspondence and statutes of various societies, organizations and parties, among them *Gmilas Chesed, Linas Hatzedek, Ezra, Hatzofim Brit Trumpeldor, Bund* and *Poalei Zion*, 1921–37; reports and correspondence on activities of the community, and a list of members, 1931–35.
(DAIFO, Ivano-Frankivs'k, UW, Stanisławów)

BUSK (pow. Kamionka Strumiłowa, woj. tarnopolskie) 1411–1843
Microfilms:
1. Receipt from the Jewish community to a monastery [L], 1732.

(TsDIAU, L'viv, Kolektsiia dokumentiv pro katolyts'ki monastyri…)

2. Castle Court decree on exempting the Jewish community from taxes to the monastery in Derewlany [L], 1734.

(NBANU, L'viv, Klasztor Bazylianów)

3. Charters of Polish kings to Busk; decrees of the *starosta* to the Jews of Busk (1746); *lustracje,* including descriptions of the Jewish houses in Busk and the surroundings (1765) [P, L], 1411–1843; statistical information, a list of inhabitants, 1820.

(NBANU, L'viv, Zb. Czołowskiego)

4. A decision of the Council of Four Lands in Jarosław on relations between communities, among them Busk, [P, L], 1758.

(NBANU, L'viv, Arch. Radzimińskich)

5. Correspondence on leasing, taxes, residence permission and tolls [G], 1819–1828.

(TsDIAU, L'viv, Namiestnictwo Galicyjskie)

BUSKO (pow. Stopnica, woj. kieleckie) 1864–1866
Microfilms:
Litigation between the Crown Treasury and a Jew, 1864–66.
(AGAD, Warszawa, RSKP)

BYCHAWA (pow. Lublin, woj. lubelskie) 1830–1864
Microfilms:
1. Reports and correspondence on the positions of rabbis, 1856–1864.
(AGAD, Warszawa, CWW)
2. Statistical description, 1830–1861.
(AP Lublin, Rząd Gubernialny, Lublin)

BYDGOSZCZ (woj. poznańskie) 1809–1937
Originals:
Payment of tax on kosher meat [G], 1809; reports on Jewish doctors 1815–64; payments to exempt various community members from military service, 1820–29; records on community elections, organization, taxation [G], 1820–58, 1886; files on the *mikve* [G], 1820, 1859–66; regulations, 1825–32; complaints to the community, 1825–90; files on maintaining order during prayers [G], 1827–83; draft of community statute [G], 1830; files on building a new synagogue [G], 1830–39; inaugurations of synagogues [G], 1834, 1884; construction of new houses [G], 1835–58; community minutes [G], 1836–40; files on acquiring *etrog* and *lulav* [G], 1836–40; reports on a Jewish agricultural colony, 1838; files on kosher wine [G], 1840–47; assistance for needy Jews [G], 1844; correspondence with the Ministry of Justice and records of legal cases, 1852–64, 1886; decisions, circulars and documents of community administration [G], 1857–83; files on *gabbaim* [G], 1860–74; files on shechita [G], 1861–65, 1880–84; requests for aid [G], 1864–93; file on food for soldiers and prisoners during Passover [G], 1865–83; files on cantors [G], 1867–84; files on religious schools [G], 1867, 1877–84; decisions of the community board [G], 1880–84; files on teachers and rabbis [G], 1880–91; files on the new cemetery [G], 1880–83; plan of a synagogue [G], 1883; invitations to community meetings, 1937;
Microfilms:
Files on Jewish doctors [G], 1816–1842; residence rights and tolerance of Jews from other places [G], 1830–59; files on decisions of the community representatives [G], 1835–79; files on elections; communal opposition to the "Bromberger Tagblatt" newspaper [G], 1882–83.

(Centrum Judaicum, Berlin)

BYDGOSZCZ, surroundings, 1855–1859
Microfilms:
Financial accounts of Jewish communities in the district [G], 1855–59.
(AP Bydgoszcz, Kgl. Reg. Bromberg Praesidialabteilung)

BYSZÓW (pow. Podhajce, woj. tarnopolskie) 1749
Register of goods stolen from a Jew, 1749.
(AP Lublin, Castr. Rel., Horodło)

CHEŁM (woj. lubelskie) 1642–1917
Originals:
Letter on *propinacja*, 1805; programs of the German Jewish theater [G], 1917.
Photocopies:
Permission to settle in Chęciny, Chełm and Kazimierz, 1677.
(Bibl. Łopacińskiego, Lublin)
Microfilms:
1. Settlement of accounts between the local community and the Dominican order in Lublin, 1642; letter from the municipality on the sale of alcohol, 1805.
(Bibl. im. Łopacińskiego, Lublin)
2. Jewish population and tax lists, 1705–08.
(Bibl. Czartoryskich, Kraków)
3. Court case between two Jews, involving debts, 1737.
(AP Kraków, Arch. Sanguszków)
4. Authorization of the burial society; excerpts from municipal records; a demand by the National Education Commission to the community for payment; poll tax records from Chełm and Bełz. 1755–86.
(AP Lublin, Księgi Grodzkie Chełmskie)
5. Decree of the Royal Treasury on the settling of accounts between the community of Chełm and monks from Krasnystaw, 1782.
(AP Lublin)
6. Settlement of a dispute between the communities of Chełm and Bełz and that of Zamość on the allocation of the poll tax; decree of the Crown Treasury on the settlement of community debts to the Krasnystaw Jesuit Order, 1782.
(AP Lublin, Castr. Rel. Man. Obl., Krasnystaw)
7. Correspondence and reports on appointment of rabbis, 1856–64.
(AGAD, Warszawa, CWW)
8. Files on the *arenda* of a *mikve*, 1875–76.
(AP Lublin, Rząd Gubernialny, Lublin)

CHEŁM, surroundings, 1710–1915
Microfilms:
1. Declaration of the Chełm and Krasnystaw *Sejmik* on the poll tax paid by Jews and Christians, 1710.
(AP Lublin, Castr. Rel. Man. Obl., Krasnystaw)
2. Instructions to the delegation from Chełm to the *Sejm* in Warsaw on the prohibition to lease *arendas* to Jews; poll tax records. 1744–81.
(AP Lublin, Księgi Grodzkie Chełmskie)

3. Denunciations of the pro-German attitude of Jews and correspondence on the release of Jews from prison and from other punishments, 1914–15.
(RGVIA, Moscow, Shtab…)

CHEŁMIK (pow. Chrzanów, woj. krakowskie) 1821–1862
Microfilms:
Correspondence on budgets, income and expenses of the community, 1821–62.
(AGAD, Warszawa, CWW)

CHĘCINY (pow. Kielce, woj. kieleckie) 1534–1867
Photocopy:
Permission to settle in Chęciny, Chełm and Kazimierz, 1677.
(Bibl. Łopacińskiego, Lublin)
Microfilms:
1. *Lustracje* of the Sandomierz province, including Chęciny, 1534–1615.
(AGAD, Warszawa, ASK)
2. General permission (including for Jews) to settle in Chęciny, Chełm and Kazimierz Dolny, 1677.
(Bibl. im. Łopacińskiego, Lublin)
3. Decisions in court cases between Jews, 1747.
(AP Kraków, Arch. Sanguszków)
4. Confirmation by King Stanisław August Poniatowski of the charter granted to the Jews [L, P], 1765.
(AGAD, Warszawa, Księgi Kanclerskie)
5. Correspondence on payment of taxes; sale and purchase of a house for the rabbi, 1819–67.
(AGAD, Warszawa, CWW)
6. Files on community debts to the Church in Jędrzejów, 1836–48.
(AGAD, Warszawa, KRzPiS)
7. Request by the community for the refund of "protection money" paid between 1817 and 1822, 1865.
(AGAD, Warszawa, RSKP)

CHMIELNIK (pow. Stopnica, woj. kieleckie) 1851–1915
Microfilms:
1. Records of loans taken by Jews for building purposes, 1851–65.
(AGAD, Warszawa KRzSW)
2. Description by N. L. Twersky of the situation of the Jews in Chmielnik during occupation of the Russian Army there [R], 1914–15.
(GARF, Moscow, Bomash)

CHMIELÓW (pow. Tarnobrzeg, woj. lwowskie) 1613
Original:
Last will and testament of a Jew, 1613.

CHOCIMIERZ (pow. Tłumacz, woj. stanisławowskie) 1896–1936
Microfilms:
1. Minutes from inspections of Baron Hirsch Foundation (JCA) schools, 1896–1904.
(TsDIAU, L'viv, Krajowa Rada Szkolna)
2. Correspondence between the community and the district authorities on the community statutes, including a copy of them, 1898–1906.

(TsDIAU, L'viv, Namiestnictwo Galicyjskie)
3. Correspondence on community elections, 1932–36.
(DAIFO, Ivano-Frankivs'k, UW, Stanisławów)

CHODAKÓWKA (pow. Rzeszów, woj. lwowskie) 1878
Microfilms:
Correspondence and reports on reorganization of elementary schools attended by Jewish pupils [G, P], 1878.
(TsDIAU, L'viv, Krajowa Rada Szkolna)

CHODECZ (pow. Włocławek, woj. warszawskie) 1826–1930.
Originals:
Copies of Jewish marriage records (fragmentary) [P, R], 1826–1903; 1928–30.
Microfilms:
Copies of inscriptions from cemeteries and synagogues, 1910.
(RGIA, St. Petersburg, Departament dukhovnykh del…)

CHODEL (pow. Lublin, woj. lubelskie) 1827–1873
Microfilms:
Statistical description of the town, 1827–50; files on founding a new Jewish community; elections of community elders; establishing a cemetery [R], 1869–73.
(AP Lublin, Rząd Gubernialny, Lublin)

CHODORÓW (pow. Bóbrka, woj. lwowskie) 1720–1939
Originals:
Two letters from the municipality to the community, on a request to extend the cemetery, 1902, 1906; drawing of a wooden synagogue, n.d.
(IKG Wien - Juedisches Museum)

Microfilms:
1. Community budget and list of tax payers, 1933–35.
(DALO, L'viv, UW, Lwów)
2. Files on payments of a military tax by the Jews, 1720–67; court case on a Jew [L], 1736; complaint of a Jew, 1758; a list of taverns, 18th cent.
(TsDIAU, L'viv, Arch. Lanckorońskich)
3. Correspondence with the district authorities regarding *chadorim* including lists of *melamdim*, 1877–1908; correspondence on the community statutes [P,G], 1898; correspondence on elections to the community board [P,G], 1903–06.
(TsDIAU, L'viv, Namiestnictwo Galicyjskie)
4. Correspondence on civil registration in the community, 1927–29; files on an investigation against the rabbi, 1931–39; files on founding a *Machzikei Hadas* society, 1932–33; files on elections of a rabbi and community board [P, Y], 1932–39; correspondence about the community budget; a list of tax payers, 1933–35.
(DALO, L'viv, UW, Lwów)
5. Correspondence about the registration of *Agudas Yisroel*, 1933.
(DALO, L'viv, Magistrat, Lwów)

CHODZIEŻ (woj. poznańskie) 1790–1891
Originals:
Two letters from the community in Chodzież to the community in Frankfurt on the Oder regarding the estate of a Jewish merchant who died in Frankfurt [H], 1790; account book of the prayer house [G], 1813–91; *memorbuch* of the tailors' society prayer house [H], 1819; records on relations between the Church and the community, 1826–36; *memorbuch* of the community prayer house [H], 1834.
Microfilms:
1. Community statutes [G], 1833–65.
(AP Poznań, Akta miast, woj. poznańskie)
2. Community accounts; upkeep of the synagogue; payment of the recruiting tax [G], 1835–41, 1872.
(AP Poznań, Gmina Żydowska, Chodzież)

CHOMIAKÓW (pow. Stanisławów, woj. stanisławowskie) 1920–1921
Microfilms:
Statistical reports on children attending school, 1920–21.
(DAIFO, Ivano-Frankivs'k, Inspektorat Szkolny, Stanisławów)

CHOMSK (pow. Drohiczyn, woj. poleskie) 1896
Microfilms:
Copies from various *pinkassim* [H], 1896.
(GARF, Moscow, Marek)

CHOROSTKÓW (pow. Kopyczyńce, woj. tarnopolskie) 1816–1936
Microfilms:
1. Listing of houses for the military tax, including a list of Jewish house owners [G], 1816.
(AP Kraków, Teki Schneidra)
2. Correspondence between the community and the district authorities regarding the community statutes, complaints against the community elections, 1896–1905.
(TsDIAU, L'viv, Namiestnictwo Galicyjskie)
3. Files on the election of a rabbi, 1913–19.
(TsDIAU, L'viv, Ministerium fuer Kultus und Unterricht, Wien)
4. Monograph on demographic and economic aspects, 1936.
(AP Wrocław, Ossolineum, WKNZNP, Lwów)

CHOROSTKÓW POLSKI (pow. Stanisławów, woj. stanisławowskie) 1930
Microfilms:
Reports by elementary school principals on social, economic, ethnic, and cultural aspects of the population [P,U], 1930.
(DAIFO, Ivano-Frankivs'k, Inspektorat Szkolny, Stanisławów)

CHOROSZCZ (pow. Białystok, woj. białostockie) 1826–1937
Originals:
Photographs of tombstones from the Jewish cemetery, 1826–1937; marriage records (fragmentary), 1931–32.

CHORZELE (pow. Przasnysz, woj. warszawskie) 1818–1871
Microfilms:
Files on the *eruv* in Jewish neighborhoods, 1818–71.

(AGAD, Warszawa, CWW)

CHORZÓW see KRÓLEWSKA HUTA

CHRÓŚCIN (pow. Wieluń, woj. łódzkie) 1534–1615
Microfilms:
Inventory of the town, 1534–1615
(AGAD, Warszawa, ASK)

CHOTYNICZE (pow. Łuninice, woj. poleskie) 1855–1892
Photocopies:
Investigation files on unauthorized Jewish schools, teaching Jewish subjects and the Russian language [R], 1855–92.
(NIAB, Minsk, Minskii okruzhnoi sud)

CHRYPLIN (pow. Stanisławów, woj. stanisławowskie) 1923–1939
Microfilms:
1. Statistical data from the civil registry office, 1923–24; files on confirmation of community statutes, and registration of various societies, 1928–39.
(DAIFO, Ivano-Frankivs'k, Starostwo Powiatowe, Stanisławów)
2. Reports by elementary school principals on social, economic, ethnic, and cultural characteristics of the population, [P,U], 1930
(DAIFO, Ivano-Frankivs'k, Inspektorat Szkolny, Stanisławów)

CHRZANÓW (woj. krakowskie) 1707–1904
Photocopies:
Statutes of the Jewish community, 1901–04

Microfilms:
1. Various legal records of the community; minute books of the synagogue and the rabbinical court [H, P], 1707–1815.
(AP Kraków, IT)
2. Collection of documents, mainly promissory notes [H, P], 1730–96
(TsDIAU, Kyiv, Arch. Tarło)
3. Files of the Department of Internal Affairs and Police concerning the Jewish communities in Kraków and Chrzanów (on rabbinate, taxes, Jewish hospital, Jewish marriage etc.), 1816–53.
(AP Kraków, Arch. Wolnego Miasta Krakowa)
4. Files on closing *chadorim* [P, G], 1868–74; *Starostwo* reports on *chadorim* [P, G], 1875–77; minutes from inspections of Baron Hirsch Foundation (JCA) schools, [G, P] 1896–1904.
(TsDIAU, L'viv, Krajowa Rada Szkolna)
5. Correspondence with the authorities on registration of vital statistics; correspondence on the position of a rabbi and on the confirmation of the community statutes [P, G], 1891–96.
(TsDIAU, L'viv, Namiestnictwo Galicyjskie)

CHYRÓW (pow. Stary Sambor, woj. lwowskie) 1802–1939
Original:
Drawing of a wooden synagogue, n.d.
(IKG Wien - Juedisches Museum)

Microfilms:
1. An inventory of the town, 1802.
(AP Wrocław, Ossolineum)
2. Correspondence with the authorities in Dobromil on transferring certain neighborhoods from the Jewish community in Chyrów to Nowe Miasto; files on a request for financial aid to build the *Beis–Talmud (yeshiva)*; correspondence about the community budget; results of community board elections; list of community board members; correspondence about legal matters and community structure, 1928–39.
(DALO, L'viv, UW, Lwów)
3. Correspondence on the registration of *Machzikei Hadas* and *Agudas Yisroel*, 1932–34.
(DALO, L'viv, Magistrat, Lwów)

CIECHANOWIEC (pow. Bielsk, woj. białostockie) 1839–1936
Originals:
Birth, marriage and death registers (fragmentary), 1847–1936.
Microfilms:
Birth, marriage and death records (fragmentary), [P, R], 1839–70; fines for evading conscription [R], 1905–06.
(AP Białystok, Lomzhinskoie Gubernskoie Pravlenie)

CIECHANÓW (woj. warszawskie) 1566–1910
Microfilms:
1. *Lustracja* of the town and its surroundings, 1566.
(AGAD, Warszawa, ASK)
2. Files on synagogues, 1818–60.
(AGAD, Warszawa, CWW)
3. Copies of inscriptions from cemeteries and synagogues, 1910.
(RGIA, St. Petersburg, Departament dukhovnykh del...)

CIEPIELÓW (pow. Iłza, woj. kieleckie) 1864–1866
Microfilms:
Files on the community budget and taxes; inventory of community goods; a list of community members who did not pay taxes on time, 1864–66.
(AP Radom, Rząd Gubernialny, Radom)

CIEPLICE (pow. Jarosław, woj. lwowskie) 1628–1759
Microfilms:
Contracts, receipts and other documents on economic activities of the Sieniawski and Czartoryski families, 1628–1759.
(Bibl. Czartoryskich, Kraków)

CIESZANÓW (pow. Lubaczów, woj. lwowskie) 1891–1937
Microfilms:
1. Correspondence with the authorities on registration of vital statistics, 1891–92; correspondence with the *Ahavas Zion* colonization society about emigration to Palestine [P, G], 1898.
(TsDIAU, L'viv, Namiestnictwo Galicyjskie)
2. Correspondence about the registration of *Agudas Yisroel*, including a statute, 1931.
(DALO, L'viv, Magistrat, Lwów)

3. A complaint against the community board president; correspondence about the community budget; renovation of the synagogue; collection of funds for a statute of Józef Piłsudski; *lustracja* of community expenses; reports and correspondence on elections to the community board, 1931–37.
(DALO, L'viv, UW, Lwów)

CIESZAWA (pow. Lubliniec, woj. śląskie)
Original:
Drawing of a wooden synagogue, n.d.
(IKG Wien - Juedisches Museum)

CIESZYN (woj. śląskie) 1637–1784
Microfilms:
Jewish land registry records, 1637–1784.
(AP Katowice, Arch. Miasta Cieszyna)

CZANIEC (pow. Biała, woj. krakowskie) 1878
Microfilms:
File on reorganization of the elementary school attended by Jewish pupils [P, G], 1878.
(TsDIAU, L'viv, Krajowa Rada Szkolna)

CZARNKÓW (woj. poznańskie) 1876–1901
Microfilms:
Synagogue statutes; records on religious education [G, H], 1876–1901.
(ŻIH, Warszawa, Prow. Poznań)

CZARNOTRZEW (pow. Ostrołęka, woj. białostockie) 1915
Microfilms:
A file on Jews suspected of spying for the Germans [R], 1915.
(AP Białystok, Rząd Gubernialny, Łomża)

CZEMPIŃ (pow. Kościan, woj. poznańskie) 1838–1872
Originals:
Community account books [G], 1838–47; *pinkassim* of the *kahal* [community record books] [G, H], 1843–62; official instructions and orders [G], 1846–47; records of the burial society [G, H], 1846–47.
Microfilms:
Files on rabbinical matters and regulation of community affairs [G], 1851–72.
(Centrum Judaicum, Berlin)

CZERNA (pow. Chrzanów, woj. krakowskie) 1878
Microfilms:
Files on the reorganization of schools attended by Jewish pupils [P, G], 1878.
(TsDIAU, L'viv, Krajowa Rada Szkolna)

CZERNAWCZYCE (pow. Brześć, woj. poleskie) 1758–1760
Microfilms:
Arenda contract, 1758, 1760.
(AGAD, Warszawa, Arch. Radziwiłłów)

CZERNELICA (pow. Horodenka, woj. stanisławowskie) 1877–1937
Microfilms:
1. File on confirming statutes of Jewish societies [G, P]; membership lists of the *Yad Charutzim, Gmilas Chesed* and other societies, 1877–86, 1927–37; files on elections to the community board, 1932–36.
(DAIFO, Ivano-Frankivs'k, UW, Stanisławów)
2. Correspondence between the community and the district authorities regarding statutes and budget [P, G], 1899–1907.
(TsDIAU, L'viv, Namiestnictwo Galicyjskie)
3. A monograph containing demographic and economic information on Jews, 1936.
(AP Wrocław, Ossolineum, WKNZNP, Lwów)

CZERNIEJEWO (pow. Gniezno, woj. poznańskie) 1795–1829
Microfilms:
Four files of litigation between Jews and non-Jews; records of a suit on a distillery contract; two files on a suit between General Lipski and a "so called" Jewish doctor; records of a Jewish *arenda;* complaint against a Jewish liquor trader [G, P], 1795–1829.
(AP Poznań, Majątek Czerniejewo-Skórzewscy)

CZERNIEJÓW (pow. Stanisławów, woj. stanisławowskie) 1896–1939
Microfilms:
1. Files on various Jewish societies, 1896, 1925–39.
(DAIFO, Ivano-Frankivs'k, Starostwo Powiatowe, Stanisławów)
2. Reports by the director of the public elementary school on economic, ethnic, social, and cultural aspects of the population [P, U], 1930.
(DAIFO, Ivano-Frankivs'k, Inspektorat Szkolny, Stanisławów)
3. Lists of members of various Jewish societies, 1933–36.
(DAIFO, Ivano-Frankivs'k, Komenda Powiatowa PP, Stanisławów)

CZERSK (pow. Grójec, woj. warszawskie) 1566–1799
Originals:
A report to the King of Prussia on efforts to raise money in Czersk to rebuild the burnt synagogue in Schokken [G], 1799
Microfilms:
Lustracja of the town, 1566.
(AGAD, Warszawa, ASK)

CZERTEŻ (pow. Żydaczów, woj. stanisławowskie) 1936–1937
Microfilms:
Files on anti-Jewish actions by Ukrainian nationalists, 1936–37
(DAIFO, Ivano-Frankivs'k, Komenda Wojewódzka PP, Stanisławów)

CZERWIŃSK (pow. Płońsk, woj. warszawskie) 1910
Microfilms:
Copies of inscriptions from cemeteries and synagogues [R], 1910.
(RGIA, St. Petersburg, Departament dukhovnykh del…)

CZERWONOGRÓD (pow. Zaleszczyki, woj. tarnopolskie) 1878
Microfilms:

Files on the reorganization of schools attended by Jewish pupils, [P, G] 1878
(TsDIAU, L'viv, Krajowa Rada Szkolna)

CZĘSTOCHOWA (woj. kieleckie) 1827–1914
Microfilms:
1. Records on the Jewish quarter and community, 1827–66.
(AP Łódź, Anterioria Rządu Gubernialnego, Piotrków)
2. Ratification of community elections and accounts; the administration of the *mikvaot*; appointments of religious officials; requests for licenses to open businesses; requests for the transfer of real estate; bequests to the community; records on the conversion of Jews to Christianity [R], 1864–1914.
(AP Łódź, Rząd Gubernialny, WA, Piotrków)
3. Jewish schools and their finances; lists of property owned by Jewish schools; Jewish teachers [P, R], 1843–1913.
(AP Łódź, Dyrekcja Szkolna, Łódź)
4. The Jewish hospital; bequests to the community for philanthropic purposes; records on various charitable activities [R], 1900–13.
(AP Łódź, Rząd Gubernialny, RO, Piotrków)
5. A request to register charitable and cultural societies [R], 1908–12.
(AP Łódź, Rząd Gubernialny, KP, Piotrków)
6. Records on anti-government demonstrations in 1905; investigations of individuals accused of misdemeanors (including membership in Jewish political parties); correspondence on surveillance of Jews suspected of criminal activity; an order expelling three foreign Jews (emissaries from Palestine) [R], 1905–14.
(AP Łódź, GZŻ, Piotrków)
7. Fines for evading conscription, 1890–1902.
(AP Łódź, Rząd Gubernialny, WP, Piotrków)
8. Files on community matters, 1820–67.
(AGAD, Warszawa, CWW)
9. Copies of inscriptions from cemeteries and synagogues [R], 1910.
(RGIA, St. Petersburg, Departament dukhovnych del...)

CZĘSTOCHOWA, surroundings, 1891–1914
Microfilms:
1. Records on the establishment of a new community in a village; the opening of a kerosene store [R], 1904–14.
(AP Łódź, Rząd Gubernialny, WA, Piotrków)
2. A report on the families of poor Jews conscripted into the army; fines for evading conscription [R], 1891–1902.
(AP Łódź, Rząd Gubernialny, WP, Piotrków)
3. An investigation of a Jew accused of printing illegal literature [R], 1904.
(AP Łódź, GZŻ, Piotrków)

CZORTKÓW (woj. tarnopolskie) 1753–1931
Photocopies:
Letter from the Ministry of Religious Affairs to the government representative in Lwów requesting information about the Jewish community, 1920–23.

(DALO, L'viv, UW, Lwów)
Microfilms:
1. Files on taxes, 1753–67; files on activities of the Jewish community [G, H, P], 1797–1851; a case regarding the beating of a Jew, 1817; correspondence on elections to the Jewish community board, 1820; a report on escape of Jews from army camps [G, P], 1824.
(TsDIAU, L'viv, Arch. Lanckorońskich)
2. Correspondence on appointment of a *dayan* [G], 1862–68; files on the *Bikur Cholim* society [G, P], 1876–1913; correspondence on elections to the community board, 1895; correspondence about the *Dorshei Tzdoko Vachesed* society, 1907–13.
(TsDIAU, L'viv, Namiestnictwo Galicyjskie)
3. Files on the closing of *chadorim* [G,P], 1868–74; reports on teaching Jewish religion in the elementary school [G, P], 1882–89
(TsDIAU, L'viv, Krajowa Rada Szkolna)
4. Correspondence with the authorities on Jews expelled from Śniatyn, 1916.
(DAIFO, Ivano-Frankivs'k, Nachal'nik Sniatynskogo Uezda)
5. Reports on meetings of the Revisionist Zionist party in the town, 1930–31.
(DALO, L'viv, UW, Lwów)

CZORTOWIEC (pow. Horodenka, woj. stanisławowskie) 1921–1938
Microfilms:
Files on various Jewish societies, 1921–38.
(DAIFO, Ivano-Frankivs'k, UW, Stanisławów)

CZUDEC (pow. Strzyżów, woj. lwowskie) 1933–1934
Microfilms:
Correspondence about the community budget and lists of tax payers, 1933–34.
(DALO, L'viv, UW, Lwów)

CZUKAŁÓWKA (pow. Stanisławów, woj. stanisławowskie) 1930
Microfilms:
Reports by the director of the public elementary school on economic, ethnic, social, and cultural characteristics of the population [P, U], 1930.
(DAIFO, Ivano-Frankivs'k, Inspektorat Szkolny, Stanisławów)

CZYSTOPADY (pow. Zborów, woj. tarnopolskie)
Microfilms:
Files on the reorganization of schools attended by Jewish pupils, [G, P] 1878.
(TsDIAU, L'viv, Krajowa Rada Szkolna)

CZYŻEWO (pow. Wysokie Mazowieckie, woj. białostockie) 1818–1935
Originals:
An application for marriage, 1935.
Microfilms:
Files on synagogues, 1818–60.
(AGAD, Warszawa, CWW)

DAWIDGRÓDEK (pow. Łuniniec, woj. poleskie), 1810
Microfilms:

A table of contracts with Jewish *arendars*, 1810.
(AGAD, Warszawa, Arch. Radziwiłłów)

DĄBIE (pow. Kalisz, woj. łódzkie) 1907–1910
Microfilms:
1. A file on a Jew sent into exile [R], 1907.
(AP Łódź, Kancelaria Gubernatora Kaliskiego)
2. Copies of inscriptions from cemeteries and synagogues, 1910.
(RGIA, St. Petersburg, Departament dukhovnykh del…)

DĄBROWA (pow. Bochnia, woj. krakowskie) 1628–1904
Microfilms:
1. Various contracts, 1628–1759.
(Bibl. Czartoryskich, Kraków)
2. Contracts of various *arendas,* 1756.
(TsDIAU, L'viv, Arch. Lubomirskich)
3. Correspondence with the *starostwo* on citizenship and the statutes of the Jewish community, 1891–96; correspondence about Jewish farmers, including lists of farmer families [G], 1822–47.
(TsDIAU, L'viv, Namiestnictwo Galicyjskie)
4. Files on the closing of *chadorim* [G, P] , 1868–74; minutes of inspections at Baron Hirsch Foundation (JCA) schools [G, P], 1896–1904.
(TsDIAU, L'viv, Krajowa Rada Szkolna)

DĄBROWA (pow. Sokółka, woj. białostockie) 1786
Photocopies:
Inventories of estates, 1786.
(NIARB, Minsk, Kollektsiia drevnikh inventarei)
Microfilms:
Correspondence with the Jewish school [R], 1864–65.
(RGIA, St. Petersburg, OPE)

DĄBROWA GÓRNICZA (pow. Będzin, woj. kieleckie) 1896–1913
1. Foundation of a charitable society [R], 1896–98.
(AP Łódź, Rząd Gubernialny, RO, Piotrków)
2. The establishment of an independent religious community; the appointment of a new rabbi; ratification of synagogue elections and accounts; complaint of a *shochet* refused permission to slaughter cattle [R], 1907–13.
(AP Łódź, Rząd Gubernialny, WA, Piotrków)
3. File on a Jew accused of possessing illegal literature and murdering a policeman [R], 1906.
(AP Łódź, GZŻ, Piotrków)

DĄBROWICA (pow. Jarosław, woj. lwowskie) 1628–1759
Microfilms:
Contracts and other financial documents of the Sieniawski and Czartoryski estates, 1628–1759; accounts, letters, tax registers [L, P], 1738, 1756
(Bibl. Czartoryskich, Kraków)

DĄBROWICA (pow. Sarny, woj. wołyńskie) 1816–1858
Microfilms:
Lists of inhabitants (*revizskie skazki)* [R], 1816–28, 1858.
(DARO, Rivne, Rovenskoe uezdnoe kaznacheistvo)

DELATYCZE (pow. Nowogródek, woj. nowogrodzkie) 1617–1767
Microfilms:
Records of *arendas* , 1617–1767.
(AGAD, Warszawa, Arch. Radziwiłłów)

DELATYN (pow. Nadwórna, woj. stanisławowskie) 1882–1936
Microfilms:
1. Reports on teaching Jewish religion in elementary schools [P,G], 1882–89.
(TsDIAU, L'viv, Krajowa Rada Szkolna)
2. Correspondence about the *Beis Yisroel, Adas Yisroel* and *Bnei Emuna* societies, 1908.
(TsDIAU, L'viv, Namiestnictwo Galicyjskie)
3. Files on various Jewish societies and parties, among them *Agudas Yisroel, Ogólno-Żydowska Partia Pracy, Gmilas Chesed, Biblioteka Żydowska*, 1908–1936; files on elections to the community board, and on rabbis, 1932–1936;
(DAIFO, Ivano-Frankivs'k, UW, Stanisławów)

DELEJÓW (pow. Stanisławów, woj. stanisławowskie) 1910–1930
Microfilms:
1. Files on anti Jewish agitation [G, P, U], 1910–11.
(DAIFO, Ivano-Frankivs'k, Prokuratoria Państwa, Stanisławów)
2. Reports by the director of the public elementary school on economic, ethnic, social, and cultural characteristics of the population [P,U], 1930.
(DAIFO, Ivano-Frankivs'k, Inspektorat Szkolny, Stanisławów)

DEMYCZE (pow. Śniatyn, woj. stanisławowskie) 1875–1877
Microfilms:
Reports of the *starostwos* in Galicia containing lists of *chadorim* and *melamdim,* [G, P], 1875–77.
(TsDIAU, L'viv, Krajowa Rada Szkolna)

DERAŻNE (pow. Kostopol, woj. wołyńskie) 1816–1828
Microfilms:
Lists of inhabitants (*revizskie skazki*), [R], 1816–28
(DARO, Rivne, Rovenskoe uezdnoe kaznacheistvo)

DĘBICA (pow. Ropczyce, woj. krakowskie) 1882–1920
Microfilms:
Reports on religious education in the elementary school [G, P], 1882–89.
(TsDIAU, L'viv, Krajowa Rada Szkolna)
Correspondence about the *Zion* and *Postęp* societies, 1895, as well as the *Gmilus Chasodim,* and *Poalei Zion* societies, 1902–20.
(TsDIAU, L'viv, Namiestnictwo Galicyjskie)

DĘBNO (pow. Opatów, woj. kieleckie) 1765
Microfilms:
Confirmation by King Stanisław August Poniatowski of the charter granted to the Jews [L, P], 1765.
(AGAD, Warszawa, Księgi Kanclerskie)

DOBRA (pow. Limanowa, woj. krakowskie) 1628–1904
Microfilms:
1. Contracts and other documents on the Sieniawski and Czartoryski family estates, 1628–1759.
(Bibl. Czartoryskich, Kraków)
2. Correspondence with the district authorities regarding the opening of a *mikve*, 1901–1904.
(TsDIAU, Namiestnictwo Galicyjskie)

DOBROMIL (woj. lwowskie) 1566–1935
Microfilms:
1. A copy from 1808 of the charters granted to the Jews in 1566 and 1612 [L, P].
(AP Wrocław, Ossolineum)
2. Files on *propinacja,* 1786–1805; a memorandum of burghers and the Jews on municipal elections, 1791; registration of farmers' claims [G, P], 1862.
(AP Kraków, Teki Schneidra)
3. Files on relief and loans to Jews for settling on agricultural colonies in Galicia [G], 1789. correspondence with the district authorities of Sanok on taverns run by Jews on lands of the nobility, including detailed tables, 1853 [G]; files on confirmation of the community statutes, on community elections and on a *lustracja* of the community, 1846–1907; correspondence with the district authorities regarding *chadorim,* including lists of *melamdim,* 1874–1908; reports and correspondence on confirmation of the community statutes, 1879 correspondence with the Ministry of the Interior on the reorganization of the community, on community elections and on community taxes, 1895.
(TsDIAU, L'viv, Namiestnictwo Galicyjskie)
4. Reports on teaching Jewish religion in elementary schools [P, G], 1882–89.
(TsDIAU, L'viv, Krajowa Rada Szkolna)
A list of community taxpayers, 1869–89.
(TsDIAU, L'viv, Ministerium fuer Cultus und Unterricht, Wien)
5. Files on community elections, budgets and taxes, and confirmation of the rabbi, 1908–35; lists of community board members for the years 1908 and 1923; correspondence on registration of the: *Zgoda, Machzikei Hadas, Shomrei Emunei Yisroel (Agudas Yisroel)* societies and their statutes, 1928–34; statistical data on members of political parties, 1930.
(DALO, L'viv, UW, Lwów)

DOBROTWÓR (pow. Kamionka Strumiłowa, woj. tarnopolskie) 1723–1784
Microfilms:
Correspondence on Jewish traders in the town [P, L, H], 1723–84.
(TsDIAU, L'viv, Arch. Lanckorońskich]

DOBRZYCA (pow. Krotoszyn, woj. poznańskie) 1830–1889
Originals:
Records of recruitment and other taxes, 1830–80; minutes of community meetings [G], 1834–89; records on poor Jews, 1843–70; an application for the position of cantor and *shochet,* [G], 1869.

DOBRZYŃ nad Wisłą (pow. Lipno, woj. warszawskie) 1610–1775
Microfilms:
1. An inventory of the *starostwo*, 1610.
(AGAD, Warszawa, ASK)
2. Confirmation by King Stanisław August Poniatowski of the charter granted to the Jews, 1765; establishment by him of a commission to settle a dispute between the community and its creditors [L], 1775.
(AGAD, Warszawa, Księgi Kanclerskie)

DOLINA (woj. stanisławowskie) 1779–1939
Microfilms:
1. Files on debts of the Jewish community, 1779 [L, G]
(TsDIAU, L'viv, Kolektsiia dokumentiv…)
2. Correspondence on colonization of Jews [G],1806–26; correspondence with the *Starostwo* on registration of Jewish vital statistics, 1891–92; correspondence about various societies including their statutes (e.g.: *Zion, Postęp, Divrei Emes, Linas Halaila*), 1895–1911; correspondence with the *Ahavas Zion* colonization society about emigration to Palestine, 1898.
(TsDIAU, L'viv, Namiestnictwo Galicyjskie)
3. Files on payment of a debt by an *arendar* from Dolina [P, G], 1798.
(TsDIAU, L'viv, Arch. Lanckorońskich)
4. Records on social, cultural and charitable societies, among them: *Achva, Talmud Tora, Ner Tamid, Gmilas Chesed, Beit-Am*, 1894–1935; files on activities of political organizations and parties, e.g. Bundist, Zionist, Revisionist Zionist and others, 1923–35; files on scout organizations, 1929–30; files on collecting funds for Palestine, 1926; correspondence with the community, reports, elections, confirmation of budgets, of rabbis etc., 1926–38; statistical data on the population, 1938.
(DAIFO, Ivano-Frankivs'k, UW, Stanisławów)
5. Files on dissemination of antisemitic pamphlets by the *Stronnictwo Narodowe* party (*Endecja*), 1936; reports and correspondence on antisemitic actions by Ukrainian nationalists, 1936–37.
(DAIFO, Ivano-Frankivs'k, Komenda Wojewódzka PP, Stanisławów)
6. List of community employee salaries, 1937–39.
(DAIFO, Ivano-Frankivs'k, Wojewódzke Biuro Funduszu Pracy, Stanisławów)

DOLINA, surroundings 1878–1935
Microfilms:
1. Reports on *chadorim* in the Dolina district, including lists of *melamdim* ,1878–81.
(TsDIAU, L'viv, Krajowa Rada Szkolna)
2. Lists of societies in the Dolina district [P, U], 1922–23;descriptions of the Dolina district including statistical data, 1934–35.
(DAIFO, Ivano-Frankivs'k, UW, Stanisławów)

DONABORÓW (pow. Kępno, woj. poznańskie) 1534–1615
Microfilms:
Inventories and accounts, 1534–1615.
(AGAD, Warszawa, ASK)

DORA (pow. Nadwórna, woj. stanisławowskie) 1937–1938
Microfilms:
Political description of the town, 1937–38.
(DAIFO, Ivano-Frankivs'k, Posterunek Policji Państwowej, Jaremcze)

DOROHÓW (woj. Stanisławów) 1936
Microfilms:
Police report on antisemitic incidents, 1936.
(DAIFO, Ivano-Frankivs'k, UW, Stanisławów)

DROHICZYN (pow. Bielsk, woj. białostockie) 1753–1913
Microfilms:
1. Files on military taxes, 1753–67
(TsDIAU, L'viv, Arch. Lanckorońskich)
2. Files on candidates for the rabbinate [R], 1886–1913.
(AP Białystok, Rząd Gubernialny, Łomża)

DROHOBYCZ (woj. lwowskie) 16th cent.–1938
Photocopies:
Family tree of L. M. Fern and F. Klinghoffer from Drohobycz.
(Private collection)
Microfilms:
1. Records of the tailors' guild, 16th–19th cent.
(Bibl. Jagiellońska, Kraków)
2. Files on *propinacja*, community schools and correspondence with the town authorities on new building projects, [G, P, L], 1685, 1759–97, 1841; a register of building permits for Jews, 1686–1780; community debts to the Catholic Seminary in Sambor, 1716–30; a report of the community's debts to a nobleman, 1780; complaints by Jews regarding *propinacja*, 1780; orders of the Austrian Emperor regarding Jewish homes, 1781; a list of Jewish residents related to propination disputes, 1785; a promissory note of the church [L], 1794; files on the illegal trade of Jews in iron [G], 1794; a report by local Jews to the district authorities on an inheritance in Tarnów [G], 1797; housing matters, 1841.
(AP Kraków, Teki Schneidra)
3. *Arenda* contract, [P, L], 1749
(TsDIAU, L'viv, Ekonomia Samborska)
4. Minutes on Jewish religious instruction in elementary schools [G, P], 1882–89.
(TsDIAU, L'viv, Krajowa Rada Szkolna)
5. Correspondence with the *Landes Gubernium* and the viceroy regarding the appointment of a committee to investigate the community, including a list of voters, taxpayers and community officials [G], 1819–59; files on various societies: *Dorshei Tov Vachesed, Poalei Tzedek, Beis Lechem* and others, correspondence with the district authorities on Jewish schools and community statutes and budget [G, P], 1874–1912; correspondence with the *Starostwo* on registration of Jewish vital statistics 1891–92; files on *shechita*, 1894–97; correspondence on the election of a rabbi, 1896
(TsDIAU, L'viv, Namiestnictwo Galicyjskie)
6. Jewish community statutes, [P, G], 1911–18
(TsDIAU, L'viv, Ministerium fuer Kultus und Unterricht, Wien)

7. Correspondence, reports, complaints etc. relating to community elections; lists of community board members, confirmation of statutes, budgets, lists of taxpayers, personal matters, 1923–38; correspondence with the police regarding censorship of a sermon, 1924; records on activities of *Poalei Zion Lewica*, 1929–32, and of the Revisionist Zionists 1930–31; a list of Zionist organization members [Y, P], 1931; correspondence about registration of societies and political parties, e.g. *Agudas Yisroel*, *Machzikei Hadas*, *Kultur Liga*, *Achva*, 1923–38; correspondence on budgetary matters and a list of taxpayers, 1938.
(DALO, L'viv, UW, Lwów)
8. Report and correspondence on accusations against Hersh Nagler, editor of the journal "Der Consument, freie Tribüne und literarische Nachrichten" for bolshevik agitation during a meeting of *Poalei Zion*, 1920.
(DALO, L'viv, Dyrekcja Policji, Lwów)
9. A report on the activities of the *Ogólno-Żydowska Partia Pracy*, 1933.
(DAIFO, Ivano-Frankivs'k, UW, Stanisławów)

DROHOBYCZ, surroundings, 1724–1955
Original:
Ratification by the Lwów Rabbinical Court of a ruling on trading rights in three villages near Drohobycz [H], 1724.
Photocopies:
Reports about activity of the Ukrainian Communist Party in the Drohobycz area, data on communists [R], 1949; reports about the activity of Jewish communities [R], 1949, 1951, 1955.
(DALO, L'viv, Drohobyts'kii obkom…)
Microfilms:
1. Correspondence with the authorities in Sanok on taverns in villages owned by the nobility, 1853; statute of the *Jüdische Volkskuche* society [G], 1888–1912.
(TsDIAU, L'viv, Namiestnictwo Galicyjskie)
2. Statistical data on members of political parties in the district of Drohobycz., 1930.
(DALO, L'viv, UW, Lwów)

DROHOMIRCZANY (pow. Stanisławów, woj. stanisławowskie) 1930
Microfilms:
Reports by the director of the public elementary school on economic, ethnic, social, and cultural characteristics of the population [P, U], 1930.
(DAIFO, Ivano-Frankivs'k, Inspektorat Szkolny, Stanisławów)

DRUJA (pow. Brasław, woj. wileńskie) 1555
Microfilms:
A charter to the Jews to lease the collecting of taxes [Rt], 1555
(RGADA, Moscow, ML)

DRZEWICA (pow. Opoczno, woj. kieleckie) 1839–1865
Microfilms:
Files on founding a new community in Drzewica, a part from Opoczno, and a list of members, 1839–65.
(AP Radom, Rząd Gubernialny, Radom)

DUBIECKO (pow. Przemyśl, woj. lwowskie) 1846–1938
Photocopies:

Files on community elections and other communal matters, including a list of candidates and lists of community taxpayers, 1924–38.
(DALO, L'viv, UW, Lwów)
Microfilms:
1. Files on the confirmation of community statutes, 1846–96.
(TsDIAU, L'viv, Namiestnictwo Galicyjskie)
2. A list of eligible voters to the *Sejm*, 1870.
(AP Kraków, Teki Schneidra)
3. Files on the *Yesodei Hatora* school and on registration of the *Mizrachi* and *Machzikei Hadas* societies, 1931–33.
(DALO, L'viv, Magistrat, Lwów)

DUBIENKA (pow. Hrubieszów, woj. lubelskie) 1785–1869
Microfilms:
1. Agreement between the burghers and the community allowing Jews to lease *propinacja* rights, 1785.
(AP Lublin, Księgi Grodzkie Chełmskie)
2. Records on taxes, on *shechita* and the *arenda* of community taxes, 1795–97.
(AP Kraków, IT)
3. Statistical description of Dubienka, 1833–59; correspondence on elections to the community board [R], 1868–69.
(AP Lublin, Rząd Gubernialny, Lublin)

DUBNO (woj. wołyńskie) 1635–1910
Originals:
Report of the Dubno police commander on Jews wishing to settle in the area of Novorossiysk, including lists of candidates [R], 1807–08.
Photocopies:
File on a Jew from Dubno prohibited from entering the capital cities, Moscow and St. Petersburg [R], 1838–57.
(GARF, Moscow, Tret'e otdelenie...)
Microfilms:
1. Files on Jewish *arendars,* on community taxes and on a court case between a Jewess and a local woman, 1635–1752.
(AP Kraków, Arch. Sanguszków)
2. Copies of documents on the devastation of the town by Cossacks, 1648; records of sales, properties, debts, taxes, 1666–68, 1731–60; copies of documents on court cases among Jews and between Jews and Christians, 1740–50.
(TsDIAU, Kyiv, Magistrat, Dubno)
3. Community regulations, 1722.
(AP Lublin, Arch. Lubomirskich z Dubna)
4. Requests of 88 Jewish traders for permission to trade in Russia [R], 1739; files on debts of the Jewish community to Catholic monasteries [R], 1845–47.
(TsDIAU, Kyiv, Kievskaia gubernskaia kantseliariia)
5. Files on debts of the Jewish community to Catholic monasteries and churches [R, P], 1742–1868; files on taxation of the Jewish community by the Church [R], 1837–1838; records on an investigation against

two Jews suspected of kidnapping poor Jewish children for the Russian army [R], 1853–63; files on the sale of a Jew's house in lieu of a fine for smuggling [R], 1854–56.
(DARO, Riwne, Magistrat, Dubno)
6. Copy of a Russian official's memorandum on a dispute between two Jews and a Russian merchant, 1762.
(AGAD, Warszawa, Księgi Kanclerskie)
7. Copies of municipal documents [R, P], 1773; complaint against *Chevra Kadisha* members [R], 1853.
(TsDIAU Kyiv, Dokumenty, sobrannye…)
8. Copy of as contract on kosher meat taxation from 1793, sent by Rabbi Ch. Z. Margolies to Shimon Dubnov, then editor of the journal "Evreiskaia Starina" [H, R].
(RGIA, St. Petersburg, "Evreiskaia Starina")
9. Correspondence on *chasidim*, [R] 1850; notes by a supervisor of Jewish schools [R], 1865–66; files on opening a *Talmud Tora* [R], 1867–68.
(TsDIAU, Kyiv, Upravlenie Kievskogo uchebnogo okruga)
10. Reports on Jewish schools [R], 1852–58.
(GAKHO, Kamianets' Podil's'kyi, Direkcia narodnykh uchilishch…)
11. Files on the leadership of a synagogue [R], 1867–68.
(DARO Riwne, Sąd Powiatowy, Dubno)
12. Correspondence of the local branch of the Society for the Attainment of Full Rights for the Jewish People in Russia on elections to the State *Duma* [R], 1905–06.
(RGIA, St. Petersburg, Obshchestvo polnopraviia…)
13. Request of a Jew for a job on Admiral Dubasow's estate [R], 1905.
(RGAVMF, St. Petersburg, Dubasov)
14. Copies of inscriptions from cemeteries and synagogues, 1910.
(RGIA, St. Petersburg, Departament dukhovnykh del…)

DUBNO, surroundings, 1743–1912
Microfilms:
1. *Arenda* contracts in villages around Dubno, 1743.
(TsDIAU, Kyiv, Arch. Zamojskich)
2. Documents on the Jews in a nearby village; permission to open a Jewish school in a village; governmental decision regarding migration of Jews from villages to towns, 1790–1866.
(AP Kraków, Arch. Młynowskie Chodkiewiczów)
3. Reports on a number of communities, synagogues, Jewish schools, and population statistics in the Kiev, Podolia and Volhynia *guberniias* [R], 1830, 1850; a list of charters by Polish kings and of permits by Russian authorities for the transformation of villages into small towns and for *propinacja* [R], 1849–52; files on prohibiting contraband merchandise in taverns [R], 1849; a report on important events in the Dubno region [R], 1912.
(TsDIAU, Kyiv, Kantseliariia…)
4. Records on the founding of hospitals and old–age homes in small towns of the Dubno district [R], 1863–64; statistical information on small towns in the Dubno district [R], 1871
(RGIA, St. Petersburg, Khoziaistvennyi departament MVD)

DUDA (pow. Święciany, woj. wileńskie), 1913–1915
Microfilms:
Files on Jews expelled from the *guberniia* for involvement in illegal emigration [R], 1913–15.
(AP Białystok, Rząd Gubernialny, Łomża)

DUKLA (pow. Krosno, woj. lwowskie) 1877–1937
Microfilms:
1. Correspondence with the district authorities regarding *chadorim,* including lists of *melamdim*, 1877–1908.
(TsDIAU, L'viv, Namiestnictwo Galicyjskie)
2. Correspondence on the registration of *Agudas Yisroel*, 1933.
(DALO, L'viv, Magistrat, Lwów)
3. Correspondence about community matters e.g. budget, taxpayers, tariffs for cemetery plots, protests against community election results, etc.; statistical reports, including lists of community board members and rabbis, 1933–37.
(DALO, L'viv, UW, Lwów)

DUNAJÓW (pow. Przemyślany, woj. tarnopolskie) 1877–1908
Microfilms:
Reports on *chadorim*, including lists of children [P, G], 1877–1908.
(TsDIAU, L'viv, Namiestnictwo Galicyjskie)

DYBKÓW (pow. Jarosław, woj. lwowskie) 1628–1759
Microfilms:
Contracts and other documents on the Sieniawski and Czartoryski family estates, 1628–1759.
(Bibl. Czartoryskich, Kraków)

DYNÓW (pow. Brzozów, woj. lwowskie) 1782–1937
Photocopies:
Community budget, 1933–35.
(DALO, L'viv, UW, Lwów)
Microfilms:
1. Inventory of the town, 1782.
(AP Wrocław, Ossolineum)
2. Complaint by Jews regarding a tax, 1838
(NBANU, L'viv, Zb. Goldsteina)
3. Correspondence with district authorities of Sanok about taverns kept by the Jews on lands of the nobility, including detailed tables [G], 1853.
(TsDIAU, L'viv, Namiestnictwo Galicyjskie)
4. Correspondence on the community budget as well as on elections of the community board and rabbis, 1925, 1933–1937.
(DALO, L'viv, UW, Lwów)

DZIAŁOSZYCE (pow. Pińczów, woj. kieleckie) 1799–1867
Microfilms:
1. Records of a dispute over an *arenda,* 1799.
(AP Kraków, IT)
2. Correspondence and reports on community budgets, appointments of rabbis, and the *Chevra Kadisha,* 1819–67.
(AGAD, Warszawa, CWW)

DZIAŁOSZYN (pow. Wieluń, woj. łódzkie) 1820–1908.
Microfilms:
1. Description of the town, 1820–61.
(AGAD, Warszawa, Komisja Województwa Kaliskiego)
2. Complaint by the community regarding welfare payments; request to receive part of the late rabbi's salary; record of a Jew wishing to convert to Christianity [R], 1899–1908.
(AP Łódź, Rząd Gubernialny, WA, Kalisz)
3. Records on two Jews sent into exile [R], 1908.
(AP Łódź, Kancelaria Gubernatora Kaliskiego)

DZIERZKOWICE (pow. Janów, woj. lubelskie) 1867
Microfilms:
Files on conversions to Christianity [R], 1867.
(AP Lublin, Rząd Gubernialny, Lublin)

DZIKÓW (pow. Lubaczów, woj. lwowskie) 1628–1930
Microfilms:
Correspondence and other records on Jewish economic activities, 1628–1728.
(Bibl. Czartoryskich, Kraków);
Files on fundraising for the Galician *kollel* in Palestine, 1928–30; community elections, 1928.
(DALO, L'viv, UW, Lwów)

DZIKÓW (pow. Tarnobrzeg, woj. lwowskie) 1682–19th cent.
Microfilms:
1. Files on Jewish debts to a Catholic monastery [L, P], 1682–1701.
(AP Kraków, Arch. Krzeszowickie Potockich)
2. Extracts from municipal records on Jews, among them contracts, deeds of sale, promissory notes and wills, 1698–1830.
(AP Kraków, IT)
3. Contracts and other records on *arendas*; a list of Jewish taxpayers; permission for Jews to establish a craft guild; a bill of sale of a plot of land to a Jew, 18th–19th cent.
(AP Kraków, Arch. Dzikowskie Tarnowskich)

DZISNA (woj. wileńskie) 1830–1865
Microfilms:
1. Files on the conversion of a Jew to Catholicism [R], 1830.
(RGIA, St. Petersburg, Rimsko-katolicheskasia kollegiia…)
2. Request by the Jewish community to build a new synagogue [R], 1865.
(RGIA, St. Petersburg, Departament dukhovnykh del…)

DZISNA, surroundings, 1861
Microfilms:
Files on Polish encouragement of Jewish participation in the uprising against the Russians and on Jewish fears of pogroms, 1861.
(GARF, Moscow, Tret'e otdelenie…)

DŹWINOGRÓD (pow. Borszczów, woj. tarnopolskie) 1762–1767
Microfilms:
Inventories of the *starostwo*, 1762–67.
(AGAD, Warszawa, ASK)

FELSZTYN (pow. Sambor, woj. lwowskie) 1931–1936
Original:
Drawing of a wooden synagogue, n.d.
(IKG Wien - Juedisches Museum)
Microfilms:
1. Correspondence on the registration of the *Machzikei Hadas* society, 1932.
(DALO, L'viv, Magistrat, Lwów)
2. A request by the Jewish community to unite with that of Sambor, 1931–33; files on rabbinical candidates, 1936.
(DALO, L'viv, UW, Lwów)

FILIPÓW (woj. białostockie) 1936–1937
Photocopies:
Correspondence about the community budget, and a list of members exempted from community taxes, 1936–37.
(AP Suwałki, Starostwo Powiatowe, Suwałki)

FIRLEJ (pow. Lubartów, woj. lubelskie) 1827–1868
Microfilms:
A statistical description of the town, 1827–1850; correspondence on conversion of Jews to Christianity [R], 1867–68.
(AP Lublin, Rząd Gubernialny, Lublin)

FORDON (pow. Bydgoszcz, woj. poznańskie) 1714–1718
Originals:
Memorbuch, n.d.
Microfilms:
Registers and accounts of trade between Sieniawa, Gdańsk and Fordon, 1714–1718
(Bibl. Czartoryskich, Kraków)

FRAMPOL (pow. Biłgoraj, woj. lubelskie) 1854–1859
Microfilms:
Statistical description of the town, 1854–59.
(AP Lublin, Rząd Gubernialny, Lublin)

FRYSZTAK (pow. Krosno, woj. lwowskie) 1898–1934
Microfilms:
1. Correspondence on communal matters, including statutes, 1898.
(TsDIAU, L'viv, Namiestnictwo Galicyjskie)
2. Files on community elections and other community matters, including budgets, 1928–32.
(DALO, L'viv, UW, Lwów)
3. Correspondence about the registration of *Agudas Yisroel*, 1933–34
(DALO, L'viv, Magistrat, Lwów)

GARWOLIN (woj. lubelskie) 1566
Microfilms:
Lustracja of Garwolin, 1566
(AGAD, Warszawa, ASK)

GAWOROWO (pow. Płońsk, woj. warszawskie) 1818–1860
Microfilms:
Files on synagogues, 1818–60
(AGAD, Warszawa, CWW)

GĄBIN (pow. Gostynin, woj. warszawskie) 1566–1910
Microfilms:
1. *Lustracja* of Gąbin, 1566.
(AGAD, Warszawa, ASK)
2. *Pinkas* of the Tora study society [H], 1792–1891.
(New York Public Library)
3. Copies of inscriptions from cemeteries and synagogues [R], 1910.
(RGIA, St. Petersburg, Departament dukhovnykh del…)

GLINIANY (pow. Przemyślany, woj. tarnopolskie) 1709–1987
Originals:
Archives of the Gliniany *Landsmannschaft* in New York [Y, E], 1900–87.
Microfilms:
1. Court document on a conflict between the Jewish community and a monastery [L], 1709.
(NBANU, L'viv, Klasztor Bazylianów)
2. Receipt from the local Jewish community to a priest from the village of Wyzłów [L, P], 1747.
(TsDIAU, L'viv, Kolektsiia dokumentiv pro katolyts'ki monastyri…)
3. Documents on litigation between the Sanguszko family and local Jews, 1775.
(AP Kraków, Arch. Sanguszków)
4. Files on financial matters of the community, 1854.
(TsDIAU, L'viv, Kolektsiia dokumentiv…)
5. Reports on *chadorim,* containing lists of children; correspondence about the *Talmud Tora* society [P, G], 1877–1911.
(TsDIAU, L'viv, Namiestnictwo Galicyjskie)
6. Minutes from inspections of Baron Hirsch Foundation (JCA) schools [P, G], 1896–1904.
(TsDIAU, L'viv, Krajowa Rada Szkolna)

GŁOBIKOWA GÓRNA (pow. Ropczyce, woj. krakowskie) 1793
Microfilms:
File on taxes [P,L], 1793
(TsDIAU, L'viv, Kolektsiia dokumentiv…)

GŁĘBOKIE (pow. Dzisna, woj. wileńskie) 1865
Microfilms:
Files on permission to found a prayer house for *chasidim*, separate from that of the *misnagdim,* 1865.
(RGIA, St. Petersburg, Departament dukhovnykh del…)

GŁOGÓW (pow. Rzeszów, woj. krakowskie) 1738–1937
Microfilms:
1. Receipts of the Jewish community [H, G, P], 1738–86.
(NBANU, L'viv, Zb. Goldsteina)
2. Correspondence about the *Chevra Kadisha Venosei Hamita* society [P,G], 1909.
(TsDIAU, L'viv, Namiestnictwo Galicyjskie)
3. Correspondence about legal matters and the budget, including a list of taxpayers, 1933–37.
(DALO, L'viv, UW, Lwów)
4. Correspondence about registration of the *Mizrachi*, 1934.
(TsDIAU, L'viv, Magistrat, Lwów)

GŁÓWNO (pow. Brzeziny, woj. łódzkie) 1822–1914
Microfilms:
1. Files on the community, its elections and its accounts, 1822–66.
(AP Łódź, Anterioria Rządu Gubernialnego, Piotrków)
2. Fines for evading conscription [R], 1897–1901.
(AP Łódź, Rząd Gubernialny, WP, Piotrków)
3. Ratification of community elections and accounts; the appointment of a new rabbi [R], 1897–1914.
(AP Łódź, Rząd Gubernialny, WA, Piotrków)
4. Police file on Jews involved in strikes and demonstrations [R], 1906.
(AP Łódź, GZŻ, Piotrków)

GŁUSK (pow. Lublin, woj. lubelskie) 1851–1864
Microfilms:
Correspondence on the appointment of a rabbi, 1856–64; statistical description, 1851–59.
(AP Lublin, Rząd Gubernialny, Lublin)

GNIEWOSZÓW (pow. Kozienice, woj. kieleckie)
Original:
Drawing of a wooden synagogue, n.d.
(IKG Wien - Juedisches Museum)

GNIEZNO (woj. poznańskie) 1737–1918
Originals:
Accounts of a women's society [G], 1840–52; community statutes [G], 1870; documents on the history of the community [G], 1858–1900.
Microfilms:
1. Records on Jewish economic activity in the town, 1737–94.
(AP Poznań, Akta miast, woj. poznańskie)
2. Records of the Girls' Zionist Club [G], 1917–18.
(ŻIH, Warszawa)

GOŁOGÓRY (pow. Złoczów, woj. tarnopolskie) 1895–1906
Microfilms:

Correspondence on the rabbi [G, P], 1895–1906; reports and correspondence on the confirmation of community statutes, 1898.
(TsDIAU, L'viv, Namiestnictwo Galicyjskie)

GORAJ (pow. Biłgoraj, woj. lubelskie) 1714–1859
Microfilms:
Records on the community's debts to the Church in Zamość, 1714–37.
(AP Lublin, Kolegiata w Zamościu)
Statistical descriptions of the town, 1819–59.
(AP Lublin, Rząd Gubernialny, Lublin)

GORLICE (woj. krakowskie) 1772–1918
Microfilms:
Request by the Jews of Gorlice to separate from the community of Żmigród and to establish a separate cemetery; files on *propinacja* [G, H, L, P], 1772–1818.
(AP Kraków, Teki Schneidra)
Reports on teaching Jewish religion in elementary schools [P, G], 1882–89.
(TsDIAU, L'viv, Krajowa Rada Szkolna)
Correspondence with *guberniia* authorities on land, housing and *propinacja* [G], 1819–22; files on the foundation of the *Chevra Kadisha, Ezra* and *Chesed shel Emes* societies [P, G], 1892–1918.
(TsDIAU, L'viv, Namiestnictwo Galicyjskie)

GORZKÓW (pow. Krasnystaw, woj. lubelskie) 1856–1864
Microfilms:
Files on the position of a rabbi, 1856–64.
(AGAD, Warszawa, CWW)

GORZYCE (pow. Jasło, woj. krakowskie) 1878
Microfilms:
Files on reorganization of the elementary school attended by Jewish pupils [P, G], 1878.
(TsDIAU, L'viv, Krajowa Rada Szkolna)

GOSTYŃ (woj. poznańskie) 1880–1889
Microfilms:
Files on elections and decisions of the community board [G], 1880–89.
(Centrum Judaicum, Berlin)

GOSTYNIN (woj. warszawskie) 1566–1910
Microfilms:
1. *Lustracja* of the town, 1566.
(AGAD, Warszawa, ASK)
2. Correspondence on the release of rabbis from army service, including a list of them, 1865–1871.
(AGAD, Warszawa, CWW)
3. Copies of inscriptions from cemeteries and synagogues, 1910.
(RGIA, St. Petersburg, Departament dukhovnykh del...)

GOSZCZYN (pow. Grójec, woj. warszawskie) 1566
Microfilms:
Lustracja of the town, 1566.
(AGAD, Warszawa, ASK)

GOWARCZÓW (pow. Końskie, woj. kieleckie) 1856–1864
Microfilms:
Reports and correspondence on appointments of rabbis, 1856–64.
(AGAD, Warszawa, CWW)

GOWOROWO (pow. Ostrołęka, woj. białostockie) 1914
Microfilms:
Complaint of a Jew [R], 1914
(AP Białystok, Rząd Gubernialny, Łomża]

GÓRA KALWARIA (pow. Grójec, woj. warszawskie) 1910
Microfilms:
Copies of inscriptions from cemeteries and synagogues, 1910
(RGIA, St. Petersburg, Departament dukhovnykh del...)

GRABOWIEC (pow. Hrubieszów, woj. lubelskie) 1747–1883
Microfilms:
1. Extract from *grod* records [L], 1747.
(AP Wrocław, Ossolineum)
2. Various receipts of the *kahal*, 18th cent.
(NBANU, L'viv, Zb. Goldsteina)
3. Statistical description of the town, 1851–59.
(AP Lublin, Rząd Gubernialny, Lublin)
4. Correspondence on irregularities in the community's administration [R], 1883.
(AP Lublin, Kancelaria Gubernatora Lubelskiego)

GRAJEWO (pow. Szczuczyn, woj. białostockie) 1905–1915
Microfilms:
Permits to Jews to open various shops and enterprises [R], 1905–14; files on the arrest and expulsion of Jews for political activities [R], 1911–15.
(AP Białystok, Rząd Gubernialny, Łomża)

GRABÓW (pow. Łęczyca, woj. łodzkie) 1910
Microfilms:
Copies of inscriptions from cemeteries and synagogues, 1910.
(RGIA, St. Petersburg, Departament dukhovnykh del...)

GRODNO (woj. białostockie) 1506–1923
Originals:
Copies of documents on the community copied by Israel Klausner in the Wilno State Archives, 1785–87; a coupon of the *Grodner Arbeter* cooperative [G, R, Y], 1919.
Drawings of a wooden synagogue, n.d.
(IKG Wien - Juedisches Museum)

Photocopies:
1. Court records about Jews, [R], 1559.
(NIAB, Minsk, Sąd Ziemski Grodnieński)
2. File on Jewish schools [R], 1842–46.
(GARF, Moscow, Tret'e otdelenie…)
Microfilms:
1. Charters given to the Jews of Grodno for *arendas*, tax collecting, etc. [Rt], 1506–68.
(RGADA, Moscow, ML)
2. Confirmation by King Jan III Sobieski of a charter given to the Jews of Grodno, 1669.
(AGAD, Warszawa, Arch. Radziwiłłów)
3. Banishment of a Jew by the *starosta's* court, for disloyalty [Rt], 1676.
(Bibl. PAN, Kraków)
4. Complaint of the Jews to the community regarding litigation with a nobleman, 1750.
(TsDIA, Kyiv, Arch. Potockich z Tulczyna)
5. Suits involving Jews, 1770–89.
(AGAD, Warszawa, Arch. Tyzenhauzów)
6. Files on debts to the community, 1788.
(RGADA, Moscow, KFE)
7. Files on the installation of a Jew as a specialist in Jewish matters at the office of the *General Gubernator* [R], 1816–84.
(RGIA, St. Petersburg, Departament narodnogo prosveshcheniia)
8. Files on debts of the Jewish community of Grodno to various Catholic monasteries in the town [R], 1831, 1838.
(RGIA, St. Petersburg, Rimsko-katolicheskaia kollegiia…)
9. Files on supervision of Jews from the Kingdom of Poland, living in Grodno; lists of Jews whose passports expired [R], 1831.
(GARF, Moscow, Tret'e otdelenie…)
10. A file on the Society for the Spread of Enlightment among the Jews of Russia [R], 1914.
(GARF, Moscow, Departament politsii…)
11. Files on illegal Jewish organizations; a list of arrested Jews [R], 1900–1904; correspondence of the Society for the Attainment of Full Rights for the Jewish People in Russia with its Grodno chapter [R], 1905–06.
(RGIA, St. Petersburg, Obshchestvo polnopraviya…)
12. Minutes of a conversation between Grodno rabbis and the *Gubernator* of Grodno on resettlement of Grodno Jews; files on the behavior of German soldiers towards the Jews of the town [R], 1915.
(TsDIAU, Kyiv, Fridman)
13. A list of people expelled from Grodno, 1923.
(DATO, Ternopil', Komenda Powiatowa PP, Trembowla)

GRODNO, surroundings, 1789–1916
Photocopies:
1. File on the evasion of military service [R], 1839–40.
(GARF, Moscow, Tret'e otdelenie…)
2. Inventories of various districts in the Grodno *guberniia*, 1789.
(NIAB, Minsk, Kollektsiia drevnikh inventarei)

Microfilms:
1. Records on resettlement of Jews from the Grodno area in the Kherson area, including a list of them [R], 1840.
(DAOdO, Odessa, Kantseliariia Novorossiiskogo i Bessarabskogo general-gubernatora)
2. Files on hospitals and old age homes in the Grodno *guberniia* [R], 1863–64.
(RGIA, St. Petersburg, Khoziaistvennyi departament MVD)
3. Documents on Jewish religious matters in the Grodno area [R], 1888–92.
(RGIA, Departament dukhovnykh del...)
4. Lists of Zionist organizations [R], 1907–16.
(TsGA, Tashkent, Turkestanskoe Okhrannoe otdelenie)

GRODZISK (pow. Nowy Tomyśl, woj. poznańskie) 1749–1929
Originals:
Charter granted to the community [G], 1749; community accounts (fragmentary) [G], 1788–1872; *pinkassim* of the *kahal* [community record books] and other records of community meetings, decisions and elections [G, H], 1779–94, 1830–69; population lists [G, H], 1810–45; taxes [G, H], 1816–43, 1852–69; personal papers of the Herzfeld family [G, H], 1828–1929; community statutes [G], 1834–44; police matters [G], 1834–46; passports [G], 1834–46 records of charitable activities [G, H], 1835–42; civil register [G, H], 1835–45; files on the appointment of a new rabbi and records of private prayer-houses [G, H], 1835–39; register of correspondence [G], 1840–43; legal matters [G], 1840–64; file on *shechita* [G], 1846; correspondence [G, H], 1851–58; files on the appointment of a cantor and a *shochet* [G, H] 1856, 1871.
Photocopies:
1. Letters of Dr. Karl Mosse, 1830–65.
(Private collection)
2. A file on *shechita* [G], n.d.
Microfilms:
Communal matters and files on litigation between a beer manufacturer and the Jewish community over the concession to serve wine in inns [G], 1800–43; various communal decisions [G], 1820–76.
(Centrum Judaicum, Berlin)

GRODZISKO (pow. Dobromil, woj. lwowskie) 1559–1746
Microfilms:
Municipal records (fragmentary), 16th-17th cent.; legal records (fragmentary), 1651–1746.
(AP Wrocław, Ossolineum)

GRÓDEK JAGIELLOŃSKI (woj. lwowskie) 1684–1939
Photocopies:
A list of Jewish merchants, entrepreneurs and homeowners [R], 1939.
(DALO, L'viv, L'vovskii obkom...)
Microfilms:
1. Confirmation by King Jan Kazimierz of the 1680 charter granting the right of settlement to Jews [P, L], 1684; a report of the district authorities on transferring the Jewish cemetery [G], 1781; permission for the community to rebuild the synagogue and private houses after a fire, 1793; a list of tax debts of residents in the surroundings [G], 1790–96; a meeting of the *gubernium* about a delay in payments of taxes by Jews, 1792–1817; correspondence on the rebuilding of 7 burnt Jewish houses, 1793; a report of the district

authorities on irregularities in registering Jewish vital statistics, 1841; a Jew's request to reside in the Christian area of the town, 1858; a list of eligible voters and community members, 1861.
(AP Kraków, Teki Schneidra)

2. Correspondence and minutes on confirmations of the statutes, 1846–1907; reorganization of the community [P, G], 1890, problems of Jewish civil registry, 1891–92; complaints of community members about elections of the community board, 1905–08; reports on *chadorim* and lists of teachers, 1877–1908; statutes of the *Talmud Tora* society, 1906–10.
(TsDIAU, L'viv, Namiestnictwo Galicyjskie)

3. Reports on teaching Jewish religion in the elementary schools [P, G], 1882–89.
(TsDIAU, L'viv, Krajowa Rada Szkolna)

4. Files on the *Mizrachi,* 1919–1921 and the *Machzikei Hadas* societies, 1932.
(DAIFO, Ivano-Frankivs'k, UW, Stanisławów)

5. Files on various community matters: elections, taxes, budget, lists of rabbis, of tax payers etc., 1924–39; correspondence on the local celebration honoring the opening of the Hebrew University in Jerusalem, 1924–25; statistical data on membership in political parties and participation by representatives of various nationalities in municipal administration, 1930–31, 1938–39; correspondence on granting travel documents to participants in the 21st Zionist Congress, 1939.
(DALO, L'viv, UW, Lwów)

GRÓJEC (woj. warszawskie) 1566–1844
Microfilms:
1. *Lustracja* of the town, 1566.
(AGAD, Warszawa, ASK)
2. Files on the Jewish inhabitants of the town (including a register of documents in the local archives on Jews), 1810–44.
(AGAD, Warszawa, KRzSW)

GRUDZIĄDZ (woj. pomorskie) 1782–1920
Originals:
Rabbinic and civil registry marriage certificates [G, H], 1846, 1901–20.
Microfilms:
Legal proceedings in the case of a theft, 1782.
(AP Kraków, IT)

GRYBÓW (pow. Nowy Sącz, woj. krakowskie) 1711–1896
Microfilms:
1. A collection of documents: accounts, real estate transactions, testimonies before the rabbinical court, obligations, *ketubot*, letters and documents from various towns in Poland and Russia, including Grybów [H, Y], 1711–1845.
(TsDIAU, Kyiv, Arch. Potockich z Tulczyna)
2. Files on the ratification of community statutes, 1846–96.
(TsDIAU, L'viv, Namiestnictwo Galicyjskie)
3. Lists of eligible voters, 1870.
(AP Kraków, Teki Schneidra)

GRZYMAŁÓW (pow. Skałat, woj. tarnopolskie) 1635–1939
Microfilms:

1. Correspondence and documents on estates of the Sieniawski family, 1635, 1713–35; circulars, accounts, decrees and *uniwersały* on inhabitants and estates of M. Sapieha, St. Siemieński, M. i A. Sieniawski, A. Czartoryski, 1663–1765.
(Bibl. Czartoryskich, Kraków)
2. Correspondence on confirmation of charters granted to the town [G], 1795–98; tax tables [G], 1842–59; correspondence with the district authorities regarding *chadorim* in the district, including names of teachers, 1874–1908; statutes of the Jewish community [G], 1875–76.
(TsDIAU, L'viv, Namiestnictwo Galicyjskie)
3. Reports and correspondence on the post of a teacher of Jewish religion in a grade school, statistics, 1910.
(TsDIAU, L'viv, Krajowa Rada Szkolna)
4. Reports, requests and correspondence on permission to open courses in Hebrew, 1925; questionnaires containing names of community board members, 1928; reports and correspondence on community elections, 1932–35; correspondence with the district authorities on statutes and elections to the board of the local branch of *Agudas Yisroel*, 1934; reports and correspondence regarding OŻPP [P, Y], 1934; a list of community taxpayers, 1936; reports by district authorities on anti-Jewish incidents, 1937; lists of rabbis and *dayanim*, citing their education and other personal data, 1937–38; an inspection report of financial and economic activity of the community, 1939.
(DATO, Ternopil', UW, Tarnopol)

GWOŹDZIEC (pow. Kołomyja, woj. stanisławowskie) 1871–1960
Original:
A drawing of a wooden synagogue, n.d.
(IKG Wien - Juedisches Museum)
Photocopies:
Reports on prayer houses [R], 1946, 1957, 1960.
(DAIFO, Ivano-Frankivs'k, Upolnomochennyi Soveta...)
Microfilms:
1. Records on ratifying the statutes of the *Bikur Cholim* society [G, P], 1871–1937; files on the statutes and subsequent liquidation of the *Gmilas Chesed* society [G, P], 1904–13, 1928–31; reports and correspondence on the ratification of statutes, registration and activities of Jewish libraries, including statutes and lists of founding members, 1921–30; reports and correspondence regarding ratification of the statutes of Jewish charitable associations aiding children, 1923–28; lists of the board members of *Hechalutz, Żydowska Rada Sieroca* and *Ochrona Młodzieży*, and of other Jewish associations, 1930–37; reports and correspondence on the activity of the Jewish community [G, P, Y], 1931–39; records of various Jewish sport associations, 1931–36; records on *Hashomer Hatzair*, 1931–37; reports about the activity of OŻPP, 1933; correspondence on Jewish agricultural associations, lists of board members and their political affiliations, 1933–38; information about elections and appointments of rabbis and *dayanim*, 1935–36.
(DAIFO, Ivano-Frankivs'k, UW, Stanisławów)
2. Minutes from inspections of Baron Hirsch Foundation (JCA) schools [G, P], 1896–1904.
(TsDIAU, L'viv, Krajowa Rada Szkolna)
3. Answers to a questionnaire on the Jews, 1922.
(NBANU, L'viv, Zb. Czołowskiego)
4. Records on the *Czytelnia Żydowska* (1924–33), *Nosei Hamita* (1924–33), *Bikur Cholim* (1926–37), *Gmilas Chesed* (1928–37), *Żydowskie Towarzystwo Rolnicze* (1932–33), *Hechalutz* (1933–37); *Hashomer Hatzair* (1933–39), *Stowarzyszenie Kupieckie* (1936–37), *Betar* (1937) societies, including their statutes

and lists of board members; correspondence with the police in Kołomyja about registration of the *Yad Charutzim* society, including statutes and a list of the founding members, 1936–37; a file on the *Żydowski Klub Sportowy 'Młot'* society, 1936–37; statutes and index cards of the *Stowarzyszenie dla Szerzenia Nauk Judaistycznych wśród Młodzieży 'Etz Chaim'* society, 1938.
(DAIFO, Ivano-Frankivs'k, Starostwo Powiatowe, Kołomyja)

HALICZ (pow. Stanisławów, woj. stanisławowskie) 1556–1939
Microfilms:
1. Two *lustracje* and an inventory of the town, 1556–1661; inventory of the *starostwo*, 1627.
(AP Wrocław, Ossolineum)
2. Excerpts from Armenian files of Stanisławów on Jewish commerce, *arenda*, loans and other matters in Halicz, 1703–09.
(NBANU, L'viv, Arch. Ossolińskich)
3. Excerpts from the decisions of the Council of Four Lands; correspondence on *Karaites* in Halicz; a list of *Karaite* families [G, H, L, P], 1775–80; statute of the *Osei Chesed Vaemes* society [G, P], 1910–13.
(TsDIAU, L'viv, Namiestnictwo Galicyjskie)
4. Minutes, contracts and requests regarding land ownership [G, L, P], 1807–53.
(DAIFO, Ivano-Frankivs'k, Sąd Magistratu, Halicz)
5. Reports on teaching Jewish religion in elementary schools [G, P], 1882–89.
(TsDIAU, L'viv, Krajowa Rada Szkolna)
6. Statutes, minutes and correspondence of Jewish associations [G, P], 1894–99, 1924–39; a membership list of *Helios*, 1921–30; reports and correspondence of Zionist organizations, 1921–30; a list of board members of the *Yad Charutzim* society, 1930–31, 1937; files on ratification of the *Gmilas Chesed* society and board member lists, 1922–31; reports and correspondence on ratification of statutes and registration of Jewish charitable associations assisting children, 1923–28; board member lists of *Hatzofim Brit Trumpeldor*, 1930–37; records of the *Makabbia*, 1931–32; reports and correspondence on appointments and salaries of rabbis and *dayanim*, 1932–35; records of the *Hatikva* society, 1932–36; reports on the activity of the *OŻPP* society, including a list of commitee members, 1933.
(DAIFO, Ivano-Frankivs'k, UW, Stanisławów)
7. Files on evaluation of war damages to the Jewish community, 1920–21.
(DAIFO, Ivano-Frankivs'k, Miejscowa Komisja Szacunkowa, Stanisławów)
8. Reports and correspondence on ratification of statutes, boards and registration of Jewish youth organizations, 1920–39; statistical data on vital statistics, 1923–24; ratification of the statutes of the *Yad Charutzim* society, including lists and reports, 1930–39; lists of Jewish association board members, 1925–39; reports and correspondence on the opening of a course in Hebrew, 1926; reports and correspondence on appointing a rabbi and board and confirming the community budget, including a list of taxpayers, 1933–34.
(DAIFO, Ivano-Frankivs'k, Starostwo Powiatowe, Stanisławów)
9. Reports by public school principals containing descriptions of social, national, cultural, economic and hygienic conditions [P, U], 1930; reports and correspondence on the legalization of *chadorim* and other Jewish schools, a list of *chadorim* and statutes of *Tarbut*, 1934–36.
(DAIFO, Ivano-Frankivs'k, Inspektorat Szkolny, Stanisławów)
10. Police reports on "political and national forces" in district councils, 1930–34; lists of Jewish association members, 1933–36.
(DAIFO, Ivano-Frankivs'k, Komenda Powiatowa PP, Stanisławów)

11. A file on an accusation against Jews suspected of distributing leaflets, in Yiddish, of the Communist Party [Y, P], 1933.
(DAIFO, Ivano-Frankivs'k, Prokuratura Sądu Okręgowego, Stanisławów)

HAŃKOWCE (pow. Śniatyn, woj. stanisławowskie) 1930–1937
Microfilms:
Lists of the *Achva* society boards members, 1930–37.
(DAIFO, Ivano-Frankivs'k, UW, Stanisławów)

HINOWICE (pow. Brzeżany, woj. tarnopolskie) 1699–1791
Microfilms:
Letters to the *wojewoda* of Volhynia on the *arenda* of plots by Jews, 1699–1791.
(TsDIAU, L'viv, Kolektsiia lystiv…)

HOLSZANY (pow. Oszmiana, woj. wileńskie) 1859–1860
Microfilms:
Accusation of a Jew for violating commerce laws [R], 1859–60.
(DAVO, Vinnytsia, Magistrat, Vinnitsa)

HOROCHÓW (woj. wołyńskie) 1793
Microfilms:
Requests by 88 Jewish merchants from Poland for permission to enter Russia [R], 1793.
(TsDIAU, Kyiv, Kievskaia gubernskaia kantseliariia)

HORODENKA (woj. stanisławowskie) 1746–1957
Microfilms:
1. Accounts, orders of payment, contracts, etc. on debts of the Jewish community [L, P], 1746.
(TsDIAU, L'viv, Kolektsiia dokumentiv…)
2. A response to a request of the Jewish community for a delay in paying taxes [G], 1798.
(AP Kraków, Teki Schneidra)
3. A letter by Prince Potocki on taxes from the Jewish community [L], 1798; correspondence with the provincial authorities about *arendas*, taxes, residence permits, etc. [G, P], 1825–28; correspondence with the district authorities about *chadorim* and lists of *melamdim*, 1883–1908, and on the designation of citizenship in civil registers, 1891–92; correspondence with the Ministry of the Interior and the Ministry of Religions about communal matters [G, P], 1895; correspondence regarding antisemitic agitation [G, P], 1898–1903; protests against results of the community elections [G, P], 1901–06; correspondence and statistical data about the community budget [G, P], 1902.
(TsDIAU, L'viv, Namiestnictwo Galicyjskie)
4. Files on ratifying the statutes of the *Hachnasas Orchim* society [G, P], 1871–88, 1921–30; statutes, minutes and correspondence on Jewish associations [G, P], 1894–99, 1924–39; file on ratification of statutes of the *Agudas Yisroel, Chevrat Bait Ivri, Talmud Tora* and *Agudas Achim* societies [G, P, U], 1895, 1920–27; file on ratification of statutes, activity and liquidation of *Gmilas Chesed,* including lists of board members [G, P], 1904–13, 1928–31; reports and correspondence on a subvention for renovating the synagogue, including a plan of the synagogue, 1921–25; files on the registration and activities of Jewish libraries, including statutes and a list of founding members, 1921–34; reports about *chadorim* [G, P], 1921–35; files on ratification of statutes and foundation of the *Koło Kobiet Żydowskich* society, 1922–30; statistical data on the Jewish population, 1923–24; reports and correspondence on ratification of statutes

and registration of Jewish charitable associations aiding children, 1923–28; reports on activities of Zionist associations and parties, among them the Revisionist Zionists 1926–27, 1935; reports on the activity of *Hashomer Hatzair* and other Jewish youth groups, 1929–1930; records on: *Towarzystwo Opieki nad Halucami i Emigrantami Palestyńskimi Ezra*, (1930–35); *Gordonia* (1930–36), *Hatzofim Brit Trumpeldor* (1930–37); reports and correspondence on the activity of the Jewish community, including voters' lists [G, P, Y], 1931–39; records of various Jewish sport associations, 1931–36; reports, statutes and board member list of OŻPP, 1932–33; records on *Hatechiya*, 1932–38; correspondence on a Jewish agricultural association, citing party affiliations of board members, 1933; reports and correspondence on *Związek Żydowski Inwalidów, Wdów i Sierot Wojennych*, 1933–37; reports about meetings organized by Jewish parties and associations, decrees aimed at preventing anti-Jewish incidents, 1934; monographs on political and social questions, 1935; a list of *Kultur Liga* board members, 1936.
(DAIFO, Ivano-Frankivs'k, UW, Stanisławów)
5. Reports on inspection of Baron Hirsch Foundation (JCA) schools [G, P], 1896–1904.
(TsDIAU, L'viv, Krajowa Rada Szkolna)
6. Answers to a questionnaire on the Jews, 1922.
(NBANU, L'viv, Zb. Czołowskiego)
7. Monthly police reports about activities of associations and political parties, 1930–1936; reports and correspondence on anti-Jewish actions by Ukrainian nationalists, 1936–37; reports about the activities of the Jewish sport associations, *Młot* and *Hapoel*, 1937.
(DAIFO, Ivano-Frankivs'k, Komenda Wojewódzka PP, Stanisławów)
8. Reports and correspondence on the legalization of *chadorim* and other Jewish schools, including a list of *chadorim*, 1934–36.
(DAIFO, Ivano-Frankivs'k, Inspektorat Szkolny, Stanisławów)
9. Reports about the activities of the Revisionist Zionists, *Poalei Zion Lewica, Hitachdut Poalei Zion, Hechalutz, Hakoach* and *Yad Charutzim*, 1935.
(DAIFO, Ivano-Frankivs'k, Komenda Powiatowa PP, Śniatyn)
10. Monographs containing economic and demographic information about the Jews, 1936.
(AP Wrocław, Ossolineum, WKNZNP, Lwów)
11. Statistical data about the Jewish population, 1938.
(DAIFO, Ivano-Frankivs'k, UW, Stanisławów)
12. Documents on the conversion of a synagogue to an oil factory and on the utilization of other synagogue buildings [R], 1946–57.
(DAIFO, Ivano-Frankivs'k, Upolnomochennyi Soveta...)

HORODENKA, surroundings, 1921–1939
Microfilms:
1. Records on the activity of the *Samopomoc* and *Stowarzyszenie Żydowskiej Młodzieży Akademickiej* associations in the district, 1921–30; a list of associations in the district [P, U], 1922–23; correspondence with the district authorities about the activities of the *Bund*, 1923; a statistical description of the district, 1935; information on the distribution of anti-Jewish brochures in the district, 1936.
(DAIFO, Ivano-Frankivs'k, UW, Stanisławów)
2. Reports and correspondence on unemployment insurance for employees of ritual slaughter houses in towns of the area, 1936–39.
(DAIFO, Ivano-Frankivs'k, Wojewódzkie Biuro Funduszu Pracy, Stanisławów)

HORODŁO (pow. Hrubieszów, woj. lubelskie) 1578–1859
Microfilms:
1. Confirmation by King Stefan Batory of an agreement between two Jewish traders, 1578.
(AGAD, Warszawa, MK)
2. Sworn testimony on Jewish houses destroyed in the fire of 1744, court ruling in a dispute between Jewish *arendars* and the local townsmen, 1765.
(AP Lublin, Księgi Grodzkie Horodelskie)
3. A statistical description, 1851–59.
(AP Lublin, Rząd Gubernialny, Lublin)

HORODŁO, surroundings, 1765.
Microfilms:
1. *Lustracja* of the royal estates [L], 1765.
(AP Wrocław, Ossolineum)

HORODYSŁAWICE (pow. Bóbrka, woj. lwowskie) 1628–1759
Microfilms:
Private agreements, receipts, contracts and other documents regarding the estates of the Sieniawski and Czartoryski families, 1628–1759.
(Bibl. Czartoryskich, Kraków)

HORYŃGRÓD (pow. Równe, woj. wołyńskie) 1816–1936
Microfilms:
1. A list of inhabitants (*revizskie skazki)* [R], 1816–28, 1858–60.
(DARO, Rivne, Rovenskoe uezdnoe kaznacheistvo)
2. Correspondence on the foundation and activities of the *Tarbut* society, 1932–36.
(DARO, Rivne, Starostwo Powiatowe, Równe)

HOSZCZA (pow. Równe, woj. wołyńskie) 1927–1936
Microfilms:
1. Files on activities of the local branch of the *Centralny Związek Rzemieślników Żydów w Polsce* [organization of Jewish craftsmen in Poland], 1927–38
2. Statutes of the *Mizrachi* and a list of board members, 1935–36.
(DARO, Rivne, Starostwo Powiatowe, Równe)

HREBENÓW (pow. Stryj, woj. stanisławowskie) 1931–1939
Microfilms:
1. Files on ratifying statutes of Jewish associations, 1931–39.
(DAIFO, Ivano-Frankivs'k, UW, Stanisławów)
2. Reports and correspondence on anti-Jewish actions by Ukrainian nationalists, 1936–37.
(DAIFO, Ivano-Frankivs'k, Komenda Wojewódzka PP, Stanisławów)

HRUBIESZÓW (woj. lubelskie) 1833–1901
Originals:
Fragment of a death register [R], 1900–01.
Microfilms:
1. Statistical description, 1833–59.

(AP Lublin, Rząd Gubernialny, Lublin)

2. Complaint by a Jew of persecution by the Jewish community for his alleged denunciation of conscription evasion by Jews [R], 1884–85.

(AP Lublin, Kancelaria Gubernatora Lubelskiego)

3. Reports and correspondence on the appointment of rabbis, their education and salaries, 1856–64.

(AGAD, Warszawa, CWW)

HUMIENIEC (pow. Sambor, woj. lwowskie) 1936

Microfilms:

Monographs containing economic and demographic information about the Jews, 1936.

(AP Wrocław, Ossolineum, WKNZNP, Lwów)

HUSIATYŃ (pow. Kopyczyńce, woj. tarnopolskie) 1753–1944

Originals:

The statutes and three handbills of *Dovevei Siftei Yeshanim*, a society for publishing old Hebrew manuscripts [H], 1902.

Photographs:

Synagogue ruin, 1944.

(Central State Archives of Film-, Photo- and Phonographic Documents of the Ukraine, Kiev)

Microfilms:

1. A list of rabbis in the town, 1753–67; records on the activity and economic situation of the *kahal* and its members [G, H, P], 1797–1851.

(TsDIAU, L'viv, Arch. Lanckorońskich)

2. Correspondence on the censorship of books and the clandestine import to Russia of prohibited books through Husiatyń [R], 1800.

(RGIA, St. Petersburg, Kantseliariia general-prokurora)

3. Excerpt from the Franciscan register of Jewish plot owners, their annual incomes and taxes, 1820.

(TsDIAU, L'viv, Metryka franciszkańska)

4. Reports about *chadorim* and teachers [G, P], 1875–77.

(TsDIAU, L'viv, Krajowa Rada Szkolna)

5. Report containing lists of *chadorim* in the district, 1880–1908; correspondence about emigrants from Russia, who passed through the town [G, P], 1890–95; correspondence with the Ministry of Interior about reorganization of the community, 1875; letters by Jews against the appointment of Berel Landman as a *dayan*, 1899–1906; correspondence with the *Starostwo* regarding changes in the statutes of the Jewish community, 1899–1907; correspondence about elections to the community board, 1900–02; statutes of the *Tzedaka Vachesed* society [G], 1909.

(TsDIAU, L'viv, Namiestnictwo Galicyjskie)

6. Correspondence about elections to the community board, 1922–25; questionnaires containing names of community board members, 1928; a list of political parties containing names of members and descriptions of their activities, 1929; records on renovation of 17th cent. synagogues in Husiatyń and Leszniów, 1931; reports and correspondence on elections of the community board, 1932–36; a report on economic and financial activity of the Jewish community, 1934–36; a list of community taxpayers [H, P], 1935; lists of rabbis and *dayanim*, their education and other data, 1937–38; a report following an inspection of the community, 1938.

(DATO, Ternopil', UW, Tarnopol)

HUSSAKÓW (pow. Mościska, woj. lwowskie) 1874–1935
Microfilms:
1. Correspondence on *chadorim*, including names of teachers, 1874–1908; correspondence on the relationship between Hussaków and the central community in Mościska, 1890.
(TsDIAU, L'viv, Namiestnictwo Galicyjskie)
2. Correspondence about the registration of *Agudas Yisroel*, 1932.
(DALO, L'viv, Magistrat, Lwów)
3. Correspondence about the community budget, including a list of taxpayers, 1935.
(DALO, L'viv, UW, Lwów)

HUSZLEW (woj. lubelskie) 1691–1700
Microfilms:
Records on the *arenda* of a tavern, 1691–1700.
(AP Lublin, Arch. Woronieckich z Huszlewa)

HUTA (pow. Suwałki, woj. białostockie) 1912–1914
Microfilms:
File on payment for medical treatment in the Jewish hospital of Suwałki, including a list of inhabitants from Huta [R], 1912–14.
(AP Białystok, Rząd Gubernialny, Łomża)

HUTA BANKOWA (DĄBROWA GÓRNICZA) (pow. Będzin, woj. kieleckie) 1877
Microfilms:
File on the conversion of a Jewish woman to Christianity [R], 1877.
(AP Łódź, Rząd Gubernialny, WA, Piotrków)

ILJA (pow. Wilejka, woj. wileńskie) 1801
Microfilms:
Reports about a glass factory in Ilja, owned by a Jew from Wilejka [R], 1801.
(RGADA, Moscow, Manufaktur-kollegiia)

IŁŻA (woj. kieleckie) 1859–1866
Microfilms:
Files on the Jewish community, accounts, documents on the foundation of the Jewish community in Wąchock and its separation from the community in Iłża, as well as excerpts from marriage and death records, 1859–66.
(AP Radom, Rząd Gubernialny, Radom)

INDURA (pow. Grodno, woj. białostockie) 18th–20th cent.
Photocopies:
Copies of the community's correspondence with the *Landsmannshaft* in the United States [Y], 1930s.
Microfilms:
Legal and financial documents; community regulations [H, Y], 18th cent.
(Bibl. PAN, Kraków)

INOWŁÓDZ (pow. Rawa, woj. warszawskie) 1825–1913
Microfilms:

1. Community records and accounts, 1825–66.
(AP Łódź, Anterioria Rządu Gubernialnego, Piotrków)
2. Records of community accounts and elections [R], 1900–13.
(AP Łódź, Rząd Gubernialny, WA, Piotrków)

INOWROCŁAW (woj. poznańskie) 1765–1846
Originals:
Litigation between two farmers [G], 1840–41; a file on Jewish colonization [G], 1846;
Microfilms:
Confirmation by King Stanisław August Poniatowski of the charter granted to the Jews [L, P], 1765.
(AGAD, Warszawa, Księgi Kanclerskie)

IWANICZE (pow. Włodzimierz, woj. wołyńskie) 1898
Original:
Jahrzeit table of the Eliasberg family [H, Y], 1898.

IWANIKI (pow. Pińsk, woj. poleskie) 1888–1894
Photocopies:
A file on the Jewish school [R], 1888–94.
(NIAB, Minsk, Minskoe gubernskoe pravlenie)

IZABELIN (pow. Wołkowysk, woj. białostockie) 1803
Microfilms:
Reports about a tannery and a hat manufacturer [R], 1803.
(RGADA, Moscow, Manufaktur kollegiia)

IZBICA KUJAWSKA (pow. Koło, woj. łódzkie) 1893–1911
Microfilms:
Records, accounts of the community [R], 1893–1910; fines for evading conscription [R], 1906–11.
(AP Łódź, Urząd Gminy, Izbica)

JABŁONICA (pow. Brzozów, woj. lwowskie) 1853
Microfilms:
Correspondence with the district authorities in Sanok about taverns in agricultural areas, among them Jabłonica, on plots belonging to Christians [G], 1853.
(TsDIAU, L'viv, Namiestnictwo Galicyjskie)

JABŁONICA (pow. Kosów, woj. stanisławowskie) 1704–1721
Microfilms:
Excerpts from court minutes concerning an assault on Jews in Jabłonica, 1704–21.
(NBANU, L'viv, Arch. Ossolińskich)

JABŁONKA (pow. Wysokie Mazowieckie, woj. białostockie) 1827–1912
Originals:
Birth, marriage and death records (fragmentary) [P, R], 1840, 1886, 1890, 1911.
Microfilms:
1. Birth, marriage and death records (fragmentary), 1827–65.
(AP Łomża)

2. Reports and correspondence on the appointment of rabbis and their relations with the communities, including a list of rabbis, 1853–56.
(AGAD, Warszawa, CWW)
3. Fine for illegal sale of alcohol by a Jew [R], 1912.
(AP Białystok, Rząd Gubernialny, Łomża)

JABŁONKA NIŻNA (pow. Turka, woj. lwowskie) 1936
Microfilms:
Monograph containing demographic and economic data on the town, 1936.
(AP Wrocław, Ossolineum, WKNZNP Lwów)

JABŁONÓW (pow. Kołomyja, woj. stanisławowskie) 1884–1939
Photocopies:
A drawing of the wooden synagogue, n.d.
(IKG Wien - Juedisches Museum)
Microfilms:
1. Correspondence on the election of a rabbi, 1884–89; correspondence about unauthorized taxes for *shechita*, 1886–87; reports and correspondence on ratification of the community statutes [G, P], 1887–97; correspondence about *chadorim,* including names of teachers, 1900–08.
(TsDIAU, L'viv, Namiestnictwo Galicyjskie)
2. Reports following inspection of Baron Hirsch Foundation (JCA) schools, including the personal files of teachers, I. Ratner and M. Abend, 1896–97.
(TsDIAU, L'viv, Krajowa Rada Szkolna)
3. A membership list of the *Żydowski Komitet Rozdzielczy* society, 1920; a file on the activity of *Poalei Zion Lewica*, 1924–25.
(DAIFO, Ivano-Frankivs'k, Starostwo Powiatowe, Peczeniżyn)
4. Answers to a questionnaire on the Jews, 1922.
(NBANU, L'viv, Zb. Czołowskiego)
5. Files on ratifying the statutes of the *Gmilas Chesed* society, 1922–30; a file on Jewish community elections and the establishment of a separate Jewish community in Mikuliczyn, 1912–14, 1923–24; records on the elections of rabbis, 1925–39; a list of *Hechalutz* board members, 1930; files on *Hatzofim Brit Trumpeldor* and other Jewish associations, 1930–37; files on Jewish sport associations, 1931–36; reports and correspondence on community board elections, 1932–36; a file on *Hatechiya*, 1932–38.
(DAIFO, Ivano-Frankivs'k, UW, Stanisławów)
6. Records on the activity of the *Gwiazda* association, statutes and a list of members, 1924–33; records on the activity of the *Gmilas Chesed* society, statutes and a list of members, 1928–38; files on *Hechalutz* and *Brith Trumpeldor*, containing lists of board members, 1933–37; records on *Histadrut Hanoar Haivri*, 1933–38.
(DAIFO, Ivano-Frankivs'k, Starostwo Powiatowe, Kołomyja)
7. Reports on the activity of the *Etz Chaim* society, 1933.
(DAIFO, Ivano-Frankivs'k, Posterunek Policji Państwowej, Śniatyn)
8. Monograph on demographic and economic data, 1936.
(AP Wrocław, Ossolineum, WKNZNP, Lwów)

JAGIELNICA (pow. Czortków, woj. tarnopolskie) 1742–1939
Photocopies:

An album of compositions, in Hebrew, by pupils of the *Tarbut* school, which was presented to Moses Herzog, President of the Jagielnicer Relief Committee in New York [H, Y], 1939.

Microfilms:

1. *Arenda* contract with a Jew from Jagielnica, 1742; files on litigation between a Jewish tavern keeper and the Lanckoroński and Potocki families [L], 1762–66; a register of tavern keepers and merchants in Jagielnica and Ułaszkowice [G, P], 1784, 1810, 1839–41; litigation between two Jews over an inheritance [H], 1785–1812; litigation between two tavern keepers [L, P], 1788–1807; an accusation of theft, 1796–97; a file on the activity and financial situation of the *kahals* in Jagielnica and other towns, and data on Jewish inhabitants [G, H, P], 1797–1851; litigation over property between Jews from Ułaszkowice and Jagielnica [G, H, P], 1806–18; an agreement about leasing an estate from A. Lanckoroński, 1812–30; complaint against sale of meat of poor quality by the *kahal*, 1813; *arenda* contract for a tavern and a mill, 1815; a file on the accusation of a Jew for assaulting a Jewish tax collector [G, L, P], 1818–22; a letter about founding new private *minyanim*, 1819; correspondence about community elections [G], 1820; an accusation of two Jews for attacking a soldier in the course of tax collecting [G, L, P], 1822; minutes on a case of horse theft by Jews [G, P], 1825; a list of merchants and *arendas* [G], 1829–35.

(TsDIAU, L'viv, Arch. Lanckorońskich)

2. Correspondence with the authorities about community elections [G, P], 1901–04.

(TsDIAU, L'viv, Namiestnictwo Galicyjskie)

3. Minutes about community elections, 1924–28; reports on inspection of Jewish communities, 1937; lists of rabbis and *dayanim*, and personal data about them, 1937–38.

(DATO, Ternopil', UW, Tarnopol)

4. Reports on elections to the board of the Jewish National Fund, 1925–28, 1931–36; files on the activity of *Hashomer Hatzair*, including a list of board members, 1930–38; statutes, lists and reports on activities of *Tarbut*, 1930–38; a file on the activity of *Gordonia*, 1933–37; reports on meetings and elections of the *Stowarzyszenie im. J. L. Pereca* [Y. L. Peretz club], 1933–38; reports of the *Merkaz Ruchani* association, including lists of members, 1935–38.

(DATO, Ternopil', Starostwo Powiatowe, Czortków)

5. Reports and correspondence on ratifying the statutes of *Agudas Yisroel*, including lists of members, 1926–28; a list of Jewish community board members, their professions and political affiliations, 1933; community budget and list of communal taxpayers, 1937.

(DATO, Ternopil', UW, Tarnopol)

JAMIELNICA (pow. Stryj, woj. stanisławowskie) 1936–1937
Microfilms:
Correspondence on anti-Jewish actions by Ukrainian nationalists, 1936–37.
(DAIFO, Ivano-Frankivs'k, Komenda Wojewódzka PP, Stanisławów)

JAMNA (pow. Nadwórna, woj. stanisławowskie) 1937–1938
Microfilms:
Description of the town and the political situation, 1937–38.
(DAIFO, Ivano-Frankivs'k, Posterunek Policji Państwowej, Jaremcze)

JAMNICA (pow. Stanisławów, woj. stanisławowskie) 1923–1924
Microfilms:
A list of Jewish inhabitants, 1923–24.

(DAIFO, Ivano-Frankivs'k, Starostwo Powiatowe, Stanisławów)

JANOWIEC (pow. Żnin woj. poznańskie) 1793
Microfilms:
A list of income from the town, 1793.
(AP Wrocław, Ossolineum)

JANÓW (pow. Drohiczyn, woj. poleskie) 1791–2001
Originals:
Correspondence, maps, minutes, video recordings [H, Y], 1919, 1928–2001.
(Archives of *Landsmannshaft* of Pińsk, Karlin, Janów and surroundings)
Photocopies:
Excerpts from municipal books on financial and commercial matters, 1791–92.
(NIAB, Minsk, Pinskaia Magdeburgia)

JANÓW (pow. Gródek Jagielloński, woj. lwowskie) 1846–1938
Microfilms:
1. Files on ratifying the statutes of the community, 1846–96; correspondence between the community and the district authorities regarding the statutes and the budget [G, P], 1898; complaints about community elections, 1906–08.
(TsDIAU, L'viv, Namiestnictwo Galicyjskie)
2. Correspondence with the district authorities regarding communal matters, among them elections; a list of board members, their ages, professions and political affiliations, 1924, 1933–38.
(DALO, L'viv, UW, Lwów)
3. Monograph, containing demographic and economic data, 1936.
(AP Wrocław, Ossolineum, WKNZNP, Lwów)

JANÓW (woj. lubelskie) 1691–1861
Microfilms:
1. Records of the community's debts to the Catholic Church in Zamość, 1691–1804.
(AP Lublin, Kolegiata w Zamościu)
2. A statistical description of Janów (1819–59), 1860–61.
(AP Lublin, Rząd Gubernialny, Lublin)
3. Files on synagogues, 1818–60; reports and correspondence on burial societies, 1822–50; correspondence about payments for burial; minutes and correspondence about illegal burial societies in Janów and Olkusz, 1853–59.
(AGAD, Warszawa, CWW)

JANÓW (woj. kieleckie) 1849–1913
Microfilms:
1. Records of the community, 1849–66.
(AP Łódź, Anterioria Rządu Gubernialnego, Piotrków)
2. Ratification of community elections and accounts [R], 1893–1913.
(AP Łódź, Rząd Gubernialny, WA, Piotrków)

JANÓW (pow. Sokółka, woj. białostockie) 1786–1789
Photocopies:
Inventory of estates containing lists of Jews, 1786, 1789.

(NIAB, Minsk, Kollektsiia drevnikh inventarei)

JANÓW (pow. Trembowla, woj. tarnopolskie) 1924–1939
Microfilms:
1. Decrees, minutes and correspondence on elections to the Jewish community board, including voting lists, 1924–25.
(DATO, Ternopil', Starostwo Powiatowe, Trembowla)
2. Questionnaires containing names of Jewish community board members, 1928; a list of community taxpayers, 1932–33; reports and correspondence on community elections, 1932–35; lists of rabbis and *dayanim*, their educations and other personal data, 1937–38; reports and correspondence on elections and appointments of rabbis and *dayanim*, 1939.
(DATO, Ternopil', UW, Tarnopol)

JARACZEW (pow. Jarocin, woj. poznańskie) 1841–1848
Microfilms:
1. Decisions of the community board [G], 1841–48.
(Centrum Judaicum, Berlin)

JARCZÓW (pow. Tomaszów, woj. lubelskie) 1840–1860
Microfilms:
1. Residence permit for a Jew [R], 1840; a statistical description of the town (1847–59), 1860.
(AP Lublin, Rząd Gubernialny, Lublin)

JAREMCZE (pow. Nadwórna, woj. stanisławowskie) 1932–1938
Microfilms:
1. Reports and correspondence on the appointment of rabbis and *dayanim* and on their salaries, 1932–35.
(DAIFO, Ivano-Frankivs'k, UW, Stanisławów)
2. Description of the town and its political situation, 1937–38.
(DAIFO, Ivano-Frankivs'k, Posterunek Policji Państwowej, Jaremcze)

JAROCIN (woj. poznańskie) 1835–1884
Originals:
Records on various community officials [G], 1835–50; a letter by the rabbi [H], 1835; a file on civil records [G], 1838–48; a file on the appointment of a new cantor and *shochet* [G], 1839–52; a register of expenses [G], 1841–44; a correspondence register [G], 1842–47.
Microfilms:
Minutes of community board meetings [G], 1834–51, 1878–84.
(Centrum Judaicum, Berlin)

JAROCIN, surroundings, 1829–79
Microfilms:
Various legal and economic records on the Jews of the Radoliński estates [G], 1829–79.
(AP Poznań, Zespół akt majątku Radolińskich, Jarocin)

JAROSŁAW (woj. lwowskie) 1628–1939
Photographs:
Teachers and schoolgirls of the *Beis Yaakov* school on an excursion, 1929.

Microfilms:

1. Private agreements, receipts, contracts and other documents regarding the estates of the Sieniawski and Czartoryski families [H, L, P], 1628–1767.
(Bibl. Czartoryskich, Kraków)

2. Confirmation by Princess Anna Ostrogska of a document by Zofia Tarnowska, permitting Jews to reside in only one house, and maintain only one tavern, 1630; complaints against Jewish inn keepers for producing vodka of bad quality, 1665; a decree by the town council prohibiting the Christian inhabitants to employ Jews or rent them apartments [L], 1664; a document by Queen Maria Kazimiera, appointing the Bishop of Jarosław as an arbitrator in conflicts between Jews and townsmen [L], 1683; orders by Prince J. K. Lubomirski, forbidding townsmen to rent apartments to Jews after the fair, 1687, and ordering their expulsion immediately after its closing, 1688; a verdict by J. K. Lubomirski on a dispute between townsmen and an *arendar*, 1701; an order by Princess T. L. Lubomirska to the mayor and the town council to respect the decree issued on 29.05.1703 in Kraków forbidding the provision of shelter in the town for Jews, 1704; an order of expulsion of a Jew, previously expelled from Przeworsk and Łańcut for various criminal offences, 1711; confirmation by Princess E. Sieniawska of a charter given to a Jew, Z. Jakubowicz, for commerce and an order to prosecute Jews of Jarosław who wished to ban and murder him, 1712.
(AP Przemyśl, Akta m. Jarosławia, DP)

3. *Arenda* contract for trade in tobacco and alcohol, 1672; a receipt by Prince Lubomirski to M. Jakowicz, an *arendar*, 1692.
(AP Kraków, Teki Sanguszków, tzw. rzymskie)

4. A decree by Princess H. Lubomirska, owner of the town, expelling Jews and limiting the rights of those remaining in the town, 1678; a decision by the Council of Four Lands on the relationships between *kahals* in Busk, Rozwadów, Sarnaki and Siemiatycze [L, P], 1758.
(NBANU, L'viv, Arch. Sapiehów)

5. Receipts issued by the *kahal* and an inventory of the Jesuit order [G, L, P], 1693–1797.
(TsDIAU, L'viv, Kolektsiia dokumentiv pro katolyts'ki monastyri…)

6. A list of documents on the city, 17th–18th cent.
(AP Wrocław, Ossolineum)

7. Miscellanea [G, H, L, P], 17th–19th cent., among them: debts of the *kahal* to the Jesuits, 1688–1773; quarterly payments for the army (including a list of home owners in the area), 1819.
(AP Kraków, Teki Schneidra)

8. Two charters granted to the Jews by Prince August Czartoryski, 1751, 1754.
(Bibl. PAN, Kraków)

9. *Lustracja* of the poll-tax on the estates of A. Czartoryski, 1766.
(AGAD, Warszawa, Arch. Potockich w Łańcucie)

10. Correspondence with provincial authorities about marriage permits [G], 1820–23; correspondence about *chadorim* in the area, including names of teachers and statistical data for 1884 on *chadorim* in various districts [G, P], 1877–1908; correspondence with the Ministry of Religion containing complaints about communal taxes [G, P], 1895; correspondence about societies for the support of merchants and tradesmen [G, P], 1897; correspondence about budget and taxes, including a list of tax payers, 1902.
(TsDIAU, L'viv, Namiestnictwo Galicyjskie)

11. Correspondence with various communities on the costs of establishing a Jewish Teachers' Seminary, 1905–06.
(TsDIAU, L'viv, Gmina Żydowska, Lwów)

12. A file on registration of the *Związek Dziewcząt Miryam* society, statutes and a list of board members, 1918–27; correspondence on registering the *Hanigun* society, including statutes, 1930–36; correspondence on registering the *Machzikei Hadas* society and a list of board members, 1932.
(DALO, L'viv, Magistrat, Lwów)

13. Files on community elections, budget, taxes and other matters, including statutes from 1897 [G, P] 1925–1933; correspondence about the *Kultur Liga*, 1926; correspondence with the district authorities on the liquidation of the *Czytelnia Naukowa* association, including statutes from 1911, 1930; statistical data on members of the town council, their political affiliations and nationalities, 1930–31; statistical reports containing names of community board members, rabbis and *dayanim*, 1937; reports and correspondence on community elections, 1938–39.
(DALO, L'viv, UW, Lwów)

14. Monograph containing demographic and economic data, 1936.
(AP Wrocław, Ossolineum, WKNZNP, Lwów)

JARYCZÓW (pow. Lwów, woj. lwowskie) 1685–1937
Originals:
A circumcision register [H], 1790–1835.
Microfilms:
1. A charter granted by King Jan III Sobieski to the town according to the Magdeburg law, charters for the Jews (confirmed in 1813) 1685, 1813.
(NBANU, L'viv, Zb. Czołowskiego)

2. Verdict of the town court regarding a dispute between the *kahal* and a Greek-Catholic priest [L], 1725.
(NBANU, L'viv, Klasztor Bazylianów)

3. Correspondence with the province authorities about residence permits for Jews [G], 1806, 1816–26; correspondence regarding taxes [G], 1820–41, and community elections, 1895.
(TsDIAU, L'viv, Namiestnictwo Galicyjskie)

4. Voting lists [G], 1860, 1867.
(AP Kraków, Teki Schneidra)

5. Reports about teaching Jewish religion in elementary schools [G, P], 1882–89.
(TsDIAU, L'viv, Krajowa Rada Szkolna)

6. Documents on the registration of the *Tarbut* society, 1923–29; correspondence about the registration of *Machzikei Hadas*, 1932; decrees, reports and correspondence about elections of the community board, 1933.
(DALO, L'viv, Magistrat, Lwów)

7. File on community board elections, 1928–29; statistical reports containing names of the members of community board and board, rabbis and *dayanim*, 1937.
(DALO, L'viv, UW, Lwów)

JASIENICA ROSIELNA (pow. Brzozów, woj. lwowskie) 1932–1936
Microfilms:
1. Correspondence on the community budget, including a list of taxpayers, 1932–35.
(DALO, L'viv, UW, Lwów)

2. Correspondence on the registration of *Agudas Yisroel*, 1936.
(DALO, L'viv, Magistrat, Lwów)

JASŁO (woj. krakowskie) 1801–1903
Microfilms:
1. Lists of eligible voters [G, P], 1867, 1870.
(AP Kraków, Teki Schneidra)
2. Correspondence on taxes, community elections, complaints against the elections, elections of rabbis [G], 1819–23; correspondence with the provincial authorities and the tax collector's office about *propinacja*, including lists of names [G, L, P], 1820–28; complaints and requests regarding residence permits [G], 1822–35; correspondence with the authorities about the *arenda* of taverns and displacement of Jews from one place to another [G], 1834–37; tax tables [G], 1842–59; correspondence with the police about Jewish refugees from pogroms in Russia and lists of emigrants to America 1881–82; correspondence with the district authorities about the designation of citizenship in civil registers, 1891–92; correspondence with the Ministry of the Interior about the reorganization of the Jewish community, 1895; correspondence about antisemitic agitation [G, P], 1898–1903.
(TsDIAU, L'viv, Namiestnictwo Galicyjskie)
3. Correspondence on the closing of *chadorim*, including lists of *chadorim* and teachers [G, P], 1868–77.

(TsDIAU, L'viv, Krajowa Rada Szkolna)

JASTRZĘBOWO (pow. Tarnopol, woj. tarnopolskie) 1935
Microfilms:
Statutes and membership list of the *Akiba* society, 1935.
(DATO, Ternopil', Starostwo Powiatowe, Tarnopol)

JASTRZĘBIE ZDRÓJ (pow. Rybnik, woj. śląskie) 1906
Originals:
An appeal by the Jewish children's hospital [G], 1906.

JAŚLISKA (pow. Sanok, woj. lwowskie) 1895–1930
Microfilms:
1. Correspondence with the district authorities about ratification of the community statutes, 1895–96.
(TsDIAU, L'viv, Namiestnictwo Galicyjskie)
2. Authorization by the district authorities to raise funds for the Galician *kollel* in Palestine, including a list of contributors, 1928–30.
(DALO, L'viv, UW, Lwów)

JAZŁOWIEC (pow. Buczacz, woj. tarnopolskie) 1850
Microfilms:
Disputes between the Jewish community and the landowners over *propinacja* [G], 1850
(AP Kraków, Teki Schneidra)

JELENIEWO (pow. Suwałki, woj. białostockie) 1928
Photocopies:
A list of community taxpayers, 1928.
(AP Suwałki, Starostwo Powiatowe Suwalskie)

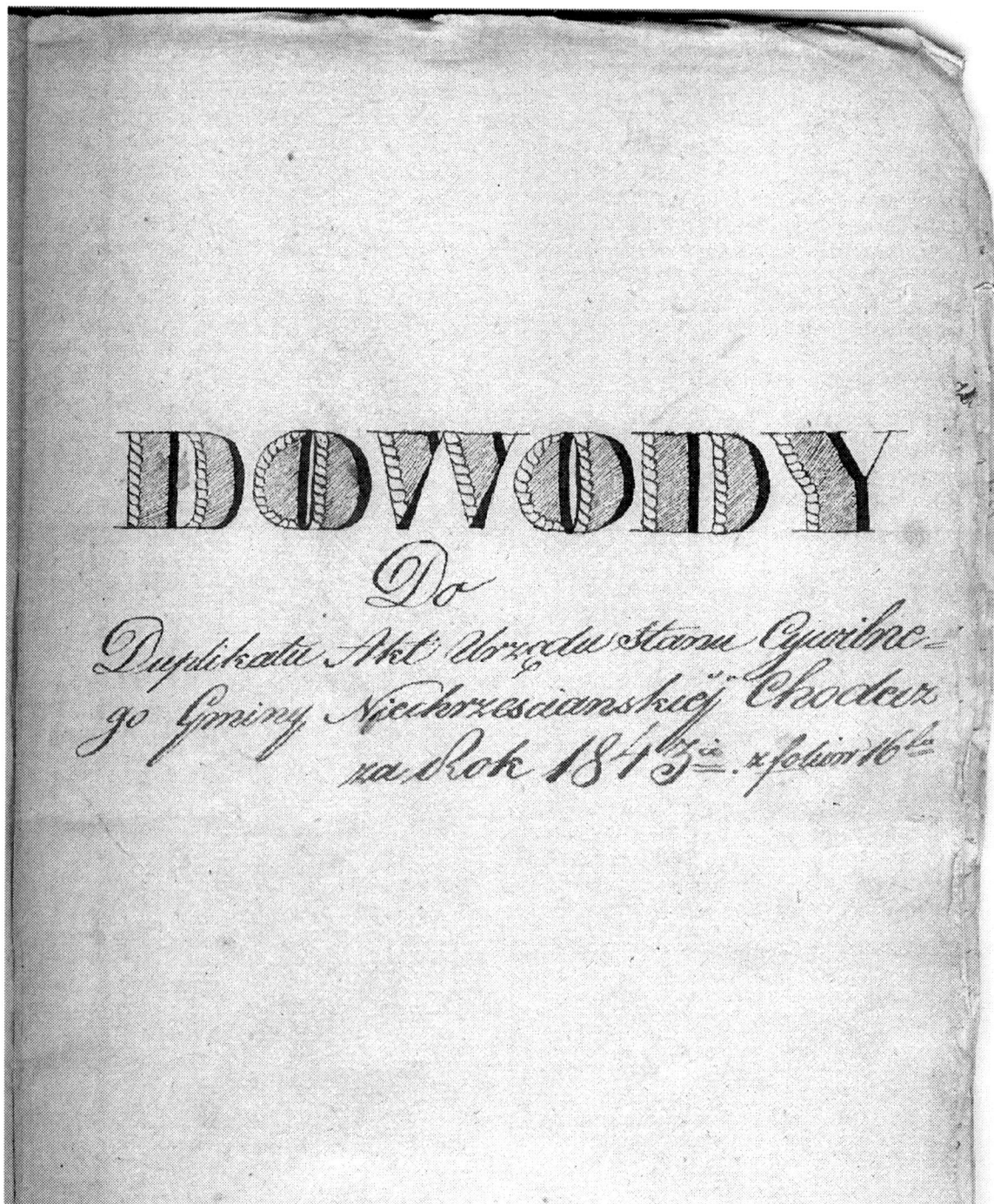

Chodecz. Jewish marriage register, 1843 (Polish)

JEZIERNA (pow. Zborów, woj. tarnopolskie) 1682–1724
Photocopies:
Inventories of Jezierna estates, 1682, 1689, 1703, 1719–24.
(NIAB, Minsk, Arch. Radziwiłłów)

JEZIERZANY (pow. Borszczów, woj. tarnopolskie) 18th–19th cent.
Microfilms:
Inventories of the town and neighbouring villages, 18th–19th cent.
(AP Wrocław, Ossolineum)

JEŻÓW (pow. Brzeziny, woj. łódzkie) 1879–1912
Microfilms:
1. Ratification of community elections and accounts; files on the construction of new synagogues; reports on the sale of seats in the synagogue; the employment of an extra official in the cemetery [R], 1879–1912.
(AP Łódź, Rząd Gubernialny, WA, Piotrków)
2. Fine for evading conscription [R], 1890.
(AP Łódź, Rząd Gubernialny, WP, Piotrków)
3. Investigations of Jews involved in anti-government demonstrations [R], 1906.
(AP Łódź, GZŻ, Piotrków)

JÓZEFÓW (pow. Puławy, woj. lubelskie) 1799–1864
Microfilms:
1. Court files about debts and the sale of a house; documents concerning taxes, 1799–1909.
(AP Lublin, Jurysdykcja dominikalna Józefowa i Opola)
2. Statistical description of the town, 1826–59.
(AP Lublin, Rząd Gubernialny, Lublin)
3. Files on candidates for the rabbinate, 1856–64.
(AGAD, Warszawa, CWW)

JUTROSIN (pow. Rawicz, woj. poznańskie) 1854–1876
Originals:
An inventory of community property [G], 1854–76.

KALISZ (woj. łódzkie) 1617–1930
Originals:
A receipt for a donation to the Orthodox vocational school [H], 1930.
Microfilms:
1. Complaint against a Jew, 1617.
(AGAD, Warszawa, Księgi Grodzkie i Ziemskie Ostrzeszowskie)
2. *Lustracja* of the *starostwo,* 1661.
(AGAD, Warszawa, ASK)
3. Permission given by King Jan Kazimierz to the guilds to exclude nonmembers, including Jews, from trade, 1662.
(AGAD, Warszawa, MK)
4. Loan to the Jews by the Jesuit order; excerpts from municipal records, 1668–90.
(AP Poznań, Kancelaria Gubernatora Kaliskiego)
5. List of Jewish inhabitants and taxes paid by them, 1705–08.

(Bibl. Czartoryskich, Kraków)

6. Confirmation by King Stanisław August Poniatowski of the charter granted to the Jews [L, P], 1765.

(AGAD, Warszawa, Księgi Kanclerskie)

7. Community petition concerning a delay in the payment of debts, 1779–80.

(RGADA, Moscow, KFE)

8. Grants of municipal rights, 1779–86.

(AP Poznań, Akta miast, woj. poznańskie)

9. Records concerning the abolition of the *kahal*; records on communal debts; appointment of rabbis; files on rabbinic education, description of the town and conflicts with *chasidim* [P, R], 1811–60.

(AGAD, Warszawa, Komisja Województwa Kaliskiego)

10. A file on Jewish houses in the town, 1811–60.

(AGAD, Warszawa, KRzSW)

11. Establishment, administration and bequests to a Jewish hospital [P, R], 1822–1914.

(AP Łódź, Rada Opiekuńcza Guberni Kaliskiej)

12. Reports, minutes and complaints concerning the *Chevra Kadisha*, files of the Jewish community, financial reports and decrees, 1822–50; a project to supply food to poor Jews and support Jewish patients in hospitals [P, R], 1848–56; reports and correspondence concerning appointments of rabbis, their education and salaries, conflicts between them and communities, names of rabbis and release from military service of students at the Rabbinical Seminary, 1823–64; files on the setting up of an *eruv*, 1818–71.

(AGAD, Warszawa, CWW)

13. Requests by Jews to convert; expulsions of nonresident Jews; requests to establish Jewish institutions [R], 1871–1912.

(AP Łódź, Kancelaria Gubernatora Kaliskiego)

14. Bequests to Jewish philanthropic institutions; opening of two Jewish schools; financial reports of the community [R], 1894–1914.

(AP Łódź, Rząd Gubernialny, WA, Kalisz)

15. A file on measures by the authorities to halt the pogroms [R], 1906.

(GARF, Moscow, Departament politsii...)

16. Statistical data about rabbis and synagogues of the Kalisz area, 1908; inscriptions from Jewish tombstones and synagogues [H, R], 1910.

(RGIA, St. Petersburg, Departament dukhovnykh del...)

KALISZ, surroundings, 1877–1914
Microfilms:
1. Statistical data on Jewish charitable institutions [R], 1877–84.

(AP Łódź, ROGK)

2. Files concerning the legal status of the Jews, Jewish cultural and charitable societies, donations to a Jewish hospital in Jerusalem, Jewish dress, a boycott of Jewish merchants, an investigation into Jewish emigration and those suspected of holding subversive political opinions [R] 1881–1914.

(AP Łódź, Kancelaria Gubernatora Kaliskiego)

3. A prohibition of Jewish settlement in villages [R], 1891–1913.

(AP Łódź, GUW, Kalisz)

4. Ratification of the elections and accounts of various communities [R], 1895–1914.

(AP Łódź, Rząd Gubernialny, WA, Kalisz)

KALWARIA ZEBRZYDOWSKA (pow. Wadowice, woj. krakowskie) 1633–1898
Originals:
School certificate for Eugenia Schnitzer from the elementary school, 1898.
Microfilms:
Circulars, accounts and decrees by M. Sapieha, St. Siemieński, M. i A. Sieniawski and A. Czartoryski concerning Jews on their properties, 1633–1765.
(Bibl. Czartoryskich, Kraków)

KAŁUSZ (woj. stanisławowskie) 1766–1960
Photocopies:
Reports on the liquidation of the Jewish cemetery [R], 1946, 1957, 1960.
(DAIFO, Ivano-Frankivs'k, Upolnomochennyi Soveta...)
Microfilms:
1. Confirmation by King Stanisław August Poniatowski of the charter granted to the Jews [L, P], 1766.
(AGAD, Warszawa, Księgi Kanclerskie)
2. A *lustracja* of the poll-tax on the estates of Prince A. Czartoryski, 1766.
(AGAD, Warszawa, Arch. Potockich w Łańcucie)
3. A permit to enlarge the synagogue [G], 1803.
(AP Kraków, Teki Schneidra)
4. Promotion of army service among young Jews, 1870; correspondence on the *Linas Hatsedek* [G, P], 1888–1912 and *Ezra* societies, 1907.
(TsDIAU L'viv, Namiestnictwo Galicyjskie)
5. Reports and correspondence about *chadorim* and Jewish private schools, including lists of teachers [P, G], 1875–81.
(TsDIAU, L'viv, Krajowa Rada Szkolna)
6. Statutes, minutes and correspondence concerning *Agudas Yisroel, Gmilas Chesed* and other Jewish associations, 1895, 1920–39; reports and correspondence about the activities of the Revisionists, *Bund, Hashomer Hatzair, Hatzofim, Brit Trumpeldor* and others, as well as a membership list of the local committee of *OŻPP*, 1923–37; minutes of a meeting honoring the inauguration of the Hebrew University in Jerusalem, 1925; documents on the collection of money for the *Yishuv* in *Eretz Yisroel*, 1926; complaints against the community leadership, and the establishment of a supervisory committee 1926–35; material on community elections, 1932–39; salaries, appointments and transfers of rabbis and *dayanim*, 1932–35; materials on the distribution of anti-Jewish pamphlets by *Stronnictwo Narodowe*, 1936; registration of the *Biblioteka Żydowska* society, 1937.
(DAIFO, Ivano-Frankivs'k, UW, Stanisławów)
7. Material on the election of a rabbi [G, P], 1913–19.
(TsDIAU, L'viv, Ministerium fuer Kultus und Unterricht, Wien)

KAŁUSZYN (pow. Mińsk Mazowiecki, woj. warszawskie) 1856–64
Microfilms:
Reports on the appointments of rabbis, their educations and salaries, 1856–64.
(AGAD, Warszawa, CWW)

KAMIEŃ (pow. Nisko, woj. lwowskie) 1724–1930
Microfilms:
1. Letters, *supliki* and reports regarding the Sieniawski estates, 1724–26.

(Bibl. Czartoryskich, Kraków)
2. Litigation between a Jew from Kamień and a Jew from Słonim [H, P, Y], 1783–86.
(Bibl. PAN, Kraków)
3. Authorization by the authorities to collect donations for Jews in Palestine and a list of donors, 1928–30.
(DALO, L'viv, UW, Lwów)

KAMIENICA (pow. Limanowa, woj. lwowskie) 1756–1770
Microfilms:
Suplika by Jews converting to Christianity, 1756–70.
(NBANU, L'viv, Arch. Ossolińskich)

KAMIEŃSK (pow. Piotrków, woj. łódzkie) 1821–1914
Microfilms:
1. Records and accounts of the community, 1821–66.
(AP Łódź, Anterioria Rządu Gubernialnego, Piotrków)
2. Ratification of the community elections and accounts 1896–1914; appointment of a new rabbi; request to open a kerosene store [R], 1900–12.
(AP Łódź, Rząd Gubernialny, WA, Piotrków)

KAMIONKA (pow. Lubartów, woj. lubelskie) 1805–1867
Microfilms:
1. Documents about 8 families of Jewish farmers [G], 1805.
(AP Kraków, Teki Schneidra)
2. Statistical description, 1845–59; material on community elections and conversion to Christianity [R], 1867.
(AP Lublin, Rząd Gubernialny, Lublin)

KAMIONKA MAŁA (pow. Kołomyja, woj. stanisławowskie) 1933
Microfilms:
Correspondence concerning the local branch of the Jewish Agricultural Society, 1933.
(DAIFO, Ivano-Frankivs'k, UW, Stanisławów)

KAMIONKA STRUMIŁOWA (woj. tarnopolskie) 1723–1919
Microfilms:
1. Various *supliki* from the *kahal* concerning *arenda* and other issues; *arenda* contract, court records [P,L,H], 1723–84.
(TsDIAU, L'viv, Arch. Lanckorońskich)
2. Reports and a list of *chadorim* in the district, 1877–1908; minutes and correspondence concerning confirmation of the community statutes [G, P], 1898.
(TsDIAU, L'viv, Namiestnictwo Galicyjskie)
3. Election of rabbis, 1913–19.
(TsDIAU, L'viv, Ministerium fuer Kultus und Unterricht, Wien)

KAMYK (pow. Częstochowa, woj. kieleckie) 1904–1906
Microfilms:
A file on the establishment of a community [R], 1904–06.
(AP Łódź, Rząd Gubernialny, WA, Piotrków)

KAŃCZUGA (pow. Przeworsk, woj. lwowskie) 1921–1937
Microfilms:
Correspondence on community elections, 1921–37; reports on erection of an *eruv*, 1929–31.
(DALO, L'viv, UW, Lwów)

KARLIN (pow. Pińsk, woj. poleskie) 1777–2001
Originals:
A letter to an official of *Kollel Pinsk* in Jerusalem concerning the donation of money for the Jews of Palestine [H], 1873; regulations of a *Talmud* study society [H], 1905.
Correspondence, maps, minutes, video recordings [H, Y], 1919, 1928–2001.
(Archives of the Landsmannshaft of Pińsk, Karlin, Janów and surroundings)
Photocopies:
Various criminal matters, 1777–85; records of legal proceedings in financial affairs between Jews and noblemen, 1782–84, 1792–94.
(NIAB, Minsk, Pinskaia Magdeburgiia)

KATOWICE (woj. śląskie) 1865–1938
Originals:
Minutes of community board meetings [G], 1865–1900; correspondence [G], 1867–1914;
a file on confirmation for girls [G], 1868; the correspondence of the *Kultuskommission* [ritual commission] [G], 1869–72; files on cantors and *shochatim,* among them, Cantor M. Backstein [G], 1870–95; material relating to education [G], 1874–1921; court verdicts [G], 1875–76; circulars on community meetings [G], 1879–90; community statutes [G], 1881, 1900; communal and state tax matters, including proceedings of an appraisal committee [G], 1881–89; statutes and reports of the Jewish Welfare Society [G], 1889–1910; statutes and reports of the burial society [G], 1889–1911; a file on the orphanage [G], 1893–94; the papers of Rabbi Jacob Cohn (relating to the Upper Silesian Rabbinic Association and the Russian Aid Society) [G], 1896–1903; community records on the construction of a synagogue [G], 1896–1911; correspondence registers [G], 1898–1914; the statutes of the society for the promotion of Jewish learning [G], 1912; community periodical,: *Wiadomości Gminne: Organ Gminy Żydowskiej w Katowicach*, No 152, August 1938.
Microfilms:
Minutes of community board meetings [G], 1876–1910.
(Centrum Judaicum, Berlin)

KAZIMIERZ DOLNY (pow. Puławy, woj. lubelskie) 1608–1864
Originals:
A decree by King Zygmunt III concerning the investigation of a Jew [L, P], 1608; cancellation of a bill of exchange [H], 1726; royal confirmations of charters to the Jews [L, P], 1739, 1765; a contract [H], 1778; deed of sale of a house and the payment of a widow's *ketuba* [H], 1802.
Microfilms:
1. Confirmation by King Stanisław August Poniatowski of the charter granted to the Jews [L, P], 1765.
(AGAD, Warszawa, Księgi Kanclerskie)
2. Litigation concerning debts [H, P], 1737.
(AP Kraków, Arch. Sanguszków, teki tzw. arabskie)
3. Files on donations to the Jewish community, 1853–64; statistical data on the community, 1860–61.
(AP Lublin, Rząd Gubernialny, Lublin)

KĄPIEL (pow. Konin, woj. łódzkie) 1831
Microfilms:
A file on the investigation of a group of criminals, among them two Jews, 1831.
(AGAD, Warszawa, WCPL)

KĘPNO (woj. poznańskie) 1780–1885
Originals:
An announcement on the adoption of family names [G], 1834; regulations dealing with commerce [G], 1885.
Microfilms:
Charters granted to the Jews by the owner of the town; a verdict by King Stanisław August Poniatowski in a dispute between the owner of the town and its inhabitants, 1780–82.
(AP Poznań, Akta miast,woj. poznańskie)

KIELCE (woj. kieleckie) 1818–1911
Microfilms:
1. Records concerning synagogues, 1818–60; correspondence on exemption from military service for Rabbinical Seminary graduates, including a list of rabbis, 1865–71.
(AGAD, Warszawa, CWW)
2. Police correspondence concerning a member of a socialist party [R], 1911.
(WAP Łódź, GZŻ, Piotrków)

KIELCE, surroundings, 1830–1949
Microfilms:
1. Files concerning an educational fund, 1830–36.
(AGAD, Warszawa, KRzPiS)
2. Documents on conversions of Jews to Christianity, 1846–66.
(AP Radom, Rząd Gubernialny, Radom)
3. Statistical data about synagogues and rabbis in the Kielce *guberniia* [R], 1908.
(RGIA, St. Petersburg, Departament dukhovnykh del...)
4. Denunciations of pro-German sentiments among the Jews and correspondence about the release of Jews from arrest and from other repressive measures [R], 1914–15.
(RGVIA, Moscow, Shtab ...)
5. Minutes of the *Okręgowy Komitet Żydowski*, Radom, including information about Jews living in various towns of the Kielce province, 1945–49.
(AP Radom, OKŻ, Radom)

KISIELIN (pow. Horochów, woj. wołyńskie) 1863–1864
Microfilms:
Documents about the foundation of a Jewish hospital and other charitable activities [R], 1863–64.
(RGIA, St. Petersburg, Khoziaistvennyi departament MVD)

KLAPKA (pow. Wieluń, woj. łódzkie) 1816
Microfilms:
A list of taxpayers, 1816.
(TsDIAU, L'viv, Arch. Lanckorońskich)

KLESZCZELE (pow. Bielsk, woj. białostockie) 1558–1561
Microfilms:
Royal decrees concerning *arendas* in Kleszczele for Jews of Brześć, 1558–61.
(RGADA, Moscow, ML)

KLESZCZÓW (pow. Piotrków, woj. łódzkie) 1900
Microfilms:
A fine for evading conscription [R], 1900.
(AP Łódź, Rząd Gubernialny, WP, Piotrków)

KLEWAŃ (pow. Równe, woj. wołyńskie), surroundings, 1680–1803
Microfilms:
1. Inventories, accounts and lists of inhabitants, 1680–1803; contracts concerning *arendas*, 1719–54; Inventories of estates in the area, 1785–92.
(Bibl. Czartoryskich, Kraków)
2. Registers, accounts, proclamations, resolutions and contracts of the Sieniawski and Czartoryski families concerning their properties in Klewań [L, P], 1706–85.
(Biblioteka Narodowa, Warszawa)
3. A *lustracja* of poll-tax paid by Jews on the properties of August Aleksander Czartoryski in Klewań, 1766.
(AGAD, Warszawa, Arch. Potockich w Łańcucie)

KLUKOWO (pow. Wysokie Mazowieckie, woj. białostockie) 1933–34
Originals:
Marriage registers, 1933; birth, marriage and death registers, 1934

KŁOBUCKO (pow. Częstochowa, woj. kieleckie) 1835–1912
Microfilms:
1. Files on the community and its accounts, 1835–99.
(AP Łódź, Anterioria Rządu Gubernialnego, Piotrków)
2. A file on "cruel acts" committed by Jews, and on the escape of two Jewish prisoners [R], 1897–99.
(AP Łódź, Kancelaria Gubernatora Piotrkowskiego)
3. Ratification of community elections and accounts; the appointment of a *dayan* [R], 1899–1912.
(AP Łódź, Rząd Gubernialny, WA, Piotrków)

KLIMONTÓW (pow. Sandomierz, woj. kieleckie) 1853–1856
Microfilms:
Reports and other materials concerning the *Chevra Kadisha*, 1822–50; reports and correspondence on the appointment of rabbis, and litigation between them and their communities, including names of rabbis, 1853–56.
(AGAD, Warszawa, CWW)

KLWÓW (pow. Opoczno, woj. kieleckie) 1865–1866
Microfilms:
A list of Jewish families, 1865–66.
(AP Radom, Rząd Gubernialny, Radom)

KNIAŻE (pow. Śniatyn, woj. stanisławowskie) 1930–1937
Microfilms:
A list of Jewish youth movements, 1930–37.
(DAIFO, Ivano-Frankivs'k, UW, Stanisławów)

KNIHININ (pow. Stanisławów, woj. stanisławowskie) 1779–1911
Microfilms:
1. Complaint of Jewish *arendars* against the owner of the *klucz*, 1779–80.
(RGADA, Moscow, KFE)
2. Minutes and correspondence with the *Beis Yisroel* society in the Knihinin colony on the construction of a prayer house, including plans, 1905–06; statutes of the *Ahavas Chesed* society in the colony [P,Y], 1911.
(DAIFO, Ivano-Frankivs'k, UW, Stanisławów)

KNIHYNICZE (pow. Rohatyn, woj. stanisławowskie) 1922–1938
Microfilms:
Statutes and membership lists of the *Merkaz Ruchani (Mizrachi)* and *Gmilus Chasodim* societies, 1922–38; reports and correspondence on rabbis, *dayanim* and community elections, 1932–36; reports on meetings of Jewish political parties and associations, 1934.
(DAIFO, Ivano-Frankivs'k, UW, Stanisławów)

KNUBOWO (pow. Pińsk, woj. poleskie) 1804–1805
Microfilms:
Report of the governor of Minsk on a complaint by peasants against a Jewish *arendar*, 1804–05.
(TsDIAU, Kyiv, Kievskii voennyi gubernator)

KNYSZYN (pow. Białystok, woj. białostockie) 1606–1847
Photocopies:
A file on an attack by Jews against a priest and on desecration of Christian artifacts [R], 1847.
(GARF, Moscow, Tret'e otdelenie…)
Microfilms:
Confirmation of a charter given to the city by King Zygmunt III, regarding the leasing of a malt-house and brewery taxes to Christians and Jews, 1606.
(AGAD, Warszawa, Księgi Kanclerskie)

KOBRYŃ (woj. poleskie) 1566–1905
Microfilms:
1. Royal charters to the Jews concerning the timber industry [Rt], 1566–68.
(RGADA, Moscow, ML)
2. Correspondence of the Association for the Attainment of Full Rights for the Jewish People in Russia with the local branch [R], 1905.
(RGIA, St. Petersburg, Obshchestvo polnopraviia…)

KOBYLIN (pow. Krotoszyn, woj. poznańskie) 1778–1903
Originals:
Charter for the Jewish community [G, P], 1778–89; statutes of the Jewish Society for Care of the Sick and of the burial society [G], 1903.

KOCIUBIŃCE (pow. Kopyczyńce, woj. tarnopolskie) 1686–1805
Microfilms:
Charters, requests and contracts concerning *arendas* [G, H, L, P, Y], 1686–1805.
(AP Lublin, Zb. Czołowskiego)

KOCK (pow. Łuków, woj. lubelskie) 1749–1859
Microfilms:
1. Material concerning damages to Jewish property by Russian troops, 1749.
(NBANU, L'viv, Arch. Sapiehów)
2. A complaint by a Jew against officials of the Radom *guberniia* [R], 1858–59.
(AGAD, Warszawa, SSKP)

KODEŃ (pow. Biała, woj. lubelskie) 1722–1913
Photocopies:
Inventories of estates, 1722.
(NIAB, Minsk, Arch. Radziwiłłów)
Microfilms:
1. Material concerning the synagogue, 1818–60.
(AGAD, Warszawa, CWW)
2. Documents and photographs of candidates for rabbinical positions [R], 1886–1913.
(WAP Białystok, Rząd Gubernialny, Łomża)

KOLBUSZOWA (woj. lwowskie) 1671–1938
Microfilms:
1. A case of a Jewess accused of blaspheming against the Virgin Mary, 1671.
(AP Kraków, Teki Sanguszków)
2. Accounts of the community, 1715; a suit against a rabbi, 1744.
(AP Kraków, Arch. Sanguszków)
3. Correspondence with the authorities regarding *chadorim,* including a list of *melamdim,* 1877–1908; reports and correspondence concerning an administrative division of the Jewish communities in the district [G, P], 1884–85; correspondence about reorganization of the community, a list of taxpayers and their professions, 1890; correspondence on approval of the community statutes, 1895–96.
(TsDIAU, L'viv, Namiestnictwo Galicyjskie)
4. Reports and correspondence concerning *chadorim* and private Jewish schools [G, P], 1878–81.
(TsDIAU, L'viv, Krajowa Rada Szkolna)
5. Material on community taxes, 1922–27; correspondence on local celebrations honoring the inauguration of the Hebrew University in Jerusalem, 1924–25; minutes and reports about community elections, 1929–30; lists of political party members who were members of the local authorities, 1930; correspondence, budgets and lists of community taxpayers [P, Y], 1931–32, 1933–35; decrees, reports and correspondence concerning the community board, 1933; registration of the *Gmilas Chesed* society, 1935; correspondence about legal community matters, 1935–37; reports of the community board, authorities, rabbis and *dayanim,* including lists, 1937; correspondence on supervision of the employees of the *Yad Charutzim* society, 1938.
(DALO, L'viv, UW, Lwów)
6. Correspondence on the registration of *Agudas Yisroel,* including statutes, 1929–34.
(DALO, L'viv, Magistrat, Lwów)

KOLBUSZOWA, surroundings, 1832
Microfilms:
An inventory of the district, 1832.
(AP Wrocław, Ossolineum)

KOLNO (pow. Łomża, woj. białostockie) 1822–1923
Microfilms:
1. Reports, minutes and complaints concerning the *Chevra Kadisha*, 1822–50.
(AGAD, Warszawa, CWW)
2. Permit for a Jewish doctor to open an obstetric practice [R], 1906; documents concerning the *arenda* of municipal incomes for the years 1912–14 [R], 1911; a contract for street illumination for the years 1913–16 [R], 1912–23; permission for a Jewish inhabitant to emigrate to Germany [R], 1912–14; order of expulsion to Grodno of an inhabitant, [R], 1913; documents about the arrest and expulsion from the *guberniia* of Jewish inhabitants suspected of clandestine emigration activity and espionage for the Germans [R], 1913–15; documents about the arrest of three Jews suspected of horse theft [R], 1914–15.a
(WAP Białystok, Rząd Gubernialny, Łomża)

KOŁACZYCE (pow. Jasło, woj. krakowskie) 1895–1896
Microfilms:
Correspondence with the governor about the community and confirmation of its statutes, 1895–96.
(TsDIAU, L'viv, Namiestnictwo Galicyjskie)

KOŁBIEL (pow. Mińsk Mazowiecki, woj. warszawskie) 1910
Microfilms:
Inscriptions from tombstones and synagogues [H, R], 1910.
(RGIA, St. Petersburg, Departament dukhovnykh del…)

KOŁKI (pow. Łuck, woj. wołyńskie) 1746
Originals:
Community regulations on financial matters, 1746.

KOŁO (woj. łódzkie) 1818–1909
Originals:
Marriage registers from Koło, Przedecz and Piotrków, 1854.
Microfilms:
1. Records concerning the delineation of the Jewish quarter, 1818–62.
(AGAD, Warszawa, Komisja Województwa Kaliskiego)
2. A request for the lease of *propinacja* in the town, 1864.
(AGAD, Warszawa, RSKP)
3. A file on the closing of the cemetery; the appointment of a new rabbi; various bequests to the community; the opening of two Jewish elementary schools; the donation of a plot of land to a Jewish school; a complaint concerning the rabbi's refusal to perform a marriage ceremony [R], 1893–1909.
(AP Łódź, Rząd Gubernialny, WA, Kalisz)
4. A request to found a charitable society; the expulsion of various individuals [R], 1904–09.
(AP Łódź, Kancelaria Gubernatora Kaliskiego)

KOŁO, surroundings, 1902–1914
Microfilms:
The ratification of the elections and accounts of various communities [R], 1902–14.
(AP Łódź, Rząd Gubernialny, WA, Kalisz)

KOŁOMYJA (woj. stanisławowskie) 1704–1960
Originals:
Posters and announcements concerning Jewish cultural and economic life [H, P, Y], 1931–32.
Photocopies:
Letters and reports about synagogues and prayer houses [R], 1946, 1957, 1960.
(DAIFO, Ivano-Frankivs'k, Upolnomochennyi Soveta…)

Microfilms:
1. Excerpts of minutes from penal cases concerning attacks on Jews, 1704–21; accusations against Jews for horse theft and burglary of churches, 1738–50.
(NBANU, L'viv, Arch. Ossolińskich)
2. Confirmation by King Stanisław August Poniatowski of the charter granted to the Jews [L, P], 1772.
(AGAD, Warszawa, MK)
3. Correspondence of the Jewish community with the authorities concerning the settlement of Jews in Kołomyja [G], 1819–37; tax tables of the Jewish communitiy [G], 1819; voting rights for the Jews [G], 1829–43; the Savings and Loan Society [G, P], 1891–92; confirmation of the community statutes and of various societies, e.g.: *Bursa Izraelicka, Agudas Achim, Ahavas Chesed, Chajtim, Naprzód ("Vorwarts"), Zeire Zion* [G, P], 1895–1912; correspondence with the *Ahavas Zion* society [P, G], 1898.
(TsDIAU, L'viv, Namiestnictwo Galicyjskie)
4. Reports on teaching Jewish religion in elementary schools [G, P], 1882–89; statutes of an elementary school of the *Israelitische Allianz* in Vienna [G, P], 1889; reports from inspections of Baron Hirsch Foundation (JCA) schools [G, P], 1896–1904.
(TsDIAU, L'viv, Krajowa Rada Szkolna)
5. Correspondence concerning pogroms [G], 1892.
(TsDIAU L'viv, Nadprokuratoria Państwowa)
6. Correspondence with community elders concerning their complaints about tax increases, 1907.
(TsDIAU, L'viv, Gmina Żydowska, Lwów)
7. File on elections of rabbis [G, P], 1913–19.
(TsDIAU L'viv, Ministerium fuer Kultus und Unterricht, Wien)
8. Files on various political, professional, cultural, charitable and sport organizations, among them: *Dror, Maskil el Dal, Beis Yisroel, Brith Trumpeldor, Tarbut, Gordonia, Safa Brura,* including statutes and lists of members, 1920–39.
(DAIFO, Ivano-Frankivs'k, Starostwo Powiatowe, Kołomyja)
9. Files on social and political organizations, including confirmations of their statutes as well as lists of leaders and members, among them, *Keren Kayemet, Linas Hatzedek, Bikur Cholim, Achdut, Mizrachi, Agudas Yisroel, Akiva, Tsofe* and others [P, Y], 1921–39; files on activities of the *Bund* 1923–34; reports of the district police concerning activities of Jewish political parties, eg. Revisionists, *Bundists* 1925–26; descriptions and statistical data on the Kołomyja district 1934–36; files about closing the *Biblioteka Żydowska* society (1932–36), sale of the journal, *Zibn Tag* [Seven Days] [P, Y], 1936.
(DAIFO, Ivano-Frankivs'k, UW, Stanisławów)
10. Budgets of the Jewish community, 1932, 1938; lists of taxpayers, 1932, 1939.

(DAIFO, Ivano-Frankivs'k, Gmina Żydowska, Kołomyja)

KOMARNO (pow. Rudki, woj. lwowskie) 1695–1938
Photocopies:
File on community board elections, 1924.
(DALO, L'viv, UW, Lwów)
Microfilms:
1. A letter to the authorities concerning fish commerce, 1695.
(TsDIAU, L'viv, Kolektsiia lystiv…)
2. A decree concerning payment of taxes for the army, 1753–67.
(TsDIAU, L'viv, Arch. Lanckorońskich)
3. Correspondence with the authorities concerning confirmation of the community statutes, 1895–96; file on the election of a rabbi [G, P], 1896.
(TsDIAU, L'viv, Namiestnictwo Galicyjskie)
4. Correspondence about community elections, 1924–33; files on the registration of *Machzikei Hadas*, 1933 and *Agudas Yisroel*, 1935; minutes and reports on approval of the community budget, including a list of taxpayers, 1933–38.
(DALO, L'viv, UW, Lwów)

KOMARÓW (pow. Tomaszów, woj. lubelskie) 1856–1864
Microfilms:
1. Reports and correspondence concerning appointments of rabbis, 1856–64.
(AGAD, Warszawa, CWW)
2. A file on a Jew sent into exile [R], 1843–44; statistical description of the town, 1860.
(AP Lublin, Rząd Gubernialny, Lublin)

KONARZEWO (pow. Poznań, woj. poznańskie) surroundings, 1801–1870
Microfilms:
Records of a suit concerning a Jew's debt to a nobleman; files on taverns and the manufacture of spirits, 1801–70.
(AP Poznań, Majątek Konarzewo)

KONIECPOL (pow. Radomsko, woj. łódzkie) 1822–1913
Microfilms:
1. Records concerning the community and its accounts, 1822–66.
(AP Łódz, Anterioria Rządu Gubernialnego, Piotrków)
2. Ratification of community accounts and elections; reports on the rebuilding of the synagogue, *mikve* and prayer-house [R], 1898–1913.
(AP Łódz, Rząd Gubernialny, WA, Piotrków)
3. Fines for evading conscription [R], 1891–1901.
(AP Łódz, Rząd Gubernialny, WP, Piotrków)

KONIN (woj. łódzkie) 1815–1913
Microfilms:
1. Jewish purchase of land for building purposes, 1815–39.
(AGAD, Warszawa, Komisja Województwa Kaliskiego)
2. Correspondence on the exemption of Rabbinical Seminary graduates from military service, 1865–71.

(AGAD, Warszawa, CWW)

3. The appointment of a new rabbi; donations to the community [R], 1893–1913.

(AP Łódz, Rząd Gubernialny, WA, Kalisz)

4. A request to open a shelter for Jewish children; records of philanthropic and literary societies; an investigation of the illegal activities of an emigration agent; files on the exiling of three Jews [R], 1895–1912.

(AP Łódź, Kancelaria Gubernatora Kaliskiego)

KONIN, surroundings, 1905–1914

Microfilms:

Financial reports of communities in the district; a license for a Jew to qualify as a rabbi [R], 1905–14.

(AP Łódz, Kancelaria Gubernatora Kaliskiego)

KONIUSZKI (pow. Przemyśl, woj. lwowskie) 1878

Microfilms:

Correspondence on reorganization of elementary schools attended by Jewish pupils [G, P], 1878.

(TsDIAU, L'viv, Krajowa Rada Szkolna)

KOŃSKIE (woj. kieleckie) 18th cent.

Originals:

Drawing of a wooden synagogue, n.d.

(IKG Wien - Juedisches Museum)

Microfilms:

1. A license for the community to build a new prayerhouse, 1780.

(AP Kraków, Arch. Dzikowskie Tarnowskich)

2. Records of Jewish debts to the city, 18th cent.

(AGAD, Warszawa, Arch. Radziwiłłów)

KOŃSKOWOLA (pow. Puławy, woj. lubelskie) 1705–1864

Microfilms:

1. *Supliki* of Jews to Princess Elżbieta Sieniawska, 1705–36; inventories and accounts, 1770–98.

(Bibl. Czartoryskich, Kraków)

2. A *lustracja* of properties of Prince A. Czartoryski, 1766.

(AGAD, Warszawa, Arch. Potockich w Łańcucie)

3. Files on Jewish debts, 1806–09.

(AP Lublin, Jurysdykcja dominikalna Końskowoli i Puław)

4. Litigation among Jewish merchants, 1808.

(AP Lublin, Jurysdykcja dominikalna Kurowa)

5. A statistical description of the town 1828–60.

(AP Lublin, Rząd Gubernialny, Lublin)

6. Reports and correspondence on the appointment of rabbis, 1856–64.

(AGAD, Warszawa, CWW)

KONSTANTYNÓW (pow. Łódź, woj. łódzkie) 1818–1914

Microfilms:

1. Files on synagogues, 1818–60.

(AGAD, Warszawa, CWW)

2. Reports on the community budget, 1825–66.
(AP Łódź, Anterioria Rządu Gubernialnego, Piotrków)
3. Ratification of community accounts and elections; the appointment of a new rabbi [P, R], 1889–1914.
(AP Łódź, Rząd Gubernialny, WA, Piotrków)
4. A fine for evading conscription, 1895–96.
(AP Łódź, Rząd Gubernialny, WP, Piotrków)

KOPRZYWNICA (pow. Sandomierz, woj. kieleckie) 1914–1916
Microfilms:
A description by Rabbi N. L. Tversky of the situation of the Jews during the Russian occupation [R], 1914–16.
(GARF, Moscow, Bomash)

KOPYCZYŃCE (woj. tarnopolskie) 1895–1934
Microfilms:
1. Reports and correspondence concerning confirmation of the community statutes, 1895–1908; correspondence between the community and the authorities about the *krupka*, 1900–07.
(TsDIAU, L'viv, Namiestnictwo Galicyjskie)
2. Statistical and financial reports on the activity of the local branch of the Kiev Committee, lists of Jews adversely affected by World War I, and of those who received assistance [R], 1916–17.
(DATO, Ternopil', Komitet pomoshchi…)
3. Reports about demonstrations against British policy in Palestine, 1934.
(DAIFO, Ivano-Frankivs'k, UW, Stanisławów)

KOPYŁÓW (pow. Hrubieszów, woj. lubelskie), surroundings, 1804–1833
Microfilms:
Documents concerning Jews in the timber trade, 1804–33.
(AP Kraków, Arch. Młynowskie Chodkiewiczów)

KORCZAKI (pow. Ostrołęka, woj. białostockie) 1913–1914
Microfilms:
A file on issuing a passport to a Jew and the registration of his family as inhabitants of the community [R], 1913–14.
(AP Białystok, Rząd Gubernialny, Łomża)

KORCZEW (pow. Sokołów, woj. lubelskie) 1740.
Microfilms:
A *suplika* of inhabitants against Jews, 1740.
(AGAD, Warszawa, Arch. Radziwiłłów)

KORCZYN (woj. białostockie) 1819.
Microfilms:
Files concerning a dispute between the community and the municipality over *propinacja* rights, 1819.
(AGAD, Warszawa, RSKP)

KORCZYN (pow. Sokal, woj. lwowskie) 1877–1908
Microfilms:

Correspondence with the district authorities on communal matters, statutes and *chadorim*, including a list of *melamdim*, 1877–1908.
(TsDIAU, L'viv, Namiestnictwo Galicyjskie)

KORCZYNA (pow. Krosno, woj. lwowskie) 1833–1839
Microfilms:
Files on community accounts and a list of taxpayers, 1933–35; complaints concerning community elections, 1938–39.
(DALO, L'viv, UW, Lwów)

KORELICZE (pow. Nowogródek, woj. nowogródzkie) surroundings, 1722–1821
Microfilms:
1. Suits filed by Jews on matters concerning *propinacja* on the estates around the town, 1722–1807.
(AGAD, Warszawa, Arch. Radziwiłłów)
2. A *uniwersał* by Princess Anna z Sanguszków ks. Radziwiłłowa to Christians and Jews coming from German states, 1722; complaints of Jewish inhabitants, addressed to the *arendar* of the city, 1821.
(AGAD, Warszawa, Arch. Radziwiłłów)

KOROLÓWKA (pow. Tłumacz, woj. stanisławowskie) 1797–1908
Microfilms:
1. Reports and testimonies in the case of a Jew accused of theft, 1797–1800.
(TsDIAU, L'viv, Arch. Lanckorońskich)
2. Correspondence with the district authorities regarding *chadorim*, including a list of *melamdim*, 1874–1908, and regarding a candidate for the rabbinate [G, P], 1899–1905.
(TsDIAU, L'viv, Namiestnictwo Galicyjskie)
3. Reports and lists of *chadorim* and *melamdim* [G, P], 1875–77; minutes and reports concerning schools of the Baron Hirsch Foundation (JCA), including personal files of teachers [G, P], 1896–1904.
(TsDIAU, L'viv, Krajowa Rada Szkolna)

KORZEC (pow. Równe, woj. wołyńskie) 1615–1939
Originals:
A photo of Jewish teachers and pupils, before 1917.
(Central State Archives of Film-, Photo-, Phonografic Documents of the Ukraine, Kiev)
Microfilms:
1. Plenipotentiary for the Korzecki family concerning affairs of Jews, 1615.
(AP Kraków, Arch. Sanguszków, teki rzymskie)
2. Material concerning tannery industries owned by Jews [R], 1801–02.
(RGADA, Moscow, Manufaktur kollegiia)
3. Files on the expulsion of Jewish innkeepers for collaboration with the enemy, including a list of inns [R], 1841.
(TsDIAU, Kyiv, Kantseliariia... general-gubernatora)
4. Reports on Jewish schools [R], 1852–58.
(DAKHO, Kamianets'-Podil's'kyi, Direktsiia narodnykh uchilishch...)
5. Correspondence with the *Talmud Tora* [R], 1893–99.
(RGIA, St. Petersburg, Obshchestvo polnopraviia...)
6. Inscriptions from synagogues and tombstones [H, R], 1910.
(RGIA, St. Petersburg, Departament dukhovnykh del...)

7. Reports and correspondence about registration of the local branch of the *Centralny Związek Rzemieślników Żydów w Polsce* society, including a list of society leaders, 1924–36; statutes, reports and correspondence on registration and activities of the local branch of the *Towarzystwo Ochrony Zdrowia Ludności Żydowskiej* (TOZ) society, 1924–38, correspondence concerning foundation of a local branch of the *Tarbut* society 1933–39.
(DARO, Rivne, Ekspozytura Starostwa Powiatowego, Równe)
8. A list of community taxpayers, 1932
(DARO, Rivne, Gmina Żydowska, Korzec)

KORYCIN (pow. Sokółka , woj. białostockie), 1786–1789
Photocopies:
Inventories of estates, 1786, 1789;
(NIAB, Minsk, Kollektsiia drevnikh inventarei)

KOSÓW (pow. Iłża, woj. kieleckie) 1853–1864
Microfilms:
Reports and correspondence concerning confirmation of rabbis, litigation between them and community boards, names of rabbis, 1853–56; reports and correspondence concerning rabbis, their education and salaries, a list of Warsaw Rabbinical Seminary graduates, and a member list of the commission in charge of examining rabbinical candidates, 1856–64.
(AGAD, Warszawa, CWW)

KOSÓW (woj. stanisławowskie), 1704–1938
Originals
Drawing of a wooden synagogue, n.d.
(IKG Wien - Juedisches Museum)
Photocopies:
File on the registration of the National Zionist Organization in Kosów, including statutes, 1927–28.
(DALO, L'viv, Starostwo Miejskie, Lwów)
Microfilms:
1. Excerpts from minutes of criminal proceedings in Stanisławów over theft in the synagogue, 1704.
(NBANU, L'viv, Arch. Ossolińskich)
2. Correspondence with the authorities on Jewish schools and *chadorim*, including a list of *melamdim* in the area, 1877–1908; documents concerning the *Tomchey Aniey Eretz Yisroel* association for the support of needy Jewish emigrants from Galicia and Bukovina to Palestine [G, P], 1883–1913; correspondence with the district authorities regarding community statutes, *shochatim* and complaints regarding communal burial taxes, 1889–1908; correspondence with the *Ahavas Zion* society [G], 1898.
(TsDIAU, L'viv, Namiestnictwo Galicyjskie)
3. Files on Jewish associations, 1921–37; correspondence with provincial authorities on activities of the *Bund*, 1923; celebrations of the inauguration of the Hebrew University in Jerusalem, 1925; material on community elections, administration, a draft budget, taxes on *shechita* of poultry and financial inspection of the community, including complaints against community leadership, 1926–36; reports on donations for Jews in Palestine, 1926; reports about the activity of the Revisionist Zionists, *Hashomer Hatzair, Histadrut Hanoar Haivri, Tzofe* and other Jewish youth movements, 1927–33; decrees, reports and correspondence about Zionist parties and associations, among them *Hitachdut Poalei Zion* [P, Y], 1932–35; reports on activity of the *Ogólno-Żydowska Partia Pracy* (OŻPP), 1933; correspondence regarding the local

leadership of the Jewish Agricultural Association, 1933; statistical data on the district, 1935; information of the district authorities about distribution of the periodical, *Zibn Tag* [Seven Days] [P, Y], 1936; distribution of anti-Jewish pamphlets by the *Stronnictwo Narodowe*, 1936; material on the inauguration of high school courses by the *Żydowskie Stowarzyszenie Szkoły Ludowej w Kosowie*, 1938.
(DAIFO, Ivano-Frankivs'k, UW, Stanisławów)

KOSMACZ (pow. Kołomyja, woj. stanisławowskie) 1921–1939
Microfilms:
1. Minutes and correspondence on the organization and statutes of Jewish associations, 1921–39.
(DAIFO, Ivano-Frankivs'k, UW, Stanisławów)
2. Files on the *Gmilas Chesed* and *Hatchiya* associations, 1929–35.
(DAIFO, Ivano-Frankivs'k, Starostwo Powiatowe, Kołomyja)

KOSTRZYN (pow. Środa, woj. poznańskie) 1896
Originals:
An appeal for donations to establish a new cemetery [G], 1896.

KOŚCIAN (woj. poznańskie) 1797–1876
Originals:
Regulations concerning the payment of Jewish state taxes, circular letters and files of individual taxpayers [G], 1797–1876; synagogue statutes and violation of them [G], 1838–65; a government ban on early burials [G], 1840; a file on kosher meat [G], 1840–65; instructions on civil registration [G], 1840–44; regulations concerning Jewish communities [G], 1842–76; the administration of the "Jews' oath" [G], 1851; an inventory of files [G], 1854.

KOWAL (pow. Włocławek, woj. warszawskie) 1765–1873.
Originals:
Marriage registers (fragmentary) [P, R], 1843–73.
Microfilms:
Confirmation by King Stanisław August Poniatowski of the charter granted to the Jews [L, P], 1765.
(AGAD, Warszawa, Księgi Kanclerskie)

KOWEL (woj. wołyńskie) 1614–1907
Microfilms:
1. Confirmation of rights and charters granted to the Jews of Kowel, 1614.
(NBANU, L'viv, Arch. Ossolińskich)
2. Files on the debts of Prince Hieronim Sanguszko to a Jew, 1684–88.
(AP Kraków, Archiwum Sanguszków, tzw. teki arabskie)
3. Confirmation of rights and charters to the Jews of Kowel by King Stanisław August Poniatowski [L, P], 1765.
(AGAD, Warszawa, Księgi Kanclerskie)
4. Reports on communities, synagogues, Jewish schools, officials and inhabitants, 1834, 1850; lists of charters by Polish kings and of permits given to Jewish inhabitants of towns by the Russian government; permits concerning *propinacja*, 1849–52; complaints by Jews, of a beating by a nobleman (1833), material on the Jewish hospital and old people's shelter [R], 1863–64; reports and correspondence concerning pogroms [R], 1905–07.

(TsDIAU, Kyiv, Kantseliariia... general-gubernatora)
5. Files on Jewish hospitals and charitable institutions [R], 1863–64.
(RGIA, St. Petersburg, Khoziaistvennyi departament MVD)

KOWEL, surroundings, 1871
Microfilms:
Statistical description of towns in the district [R], 1871.
(RGIA, St. Petersburg, Khoziaistvennyi Departament MVD)

KOZIENICE (woj. kieleckie) 1767–1945
Microfilms:
1. Confirmation by King Stanisław August Poniatowski of the charter granted to the Jews [L, P], 1767.
(AGAD, Warszawa, MK)
2. Reports and correspondence on the appointment of rabbis and conflicts between them and their communities, including names of rabbis, 1853–56.
(AGAD, Warszawa, CWW)
3. Correspondence between the Jewish Committees of Jedlińsk and Kozienice about threats by a right wing underground oraganization, 1945.
(AP Radom, OKŻ Radom)

KOZIN (pow. Dubno, woj. wołyńskie) 1905–1907
Microfilms:
Reports and correspondence on pogroms and measures taken by the authorities [R], 1905–07.
(TsDIAU, Kyiv, Kantseliariia... general-gubernatora)

KOZINIEC (pow. Wadowice, woj. krakowskie) 1777
Microfilms:
Complaints by Jews to the owner of the town, 1777.
(TsDIAU, L'viv, Arch. Lanckorońskich)

KOZŁÓW (pow. Tarnopol, woj. tarnopolskie) 1752–1908
Microfilms:
1. Contracts concerning Jewish *arendas* in towns on properties of the Radziwiłł family; confirmation of a rabbi's election [L, P], 1752–53.
(AGAD, Warszawa, Arch. Radziwiłłów)
2. Correspondence with the authorities on vital statistics registration, 1896–1903; complaints against the community board, 1905–08.
(TsDIAU, L'viv, Namiestnictwo Galicyjskie)

KOZOWA (pow. Brzeżany, woj. tarnopolskie) 1846–1906
Microfilms:
Correspondence with the district authorities and confirmation of the community statutes; 1846–97; complaints against a candidate for the rabbinate, 1902–06.
(TsDIAU, L'viv, Namiestnictwo Galicyjskie)

KOŹMIN (pow. Krotoszyn, woj. poznańskie) 1753–1926
Originals:

Contracts for the acquisition of various community properties [G], 1808; memoranda from the municipality concerning the distribution of safe conduct passes to Jews [G], 1820; community records concerning statutes, rules concerning the conduct and duration in office of community employees and the election of various commissions, [G], 1834–46; municipal supervision of various religious practices [G], 1837,1841; a community civil register [G], 1838; a proposal for the cancellation of community debts [G], 1839; accounts of the Jewish school [G], 1844, 1902–05; population lists [G], 1847–49; *memorbuch* [H], 1851; the conversion to Judaism of a baker's apprentice [G], 1855; lesson plans and attendance records of the Jewish school [G], 1871–1917; accounts of a young women's association [G], 1890–04; a community budget [G], 1904–05; files on religious instruction at the municipal school [G], 1907–18; a letter by Rabbi Menashe Feilchenfeld to the rabbi of Koźmin [H], 1926.

Microfilms:
1. The designation of Jewish rights and taxes by the owner of the town; charters and other documents relating to the legal status and economic activities of the Jews, 1753–1813.
(AP Poznań, Akta miast, woj. poznańskie)
2. Correspondence with the municipal authorities regarding the sale of alcohol [G], 1815–22; community board minutes [G], 1840–89.
(Centrum Judaicum, Berlin)

KOŹMINEK (pow. Kalisz, woj. łódzkie) 1821–1910
Microfilms:
1. Description of the town, 1821–22.
(AGAD, Warszawa, Komisja Województwa Kaliskiego)
2. Copies of inscriptions from synagogues and tombstones [H, R], 1910.
(RGIA, St. Petersburg, Departament dukhovnykh del…)

KOŻANGRÓDEK (pow. Łuniniec, woj. poleskie) 1936
Microfilms:
Monographical series including demographical and economical data on Jews in the town, 1936.
(AP Wrocław, Ossolineum, WKNZNP, Lwów)

KÓRNIK (pow. Śrem, woj. poznańskie) 1781–1863
Originals:
Minutes and accounts of the Jewish community [G, H], 1781–1824; decrees concerning taxes [G], 1811; a file on financial matters [G], 1834–55; a file on the men's section of the synagogue, 1856.
Microfilms:
Minutes of community board meetings [G], 1834–63.
(Centrum Judaicum, Berlin)

KRAKOWIEC (pow. Jaworów, woj. lwowskie) 1895–1936
Microfilms:
1. Correspondence on the election of a rabbi [G, P], 1895–96; correspondence with the *starostwa* about the community and the confirmation of its statutes, 1895–96.
(TsDIAU, L'viv, Namiestnictwo Galicyjskie)
2. Correspondence with the district authorities about the community statutes and other matters, including a budget and a list of community taxpayers [P, Y], 1927–36.
(DALO, L'viv, UW, Lwów)

KRAKÓW–KAZIMIERZ (woj. krakowskie) 14th–1939
Originals:

Ratification by the *wojewoda* of an agreement between the community and the municipality [L], 1485; an order by King Zygmunt to punish those responsible for an assault on Jews [L], 1530; a copy of a letter from Pope Paul III protecting the Jews and their rights [L], 1540; confirmation by King Zygmunt August of an agreement between the municipality and the community, 1553; a dispute between a Christian and a Jew over a debt [L], 1586; partial copy of a petition by the community, quoting the Pope's letter of 1540 [L], 1596;

1600's

Decrees by King Zygmunt III regulating Jewish trade (1588) [L, P], 1601, 1608; a report on litigation between the municipality and the Jewish community [L], 1616; a decree by the Kazimierz municipality concerning an anti-Jewish riot [L, P], 1616; a verdict of the royal court against participants in an anti-Jewish riot, 1619; an agreement between the community and a convent in Bochnia concerning the lease of land, 1619; ratification by the archbishop of an agreement between the community and a priest [L], 1627; an order by King Jan Kazimierz to the community to enforce the payment of a debt owed by a Jew, 1657; a decree by him concerning payment for imports [L], 1658; confirmation of the status of the Jews, 1659; a charter granted to the Jews by King Michał Korybut [L], 1669–73; an order by King Jan Sobieski to the community to pay the pension of a royal official, 1677; a summary of the royal charters granted to the Jews, 1678; a copy of an order by King Jan Sobieski to the municipality to allow Jews to return to the city and trade after the plague, and an order by him to the magistrate to keep an agreement with the community, 1678; a one year's exemption from tax granted to the community by the *wojewoda,* 1679; rules of judicial proceedings concerning the Jews, 1688; a list of official documents held by the community, 1690; a promissory note of the community to an official in Poznań, 1690–91; the verdict of the Breslau municipality in a case of a debt owed by a Jew from Kraków [L], 1699; an order by an official of the royal treasury to the community to pay a tax debt, 1699; confrmation by King August II of charters to the Jews of Kazimierz [L], 1699;

1700's–1900's

Confirmation by King August II of the charter granted to the Jews [L, P], 1742; a page from the community minute book [H], 1771; correspondence with the Berlin Jewish community [G, H], 1815–17; information about Jewish participation in the "January" uprising [H], 1863–64; statutes of the community [G, P], 1869, 1897; speeches and newspaper clippings concerning *Maccabi-Kraków* [H, P], 1909–39; letters from the secretariat of the *Akiva* youth movement, 1937; newspaper clippings and letters about the Hebrew gymnasium, 1920s–1930s; copies of documents, photos, letters and articles by the Polish-Jewish journalist, Felicja Infeld-Stendigowa, 1895–1945.

Photocopies:

1. Copies of decrees by King Carl X of Sweden concerning the Jews of various communities in Poland, including Kraków [G], 1655–57.
(Riksarkivet and Kammararkivet, Stockholm)
2. Testimony by several Jews to King Władysław Jagiełło that a loan granted by them has been paid [L], 1398; decrees by King Zygmunt I relating to Jewish trade, 1521, 1527; grant of protection to the Jews by King Zygmunt August, confirming previous documents of 1485 and 1527 [L], 1562; a charter issued by him, limiting the acquisition of real estate by the Jews of Kazimierz and permitting the collection of taxes for fabric imported by the Jews, 1566; a decree by him forbidding Jews, converts, heretics and suspected heretics to hold public office in Kazimierz, 1567; a charter by King Jan Kazimierz confirming all previous

charters and decrees for the town Kraków and a decree requiring the Jews and the town of Kraków to share the costs of renovating the bridge between Kraków and Kazimierz, 1649; a regulation by the Council of the Four Lands concerning Kraków, 1717.

(AP Kraków, DP)

Microfilms:

1. Legal documents concerning both the community and individual Jews (incl. decrees, charters and tax records) [L, P], 14th–17th cent.; a collection of verdicts given by the High Court and of charters to the town, 1530–1606.

(Biblioteka Narodowa, Warszawa)

2. A contract for the sale of a house [L], 1405; letter of protection for a Jew from Kraków by Emperor Carl V [G], 1551; confirmation in 1635 by King Jan Kazimierz of a charter given to the Jews of Małopolska, including Jews of Kraków by King Kazimierz Wielki in 1367 and confirmed by King Zygmunt August in 1559 [L], 1633

(AP Przemyśl, DP)

3. Court records and legal documents concerning individual Jews [G, H, P], 1550–1834; records of the rabbinical court [H, P], 1665–1805; regulations concerning the Jews and their economic life, 16th–18th cent.; a list of all the Jews in Kraków [G], 1796; the minutes and account books of various Jewish guilds, 1833–66.

(AP Kraków, Akta Żydowskie)

4. A copy of *Privilegiorum Libertatis* [L], 1580–86; a collection of rights and charters for the town [L, P], 1694; *arendas* and litigation between the Jewish community and the municipal authorities, 1730–39, 1784; taxes paid by the community, 1793; complaints of townsmen, 18th cent.

(AP Wrocław, Ossolineum)

5. Documents concerning *propinacja* and debts [H, Y], 1583–91.

(TsDIAU, L'viv, Magistrat, Lwów)

6. Files on a number of Jews, 1587–90; a charter by King August III to Krzysztof Radziecki to act as judge of the local Jews, 1745; *suplika* of the synagogue in Kraków, n.d.

(AGAD, Warszawa, Arch. Radziwiłłów)

7. Confirmation by King Zygmunt III of the charter granted to the Jews [L], 1588; promissory notes signed by the community, 1658; a request by Christian guilds for official protection in a Jewish suit against them, 1756; confirmation by King August III of the brewers' guild statute limiting Jewish manufacture and sale of beer, 1758; the decision of King Stanisław August Poniatowski in a dispute between the brewers' guild and Jewish *arendars* [L, P], 1768; confirmation by him of the charter granted to the Jews of Kazimierz by former kings, as well as three letters of protection [L, P], 1765–92.

(AGAD, Warszawa, Księgi Kanclerskie)

8. Evidence in a suit between the shoemakers' guild and a Jew, 1596.

(AP Kraków, Cech Szewców)

12. Records of the *wojewoda's* court for the Jews [L, P], 1620–42; royal records concerning the Jews [L, P], 1524–1765.

(AP Kraków, Inscr. Castr. Cracoviensa)

9. Files of the tailors' guild in Kraków and Kazimierz, 1630–1820.

(Bibl. Jagiellońska, Kraków)

10. Records of taxes paid to the Swedish Commissar in Kraków by Jews [G], 1657.

(Kammararkivet, Stockholm)

11. Circulars, accounts, decrees and *uniwersały* concerning inhabitants and their properties in Kraków, 1663–1765; registers of Jewish inhabitants and taxes paid by them in Kraków and Kazimierz, 1705–08; *supliki* to Elżbieta Sieniawska from a Jew of Kraków, 1705–1736; accounts, contracts and reports concerning property of the Sieniawski family, 1709–28; accounts of profits from properties in Kraków, 1761–63.
(Bibl. Czartoryskich, Kraków)

12. Documents on various financial matters [G, H, L, P], 1680, 1698, 1773–76.
(AP Kraków, Teki Schneidra)

13. A letter by a Jew in Stanisławów to a merchant in Kraków concerning commercial matters, 1685.
(TsDIAU, L'viv, Kolektsiia lystiv…)

14. Files on taxes paied by Jews of Kraków, 1705–06; various documents concerning *propinacja*, 1705–16.
(AP Kraków, Varia)

15. Inventories concerning management of properties and Jews of Kazimierz, 1730.
(AGAD, Warszawa, Zb. Popielów)

16. Litigation between a nobleman and a Jewish salt merchant, 1762–83.
(AP Kraków)

17. *Arenda* contract, 1763; various legal records, 17th–18th cent.; legal proceedings between the municipality of Kazimierz and Jews over quarters for soldiers, 1783; appeal concerning financial matters, 1785; the records of the "Koscherfleisch–Kommission" [G], 1797–1802; documents concerning Jewish merchants, 1821–24; a file on the community's participation in rebuilding the town, 1828–42.
(AP Kraków, IT)

18. A court case between the town of Kraków and the Jews of Kazimierz, 1780.
(Bibl. im. Łopacińskiego, Lublin)

19. Birth and death registers, 1788–1855; banns, marriage and divorce registers, 1798–1842.
(AP Kraków)

20. Instructions issued by the Austrian Emperor concerning taxes on kosher meat, 1796–97.
(AP Kraków, Teki Sanguszków)

21. Legal documents limiting Jewish commerce and property in Kazimierz [G], 18th–19th cent.
(NBANU, L'viv, Arch. Ossolińskich)

22. Regulations concerning the legal status of the Jews; files on the Jewish community, and on charitable and educational institutions; taxes paid by Jews; Jewish building projects [G, P], 1816–53.
(AP Kraków, Arch. Wolnego Miasta Krakowa)

23. A request of the *kahal* to cancel taxes, 1820; an obligation of a Jew to pay 1720 zloty to a convent in Kraków 1830–32; obligations of the Kazimierz community towards the Augustinian monastery in Olkusz, 1845–48.
(AGAD, Warszawa, KRzPiS)

24. Records of the Jewish furriers' guild, 1837–40.
(AP Kraków, Izba Rzemieślnicza)

25. <u>The Jewish Community</u>
<u>Synagogues</u>: the 'old' synagogue in Kazimierz - restoration plans and architectural sketches, 1838–39; the 'New' or *Remu* synagogue - lists of members, elections, inventories, 1887–1925; the 'Wysoka' synagogue - lists of members, elections, 1887–1920; the *Kupa* synagogue - elections, 1893–94; the *Eizyk* synagogue - correspondence, elections, 1899–1936; *Synagoga Izraelitów Postępowych* - construction plans, statutes, correspondence [G, P], 1912–39;

Community administration: minutes of various community departments, 1843, 1899–1912; a register of Kazimierz community properties, 1861; minutes and correspondence of the community board, and an inventory of community property, 1870–1939; correspondence [G, P], 1871–99, 1917–22; correspondence of the community presidium with the municipal authorities, 1900–36; correspondence of the community board with other Jewish communities in Poland [P, Y], 1923–36;

Finances and taxes: files on the Kazimierz community budget and taxes [G, P], 1854–57; a list of kosher meat taxpayers, 1858–59; a register of community members' incomes, 1897;

Membership and elections: a list of community members, including those living elsewhere, 1856; community elections - minutes, correspondence and lists of voters, 1874–1900; voting lists citing addresses and professions, 1929, 1935;

Welfare: files on a Jewish hospital [G, P], 1866–72; files on charity, a list of the needy, 1890–93; statutes of various charitable societies [G, P, Y], 1912–37;

Education: files on the Jewish educational system [G, P], 1866, 1872; files on Jewish schools in Kraków, a list of students, teaching programs, correspondence with municipal authorities, 1874–78, 1889–93;

Statutes: files on statutes of the Jewish community [G, P], 1869–83; drafts of changes in the community statutes [G, P, Y], 1897–1914, 1925–26.

Varia: Minutes of representatives of *Zbór Izraelicki*, 1891–95; agenda of the debates of the Jewish religious board, 1899–1929; correspondence on the publication of Majer Bałaban's historical works, 1912–35; minutes of the commission for protection of Jewish monuments in Kraków, 1922;

(ŻIH, Warszawa, Gmina Żydowska, Kraków)

26. Files on confirming the statutes of the community, 1846–96; minutes and correspondence on the draft of statutes for a Jewish school in Kraków, 1853–54; a report of the *starostwa* in Kraków on anti–Jewish incidents and societies, 1871; correspondence and/or statutes about the following societies: *Czytelnia Izraelicka, Hizaharu Bivnei Aniyim, Agidas Achim – Bruder Bund, Agudas Yeschorim* [G, P], 1871; *Hachnasas Kala* [G, P], 1871–1912; *Israelitischen Leseverein* [G, P], 1873–74; *Zion* [G, P], 1890–1902; *Stowarzyszenie Posługaczy Żydowskich*, 1895; *Chayatim* [G, P, Y], 1895–1906; *Aufiml* 1903–04; *Bank Ludowy w Krakowie*, 1903–10; *Machzikei Cholim* [P, Y], 1903–12; various societies to assist school children and students [G, P], 1904–07; *Achva* 1906–11; *Allgemeinen jüdischer Arbeiterverband* [G, P], 1906–12; *Poalei Zion* [G, P], 1907–12; *Salomon Halberstamms Bethaus, Berush Meisels Beis Medrash, Salomon Deiches Beis Medrash* [G, P], 1908; *Beis Yisroel, Adas Yisroel, Bnei Emunah*, 1908; *Żydowski Związek Demokratyczny*, 1908; correspondence with the municipal authorities regarding *chadorim*, including lists of melamdim (among them a woman), 1876–1908; correspondence on supporting Jewish schools [G, P], 1880; correspondence on pension payments for university teachers [G, P], 1886–87; minutes of the executive committees of the Baron Hirsch Foundation (JCA) (vol. 2) in Lwów and Kraków, 1892; files on kosher slaughter–houses, 1894–97; correspondence with the *starostwa* on community statutes, 1895–96; correspondence with the municipal authorities on providing kosher meals for Jewish prisoners [G, P], 1896, and regarding the positions of Rabbis Chaim Leib Horowitz and Osias Thon, 1899–1904; correspondence regarding Rabbi Chaim Leib Horowitz's opposition to changes in the marriage registration procedure [G, P], 1900–07; correspondence with the police administration about meetings of different associations, 1905.

(TsDIAU, L'viv, Namiestnictwo Galicyjskie)

27. Reports on teaching Jewish religion in elementary schools [G, P], 1882–97; minutes of the executive committees of the Baron Hirsch Foundation (JCA) (vol. 1) in Lwów and Kraków, 1892. (TsDIAU, L'viv, Krajowa Rada Szkolna)

28. Correspondence with the command of the Polish Army on cancelling the distribution of the journal *Nowy Dziennik* in Kraków because of accusations in it that the army was responsible for the pogroms in Lwów, 1919.
(DALO, L'viv, Dyrekcja Policji, Lwów)
29. Reports of *"Achduth Bnai Brith"* and *"Solidarność" Bnai Brith* in Kraków, 1928; correspondence of *"Achduth Bnai Brith"* in Kraków with *"Achduth Bnai Brith"* in Stanisławów on financial and organizational subjects, 1930–33.
(DAIFO, Ivano-Frankivs'k, Towarzystwo *Achduth B'nai B'rith,* Stanisławów)
30. Correspondence on the registration of WIZO in Kraków and its expansion in the Lwów province, 1935; correspondence on the registration of *Związek Zebulon* in Kraków to prepare Jewish emigrants from Poland for maritime professions in Palestine, 1938.
(DALO, L'viv, UW, Lwów)

KRAKÓW, surroundings, 1765–1924
Microfilms:
1. A *lustracja* of royal estates in the province, 1765; a census of the Jews in the province, 1790–92.
(AP Kraków, KCWWK)
2. Documents on the organization of *kahals* in the Kraków area and problems caused by new administrative divisions, 1810–11.
(AGAD, Warszawa, CWW)
3. Documents concerning new projects of tax collection (*koszerne, świeczkowe, familijne*), correspondence and admonitions regarding tax collection, addressed to *kahals*, 1810–16; correspondence concerning debts of the Kazimierz *kahal* to the St. Cross church and old people's home in Grabów, 1810–19.
(AGAD, Warszawa, KRzPiS)
4. Files of the Department of Internal Affairs and Police concerning the communities in Kraków and Chrzanów (rabbinate, taxes, Jewish hospital, rules of Jewish marriage etc.) 1816–53;
(AP Kraków, Arch. Wolnego Miasta Krakowa)
5. A collection of poems describing the events of 1846.
(Bibl. Jagiellońska, Kraków)
6. A list of Jewish communities and their inhabitants in the Kraków district , 1879, 1895.
(ŻIH, Warszawa, Gmina Żydowska, Kraków)
7. A list of Jewish communities in the Kraków region, 1922 and correspondence concerning their statutes, 1922–24;
(DALO, L'viv, UW, Lwów)

KRASICZYN (pow. Przemyśl, woj. lwowskie) surroundings, 1730–1735
Microfilms:
An inventory of the Krasiczyn estates, 1730–35.
(AP Wrocław, Ossolineum)

KRASNE (pow. Jarosław, woj. lwowskie) 1628–1759
Microfilms:
Private contracts, receipts and files concerning properties and interests of the Sieniawski and Czartoryski families,1628–1759.
(Bibl. Czartoryskich, Kraków)

KRASNOBRÓD (pow. Zamość, woj. lubelskie) 1835–1859
Microfilms:
1. A municipal document concerning a Jewish house, n.d.
(AP Kraków, IT)
2. Statistical description,1835–59.
(AP Lublin, Rząd Gubernialny, Lublin)

KRASNOPOL (pow. Suwałki, woj białostockie) 1853–1856
Microfilms:
Reports and correspondence of government offices on the confirmation of rabbinical appointments and conflicts between rabbis and communities, as well as a list of rabbis, 1853–56.
(AGAD, Warszawa, CWW)

KRASNOSIELC (pow. Maków Maz., woj. warszawskie) 1818–1913
Microfilms:
1. File on extraction of a passport fee from a Jewish inhabitant [R], 1906–13.
(AP Białystok, Rząd Gubernialny, Łomża)
2. Files on synagogues, 1818–60.
(AGAD, Warszawa, CWW)

KRASNYSTAW (woj. lubelskie) 1717–1879
Microfilms:
1. An order by King August II forbidding Jews to live in the town, following complaints by non–Jewish inhabitants, 1717.
(AP Lublin, Księgi Grodzkie Krasnostawskie)
2. Records on Jewish inhabitants in the town, 1822–60.
(AGAD, Warszawa, KRzSW)
3. A project to distribute kosher food to poor Jews and assist Jewish hospital patients [P, R], 1848–56; correspondence on the exemption of Rabbinical Seminary students from army service, and a list of rabbis, 1856–71.
(AGAD, Warszawa, CWW)
4. Files on the appointment of rabbis and confirmation of the budget [R], 1868–70; files on *arenda* of incomes from the synagogue, cemetery, circumcisions and weddings [R], 1878–79.
(AP Lublin, Rząd Gubernialny, Lublin)

KRASNYSTAW, surroundings, 1710–1744
Microfilms:
1. Instructions issued by the *Sejmik* concerning the poll tax paid by Christians and Jews, 1710.
(AP Lublin, Księgi Grodzkie Krasnostawskie)
2. A file concerning a prohibition to lease the *arenda* of estates to Jews, 1744.
(AP Lublin, Księgi Grodzkie Chełmskie)

KRAŚNIK (pow. Janów, woj. lubelskie) 1737–1886
Microfilms:
1. Records of the community's debts to the Catholic Church in Zamość, 1737–86.
(AP Lublin, Kolegiata w Zamościu)

2. Statistical description of the town, 1835–59; correspondence on a complaint against the treasurer of the community [R], 1869.
(AP Lublin, Rząd Gubernialny, Lublin)

KROBIA (pow. Gostyń, woj. poznańskie) 1841–1881
Originals:
Records of a suit involving a local Jew [G], 1841–58; register of synagogue donations [G], 1847–48; correspondence with the authorities concerning tax refunds and other matters [G], 1864–69; printed announcements and circulars from communities, organizations and government offices [G], 1861–81.

KROCZYCE (pow. Olkusz, woj. kieleckie) 1761–1762
Microfilms:
Arenda contracts, 1761–62.
(AP Kraków, Podhorce II)

KROMOŁÓW (pow. Zawiercie, woj. kieleckie) 1828–1914
Microfilms:
1. Community tax records; the reorganization of religious districts; ratification of community elections and accounts; the appointment of a rabbi [R], 1860–1914.
(AP Łódź, Rząd Gubernialny, WA, Piotrków)
2. Accounts of the community, 1828–63.
(AGAD, Warszawa, CWW)

KROSNO (woj. lwowskie) 1776–1939
Microfilms:
1. An agreement between the community in Rymanów and municipal authorities in Krosno permitting Jews to participate in fairs in exchange for a tribute to the mayor and municipal board, 1776.
(AP Kraków, Teki Schneidra)
2. Correspondence about the community and a list of communal taxpayers, 1922–35; correspondence about the *Kultur Liga*, 1926; files on community elections, 1928–33; a list of political party members, citing their nationalities, 1930; reports and correspondence on community elections, including lists of community board members, rabbis and *dayanim*, 1937–39.
(DALO, L'viv, UW, Lwów)
3. Correspondence on the registration of the *Mizrachi* and statutes, 1931.
(DALO, L'viv, Magistrat, Lwów)

KROSNO, surroundings, 1877–1935
Microfilms:
Correspondence with the authorities regarding *chadorim* in the area and a list of *melamdim*, 1877–1908; correspondence about the *Zion* society, including statutes, 1908.
(TsDIAU, L'viv, Namiestnictwo Galicyjskie)

KROŚCIENKO (pow. Dobromil, woj. lwowskie) 1918–1930
Photocopies:
Documents of the Ministry of Interior on the pogroms, 1918–19.
(AAN, Warszawa, MSW)
Microfilms:
Authorization by the authorities to collect money for Galician Jews in Palestine, 1928–30.
(DALO, L'viv, UW, Lwów)

KROŚNIEWICE (pow. Kutno, woj. warszawskie) 16th–1960
Originals:
A letter containing information on the history of the Jews in the 16th, 19th and 20th cent., 1960.

KROTOSZYN (woj. poznańskie) 1684–1899
Originals:
Files on the community's debts to the Church and other institutions [G, P], 1747–1879; records concerning various taxes and state bonds [G], 1827–42; pages from a circumcision register [G, H], 1833–69; files on community real estate [G], 1834–45; records on synagogues and religious worship [G], 1834–71; G], 1834–50; a file on relations between the community and the butchers' guild [G], 1835–57; litigation between the Thurn and Taxis family and the community [G], 1838–44; the statutes of a benevolent society [G], 1891, and of the local branch of *Bnai Brith* [G], 1899.
Microfilms:
1. Burial register [H], 1684–1830.
(Private Collection)
2. Various municipal and guild statutes; community regulations; correspondence and financial records (fragmentary) concerning the community, 1728–92 .
(AP Poznań, Akta miast, woj. poznańskie)
3. Community minute book [H], 1777.
(YIVO, New York)

KRÓLEWSKA HUTA (CHORZÓW since 1934, pow. Katowice, woj. śląskie) 20th cent.
Originals:
Documents, letters and sermons of Rabbi Dr Salomon Goldschmidt [G, H] during the period preceding WW I.

KRUHÓW (pow. Złoczów, woj. tarnopolskie) surroundings, 1783–1818
Microfilms:
Arenda accounts and contracts, 1783–1818.
(AP Kraków, Arch. Młynowskie Chodkiewiczów)

KRUKI (pow. Ostrołęka, woj. białostockie) 1914
Microfilms:
Files on the arrest of Jews suspected of causing damage to telegraph equipment [R], 1914.
(AP Białystok, Rząd Gubernialny, Łomża)

KRUKIENICE (pow. Mościska, woj. lwowskie) 1846–1935
Microfilms:
1. Files on confirmation of community statutes, 1846–96; reports and correspondence concerning community elections, 1933.
(TsDIAU, L'viv, Namiestnictwo Galicyjskie)
2. Correspondence on the community budget, including a list of taxpayers, 1933–35.
(DALO, L'viv, UW, Lwów)

KRYŁÓW (pow. Hrubieszów, woj. lubelskie) 1818–1859
Microfilms:
A statistical description, 1818–59.
(AP Lublin)

הזכרת נשמת	הזכרת נשמות
האשה שרה בת החי'ר' משה	האשה גאדע בת הח"ר' אהרן
האשה גיטל בתחח"ר' אברהם	האשה דינה בת הח'ר' ישרא'
האשה פרי'דא בת החד'ר'דוב	האשה חוה בת הח'ר' דוב
האשה מרים בתהחיר'אהרן	האשה אדיל בת הח'ר' שמעון
האשה מינדל בתהחד'ר'ישרא'	האשה חוה בת החד'ר' זעליג הכהן
האשהמ'הענא בתהחי'ר' יצחק	האשה חיי'שרה בתהח'ר' משה
האשה רחל בת החי'ר' משה	האשה רוזא בת הח'ר' דוב
האשה פריידא בתהח'ר'פינחס	האשה רחל בת הח'ר' אשר
האשה שרה בתהחי'ר' יעקב	האשה פוגל בתהח'ר' צבי
האשה יטא בת החי'ר'יצחק	האשה הייצבע בתהח'ר' יודא
האשה צירל בת החד'ר' גרשון	האשה שרה בת הח''ר' שמוא'
האשה רבקא בתהחד'ר'אברהם	האשה בילא בת החי'ר' שרגא
האשה טרנא בתהחד'ר' משה	האשה העגדל בת הח'ר' מרדפי הכהן
האשה פוגל בת הח'ר' מאיר	האשה רעכל בת הח'ר' משה
האשה קילא בתהחד'ר' שלמה	האשה בילא בת הח'ר' חיים
האשה מרים בתההד'ר' צבי	האשה מלכה בת הח'ר' איה
האשה פיגלה בת הח'ר' צבי	הבתולה רוזא בת הח'ר' מיכא'
האשה גנעגדעל בתהח'ר' צבי	האשה ראכמה בתחח'ר' שלמה
האשה גנעגדעל בתהח'ר' שמעון	האשהראכמה בת הח'ר' יעקב

Chodzież. Memorbuch of the tailor's society prayer house. 1819 (Hebrew)

KRYNKI (pow. Grodno, woj. białostockie) 1566–1934
Photographs of tombstones from the Jewish cemetery, 1758–1934.
Microfilms:
A charter for *arenda*, 1566–68.

KRYSTYNOPOL (pow. Sokal, woj. lwowskie) 1730–1939
Microfilms:
1. Various documents and accounts [H, P], 1730–96.
(TsDIAU, Kyiv, Arch. Tarło)
2. Correspondence on the registration of the *Mizrachi*, including statutes and a list of board members, 1922, and of *Machzikei Hadas*, including a list of board members, 1932.
(DALO, L'viv, Magistrat, Lwów)
3. Reports and correspondence on community budget and elections, including a list of board members, 1930–38; reports and correspondence on examinations in the Polish language for rabbis and dayanim, 1938–39.
(DALO, L'viv, UW, Lwów)

KRZEMIENIEC (woj. wołyńskie) 1557–1939
Microfilms:
1. Contracts and royal documents relating to Jewish *arendas* of inns, customs payments, breweries etc., 1557–71; *supliki* of the Jews, 1745, 1790; material from legal proceedings between Jews and a nobleman, 1755–59; summons in the case of Jewish *arendars* and a merchant from Hungary, 1784.
(AP Kraków, Archiwum Sanguszków, tzw. teki arabskie i rzymskie)
2. A request concerning compensation to a Jew for losses sustained by him [Rt], 1565.
(RGADA, Moscow, ML)
3. Accounts of the poll-tax and other taxes from villages and towns of the district, 1627–1759.
(NBANU, L'viv, Arch. Sapiehów)
4. *Regesta* from court books, referring to Jews [U], 1631–47; a report on synagogues, Jewish schools, officials and inhabitants in the district, 1834, 1850; correspondence of Isaak Ber Levinsohn, author and *maskil*, concerning permission to transfer Jews to the Cherson area, including a list of families, 1834; permit for Jews in the district to dwell in the zone adjoining the border, 1834; documents about aid for Jewish victims of a fire, 1835; documents on the collection of funds to construct a synagogue in Jerusalem, 1837–38; correspondence with the authorities on the election of Jews to the municipal board, including lists, 1842; material on Jewish community debts to monasteries, 1845–47; a list of charters by Polish kings and permits by Russian authorities to Jews, concerning *propinacja*, 1849–52; complaint by a Jewish merchant about excessive payment of the *krupka* to the Jewish community, 1879–80; correspondence on the pogroms, 1905–07; statistical data on the district [R], 1912.
(TsDIAU, Kyiv, Kantseliariia... general-gubernatora)
5. Records of litigation between between the community and a non Jew, 1753.
(AP Łódź, Zb. Bartoszewiczów)
6. Memoranda on the delay of debt payments, 1779, 1784, 1786, 1794.
(RGADA, Moscow, KFE)
7. An investigation of a *cherem* against the Jewish leaseholder of an inn, including a list of the Jews suspected of involvement [R], 1835; reports and correspondence on clandestine collecting of funds for the Jews in Jerusalem, including lists of donors [H, R], 1837–41; an investigation into the alleged return to Judaism of a convert to Christianity [G, H, R], 1841–51; material on a census of the Jews [R], 1847–48;

contracts, minutes and reports on a Jewish hospital [R], 1857–1939; construction plans of wooden shops around the great synagogue, 1925; minutes and construction plans of the prayer-house of the *Stary Beis Hamidrash* association, 1927–28; minutes and correspondence on the construction of a Jew's house, 1929.
(DATO, Ternnopil', Magistrat, Krzemieniec)

8. A report on the situation of Jewish schools [R], 1852–58.
(DAKhO, Kamianets'-Podil's'kyi, Direktsiia narodnykh uchilishch…)

9. Statistical data concerning the Jewish hospital and old people's shelter, 1863–64, and on towns in the district, 1871.
(RGIA, St. Petersburg, Khoziaistvennyi departament MVD)

10. Correspondence with the local branch of the Society for the Attainment of Full Rights for the Jewish People in Russia about elections to the *Duma* [R], 1906–07.
(RGIA, St. Petersburg, Obshchestvo polnopraviia…)

11. Copies of inscriptions on Jewish tombstones and synagogues [R], 1910.
(RGIA, St. Petersburg, Departament dukhovnykh del…)

12. Minutes, correspondence and curriculum vitae of teachers at Jewish elementary schools, 1919–25; statistical report on a Jewish religious school, 1930, and on the *Chinuch Yeladim* school, including a list of teachers in Jewish schools, 1931–35; instructions by the educational authorities of Volhynia regarding improvements in Jewish private schools, as well as a list of Jewish private schools in the district, 1931–35.
(DATO, Ternopil', Inspektorat Szkolny, Krzemieniec)

13. Files of the *Tarbut* school in Krzemieniec, including minutes, reports, course programs, governmental instructions, budgets, statutes and lists of pupils, teachers and parents [H, P], 1923–38
(DATO, Ternopil', Prywatne Koedukacyjne Gimnazjum *Tarbut*, Krzemieniec)

14. Budget of the *Towarzystwa Opieki nad Żydowskimi Sierotami i Opuszczonymi Dziecmi na Wołyniu* for support of orphans in the Krzemieniec district for the school year 1929/1930, including a list of the children supported by the association, 1928; general data about the district, 1937; a list of communities, inhabitants and voters in the district, 1937; a report on the kindergarten and nursery school maintained by the *Tarbut* association 1937.
(DATO, Ternopil', Starostwo Powiatowe, Krzemieniec)

KRZEPICE (pow. Częstochowa, woj. kieleckie) 1822–1914
Microfilms:
1. Construction of a synagogue, 1822–42; records and accounts of the community,.
1822–66.
(AP Łódź, Anterioria Rządu Gubernialnego, Piotrków)
2. Reports and correspondence on the appointments of rabbis [P, R], 1856–64.
(AGAD, Warszawa, CWW)
3. Ratification of community elections and accounts [R], 1888–1914.
(AP Łódź, Rząd Gubernialny, WA, Piotrków)
3. Fines for evading conscription [R], 1897–1902.
(AP Łódź, Rząd Gubernialny, WP, Piotrków)

KRZESZÓW (pow. Biłgoraj, woj. lubelskie) 1856–1864
Microfilms:
A statistical description, 1856–64.
(AP Lublin, Rząd Gubernialny, Lublin)

KSIĄŻ (pow. Śrem, woj. poznańskie) 1846
Originals:
Register of a marriage [G], 1846.

KSIĄŻ WIELKI (pow. Miechów, woj. kieleckie) 1818–1850
Microfilms:
1. Correspondence on the Jews' difficult economical situation, and a list of unpaid debts and taxes, 1818.
(AGAD, Warszawa, KRzPiS)
2. Reports and complaints concerning burial societies, 1822–50.
(AGAD, Warszawa, CWW)

KUKIZÓW (pow. Lwów, woj. lwowskie) surroundings, 1744
Photocopies:
An inventory of the town, 1744.
(NIAB, Minsk, Arch. Radziwiłłów)

KULIKÓW (pow. Żółkiew, woj. lwowskie) 1874–1939
Microfilms:
1. Correspondence with the district authorities regarding *chadorim*, including a list of *melamdim*, 1874–08; correspondence between the community and the authorities regarding the election of a rabbi, 1900–08.
(TsDIAU, L'viv, Namiestnictwo Galicyjskie)
2. Correspondence and documents on community matters, e.g. budget and lists of taxpayers [P, Y], 1931–35; decrees, reports and correspondence about community elections, including lists of community board members, 1933–39.
(DALO, L'viv, UW, Lwów)

KUDRYŃCE (pow. Borszczów, woj. lwowskie) 1898–1906
Microfilms:
Correspondence between the community and the authorities on community statutes, 1898, and on irregularities in community elections, 1905–06.
(TsDIAU, L'viv, Namiestnictwo Galicyjskie)

KURÓW (pow. Puławy, woj. lubelskie) 1707–1860
Microfilms:
1. Records of financial transactions involving salt, and testimony of an assault on a Jew, 1707–50.
(AP Kraków, Zb. Rusieckich)
2. Files concerning inheritances, 1805, and nonpayments of debts [H, L, P], 1801–10.
(AP Lublin, Jurysdyka dominikalna Kurowa)
3. A statistical description of the town, 1828–60.
(AP Lublin, Rząd Gubernialny, Lublin)
4. Reports and correspondence of government offices concerning appointments of rabbis and litigation between them and community boards, as well as lists of rabbis, 1853–56.
(AGAD, Warszawa, CWW)

KUTNO (woj. warszawskie) 1848–1855
Originals:
Marriage registers, 1848, 1855.

KUTY (KUTÓW) (pow. Kosów, woj. stanisławowskie) 1715–1938
Microfilms:
1. Confirmation by King Stanisław August of a charter given to the Jews in 1715 [L, P], 1765.
(AGAD, Warszawa, Księgi Kanclerskie)
2. Files on enlarging the cemetery, 1777; on taxes (containing descriptions of houses), 1784–1818 and on the imported wine trade [G], 1792–93; lists of eligible voters [G], 1862.
(AP Kraków, Teki Schneidra)
3. Correspondence with the authorities on *chadorim*, including a list of *melamdim*, 1877–1908, about the statutes, 1897 and the *mikve*, 1904–08.
(TsDIAU, L'viv, Namiestnictwo Galicyjskie)
4. Material on confirming: the *Talmud Tora* society statutes [G, P], 1893, 1920–30; and the *Agudas Yisroel* statutes, 1895, 1920–27; files on the *Gmilus Chasodim* society, including a list of members [G, P], 1904–31; an appeal by the community to the Jews about their participation in the elections to the *Sejm* and Senate [H, P], 1923; files on confirming the statutes of various Jewish associations, and membership lists, 1923–37; reports and correspondence on community elections and the raising of salaries for community board members [H, P], 1932–38; reports on the activity of various scout associations, 1929–30; files on *Hatzofim Brit Trumpeldor*, and on the *Bikur Cholim* Society, 1930–37; files on the appointment of a rabbi and his salary and those of his assistants, 1932–38; reports on *Histadrut Hanoar–Haivri*, *Hashomer Hatzair* and *Hatzofe*, 1933.
(DAIFO, Ivano-Frankivs'k, UW, Stanisławów)

KUŹNICA (pow. Sokółka, woj. białostockie) 1630–1789
Photocopies:
An inventory of the town, 1786, 1789;
(NIAB, Minsk, Kollektsiia drevnikh inventarei)
Microfilms:
A *lustracja*, 1630.
(AP Białystok, Rząd Gubernialny, Łomża)

LACHOWCE, surroundings (pow. Ostróg, woj. wołyńskie) 1627–1759
Microfilms:
Accounts and taxes paid by Christians and Jews in the towns and villages of the Lachowicki *klucz*, 1627–1759.
(NBANU, L'viv, Arch. Sapiechów)

LACHOWICE (formerly LUBNICA, pow. Żywiec, woj. krakowskie) 1652–1785
Microfilms:
1. Files on complaints, extracts from municipal books, inventories, accounts, *supliki* and *arenda* contracts concerning estates of the Sieniawski and Czartoryski families in Lubnica [H, L, P], 1652–1766.
(Bibl. Czartoryskich, Kraków)
2. Registers, accounts, *uniwersały*, decisions and contracts regarding the Sieniawski–Czartoryski estates [L, P], 1706–85.
(Biblioteka Narodowa, Warszawa)
3. Summary of accounts concerning estates in Lubnica, 1708–29; inventories of the lubnicki *klucz*, 1733.
(AP Kraków, Arch. Krzeszowickie Potockich)

4. A letter of the *wojewoda* to the municipal authorities of Lwów about a dispute over property of a Jew from Lubnica, 1754–62.
(TsDIAU, L'viv, Kolektsiia lystiv...)

LACHOWICZE (pow. Baranowicze, woj. nowogródzkie), 1855–1892
Microfilms:
Court files on unqualified teachers in Jewish schools [R], 1855–92.
(NIAB, Minsk, Minskii okruzhnoi sud)

LASZKI (pow. Jarosław, woj. lwowskie) 1699–1726
Microfilms:
Orders of payment, letters and registers concerning estates of the Sieniawski family [H, P], 1699–1726.
(Bibl. Czartoryskich, Kraków)

LĄDEK (pow. Konin, woj. łódzkie) 1844–1904
Microfilms:
1. A certificate of citizenship [G], 1844.
(ŻIH, Warszawa, Synagogen–Gemeinde)
2. Minutes of the community board [G], 1860–86.
(Centrum Judaicum, Berlin)
3. A case concerning the smuggling of Jewish emigrants across the border, 1903–04.
(AP Łódź, Kancelaria Gubernatora Kaliskiego)

LELÓW (pow. Włoszczowa, woj. kieleckie) 1792
Microfilms:
A letter of safe conduct from King Stanisław August Poniatowski to a Jewish couple engaged in trade [L] 1792.
(AGAD, Warszawa, Księgi Kanclerskie)

LEMIESZEWICZE (pow. Pińsk, woj. poleskie) 1906
Photocopies:
A report on an unauthorized *cheder* [R], 1906.
(NIAB, Minsk, Direktsiia narodnykh uchilishch)

LESKO (LISKO, woj. lwowskie) 1611–1936
Microfilms:
1. Extracts from records of the local courts, 1611–61.
(AP Wrocław, Ossolineum)
2. A charter for the town, 1612; a *suplika* of the community, 1771.
(AP Kraków, Teki Schneidra)
3. Charters, *supliki* and *arenda* contracts concerning Jews [G, H, L, P, Y], 1686–1805.
(AP Lublin, Zb. Czołowskiego)
4. Correspondence with the authorities regarding *chadorim* and a list of *melamdim*, 1877–1908; correspondence with the *Ahavas Zion* society [G, P], 1898.
(TsDIAU, L'viv, Namiestnictwo Galicyjskie)
5. Correspondence on a local celebration of the inauguration of the Hebrew University in Jerusalem, 1924–25; correspondence about the *Kultur Liga*, 1926; decrees, reports and correspondence concerning the

community and the general elections, including the community budget and a list of taxpayers [P, Y], 1928–36.
(DALO, L'viv, UW, Lwów)
6. Correspondence about the registration of *Szlomej Emunej Izrael* (*Agudas Yisroel*) and *Tzeirei Emunei Yisroel*, 1925; correspondence about the registration of *Machzikei Hadas* and a list of members, 1932.
(DALO, L'viv, Magistrat, Lwów)

LESZNIÓW (pow. Brody, woj. tarnopolskie) 1739–1908
Microfilms:
1. A request by 88 Jewish merchants from Poland to enter Russia with merchandise [R], 1739.
(TsDIAU, Kyiv, Kievskaia gubernskaia kantseliariia)
2. Correspondence between the community and the authorities regarding statutes and *chadorim*, including a list of *melamdim* [G, P], 1877–1908; official reports about the community [G, P], 1890; correspondence between the community and the authorities regarding the rabbi's complaints about his salary [G, P], 1903–08.
(TsDIAU L'viv, Namiestnictwo Galicyjskie)

LESZNO (woj. poznańskie) 1630–1859
Originals:
A register of the community's debts to the nobility and the clergy [H], 1755–85; a letter concerning collection of money for people damaged by fire [H], 1767; civil register–data concerning certain Jewish families [G], 1788–1921; a list of the property of a Jewish merchant who died in Frankfurt [H], 1785; a letter of protection [G], 1798; an invitation to a medical exam [G], 1802; the *memorbuch* of the "Joseph Schul" (fragmentary) [H], 1835; statutes and records of a benevolent society [G], 1854; records of the *Salomon–Josef–Johanna Wollheim Stiftung* [charitable foundation] [G], 1859; Dr. Świderski: "Dzieje gminy żydowskiej miasta Leszno" (History of the Jewish community of Leszno), 1971.
Microfilms:
1. A document issued by the owner of the town concerning Jewish rights, 1630; endowment of a plot to a Jewish physician, 1670; files on the sale of real estate to Jews [G, P], 1670–1730; a decree issued by a parish priest and the *wojewoda* of Poznań to the Jews of Leszno, ordering payment for the construction of a clock and the townhall's tower [G], 1689; records concerning taxes and levies imposed on Jews [G, P], 17th–18th cent; a document by the owner of Leszno regulating Jewish trade in the town [G], 1701; an injunction against dealing in stolen goods [G], 1721; correspondence of Jewish merchants with the municipal authorities [G], 1722–1810; confirmation of charters granted to the Jews by King Stanisław Leszczyński, 1737; a claim by a Jew that his municipal rights were violated, 1742; a case concerning the rights of Jewish and non-Jewish musicians, based on an agreement from 1661[G], 1745; a merchant's correspondence register [G, H], 1755–61; relations between Jewish and non-Jewish traders [G, H], 1755–61; an appeal in litigation between two Jews [G], 1760; correspondence concerning Jews of Leszno [G], 1763–1837; correspondence with the owner of the town concerning a fire, files on collection of money for the needy, excerpts from municipal books describing the damages caused by the fire and a request for a reduction of taxes [G, L, P], 1767; Jewish imports, exports and trade in salt and textiles [G, P], 1773–83; a file on the investigation of a Jew [G], 1780; an agreement between the owner of the town and the inhabitants after a fire [G], 1790; a letter requesting the return of surplus tax payments [G], 1792; a list of Jewish furriers barred from commerce [G], 1793; a list of Jewish merchants [G], 1793; a file concerning a Jewish agent [G], 1793–99; a copy of the charter granted to the Jews in 1738, 1812.
(AP Poznań, Akta miast, woj. poznańskie)

2. A letter to the community of Mantua, Italy, requesting assistance after a fire [H], 1791.
(Archivio Della Communitá di Mantova)

LEŻAJSK (pow. Łańcut, woj. lwowskie) 1623–1939
Microfilms:
1. Confirmation by King Zygmunt III of an agreement between the community and the shoemakers' guild [L, P], 1623.
(AGAD, Warszawa, MK)
2. Confirmation by King Stanisław August Poniatowski of the charter granted to the Jews [L, P], 1765.
(AGAD, Warszawa, Księgi Kanclerskie)
3. An investigation of complaints by Jews of Leżajsk and the area against the rabbi [G] 1782; decisions by the authorities regarding lease of a tavern to 23 Jewish residents [G], 1787; military taxes [G], 1788; tables, minutes and taxes relating to *propinacja*, 1798–1805;
(AP Kraków, Teki Schneidra)
4. Correspondence with the authorities on *chadorim*, including a list of *melamdim*, 1874–1908.
(TsDIAU, L'viv, Namiestnictwo Galicyjskie)
5. Files on complaints against rabbis [G, P], 1913–19.
(TsDIAU, L'viv, Ministerium fuer Kultus und Unterricht, Wien)
6. Minutes of the *Hitachdut* society, including a list of members, 1930–32; reports and correspondence on the tax for *shechita*, 1931; correspondence, community budget and a list of tax payers [P, Y], 1931–35; examination of the local rabbi in the Polish language, 1938–39.
(DALO, L'viv, UW, Lwów)
7. Correspondence on registration of the *Mizrachi*, statutes and a list of board members, 1932.
(DALO, L'viv, Magistrat, Lwów)

LIDA (woj. nowogródzkie) 1904–1915
Originals:
A letter and a certificate given to the Lida *yeshiva* by Baron David Ginzburg following his visit [H, R], 1908. Photographs of the cemetery and the town during Worl War I, 1916.
Photocopies:
A Communist proclamation to the Jews of Lida and minutes of a meeting of Jewish Communists in Lida [R, Y], 1920.
(NARB, Minsk, Tsentral'nyi komitet…)
Microfilms:
1. Files on disorders and pogroms during mobilization of the reserves [R], 1904–06.
(GARF, Moscow, Departament politsii…)
2. Correspondence of the Association for the Attainment of Full Rights for the Jewish People in Russia with the local branch about elections to the *Duma* [R], 1906.
(RGIA, St. Petersburg, Obshchestvo polnopraviia…)
3. Decrees ordering Jews to purchase copper and gold coins and other raw materials [R], 1915.
(RGIVA Moscow, Shtab Dvinskogo voennogo okruga)

LIMANOWA (woj. krakowskie) 1874–1908
Microfilms:
1. Correspondence with the authorities regarding *chadorim*, including a list of *melamdim*, 1874–1908; correspondence between the community and the authorities regarding reorganization of the community, a

text of the statutes and a list of members from the neighbouring villages [G, P], 1876–82; correspondence with the authorities regarding elections of a rabbi, 1904–08.
(TsDIAU L'viv, Namiestnictwo Galicyjskie)
2. Proclamations, reports and correspondence concerning *chadorim* and private Jewish schools [G, P], 1878–81.
(TsDIAU L'viv, Krajowa Rada Szkolna)

LIPICA DOLNA (pow. Rohatyń, woj. stanisławowskie) 1893–1937
Microfilms:
Confirmation of statutes of the *Haskel Vadaas* and *Merkaz Ruchani* associations [G, P], 1893, 1920–30; registers of Jewish associations, 1930–37.
(DAIFO, Ivano-Frankivs'k, UW, Stanisławów)

LIPICA GÓRNA (pow. Rohatyń, woj. stanisławowskie) 1893–1938
Microfilms:
Confirmation of statutes of the *Haskel Vadaas* and *Merkaz Ruchani* associations [G, P], 1893, 1920–30; statutes, minutes and correspondence concerning Jewish associations in Lipica Górna, 1930–38.
(DAIFO, Ivano-Frankivs'k, UW, Stanisławów)

LIPNICA DOLNA (pow. Jasło, woj. krakowskie) 1878
Microfilms:
Reports and correspondence on the reorganization of elementary schools attended by Jewish pupils [G, P], 1878.
(TsDIAU, L'viv, Krajowa Rada Szkolna)

LIPNO (woj. warszawskie) 1856–1910
Microfilms:
1. Reports and correspondence on the appointment of rabbis, their education and salaries; a list of graduates of the Rabbinical Seminary and of the commission examining candidates for positions of rabbi and *dayan*, 1856–64; correspondence on the release from military service of Rabbinical Seminary graduates, 1865–71.
(AGAD, Warszawa, CWW)
2. Copies of inscriptions from tombstones and synagogues [H, R], 1910.
(RGIA St. Petersburg, Departament dukhovnykh del…)

LIPSK (pow. Baranowicze, woj. nowogrodzkie) 1786–1789
Photocopies:
Inventories of estates, 1786–89.
(NIAB, Minsk, Kollektsiia drevnikh inventarei)

LISIATYCZE (pow. Pińsk, woj. poleskie) 1906
Photocopies:
A report on an unauthorized *cheder* [R], 1906.
(NIAB, Minsk, Direktsiia narodnykh uchilishch…)

LUBACZÓW (woj. lwowskie) 1643–1937
Microfilms:
1. A letter by King Władysław IV to the Tsar Mikhail Fedorovich concerning a false denunciation of Jewish merchants from Poland [R], 1643.

(RGADA Moscow, Snoshenia Rossii s Pol'shei)

2. Circulars, accounts, inventories, decrees and *uniwersały* of M. Sapieha, St. Siemienski, M. and A. Sieniawski and A. Czartoryski concerning estates and inhabitants of Lubaczów [L, H, P], 1659–1757.

(Bibl. Czartoryskich, Kraków)

3. Files on debts and debt payments by the Jewish community [L, P], 1727–28.

(TsDIAU, L'viv, Kolektsiia dokumentiv…)

4. A request concerning construction of a house [G], 1786; lists of eligible voters and community members [G, P], 1861, 1870.

(AP Kraków, Teki Schneidra)

5. Correspondence about the *Agudas Achim* society and a text of the statutes, 1904.

(TsDIAU L'viv, Namiestnictwo Galicyjskie)

6. Correspondence on celebrations honoring the inauguration of the Hebrew University in Jerusalem, 1924–25; correspondence concerning the *Kultur Liga*, 1926; files concerning community elections, 1928–33; registers of local administrative personnel, their political affiliations and nationalities, 1930–31; files on the community budget and legal matters, including lists of community board members, rabbis and *dayanim*, 1932–1937.

(DALO, L'viv, UW, Lwów)

7. Correspondence concerning the registration of *Agudas Yisroel* and *Machzikei Hadas*, including lists of members, 1930–34.

(DALO, L'viv, Magistrat, Lwów)

LUBARTÓW (woj. lubelskie) 1545–1939
Originals:
Letters from the community to a former resident living in the United States [Y], 1921–39.
Microfilms:
1. Various local records (incl. material on the Jews): fragments of court records, inventories, property registers, etc. [L, P], 1545–1642, 1714–1827.

(AP Lublin, K. M. Lubartów)

2. Records of income from Lubartów *arendas,* 1720–59; accounts, 1730–1796; litigation between Jews and a non-Jew, 1762; documents concerning payment of community debts in exchange for income from the *krupka*, 1778, various documents concerning debts and other financial matters [H, L, P], 1778–89; receipt of a loan, 1789; judicial proceedings against the community, 1796–99; a letter to the community concerning *arendars*, 1797; decrees and judicial proceedings concerning *shechita* and the kosher meat tax [G, L, P], 1797–1820; a verdict in a conflict between the owner of the estates and the community over the *krupka*, 1815.

(AP Kraków, Arch. Sanguszków, teki tzw. arabskie)

3. A letter by a rabbi concerning the settlement of Jews' debts, 1766.

(AP Lublin, Księgi Grodzkie i Ziemskie Lubielskie)

4. A statistical description, 1841–59.

(AP Lublin, Rząd Gubernialny, Lublin)

5. Reports and correspondence of the authorities concerning the appointment of rabbis, their education and salaries, litigation between them and their communities, as well as a list of Rabbinical Seminary graduates and of the commission examining candidates for positions of rabbi and *dayan*, 1853–64.

(AGAD, Warszawa, CWW)

LUBIEL (pow. Pułtusk, woj. warszawskie) 1706–1785
Microfilms:
Registers, accounts, *uniwersały*, and decrees by the Czartoryski family concerning inhabitants of Lubiel [L, P], 1706–85.
(Biblioteka Narodowa, Warszawa)

LUBLIN (woj. lubelskie) 1518–1942
Originals:
Documents concerning property and loans [H, P], 1781, 1812–63; birth and death register (fragmentary), 1833–90; receipts and other documents concerning activities of Jews, 1898, 1903, 1926–38; a receipt of the *Tomchei Noflim* society [H], 1929; announcements of the rabbinate and the local kashrut commission [Y], 1934
Photocopies:
A letter from the community to a Court Jew at Aurich, asking for financial support [H], 1708–09;
Microfilms:
1. An order by King Zygmunt I restricting Jewish trade, 1518; a 19th cent. copy of his 1535 grant to a Jewish couple to settle in Lublin; confirmation by him of the city elders' right to try Christian and Jewish traders, 1541; a complaint of the burghers against the *starosta* and the Jews in charge of mills, 1576; an order by King Zygmunt III to Jewish and Christian traders to pay their dues to the municipality, 1596; an order by King Władysław IV to the municipality to settle debts owed a Jewish merchant, 1637; a decree by King Jan Sobieski forbidding Jews to trade on Sundays and Christian holidays and requiring them to remain within the walls of the city, 1679; the right of free trade granted to the Jews by Jan Sobieski, 1696; confirmation by King August III of the charter granted to a Jew to build a synagogue, 1736; a letter of protection granted to the Jews by King Stanisław August Poniatowski [L, P], 1781.
(AP Lublin, Dokumenty m. Lublina)
2. A charter by King Zygmunt I forbidding Jewish trade in Lublin and nominating a commission to investigate other controversial issues [L], 1521; letters concerning a request to expel a Jew from Lublin, 1535; confirmation by King Zygmunt August of the 1541 charter concerning courts for Jews and Christians and trade in beer and wax [L], 1552; minutes of the *wojewoda's* court for the Jews, 1613–1781; documents of the tailors' guild, 1615–1789; copy of a town council memorandum concerning Jews, 1701; a letter from King Jan Sobieski to the mayor, resolving a controversy between the merchants and the Jews, 1696; the case of a convert to Christianity murdered by Jews, 1699;
1700 's-
A memorandum of the municipality concerning relations between the burghers and the Jews, 1701; confirmation of Jewish charters, 1736; a decree concerning Jews from the suburbs of Wieniawa and Czechówka, 1741; records of disputes between the community, burghers and nearby towns [L], 1741–42; documents concerning the right of Jews to settle in Lublin and their relations with local merchants, 1741; legal documents concerning the expulsion of Jews [L], 1744; a promissory note given by Jews to a priest from Chodel, 1748; a decree limiting Jewish rights, 1759; proclamations of the municipality concerning the expulsion of Jews from the town, 1759–73; documents on litigation between the Jews and certain noblemen [L], 1761–81; a decree of King Stanisław August Poniatowski concerning the Jews, after 1764; a letter from the merchants' association of Poznań to the merchants' association in Lublin against the Jews, 1765; excerpts from a decree against the Jews [L], 1767; a proclamation by the citizens of Lublin calling for the expulsion of the Jews [L], 1773; a memorandum to the *starosta's* office reminding him of his duty to prevent Jews from trading in Lublin, 1774; the papers of a local merchant involved in a dispute with the

Jews, 1774–82; records of municipal income (incl. from the Jews), 1776; an extract from a municipal decree concerning the Jews, 1777; an agreement on payments due from Jews acquiring shops and houses from non-Jews, 1778; the transfer of Jewish debts from the Dominican monastery to the National Educational Fund, 1779;

a decree by King Stanisław August Poniatowski forbidding Jewish merchants to live and trade in Lublin, 1780; litigation between the community and the local merchants' association, 1780–95; documents on litigation between the municipality and the Jews, 1780; a memorandum of the municipality to the Police Department regarding the Jewish quarter, 1781; various guild decisions concerning expulsion of the Jews, 1781; disputes and agreements between the tailors' guild and Jewish tailors, 1781–96; files of the Police Department regarding agreements with the Jews, 1784; verdict of a tribunal in a dispute between municipality of Kraków and the Jews of Kazimierz, involving the Jews of Lublin as well, 1792; litigation between Christian coppersmiths and a Jew, 1792;

(Bibl. im. Łopacińskiego, Lublin)

3. Records of charters (fragmentary), 1531–1635; *lustracje* 1564–1660; records concerning taxes paid by Jews (fragmentary), 1618–1760; consular records (fragmentary), 1691–1793; municipal proclamations concerning Jewish rights [L, P], 1724–26.

(AP Lublin, Księgi Miejskie, Lublin)

4. Confirmation by King Stefan Batory of a charter to the shoemakers' guild, listing certain charters of the Jews, 1576; confirmation by King Stanisław August Poniatowski of charters granted to the Jews [L, P], 1765; royal nomination of a commission to solve a dispute between the community and inhabitants of the suburbs, 1774; letters of protection granted to individual Jews by King Stanisław August Poniatowski [L, P], 1775, 1792.

(AGAD, Warszawa, Księgi Kanclerskie)

5. A charter allowing the establishment of a new neighbourhood beside the Jewish quarter, 1604; a proclamation by King Władystaw IV permitting the Jews to build three gates to protect their quarter, 1634; details of rents paid to the *starosta,* 1738.

(AP Lublin, Księgi Grodzkie Lubelskie)

6. Records of Jewish taxes, 1626, 1668.

(AP Wrocław, Ossolineum)

7. Private agreements, accounts, contracts correspondence and documents concerning properties and businesses of the Sieniawski and Czartoryski families in Lublin, including files and registers of Jewish inhabitants and taxes paid by them, 1628–1759.

(Bibl. Czartoryskich, Kraków)

8. A verdict concerning Jewish disrespect of the Sunday rest, delays in the payment of taxes and evasion of the law [L], 1659.

(AP Przemyśl, Akta m. Przemyśla)

9. Two charters granted to the Jews by the *starosta* [L, P], 1675, 1686.

(AP Lublin, Księgi Grodzkie Krasnostawskie)

10. A letter by A. Lubomirski concerning debts of Jews from Lublin, 1713; a court case between a Jew and a nobleman [L, P], 1759–62; a verdict in litigation between a nobleman and a Jew, 1784; files on legal proceedings concerning debts [L, P], 1790–91.

(AP Kraków, Arch. Sanguszków, teki tzw. arabskie)

11. A complaint sent by a Jew to the municipality, 1756.

(AP Kraków, IT)

12. Requests by the *kahal* and synagogues to delay repayment of a debt, 1781, and to arrange installments for the payment of debts, 1794.
(RGADA, Moscow, KFE)

13. A register of inhabitants and taxes, 18th cent.
(AP Lublin, Advocatalia)

14. A file on a dispute concerning the lease of a mill, 1812.
(AGAD, Warszawa, RSiRMKW)

15. Registers of seats in the women's section of the Great Synagogue [H], 1815–1930; the "new *pinkas"* – a register of seats in the "upper" synagogue [H], 1823–1910; *pinkas* of the Saul Wahl synagogue [H], 1866–68; divorce registers [P, R, H], 1866–76, 1910–42; a register of seats in the new synagogue [H], 19th cent.; copies of verdicts concerning name changes among Jews, 1911–14; various documents of the rabbinate [H, Y], 1914–17; correspondence of Rabbi Meir Shapira [H, P, Y], 1919–34; flyers and receipts from various religious institutions in Jerusalem [E, Y], 1920s–1930s; minutes of the community board, 1923; communal correspondence [P, Y], 1923–35; a proposal for an institution to care for orphans and the elderly, 1928; congratulatory telegrams honoring the cornerstone laying of *Yeshivas Chachmei Lublin* [H, P, Y], 1924; press clippings relating to the *yeshiva* and Rabbi Shapira [E, G, H, P, Y], 1926–27, 1929–34; a visitors' book of the *yeshiva* [H, P, Y], 1932–37; a register of candidates to the *yeshiva* [H, P], 1934–36; a register of donations to the *yeshiva* and a plan of the *daf hayomi* of the *Talmud* [H], 1935–38; a correspondence register of the *yeshiva* [H, P], 1936; a proclamation of the Judenrat concerning sanitary conditions in the ghetto, 1941.
(AP Lublin, Gmina Żydowska, Lublin)

16. Files on the Jewish community and correspondence with the government commission for religious affairs, 1822–43; minutes, complaints and other materials concerning burial societies, 1822–50; a project to distribute kosher food to poor Jews and to support Jewish hospital patients [P, R], 1848–56; reports and government correspondence on the appointments of rabbis and disputes between them and their communities, as well as a list of rabbis, 1853–56; correspondence on exemption from army service of Rabbinical Seminary graduates, 1865–71.
(AGAD, Warszawa, CWW)

17. Files on community financial matters, including accounts of the community, 1830–36.
(AGAD, Warszawa, Akta m. Przemyśla)

18. Files on awards for Jews who rendered service to the city, 1845–49; files on a shelter for needy Jews, 1862–66; correspondence on the establishment of evening courses for adult Jews [R], 1867; correspondence on rabbis derelict in their duties towards Jews hospitalized in the military hospital [R], 1867; correspondence on conversion of a Jewess to Christianity [R], 1867; correspondence on the decision not to register Jewish marriages in the civil register [R], 1869–70; a request of a grant for the rabbi [R], 1870–71; correspondence concerning collection of taxes for community expenses; files on flour for *matzot* [R], 1871; an application by a graduate of the Rabbinical Seminary in Zhitomir to the rabbinate in Lublin [R], 1872–73; files on establishment of a special committee to supervise a synagogue and the cemetery [R], 1872–73.
(AP Lublin, Rząd Gubernialny, Lublin)

19. A request by a Jew for the refund of illegally exacted taxes [R], 1858.
(AGAD, Warszawa, SSKP)

20. A file on the special prayer for the reigning Tsar and his family to be recited in synagogues, as well as a translation of the prayer [R], 1868; correspondence concerning a complaint by a Jew following his exclusion from the community, and denunciations of community members for misappropriations and

political unreliability [R], 1869–70; files on the prohibition of Jewish traditional dress [R], 1871; a complaint by the director of a Jewish school aginst a teacher of the Hebrew language for speaking out against instruction in Russian [R], 1875; secret correspondence concerning the prevention of pogroms and violation of public order [R], 1881; correspondence about violent encounters between Christians and Jews [R], 1881; files on the arrest of a Prussian citizen for inciting peasants to conduct pogroms [R], 1881–82; files on the decision to open a private Jewish school for girls, 1885.

(AP Lublin, Kancelaria Gubernatora Lubelskiego)

21. A permit for the *Yeshivas Chachmei Lublin* association to solicit funds throughout Poland, 1933–38.

(DALO, L'viv, UW, Lwów)

LUBLIN, surroundings, 1595–1915
Microfilms:
1. Records and accounts of various *arendas* granted by the Orzechowski family, 1595–1756.
(Bibl. im. Łopacińskiego, Lublin)
2. *Arenda* contract, 1708.
(AP Kraków, Arch. Podhoreckie Potockich)
3. The allocation to the army of taxes paid by Jews, 1716.
(AP Lublin, Księgi Grodzkie Chełmskie)
4. *Lustracja* of the *województwo*, 1764.
(AGAD, Warszawa, ASK)
5. A list of Jewish debts to be liquidated by the Crown Treasury Commission, 1765; a letter on how to collect taxes for payment of Jewish debts in the *województwo* of Lublin, 1766; a register of Jewish houses in the *województwo* for taxation purposes, 1789.
(AP Lublin, Księgi Grodzkie i Ziemskie Lubielskie)
6. An order of the Civil and Military Commmission concerning the registration of Jews for tax purposes, 1790.
(AP Lublin, Księgi Miejskie, Modliborzyce)
7. Records concerning the settlement of Jews on the Tarnówka estates, 1791.
(AP Lublin, Księgi Grodzkie Chełmskie)
8. Files on synagogues in various towns of the *guberniia*, 1818–60; reports and correspondence of the authorities concerning confirmation of rabbinical appointments, qualification exams in rabbinical schools, fee exemptions, examinations and lists of rabbis, *dayanim* and their deputies, 1823–53; files on payment of a fee for kosher slaughtering and the appointment of someone responsible for distributing food to the poor [P, R], 1848–56; files on corruption in the Lublin *guberniia* [P, R], 1848–56.
(AGAD, Warszawa, CWW)
9. Files on *propinacja* and on acquisition and lease of landed properties by Jews, 1842–64; files on the abolishment of the *kahal*, 1843–44; files on the conversion of Jews to Christianity, 1844–66; files on the establishiment and reorganization of communities, 1845–66; files concerning prohibition of traditional Jewish dress [P, Y], 1846–54; a file on a diversion of the Bystrzyca river, which hindered the operation of a flour mill, 1846–61; files on establishment of community districts and their functioning, registration of rabbis, rabbinical candidates and a list of community districts, 1848–67; files on the expulsion of Jews suspected of fraud, 1852–55; files on the printing, distribution and censorship of Jewish books, 1855–66; files on rabbinical candidates and elections in towns of the *guberniia*, 1858–61; a statistical description of towns in the *powiat*, 1861; files on abolishment of restrictions on land acquisition by Jews, 1862–63; files on rabbis in the *guberniia*, 1864–65; reports of *powiat* authorities on the exemption from conscription of

rabbinical candidates and rabbis, lists and minutes on elections of rabbis and complaints against rabbis [R], 1867–72; correspondence about the introduction of rabbinical registers, and circulars concerning introduction of civil registers [R], 1869–71; correspondence about the setting of uniform prices for burial services in the *guberniia* [R], 1878–82; files on the proposal to incorporate neighboring villages into the Lublin community [R], 1891.
(AP Lublin, Rząd Gubernialny, Lublin)
10. Statistical data on synagogues and rabbis in towns of the *guberniia*, 1908.
(RGIA, St. Petersburg, Departament dukhovnykh del...)
11. Files on persecution of Jews in military zones [R], 1914–15.
(GARF, Moscow, Katsenel'son)

LUBOML (woj. wołyńskie) 1704
Microfilms:
Various accounts, 1704.
(TsDIAU, Arch. Lubomirskich)

LUBRANIEC (pow. Włocławek, woj. warszawskie) 1784–1795
Microfilms:
1. Records of the city board, relating to Jews, 1784–95.
(AGAD, Warszawa, Arch. Radziwiłłów)
2. Confirmation by King Stanisław August Poniatowski of the charter granted to the Jews [L, P], 1792.
(AGAD, Warszawa, DPP)

LUBSZA (pow. Rohatyn, woj. stanisławowskie) 1936
Microfilms:
Monographs containing demographic and economical data, 1936.
(AP Wrocław, Ossolineum, WKNZNP, Lwów)

LUBYCZA KRÓLEWSKA (pow. Rawa Ruska, woj. lwowskie) 1769–1935
Microfilms:
1. A partial inventory, 1769
(AP Wrocław, Ossolineum)
2. Correspondence about the community budget, 1933–35.
(DALO, L'viv, UW, Lwów)

LUCZYN (pow. Zdołbunów, woj. wołyńskie) 1882
Microfilms:
A letter from the governor concerning an assault on a Jewish innkeeper [R], 1882.
(TsDIAU, Kyiv, Kantseliariia... general-gubernatora)

LUDWINÓW (pow. Bielsk, woj. białostockie) 1807–1809
Microfilms:
Personal documents and letters of protection for Jews, 1807–09.
(AP Białystok, Rząd Gubernialny, Łomża)

LUDWIPOL (pow. Kostopol, woj. wołyńskie) 1913–1914
Microfilms:
Files on Jewish associations and cooperatives, including lists of members and administrators [R], 1913–14.

(TsDIAU, Kyiv, Podol'skoe gubernskoe zhandarmskoe pravlenie)

LUTOMIERSK (pow. Łask, woj. łódzkie) 1821–1913
Drawing of a wooden synagouge, n.d.
(IKG Wien - Juedisches Museum)
Microfilms:
1. Community records and accounts; support for the Jewish poor at Passover time, 1821–66.
(AP Łódź, Anterioria Rządu Gubernialnego, Piotrków)
2. Fines for evading conscription [R], 1894–1901.
(AP Łódź, Rząd Gubernialny, WP, Piotrków)
3. Ratification of community elections and accounts [R], 1902–13.
(AP Łódź, Rząd Gubernialny, WA, Piotrków)

LUTOWISKA (pow. Lesko, woj. lwowskie) 1846–1936
Microfilms:
1. Confirmation of the community statutes and correspondence on the election of a rabbi, 1846–96.
(TsDIAU, L'viv, Namiestnictwo Galicyjskie)
2. Minutes and correspondence on changes in the statutes and raising communal taxes, 1921–24; correspondence regarding registration of the Shalom Aleichem Drama Club, text of the statutes and a list of members, 1929–35; correspondence about community matters, the community budget and lists of taxpayers, [P, Y], 1931–36; a file on an examination in the Polish language for a rabbinical candidate and on the election of a rabbi, 1932–36.
(DALO, L'viv, UW, Lwów)

LUTUTÓW (pow. Wieluń, woj. łódzkie) 1910–1914
Microfilms:
1. Copies of inscriptions on tombstones and synagogues [H, P, R], 1910.
(RGIA, St. Petersburg, Department Religious Affaires of Foreign Religions)
2. Proceedings concerning the illegal destruction of guild certificates [R], 1913–14.
(AP Łódź, Rząd Gubernialny, WA, Kalisz)

LWÓW (woj. lwowskie) 1425–1948
Originals:
Documents concerning various aspects of Jewish communal life [H], 1616–1724; a royal decree regulating litigation between the municipality and Jewish communities [L], 1732; a deed of sale of a synagogue seat [H], 1784; a proposal of new community regulations, made by Galician *chasidim* [H], 1854; statutes of the *Chesed ve Emes* society [G], 1871; records of charitable associations [G], 1878–85; the minutes and decisions of an assembly of Orthodox rabbis opposed to the Reform movement, 1870s; statutes and reports of various burial societies [H, Y], 1886, 1894–95; an announcement by the Jewish theater in Lwów of a play by J. L. Landau, '*Herodes der Große*' [G], 1890; a file on organizing a library [G], 1898–1901; a report on the activity of the community board [G], 1898–1904; a publication by Jacob Caro in honor of Emperor Franz Josef's golden jubilee [H], 1898; a poster announcing the death of Salomon Buber, 1906; manifest of the Jewish Conservative Election Committee [Y], before 1914; records on assistance for the victims of the pogrom [H, P, Y], 1918–19; various publications about the pogrom in Lwów [G, P], 1918–19; statutes of a Jewish women's association 1925; a *chasidic* manifest against immodest dress among women in synagogues, 1920s.

Photocopies and Photographs:

1. A court decree, confirmed by King Zygmunt III, regulating relations between Jewish and non-Jewish merchants (1521, 1538, 1540), 1591; a court decision in litigation between a Jewish and a non-Jewish merchant, 1635.

(AGAD, Warszawa, DP)

2. A letter by I. Löwel, the community's advocate, to King August II [G], 1728; photographs from the pogrom in Lwów, 1919; a police document concernig the *Ognisko* organization, 1910.

3. Register of donations, sale and acquisition of real estate in Lwów [G, L, P], 1787–91.

(DALO, L'viv, Magistrat, Lwów)

4. Registration and statutes of the Zionist Organization in Lwów, 1927–38.

(DALO, L'viv, Lwowskie Starostwo Miejskie)

5. Information and minutes of JEAS (Polish version of HIAS) on emigration to Argentina and Canada [P, Y], 1929, 1937, 1939.

(TsDIAU, L'viv, Żydowskie Centralne Towarzystwo Emigracyjne – JEAS)

6. Register of Jewish merchants, businessmen and homeowners [R], 1939; investigation files from the years 1941–44 [R], 1944; report about Jewish religious communities [R], 1947; a list of Communist Party members, including social status and nationality [R], 1947–48.

(DALO, L'viv, L'vovskii obkom…)

7. Reports on "Jewish" *actions*, a list of Ukrainian policemen and letters to the authorities [G], 1942.

(DALO, L'viv, Prezydium Dyrekcji Policji, Lwów)

Microfilms:

1. Lwów Jewish community files, 1787–1939

Community Board Activities: Correspondence regarding inheritances and foundations [G, P], 1798–1903; statutes, community civil registrations, reports on activities of the community board, taxes, reports on the budget [G, P], 1833–1930; correspondence with the magistrate regarding elections to the communtiy council, including lists of voters, minutes, posters, names of elected community board members [G], 1877–1907; reports on the activity of the community council by Wiktor Chajes, 1927;

Institutions and religious functionaries: Minutes and correspondence regarding: conscription [G], 1793–97, community schools and the Abraham Kohn school for boys and girls [G, P], 1793–1921, synagogues [G, P], 1807–1913, the hospital [G, P], 1809–1914, the abbattoir [G], 1813, rabbis [G, P], 1827–1939, the Temple, 1898–1903, programs for religious instructions in public schools, Jewish religion teachers in public schools, the seminar for teachers of the Jewish religion and training programs [G, P], 1901–11, the orphanage, 1902–07, a society of women to help the orphanage, 1902–05, societies to help sick and poor students, 1902–07, burial matters, 1902–38, *mohalim*, 1905, *chadorim*, 1906–11, foundation of a Theological Institute, 1907, the community library, including lists of books, 1907–18;

Name lists and Statistical data: Lists of tax payers, citing professions [G, P], 1787–1870; statistical data [G], 1845;

Varia: Correspondence regarding requests for marriage licences [G], 1797–1844; correspondence regarding permits to settle ouside the Jewish neigbourhoods, lighting the Jewish neighbourhoods, permits to use public parks and protests against restriction of Jewish civil rights [G], 1797–1863, orders and instructions [G], 1803–38; correspondence of the *Shomer Yisroel* society regarding the 1873 elections to the Parliament [P, U, G]; 1873–74, correspondence regarding the conversion of a young female, 1896; correspondence regarding the publication of Salomon Buber's memoirs, 1904; minutes of a conference of communities with the Minister of Education [G, P], 1927;

(TsDIAU, L'viv, Juedische Gemeinde Lwów)
2. A charter by King Władysław II to a Jew regarding the foundation of a new village [L], 1425; decrees by King Zygmunt I restricting commerce by the Jews [L], 1521–27; a decree by King Władysław IV confirming an *arenda* contract between the municipality and a Jew, 1633; a decree of King Jan Kazimierz that all inhabitants of Lwów are to enjoy all rights and charters irrespective of nationality, 1661; a decree by King Michał Korybut Wiśniowiecki concerning anti-Jewish riots [L], 1670.
(TsDIAU, L'viv, DP)
3. Excerpts from books of the Castle Court in Lwów, 1440–1500.
(TsDIAU, L'viv, Sąd Grodzki, Lwów)
4. Charters and decrees by the municipality concerning the Jews [L], 1488–1658; receipts confirming payments of debts to Jews, 1710, 1731; contracts between the Armenian community and Jews on the rental and sale of apartments around the Armenian church, 1716–20; a register of Jewish debts to the Trinitarian order, 1749–53.
(NBANU, L'viv)
5. Decrees and charters granted to the Jews of Lwów, 1521–91; municipal records (fragments concerning Jews), 1628–1724; a letter to the local Jesuit order after anti-Jewish riots, 1641; *lustracje* of the town's inhabitants, 1661–62, 1765; records of local finances, 1780; confirmation by King Stanisław August Poniatowski of the merchant guild's statutes, 1767.
(AP Wrocław, Ossolineum)
6. Charters and decrees of the municipality concerning the Jews [L], 1521–91; anti-Jewish pamphlets, 1539, 17th cent.; registers, accounts, *universały*, decrees and contracts of the Sieniawski–Czartoryski family concerning their properties in Lwów [F, L, P], 1706–85; a decree concerning accounts from the markets, 1789; correspondence of Hugo Kołłątaj, end 18th cent. – begining 19th cent.
(Biblioteka Narodowa, Warszawa)
7. A letter by King Zygmunt II August to the municipality, requesting assignment of a plot to a Jewish merchant, 1571; a letter by King Stefan Batory regarding real estate [L], 1577; a letter by the municipality to the town delegates to the *Sejm* concerning laws on commerce and leasing, 1577; letters by royal officials concerning administration of a Jew's inheritance and agreements with Jews, 1584–94.
1600's:
A letter by King Zygmunt III concerning contracts with Jewish merchants, 1600; a letter concerning an agreement between the Jesuit order and the Jews for the acquisition of a plot to construct a church and monastery, 1600–07; a letter by King Zygmunt III to the municipality concerning agreements between Jesuits and Jews, 1606–07; letters by the royal chancellor to the municipality and the Carmelite order requiring them to sign an agreement with the Jewish merchants, 1620–34; a letter by King Władysław IV to the municipality concerning a complaint by the Jews on restrictions of commerce, 1637; letters concerning a dispute between the municipality and the Jews, 1637–42; letters by K. Wiśniowiecki, *wojewoda ruski* to the municipal council, reminding them that the Jews are under the *starosta*'s jurisdiction, 1638; a letter by King Jan Kazimierz regarding the return of confiscated objects, 1648; letters about anti-Jewish riots in Lwów, 1655–88; a letter by the municipality of Poznań to the municipality of Lwów, regarding misappropriation by a Jewish *arendar* of income from royal customs, 1690; a letter concerning a dispute between a merchant from Gdańsk and a Jewish merchant from Lwów, 1696; a letter by King August II to the municipality requesting cessation of disputes with Jewish merchants, 1699;
1700's:
Letters by *wojewoda,* S. Poniatowski about anti-Jewish riots caused by students, 1732–33; letters by *wojewoda,* A. Czartoryski to the municipality requesting measures against anti-Jewish riots, 1733–73; a

letter by *hetman*, J. Potocki about the entry of Jewish merchants to deliver fabric for his soldiers, 1734; letters of chancellor, Załuski requesting the settling of a dispute between noblemen, clergy and Jewish merchants, 1736–45; a letter from the Lublin municipality to the Lwów municipality concerning taxes collected from the butchers' guild in Lwów, 1738; letters about a dispute between the city and the Jews, 1752–59; a letter to the mayor of Lwów, requesting delay of a verdict concerning a Jew, 1757; a letter from the municipality of Lublin to the municipality of Lwów regarding rights and duties of Jewish merchants from Lwów, 1759; a letter of priest, S. Mikulski about conversion of Jews (Frankists) to Catholicism, 1759. (TsDIAU, L'viv, Kolektsiia lystiv…)

8. Confirmation by King Henryk Walezy (Henri de Valois) of an agreement with the Jews concerning local *arendas* [L, P], 1574; confirmation by King Zygmunt III of an agreement between the senate and inhabitants of Lwów (incl. the delineation of the Jewish quarter), 1604; confirmation by King Jan Kazimierz of the furriers' guild statutes barring Jewish membership in the guild, 1662; confirmation by King Stanisław August Poniatowski of the charter granted to the Jews [L, P], 1765.
(AGAD, Warszawa, Księgi Kanclerskie)

9. Decrees of the Assessor's court in two suits between burghers and Jews concerning trading rights [L, P], 1591–1635.
(AGAD, Warszawa, DP)

10. Private agreements, accounts, files on import of merchandise and contracts concerning properties and interests of the Sieniawski and Czartoryski families [H, L, P], 1628–1765; register of inhabitants and taxes paid by them, 1705–08.
(Bibl. Czartoryskich, Kraków)

11. Description of Chmielnicki's siege of Lwów, and of the city's refusal to deliver the Jewish inhabitants to him, 1648; an agreement between a Jew and an Armenian and an *arenda* contract [L, P], 1688, 1754; Jewish oaths – excerpts from the files of the *kahal* [L], 18th cent., a verdict of the Armenian court forbidding the rental of apartments to Jews, 1700; a receipt for goods received, 1732.
(NBANU, L'viv, Arch. Ossolińskich)

12. An agreement between the *kahal* and the municipality concerning commerce in the town, 1654; information about a deceased Jew from Palestine, 17th cent.; loans by the Jesuit order to the *kahal*, 1688–1728; a receipt issued by the *kahal* of Lwów, 1714; excerpts from municipal records [L], 1759. (TsDIAU, L'viv, Magistrat, Lwów)

13. Charters, requests, *arenda* contracts and a register of *krupka* payments [G, H, L, P, Y], 1659–1805.
(AP Lublin, Zb. Czołowskiego)

14. A letter by W. K. Koc concerning anti-Jewish riots in Lwów, 1664.
(Oesterr. National Bibliothek, Wien)

15. *Chadorim:* A register of *chadorim*, 1701; reports, correspondence and instructions regarding the closing of *chadorim,* including lists of them and of the melamdim [G, P], 1868–77; a list of *chadorim* and a circular by the community board regarding holidays for Jewish pupils in the elementary and secondary schools, 1913–14;

Jewish schools: Material on the organization of Jewish schools, including lists of schools and teachers [G, P], 1855–1900; instructions, reports and correspondence regarding the Jewish "main" school in Lwów, including a list of teachers [G, P], 1872–73; a report following the inspection of Jewish schools [G, P], 1872–73; correspondence with the Jewish community about Jewish schools in Lwów, 1874; reports and correspondence on the activity of the Jewish schools, including lists of teachers [G, P], 1876–83; a report on the activity of the Bernstein vocational school, 1886–90; reports concerning the organization and activities of elementary schools with Hebrew as the language of instruction, 1890; minutes of the Baron

Hirsch Foundation (JCA) executive committee, vol. I, 1892; material on the establishment of a shelter for poor girls adjacent to the Jewish girl's school, 1899; material on the activities of Jewish schools for girls and boys, including a list of teachers [G, P], 1903–06; a file on a model text for teaching Hebrew [P, H], 1907–20; a list of parents whose children did not attend the A. Kohn Jewish boys' school, 1910.; material on a textbook for teaching Bible, by Dr. D. Rosenman, 1919–20;

General schools: Statistical data concerning Jewish pupils in Polish schools [G, P], 1855–96; material on competition for the post of Hebrew and religion teacher in the Czacki school [G, P], 1876–83; an order against spreading socialist ideas in high schools and correspondence with high schools in Lwów about the distribution of socialist periodicals among Jewish youth, 1880; a list of Jewish pupils attending the Evangelical school during the years 1882–85; material on the Staszic school for girls, 1885–1920; a report on the participation of Jewish secondary schools students in the *Kółko Społeczne* Association, 1903; a statistical report and lists of students at commercial schools [G, P], 1915–20;

Teacher's Seminary: proposed statutes for a Seminary to train teachers of Jewish religion in non-Jewish schools, 1882; correspondence about establishing the Seminary, 1885; additional correspondence on establishing the Seminary, statutes, a list of teachers and students, papers by graduates and disciplinary statutes for employees of the Jewish community [G, P], 1902–03; proposed statutes and proposals for reorganization of the Seminary [G, P], 1910–14.

(TsDIAU, L'viv, Krajowa Rada Szkolna)

16. Two letters to Jan Szembek, defending and attacking the Jews of Lwów, 1714, 1718.

(AP Kraków, Zb. Czartoryskich)

17. A circular issued by Prince Czartoryski concerning the Jews, 1749.

(AP Kraków, Arch. Podhoreckie Andrzeja Potockiego)

18. A verdict regarding a suit of the *kahal* against the Bazilian monastery [L], 1770.

(NBANU, L'viv, Klasztor Bazylianów)

19. Economics and finances: Correspondence with the authorities concerning the Jewish quarter and Jewish residence in non-Jewish areas, including a register of Jewish property (1608–36) and lists of Jewish inhabitants (1796, 1817–20) [G, P, L], 1783–1846; correspondence with the regional authorities concerning *arenda* contracts and a list of leaseholders [G, L, P], 1784–86; correspondence concerning *arenda*, mainly of the Dembowski family [G, L, P], 1806–08; correspondence concerning apartments of Jews, foundations and incomes from synagogues [G, L], 1807–16; correspondence concerning the *krupka* [G], 1819–41; correspondence on fundraising for the Jews in Palestine [G, H], 1836–38; correspondence on the use of fines paid by Jews for the creation of a fund to assist needy Jews [G], 1844–59; an order to execute the will of a Jewish merchant from Odessa for the benefit of the Jewish community of Lwów [G], 1847;

Criminal matters: Investigation of a bribe suspicion [G], 1793; correspondence with the municipality on sending Jewish prisoners to work on Jewish holidays [G], 1797; material on smuggling and a list of those involved [G], 1802; the investigation file of a Jew, S. Schorr [G], 1804; the investigation file of a Jew accused of bribery in order to avoid military service [G], 1828–32; correspondence with the municipality regarding permission to serve kosher meals to Jewish prisoners [G, P], 1896;

Censorship: correspondence with the censor on the confiscation of *chasidic* books, including letters by Joseph Perl [G, L], 1814–38; a pronouncement of the court regarding the "negative" influence of the *Choshen Mishpat* [G, L] 1823; correspondence on Jewish bookshops and the distribution of forbidden books [G], 1834; appointments and reports of censors, including the text of a work by Rabbi Zvi Hirsch Chajes on oral law [G, H], 1836–46;

Societies: Correspondence and/or statutes of the following societies and associations: *Helvuyas Homes– Agidas Kodesz (Halvayas Hames–Agudas Kodesh)* [G, P], 1864–1913; *Sheeris Yehuda* [G, P], 1866; the

Jewish orphanage, including a list of women active in it, 1868–69; *Kimcha Depischa* [G, P], 1872–1912; *Shomrei Shabbos* [G, P], 1872–1914; *Zovchei Tzedek,* butchers' association [G, P], 1876–1911; *Machzikei Hadas* [G, P], 1878–1908; *Ahavas Chesed shel Emes* [G, P], 1878–1914; *Tzeirim Ktanim* [G, P], 1884; *Lomdei Mishnayos Vatikim* [G, P], 1890–1910; the *Commis–Unterstuetzung* merchants' society [G, P], 1890–1912; *Agudas Morem* [G, P], 1891–1909; *Michyah* 1893; a kosher slaughter–house, 1894–97; *Agudas Achim* [G, P], 1895–1913; *Mechasei Gagos,* 1896; the *Siła* workers organization [G], 1901; a tailors' society [G, P, Y], 1901–06; a women's society to support poor school children, 1903–04; *Zion,* 1903–1910; *Cherut,* 1904–11; *Poalei Zion,* 1904–14; *Shira Chadasha,* 1905–11; *Tchiyas Zion* [G, P], 1906; *Safa Berura,* 1906–13; *Agudas Huraw Yisacher Yehuda,* 1907; a library society, 1907–13; *Juedischer Artisten Abraham Goldfaden* [G, P], 1908; *Agides Chaim* [G, P], 1908–10; *Israelitischer Heirats–Stipendium–Verein* [G, P], 1908–11;

General; Correspondence on limiting bestowal of the title *morenu,* including a letter by Herz Homberg [G], 1793; correspondence with regional authorities concerning synagogues and *minyanim* [G], 1819–41; propositions to the Austrian authorities by Rabbi Abraham Kohn and other community representatives on improving the situation of the Jews and the rabbinate [G], 1847; correspondence between the authorities and district rabbis regarding religious instruction [G], 1849–61; a report by the municipality to the Austrian authorities about the excessive number of Jews in Lwów [G], 1859; correspondence with the municipality and Ministry of Religion about community statutes, including letters of protest [G, P], 1869–97; correspondence on abolishing the prohibition to accept Jews to the public hospital and on the right of the Jewish hospital to receive the belongings of patients who died there, 1873; correspondence with the municipality and the Ministry of Religion about *chadorim,* including a list of *melamdim* [G, P], 1874–1908; correspondence on the establishment of a Jewish Theological Institute, including letters from communities and rabbis, objecting to it [G], 1908–09;

(TsDIAU, L'viv, Namiestnictwo Galicyjskie)

20. Relations with the authorities: Orders prohibiting public meetings by Jews [G], 1793–1818; correspondence on foreign Jews entering East Galicia [G, P], 1801; correspondence concerning Jewish dress and abolishing the use of Hebrew and Yiddish in all public correspondence [G, P], 1811–14; government instructions on the conditions under which Jews may study in Vienna and a prohibition to summon Jews to court on Jewish holidays [G, L], 1818; correspondence on permission for Jews to dwell and trade in non-Jewish quarters of the city [G], 1818–19, 1852–91; government edicts holding the heads of the community responsible for contraband merchandise found in the synagogue, and forbidding Jewish leaseholders from using the Imperial emblems [G], 1823–27; prohibitions of Jewish celebrations during Lent, and of the adoption of non-Jewish children by Jews [G], 1824–28; correspondence regarding the passage of responsibility for Jewish affairs from the government administration to the municipality [G], 1826–28; correspondence concerning illegal marriages and adoptions [G] 1830–44; correspondence between the governor's office and the community concerning registration of all the Jews belonging to the community and expulsion of the others [G], 1838–39; correspondence between the district authorities and the police concerning the boundaries of the Jewish quarter [G, P], 1842–61; correspondence, minutes and protests concerning registration of Jews and their rights as inhabitants of the town [G], 1845–59; correspondence with the Jewish community concerning permission for Jews from Brody to stay in Lwów [G], 1848; correspondence with the police and the district authorities concerning Christian employees in Jewish households and young Jews converting to Christianity [G, P], 1852–54; correspondence with the authorities regarding permission for community members to emigrate to Saxony and London [G, P], 1861; correspondence regarding complaints by Jews of violations of their political rights during elections and about declaring Hebrew as a mother tongue, 1911; correspondence on investigations of citizenship in

conjunction with conscription to the army [G, P], 1916–18; correspondence about relocation to Lwów of Jews from various towns in Austria, 1918–20;

Welfare and health: Correspondence on the hospital of the Jewish community, a prohibition for Jews to be employed as pharmacists and the activity of the Jewish orphanage [G, P] 1829–75; correspondence on collecting funds to acquire kosher food for soldiers, prisoners and the poor [G, H], 1850–63; correspondence with the authorities concerning a fund to support poor Jewish girls [G, P], 1862–66; reports on the acquisition of shoes for poor Jewish pupils and assistance for needy Jews during Passover [G], 1866–67; correspondence on dowries for poor Jewish girls, financed by the I. Lewkowicz foundation, 1869–77; a financial report on the distribution of funds among an orphanage, a *Talmud–Tora* and needy Jews, 1871; correspondence with the governorship and the community about a subvention for the Jewish orphanage and about community accounts (1880) [G, P], 1874–84; minutes on the activities of charitable societies and on private matters, statutes of associations and *minyanim* [G, P], 1881–88; a file on private foundations supporting the needy and on the prohibition to teach Hebrew without the necessary qualifications, 1882–86; minutes, reports and correspondence concerning the I. Libhaber foundation for poor Jews [G, H, P], 1885–87; proceedings of the *Pierwsze Izraelickie Stowarzyszenie Pań we Lwowie* for providing free meals to poor students, including a list of members, 1885–98; reports and correspondence concerning summer camps for poor children, 1888–90; financial reports of the *Fundusz Wyżywienia Uczniów Izraelickich* (Fund for Support Jewish Students) and a list of *chadorim*, 1894–96; a financial report of the Jewish orphanage and day-nursery for children [G, P], 1896; a list of practicing physicians, 1897–99; instructions for pharmacists on the acceptance of apprentices and a list of dental technicians and obstetricians, 1905–09; a list of Jewish midwives, 1925–26; statutes of charitable associations and foundations, 1929;

Economics and finances: A case of non-payment of community taxes [G], 1843–45; a list of community real estate and correspondence on registering houses belonging to Jews [G, P], 1843–51; a letter by a Jewish merchant concerning his donation to the police and a request for permission to trade in uniforms and mead [G], 1846; correspondence with the district authorities concerning the prohibition of commerce on Sunday and during prayers in churches [G], 1852; correspondence on payment for plots in the Jewish cemetery [G], 1858–61; a Jew's request to reduce the tax on his house, 1858–60; correspondence on income from community real estate [G], 1861; files on litigation between the municipality and Jews concerning *propinacja* and *arenda* of inns in the suburbs [G, P], 1864–75; correspondence on the prohibition of begging and Jewish trade in Christian religious artifacts, 1882; correspondence with the community board concerning taxes [G, P], 1887–88, 1900–02; a list of potential tavern keepers, 1905–06; a list of real estate owners, 1912–14; a complaint by members of the Jewish community against the community board over the amount of the religious tax, 1920–23; an appraisal of the Jewish community's expenses, 1929; correspondence on the reduction of taxes and a list of Jews from Sambor possessing real estate in Lwów, 1929–31;

Community administration: Correspondence on the admission of new members [G], 1849–62; correspondence on assistance for the rabbi's widow and for an employee of the Jewish school [G], 1850–69; minutes and correspondence with the governor of Galicia about elections to the community board and complaints by community members, including statutes for the Orthodox community and a list of community board members [G, P], 1872–89; a file on the election of a rabbi and an election list [G, P, Y], 1875; reports and correspondence concerning administrative changes and community statutes, as well as statutes of synagogues [G, P], 1875–83, 1906–10; a report on ritual institutions of the Jewish community [G, P], 1878–80; reports on the activity of the Jewish community [G, P], 1900–08;

Education: Correspondence on the establishment of a Jewish vocational school and a fund to support poor Jews [G, P], 1861–62; correspondence with the municipality on the allocation of firewood for teachers of Jewish schools, including a list of teachers, 1871–79; reports and correspondence on the registration of Jewish associations and *chadorim*, as well as a list of *chadorim,* pupils and religion teachers [G, H, P], 1874–84; reports and correspondence on decrees permitting the running of religious schools, on salaries of rabbis and requests regarding conversions to Christianity [G, P], 1876–77; instructions, reports and correspondence concerning permission for *melamdim* to open new *chadorim* after an epidemic, inspection of *chadorim*, assistance for poor Jews and certificates for *melamdim* to teach in *chadorim* [G, P], 1880–1913; correspondence with the governor of Galicia concerning changes in the M. Bernstein Foundation for vocational instruction [G, P], 1880–85; a report on the establishment of a private school for Jewish girls, 1904–06; material on the establishment of the A. Kohn girl's school [G, P], 1916–17; material on a boarding school for Jewish orphans, 1925–32; correspondence with *Agudas Yisroel* about the *Yesodei Hatora* and *Beis Yaakov* schools, including a list of *Agudas Yisroel* members in Lwów, 1933–37;

Religion: Correspondence with the community concerning private *minyanim* and salary for the rabbi [G, P], 1861–70; reports and correspondence about locations of prayer houses [G, P], 1883–84; closing of private prayer houses [G, P], 1888–1908; reports and correspondence on the election of a rabbi, including a list of *chadorim*, 1899–1906; correspondence about the *Beis Toras Moses* synagogue [G, P], 1901–37; correspondence on release from civil duty of an Orthodox journalist and release from conscription of rabbinical candidates, a rabbi and a teacher of Jewish religion [G, P, R], 1916–18; correspondence on raising the salaries of rabbis and associate rabbis [G, P], 1918;

General: A report on a street fight between Jews and Christians, 1863; correspondence concerning refugees from pogroms in Russia, coming to Galicia [G, P], 1882; correspondence with the director of the Jewish theater in Lwów about relocation, 1895–98; files on a dispute between executives of the Jewish community and the *Or Hayosher Meforshei Hayom* society over ownership of a synagogue, including statutes of the society (1891) [G, P, Y], 1901–26; a file on conversions of Jews to Christianity, 1911–13; results of the census, 1918; a report about damages to the Jewish community caused by the Polish army (between November 1, 1918 and July 31, 1919), 1919; a file on the activity of the Jewish Committee for assistance to victims of the pogrom in November 1918; 1919–20; correspondence about the *Bimah Lwuwit* society for spreading the Hebrew language, 1923; correspondence about registration of the *Hakoach,* sports society and a list of the board members, 1937.

(DALO, L'viv, Magistrat, Lwów)

21. Correspondence with the district court about the oath on the *Tora* in criminal cases when one of the parties is Jewish, including a register of oaths and judges [G], 1864.

(TsDIAU, L'viv, Najwyższy Sąd Krajowy, Lwów)

22. Correspondence of *Rada Ruska* about the 1873 parliamentary elections and possible alliances with Jewish organizations [G, R, U], 1873.

(TsDIAU, L'viv, Rada Ruska)

23. Education: Copies of circulars concerning *chadorim* (1878–80) sent to the Kraków provincial authority, 1880, 1925; files on evening courses for Jewish working youth, 1923–24; correspondence about a Seminary for teachers of the Hebrew language, 1925–26; correspondence with the municipality about the parents' committee of the girl's secondary school, including statutes and lists of founding members, 1932; correspondence on the closing of Hebrew seminars, 1938–39;

Community administration: A report on the activity of the Jewish community leadership (1919–24), 1924; a community report listing ritual objects in the synagogues, 1927; reports and correspondence, including complaints on elections to the community board [P, Y], 1927–38; reports and correspondence on the economic activity of the community and the functioning of the Jewish hospital, including a list of community taxpayers [G, P], 1933–37;

Religion and the Rabbinate: Material on burials in Zamarstynów and in Lwów, 1925–28 correspondence regarding travel documents for Rabbi R. Freundlich of the Austrian army, 1926; correspondence regarding conversion of Jews to Christianity, 1928–37; correspondence about candidates for the rabbinate, including a list of candidates turned down for the post of rabbi 1928–32;

Cultural activity: Correspondence about the use of Hebrew and Yiddish, 1922–26; correspondence with the police about the *Chwila*, 1925 and *Inser Morgen*, 1927, newspapers; correspondence about connections of the *Trupa Wileńska* theater with communists, 1928; correspondence on a visit by Chaim Nachman Bialik, 1930–31; a decree forbidding the performances of the Yiddish plays *Sztempelbrider* by R. Duszyński, *Missisipi* by T. Malach and *Midas Hadin* by D. Bergelson, 1935; general reports and correspondence regarding the Yiddish theater, 1934–36;

Societies: *Yad Charutzim* – statutes, correspondence, election posters etc [G, P], 1921–39; correspondence on the foundation of a Jewish sports club, 1924–39; authorization by the Ministry of Interior for a charitable society, *Rambam*, to assist needy Jews in Eretz Israel, 1925–26; correspondence on a fundraising drive of the Jewish Women's Association, 1926–33; *Tarbut* – correspondence and statutes, 1926–34; a membership list of the Merchants and Manufacturers' Association (President – W. Chajes), 1927; the *Rekord* sport club – correspondence, 1928; a report from the *Stowarzyszenie Rygorozantów* society for the support of Jewish academic youth, 1930–31; newspaper clippings on Jewish students active in the Sz. J. Abramowicz Dramatic Club, 1930–31; correspondence, statutes and board membership of a society of graduates of the Dr. A. Korkis technical school, 1938;

Zionist organizations: Correspondence and reports relating to the following organizations: *Hashomer*, 1924; *Poalei Zion*, 1927; *Poalei Zion Left*, 1928–32; *Hitachdut Akademaim Zionim*, 1930; *Mizrachi*, 1930–31; *Hitachdut Hanoar Haivri*, 1930–31; *Hashomer Hatzair*, 1930–31; Revisionist Zionists, 1930–31; *Keren Hayesod* and *Keren Kayemet*, 1931; the Zionist Organization, including membership lists, 1931; *Bnei Akiva*, 1932;

Political activity: Correspondence with the police about Communist activity, 1925; a report about various national minorities and their press, 1927; correspondence about prohibiting Jewish protests against pogroms in Romania, 1927; a report about Jewish parties and representatives in the Polish parliament, 1928; correspondence about organizational efforts of Jewish bakers, 1928.
(DALO, L'viv, UW, Lwów)

24. Correspondence about the establishment of a Seminary for teachers and rabbis [G], 1893–1911;
(TSKHIDK, Moscow, Israelitisch–theologische Lehranstalt Wien)

25. Correspondence between the Alliance Israélite Universelle and the Jewish community [F, H], 19th–20th cent.
(AIU, Paris)

26. Correspondence about the conscription of Rabbi L. M. Lutwak and about tax matters [G, P], 1909–18; a file on awarding a medal to the vice–president of the Jewish community [G, P], 1917.
(TsDIAU, L'viv, Ministerium fuer Kultus und Unterricht, Wien)

27. Correspondence about falsifications of election results and regulations for election committees, 1913.
(TsDIAU, L'viv, Sąd Krajowy, Lwów)

28. A financial report of a fund for Jewish schools [G], 1915–18.
(TsDIAU, L'viv, Ministerium fuer Kultus und Unterricht,Wien)

29. Reports about the pogrom of November 1918 and attacks on Jews by Polish soldiers, including lists of victims, 1918–19; investigations of various publications relating to the pogrom and the Polish army's role

in it, 1919; files on registration of the periodicals, *Folksblatt* and *Chwila*, 1918–19, and *Haor* and *Der Batlan*, 1925, 1927; a report on the arrest of three men for anti-Polish views [G, P], 1918–19; correspondence on translating shop signs in foreign languages (including Hebrew) into Polish, 1919, and on conducting public meetings in Yiddish, 1926 ; reports about the Jewish literary–scientific club, *Juventus*, including a list of members, 1919; correspondence concerning the activities of Jewish *Sejm* members on behalf of Jewish prisoners in the Brygidki prison, 1919; a complaint by the Jewish community about the desecration of the Jewish cemetery by soldiers, 1919–20; a list of Ukrainian and Jewish political parties, 1920; a report concerning a protest by Polish civil servants against employment of Ukrainians and Jews, 1920; correspondence regarding the authorization of public meetings of Jewish political parties and committees, 1920–24; correspondence on a society for emigration of Jewish workers, a parliamentary office of Jewish senators and *Sejm* members and a mutual aid society of Jewish polytechnic students, 1921–25, 1935; correspondence concerning a demand by Polish academic youth to limit the number of Jewish students studying law and philosophy, 1922; correspondence on authorizing meetings of Jewish academic youth, 1926–27; files on confiscations of alleged anti-Polish publications,1927–28; a report from a meeting of *Agudas Yisroel*, 1928; a register of Jews living in Lwów, 1930–34; investigation files against suspects accused of beating Jews, 1935–36; correspondence regarding anti-Jewish actions by members of the *Stronnictwo Narodowe* and on protest strikes of Jewish shop proprietors, including a list of tobacco shop proprietors, 1936–39.
(DALO, L'viv, Dyrekcja Policji, Lwów)
30. Minutes of the Odessa city council regarding the pogrom in Lwów, 1918–19.
(DAOdO, Odesa, Odesskaia gorodskaia duma)
31. Reports about the activities of: *Poalei–Zion*, 1925–26; the Revisionist Zionists, 1928, 1932; the general Zionist organization, *Achva*, 1929; the Zionist organization of academic youth, *Haschachar*, 1932; Berl Locker, representative of the Jewish Agency in London, 1932; the *Bund*, 1932; the IV conference of Jewish cooperatives from Galicia in Lwów, 1932; the *Hitachduth* party, 1932–33; the *Żydowska Partia Pracy*, 1932–33; *Brit Trumpeldor*, 1933; the *Ogólno-Żydowska Partia Pracy*, 1933; various Jewish economic organizations, 1934; a conference of the Zionist Organization of East Galicia in Lwów, 1934.
(DAIFO, Ivano-Frankivs'k, UW, Stanisławów)
32. Reports of the *Leopolis Achduth–Bnai Brith* in Lwów, 1927–30;
33. Information on the unification of *Hitachdut* and Poalei Zion–Left under the name *Zjednoczona Socjalistyczna Partia Hitachdut Poalej Zion*, 1933.
(DATO, Ternopil', Komenda Powiatowa PP, Trembowla)
34. A list of homeowners in Lwów [U], 1939; a decree relating to the construction of the Jewish theater in Lwów [R], 1940; a resolution of the Communist Party of the Ukraine against the influence of Polish, Jewish and Ukrainian nationalists on the youth [U], 1940; statistical data regarding the nationalities of lecturers and students at academic institutions [U], 1944; excerpts from speeches containing antisemitic remarks [R, U], 1945; information on the violation of Soviet law by Jews [R], 1945; material on: Lwów as a transit point for illegal emigration of Jews from Russia to Poland, organized by the Zionist underground organization, *Ichud;* the activity of *Hashomer Hatzair* including a list of activists arrested; crimes comitted by the Nazis in the Lwów district; the commissar for Jewish affaires, Seiss Inquart, etc. [R], 1946; excerpts from minutes of meetings by local intelligentsia about the fate of the Jews during the war [U], 1946.
(DALO, L'viv, L'vovskii obkom…)
35. Investigations of: Jews accused of financial misdeeds [P, R, U], 1941; falsification of partisan documents [R], 1945; denunciations of Jews to the German authorities during the occupation [R, U], 1945;

persons accused of inspiring anti-Jewish violence [R], 1945–46; private industry organized by a Jew [R], 1946–47.

(DALO, L'viv, Prokuror…)

LWÓW, surroundings, 1599–1938

Microfilms:

1. Files on the Dominican order in the Western Ukraine, 1599.

(Biblioteka Narodowa, Warszawa)

2. *Lustracja* of the Lwów area, 1765.

(AP Wrocław, Ossolineum)

3. Correspndence concerning taxes from various communities [G], 1819–21; correspondence concerning Jewish farmers, including a tax–register (1789–1822) and names of farmers and their families [G], 1822–47; correspondence about the financial matters of various communities [G, P], 1902.

(TsDIAU, L'viv, Namiestnictwo Galicyjskie)

4. Files on collecting money in various communities of the Lwów area for the Galician community in Eretz Yisroel, 1928–30; material on a ministerial investigation of the behavior of Jewish civil servants and teachers in East Galicia during the Ukrainian invasion, including a list of candidates rejected for various government positions [G, P], 1919–25; correspondence concerning elections in the Jewish communities of the Lwów area, 1927–28; a report from the Volhynian regional administration about the refusal of Jews and Ukrainians to celebrate the 10th anniversary of independent Poland, 1928; a report by the district authorities concerning a conference of Jewish merchants from Galicia, 1930; reports from: -a meeting of the *Mizrachi* party board for East Galicia, 1930–31; -a general conference of the General Zionists of East Galicia, *Ahava*, 1930–31; -a conference of *Keren Hayesod,* including a list of the delegates from Galicia, 1930–31; -a general conference of Revisionist Zionists of East Galicia and WIZO, 1931; correspondence regarding permission to perform plays in Yiddish in towns of the province, excluding Lwów, 1921–26 correspondence concerning the Association of Galician Rabbis, a secret conference in Gródek Jagielloński and a conference of Orthodox rabbis from Galicia in Lwów, 1927; reports and correspondence on the activity of a fund for Jewish pupils in Galicia and Bukovina [G, P], 1930–38; correspondence of the Association of Galician Rabbis with the district authorities in Bóbrka concerning disciplinary action against Rabbi S. Eichenstein and the recognition of Dr. D. Kahane's rabbinical certificate, 1931–37; a statistical report containing names of community board members, rabbis and assistant–rabbis in the province of Lwów, 1937.

(DALO, L'viv, UW, Lwów)

LWÓWEK (pow. Nowy Tomyśl, woj. poznańskie) 1558–1904

Originals:

Copies from municipal records (incl. charters granted to the community, 1725) [G], 1797–99; records of the community's debts to the Church and the nobility [G], 1826–52; a file on the execution of the law of 1833 [G]; records of payments by Jews leaving the community or living elsewhere [G], 1836–44; the community minute book [G], 1838–80.

Microfilms:

1. Local records (fragmentary), 1558–1759; various documents and charters concerning the Jews, 1649–1772; real estate records, 1778.

(AP Poznań, Arch. Miasta Lwówek)

2. Files on the election of community elders [G], 1778–99; the construction of a synagogue [G, P], 1795–1822; records of litigation between the owners of the town and Jews concerning lease of land and taverns,

the production and sale of liquor, foodstuffs, textiles and the payment of taxes [G, P], 1804–59; financial records concerning Jews involved in tavern keeping and the sale of liquor, lumber, wheat, cattle and land [G, P], 1805–47.
(AP Poznań, Majątek Lwówek)
3. Files concerning the Jews [G], 1834–90.
(AP Poznań, Distriktamt)
4. Minutes and decisions of the community board [G], 1844–1904.
(Centrum Judaicum, Berlin)

ŁABISZYN (pow. Szubin, woj. poznańskie) 1863
Originals:
An appeal for the construction of a new synagogue [G], 1863.

ŁAGIEWNIKI (pow. Krotoszyn, woj. poznańskie) 1866
Originals:
A share to raise funds for a new Jewish cemetery [H], 1866.

ŁAGÓW (pow. Opatów, woj. kieleckie) 1849–1866
Microfilms:
Files on *propinacja*, rental agreements, auctions and finances, 1849–66.
(AP Radom, Rząd Gubernialny, Radom)

ŁANCZYN (pow. Nadwórna, woj. stanisławowskie) 1921–1939
Microfilms:
1. Statutes, minutes and correspondence concerning Zionist organizations, 1921–30; minutes, reports and correspondence concerning elections to the community board, 1932–36; files on Jewish associations, including a list of the founders of the *Gmilus Chasodim* society, 1932–39.
(DAIFO, Ivano-Frankivs'k, UW, Stanisławów)
2. Statutes of the Jewish community [G, P], 1922–23.
(DALO, L'viv, UW, Lwów)

ŁANOWICE (pow. Sambor, woj. lwowskie) 1663–1765
Microfilms:
Circulars, accounts, instructions and *uniwersały* by M. Sapieha, St. Siemieński, M. i A. Sieniawski and A. Czartoryski concerning properties and inhabitants, 1663–1765.
(Bibl. Czartoryskich, Kraków)

ŁAŃCUT (woj. lwowskie) 1683–1937
Originals:
A warrant for the arrest of a Jewish businessman, 1683.
Microfilms:
1. *Arenda* contract and a document on a loan from the church to the *kahal* for the Jewish school, 1776.
(AP Kraków, Teki Schneidra)
2. Files on confirming the statutes of the Jewish community 1846–96; correspondence with the authorities regarding *chadorim*, including a list of *melamdim*, 1874–1908; correspondence about the *Zion* society, including statutes [G, P], 1894.
(TsDIAU, L'viv, Namiestnictwo Galicyjskie)
3. Reports and correspondence on *chadorim* and private Jewish schools in the district [G, P], 1878–81.

(TsDIAU, L'viv, Krajowa Rada Szkolna)

4. Correspondence with the district authorities about confirming the statutes of the Society for the Care of Jewish Orphans, 1923–27; reports and correspondence about activity of the Jewish community, a list of community board members and the statutes of 1895, 1924–30; authorization by the authorities to collect money for Polish–Galician Jews in Palestine and a list of donors, 1928–30; correspondence about the *Kultur Liga*, 1926; files on elections to the community board and the municipality, 1928–33; correspondence about community matters, including a budget and list of taxpayers, 1933–34; a statistical report containing lists of board members, rabbis and *dayanim*, 1937.

(DALO, L'viv, UW, Lwów)

5. Correspondence about registration of the *Machzikei Hadas* society, 1934.

(DALO, L'viv, Magistrat, Lwów)

ŁAPSZYN (pow. Brzeżany, woj. tarnopolskie) 1700–1738
Microfilms:
Accounts, inventories and tax registers from properties of the Sieniawski family, 1700–38.
(Bibl. Czartoryskich, Kraków)

ŁAPY (pow. Wysokie Mazowieckie, woj. białostockie) 1926
Originals:
Extracts from birth and death registers, 1926.

ŁASK (woj. łódzkie) 1787–1913
Microfilms:
1. Various legal matters between the community, municipality and the town's owner, as well as charters, decrees and agreements, 1715–1815.
(AP Kraków)
2. An agreement between the *kahal* of Łask and Jews from Widawa [H, P], 1787.
(AGAD, Warszawa, Archiw. Lubomirskich z Małej Wsi)
3. Community records and accounts; records of homes purchased from Christians, 1816–66.
(AP Łódź, Anterioria Rządu Gubernialnego, Piotrków)
4. On the *eruv* in the Jewish quarter and conflicts between Jews and Christians because of it, 1818–71.
(AGAD, Warszawa, CWW)
5. Fines for evading conscription [R], 1891–1902; bequests to communal charities [R], 1904–13.
(AP Łódź, Rząd Gubernialny, WP, Piotrków)
6. Ratification of community elections and accounts; files on the lease of the *mikve* and restoration of the synagogue; ratification of the appointment of new cantors, 1897–1913 [R]; expenses for medical care of needy Jews [R], 1899–1903; election of a Jew to the municipal administration [R], 1902–03; a complaint against the community [R], 1902–04; investigation files against those accused of distributing illegal proclamations [R], 1906–07; files concerning the relocation of a Jew to the community of Widawa [R], 1906–07.
(AP Łódź, Rząd Gubernialny, WA, Piotrków)
7. Files about transfer of money to the Jewish community for distribution among poor Jews [R], 1904–05.
(AP Łódź, Rząd Gubernialny, RO, Piotrków)
8. An investigation of an individual suspected of inciting a strike [R], 1905; files on confiscation of a shipment of illegal publications at the railway station [R], 1905–06.
(AP Łódź, GZŻ, Piotrków)

Kraków. One year's tax exemption for the community. 1679 (Polish)

9. A request to register a Jewish library [R], 1913.
(AP Łódź, Rząd Gubernialny, RO, Piotrków)

ŁASK, surroundings, 1889–1909
Microfilms:
1. Fines for evading conscription [R], 1892–1902.
(AP Łódź, Rząd Gubernialny, WP, Piotrków)
2. Correspondence concerning *chadorim,* 1889–98.
(AP Łódź, Dyrekcja Szkolna, Łódź)
3. An order to exile three Jews [R], 1908–09.
(AP Łódź, Kancelaria Gubernatora Kaliskiego)

ŁASZCZÓW (pow. Tomaszów, woj. lubelskie) 1730–1796
Microfilms:
1. Files on legal and financial matters [H, P], 1730–96.
(TsDIAU, Kyiv, Arch. Tarło)
2. Inventory of the town, 1749.
(NBANU, L'viv, Zb. Czołowskiego)

ŁATOWICZE (pow. Oszmiana, woj. wileńskie) 1744
Microfilms:
Confirmation by King August III of the charter *de non tolerandis Judaeis,* granted to the town [L], 1744.
(AGAD, Warszawa, Księgi Kanclerskie)

ŁAWOCZNE (pow. Stryj, woj. stanisławowskie) 1894–1937
Microfilms:
Statutes, minutes and correspondence of Jewish associations [G, P], 1894–99, 1924–37.
(DAIFO, Ivano-Frankivs'k, UW, Stanisławów)

ŁĘCZNA (pow. Lubartów, woj. lubelskie) 1699–1910
Microfilms:
1. Orders of payment, letters and registers concerning property of the Sieniawski family [H, P], 1699–1726.
(Bibl. Czartoryskich, Kraków)
2. Documents concerned with the civil registration of Jews, 1812–56.
(AP Lublin)
3. Excerpts from civil registers, 1812–56.
(Private collection)
4. Statistical description of the town (1829–60), 1860–61.
(AP Lublin, Rząd Gubernialny, Lublin)
5. Copies of inscriptions on tombstones and synagogues, 1910.
(RGIA, St. Petersburg, Departament dukhovnykh del...)

ŁĘCZYCA (woj. łódzkie) 1765–1912
Microfilms:
1. Confirmation by King Stanisław August Poniatowski of the charter granted to the Jews [L, P], 1765.
(AGAD, Warszawa, Księgi Kanclerskie)
2. A complaint against a community elder, 1790.
(AGAD, Warszawa, Castr. Obl., Łęczyca)

3. An investigation of a complaint made by the community, 1790.
(AP Wrocław, Ossolineum)
4. Reports and correspondence concerning appointments of rabbis and conflicts between them and the communities, 1853–56.
(AGAD, Warszawa, CWW)
5. Records of the Jewish shelter [R], 1878.
(AP Łódź, ROGK)
6. Various bequests to the community [R], 1896–1910; appointment of a new rabbi [R], 1907–08.
(AP Łódź, Rząd Gubernialny, WA, Kalisz)
7. A letter by the Jewish community to the archbishop of Warsaw [R], 1887; the registration of various philanthropic and cultural societies [R], 1909–12.
(AP Łódź, Kancelaria Gubernatora Kaliskiego)

ŁĘCZYCA, surroundings, 1658–1914
Microfilms:
1. A decision of the *sejmik,* fixing tax rates in the *województwo* (incl. for Jews), 1658.
(AGAD, Warszawa, Księgi Grodzkie Łęczyckie)
2. Ratification of the elections and accounts of communities in the district [R], 1895–1914.
(AP Łódź, Rząd Gubernialny, WA, Piotrków)

ŁĘCZYN (pow. Kostopol, woj. wołyńskie) 1686
Microfilms:
Records of a suit between the community and the Dominican order in Lublin, 1686.
(Bibl. im. Łopacińskiego, Lublin)

ŁOKACZE (pow. Horochów, woj. wołyńskie) 1634–1864
Microfilms:
1. *Arenda* contract [H, P], 1634.
(AP Kraków, Teki Sanguszków tzw. rzymskie)
2. Files on financial matters, 1713–1729.
(AP Kraków, Teki Sanguszków tzw. arabskie)
3. Decrees and charters concerning inhabitants of the town and surroundings, including Jews, 1724–27.
(AP Kraków, Teki Sanguszków)
4. Files on the founding of Jewish hospitals and old-age homes [R], 1863–64.
(RGIA, St. Petersburg, Khoziaistvennyi departament MVD)

ŁOMAZY (pow. Biała Podlaska, woj. lubelskie) 1853–1856
Microfilms:
Reports and correspondence concerning appointments of rabbis and conflicts between them and the community, 1853–56.
(AGAD, Warszawa, CWW)

ŁOMŻA (woj. białostockie) 1810–1927
Originals:
Extracts from birth and death records [P, R], 1859, 1878, 1901, 1927.
Photocopies:
Regulations and information concerning conscription of Jews including a list of conscripts, 1850–52.

(AP Suwałki, Akta miasta Suwałki)
Microfilms:
1. Reports, complaints and correspondence concerning reorganization of the community, 1810–12; reports and correspondence concerning appointment of rabbis and their salaries, and litigation between them and the community, 1853–64; files concerning the community and its accounts, 1857–67.
(AGAD, Warszawa, CWW)
2. Birth, marriage and death records (fragmentary), 1827–65.
(AP Łomża)
3. The case of a Jew exiled on false evidence, 1855–64.
(AGAD, Warszawa, KRzSW)
4. A request for a trading license [R], 1858.
(AGAD, Warszawa, SSKP)
5. Decrees, circulars and reports on the prohibition of religious services on Sabbath and holidays in private homes, fines for the disobedient and a list of home owners [R], 1858–83; personal files and photos of rabbinical candidates [R], 1886–1913; requests for business licenses [R], 1903–16; a file concerning medical treatment of a Jew [R], 1906; files on admission of Jews to the posts of municipal physician and midwife [R], 1906–14; a register of communal taxes for 1914 and *arenda* contracts [R], 1912–16; community accounts and a list of Jews [R], 1914; requests concerning registration of mortgages [R], 1914; a request for exemption from communal tax [R], 1914; files on expulsion from the military zone of Jews involved in trade of military equipment [R], 1915; files on the arrest of politically unreliable Jews [R], 1915; files on deportation of Jews suspected of espionage and trade in stolen equipement [R], 1915.
(AP Białystok, Rząd Gubernialny, Łomża)
6. A request for legal costs to be paid after litigation, 1865–66.
(AGAD, Warszawa, RSKP)
7. Request for permission to produce and distribute currant-wine [R], 1914–15.
(RGIA, St. Petersburg, Glavnoe upravlenie neokladnykh sborov…)

ŁOMŻA, surroundings (*guberniia*) 1903–1923
Microfilms:
1. Requests for business licenses [R], 1903–05; register of communal taxes for 1914, a list of *"okręgi bóżnicze"* (parochial districts) of the *guberniia*, a list of Jewish communal buildings, a decree concerning rules for shipping parcels by the Jewish communities [R], 1907–15; correspondence with the gendarmerie about lists of Jewish communities, boards, associations and communal institutions [R], 1911; community accounts and a list of Jews [R], 1914; correspondence about Jewish inhabitants of the *guberniia* suspected of smuggling emigrants across the border [R], 1915–16.
(AP Białystok, Rząd Gubernialny, Łomża)
2. Statistical data about synagogues and rabbis [R], 1908.
(RGIA, St. Petersburg, Khoziaistvennyi departament MVD)
3. Files on persecutions of Jews in military zones during WW I [R], 1914–15.
(GARF, Moscow, Katsenel'son)
4. A list of persons expelled from the district, 1923.
(DATO, Ternopil', Komenda Powiatowa PP, Trembowla)

ŁOPATYN (pow. Radziechów, woj. tarnopolskie) 1877–1908
Microfilms:

Correspondence between the community and the authorities regarding *chadorim*, including a list of *melamdim* [G, P], 1877–1908.
(TsDIAU, L'viv, Namiestnictwo Galicyjskie)

ŁOPUSZNA (pow. Rohatyn, woj. stanisławowskie) 1930–1937
Microfilms:
Registers and lists of Jewish associations, 1930–37.
(DAIFO, Ivano-Frankivs'k, UW, Stanisławów)

ŁOSICE (pow. Siedlce, woj. lubelskie) 1780–1860
Microfilms:
1. A contract for an *arenda*, 1780.
(AP Kraków, IT)
2. A letter of protection granted to a Jewish merchant by King Stanisław August Poniatowski, 1792.
(AGAD, Warszawa, Księgi Kanclerskie)
3. Files on synagogues, 1818–60.
(AGAD, Warszawa, CWW)

ŁOWICZ (woj. warszawskie) 1812–1871
Microfilms:
1. Files concerning Jewish houses, 1812–61.
(AGAD, Warszawa, KRzSW)
2. Files on the erection of an *eruv* and ensuing conflicts with Christian neighbours, 1818–71; files on exempting graduates of the Rabbinical Seminary from military service, including a list of rabbis, 1865–71.
(AGAD, Warszawa, CWW)

ŁÓDŹ (woj. łódzkie) 1880–1939
Originals:
The account books of two Jewish merchants [G, P], 1905, 1933; account books and minutes of the Hebrew Language Society [*Lomdei Safa Ivrit*] [H, R], 1911–1912; marriage announcement, 1938; a ledger containing evaluations of children learning at the private religious school, *Orchot Noam*, 1939; a poster announcing the exhibition of a painting, *Shivat Zion* [P, Y], n.d.
Microfilms:
1. Jewish community records:
Community minutes and reports; records of community elections; community correspondence; files on personal matters and on civil records; population records; community budgets and financial reports; records of income and expenditure; records of communal taxes; requests for financial aid during World War I; records of transactions concerning real estate in the town; records of the rabbinate; files on synagogues and prayer houses; records concerning the *mikve*; ritual slaughter; documents and correspondence concerning the supply of money and food for the poor at Passover time; files of the Commission for Ritual Matters; records concerning Jewish schools and *chadorim*; files on the *Talmud Tora*; files on the community delegates to the School Council; files on the establishment and the activities of various Jewish charitable and medical institutions (the poor shelter, orphanages, home for the mentally disturbed etc.); records of the Jewish cemetery; files on the staff of the cemetery and their wages; records of burial costs; files on the desecration of graves by soldiers; records concerning the Commission for Burial Matters; files concerning emigration; records concerning theft in the community; civil records and statistics concerning the Jewish population; help granted to the victims of the pogroms in the Ukraine; files on anti Jewish outbursts;

records of those wishing to leave the community; bulletins of the Jewish Press Agency; files concerning the election of Jews to the Town Council; files on community participation in various non-Jewish celebrations; records of Jews conscripted into the army; files on the Commission for the Registration of War Casualties; records of the Committee for the Support of the Wounded Soldiers [P, R], 1885–1935.
(AP Łódź, Gmina Żydowska, Łódź)

2. Records concerning the community and its officials; correspondence dealing with the community's finances; files on the Jewish cemetery, *chadorim* and Jewish schools; records of synagogues; contributions to the Jewish hospital in Piotrków; files on the construction of the Jewish hospital; the establishment of a Jewish maternity home; various societies and charitable institutions; records concerning the rabbi and the supply of kosher food; licenses for Jews to settle in the town; licenses for Jews to buy land for building purposes; files on the size of the Jewish population and its participation in local life; files on legislation concerning Jewish dress (incl. fines for breaking the law and taxes paid for permission to dress traditionally); medical certificates for burial purposes; verdicts in criminal cases [P, R], 1818–1914.
(AP Łódź, Akta Magistratu, Łódź)

3. Files on the community; records on the purchase of property and land by Jews, 1836–66.
(AP Łódź, Rząd Gubernialny, Piotrków)

4. Documents, reports and correspondence on Jewish schools and *chadorim*; inventories and descriptions of various schools; class registers [R], 1864–1915.
(AP Łódź, Łódzka Dyrekcja Szkolna)

5. Files on illegal trading activities by Jews; various official requests (incl. for opening businesses); files on synagogues, prayer houses, schools and *chadorim*, records of Jews under police observation; files on medical services; a file on the *Hazamir* society; records concerning various educational and professional societies; the appointment of a new rabbi; files concerning the registration of merchants [R], 1869–1913.
(AP Łódź, Policmajster Łodzi)

6. Ratification of community elections and accounts; records concerning the *arenda* of synagogue income; files on arrears in taxes paid by Jews; financial aid for the Jewish poor; donation and contribution to charitable institutions, schools and synagogues; the appointment of new rabbis; files on the construction and renovation of the synagogue and the Jewish hospital; records concerning the establishment of new synagogues and *chadorim*; licenses for the establishment of various cultural and charitable societies; files on Jewish guilds; various complaints concerning the community; requests for licenses to build houses, warehouses and factories; a request to permit a conversion to Christianity [R], 1871–1914.
(AP Łódź, Rząd Gubernialny, WA, Piotrków)

7. Files on the construction of Jewish hospitals, shelters and other charitable institutions (incl. licenses, correspondence, donations and legacies); donation of money, land and estates to the community [P, R], 1881–1911.
(AP Łódź, Rząd Gubernialny, RO, Piotrków)

8. Files on synagogues and cemeteries; a request to establish a society of merchants; various financial requests; complaints against Jews; proceedings against Jews who built in unauthorized areas; fines for evading conscription; files on the poverty suffered by the families of Jews conscripted into the army [R], 1890–1903.
(AP Łódź, Rząd Gubernialny, WP, Piotrków)

9. Material on a prohibition of performances by Yiddish theaters [R], 1899–1907; a file on the production and distribution of currant wine [R], 1914–15.
(RGIA, St. Petersburg, Glavnoe upravlenie neokladnykh sborov…)

10. A report "On secret Jewish organizations in the western part of the Russian Empire, Łódź" (1900) [R], 1900; .
(GARF, Moscow, Departament politsii...)
11. Accusations against Jews of membership in illegal organizations and political parties (incl. the *Bund*); files on those accused of the possession and distribution of illegal, anti-government literature; documents concerning the organization of demonstrations and meetings on May 1, 1905 and on other occasions; files on those arrested for organizing strikes in 1905; records of investigations into the political orientations of certain Jews; documents concerning the collection of funds for the *Bund* and other parties; a file on a meeting of *Poalei Zion* in 1910 [R], 1903–1912.
(AP Łódź, GZŻ, Piotrków)
12. Correspondence concerning measures to prevent pogroms [R], 1906; files of an association of political prisoners and deportees, stenograms of the department investigating revolutionary movements among Jews and memoirs concerning Jewish members of revolutionary movements [R], 1931;
(GARF, Moscow, Vsesoiuznoe obshchestvo...)
13. Requests to register cultural, charitable, religious and professional societies; confirmation of the establishment of a Jewish orphanage [R], 1906–14.
(AP Łódź, Rząd Gubernialny, KP, Piotrków)
14. Correspondence on the causes of pogroms; a statement concerning acts of sabotage committed by Jews; various petitions and complaints made by Jews; correspondence concerning a Jew under arrest; a case of a Jew using false medical certificates to evade conscription; licenses to publish Jewish journals [R], 1906–14.
(AP Łódź, Kancelararia Gubernatora Piotrkowskiego)
15. Files on various Jews sent into exile [R], 1907–08.
(AP Łódź, Kancelararia Gubernatora Kaliskiego)
16, Report of the community about closing *chadorim,* sent to the authorities of the Łódź educational district [R], 1913.
(RNB, St. Petersburg, Kamenetskii)

ŁÓDŹ, surroundings, 1883–1914
1. Files on educational matters concerning Jews in the district [R], 1883–85.
(AP Łódź, Urząd Gminy, Chojny)
2. Records concerning Jewish communities in the district; files on Jews evading conscription [R], 1889–1914.
(AP Łódź, Rząd Gubernialny, Piotrków)
3. Correspondence concerning *chadorim*, 1889–99.
(AP Łódź, Łódzka Dyrekcja Szkolna)
4. Fines for evading conscription; the complaint of a Jew against the village militia [R], 1895–1902.
(AP Łódź, Rząd Gubernialny, WP, Piotrków)
5. A file on the request of the Jews of a local village to join the Łódź community, 1908.
(AP Łódź, Rząd Gubernialny, WA, Piotrków)
6. Files on Jews under police observation [R], 1908.
(AP Łódź, GZŻ, Piotrków)

ŁUCK (woj. wołyńskie) 1503–1937
Photographs:
Old synagogue, 1916–17.
(Central State Archives of Film-, Photo-, and Phonographic Documents of the Ukraine, Kyiv)

Microfilms:
1. Charters by the Lithuanian Duke Alexander for the Jews [Rt], 1503.
(Bibl. Łopacińskiego, Lublin)
2. Charters by King Zygmunt I to a Jew from Łuck for the *arenda* of tolls in Kiev [Rt], 1506–10.
(RGADA, Moscow, ML)
3. Excerpts from books of the Castle Court in Łuck concerning Jews [Rt], 1553–1611.
(TsDIAU, Kyiv, Lutskii grodskii sud)
4. Copies of excerpts from books of the Castle Court in Łuck concerning Jews [P, Rt], (16th–18th cent); material on a blood libel, 1701.
(TsDIAU, Kyiv, Dokumenty, sobrannye…)
5. A testimony of a Jew concerning the *arenda* of tolls, 1588; a document concerning litigation between a nobleman and a Jewish *arendar*; 1638; a document concerning a loan, n.d. – 17th cent.
(AP Kraków, Teki Sanguszków, tzw. rzymskie)
6. Documents and registers of Jewish inhabitants and taxes, 1705–08.
(Bibl. Czartoryskich, Kraków)
7. A permit to construct a new synagogue, granted by the bishop of Łuck and Brześć [L], 1760; excerpts from books of the Castle Court in Łuck, 1774.
(NBANU, L'viv, Zb. Baworowskich)
8. Excerpts from minutes of the Łuck tribunal concerning taxes paid by a Jewish leaseholder, 1736; files on debts, 1767.
(TsDIAU, Kyiv, Arch. Zamojskich)
9. An appointment by King Stanisław August of a commission for the settlement of litigation between Jewish merchants and citizens of Łuck, 1792.
(AGAD, Warszawa, Księgi Kanclerskie)
10. A complaint of a wine merchant against the illegal import of alcohol in Łuck [R], 1838–39; a request by the Jewish community to vouch for Jews accused of arson [R], 1850; files of a Kiev Society for Protection of Monuments and Works of Art on renovation of the Łuck synagogue [R], 1906–14.
(TsDIAU, Kyiv, Kantseliariia... general-gubernatora)
11. A report about Jewish schools [R], 1852–58.
(DAKhO, Kamianets'-Podil's'kyi, Direktsiia narodnykh uchilishch…)
12. Files on Jewish hospitals and charitable institutions [R], 1863–64.
(RGIA, St. Petersburg, Khoziaistvennyi departament MVD)
13. Correspondence about elections to the State *Duma* [R], 1905–06.
(RGIA, St. Petersburg, Obshchestvo polnopraviia…)
14. Files on religious personnel and prayer houses of Karaites in Łuck [R], 1908; texts of inscriptions on synagogues and tombstones [H, R], 1910.
(RGIA, St. Petersburg, Departament dukhovnykh del…)
15. Files of the Jewish community board in Łuck: lists of voters, reports, correspondence, budget, elections, taxes and other documents [P, Y], 1928–37.
(DAVO, Luts'k, Gmina Żydowska, Łuck)

ŁUCZA (pow. Peczeniżyn, woj. stanisławowskie) 1920
Microfilms:
Decrees and correspondence on drafting Jews for military service, including a list of draftees, 1920.
(DAIFO, Ivano-Frankivs'k, Starostwo Powiatowe, Peczeniżyn)

ŁUKAWKA (pow. Opatów, woj. kieleckie) 1862–1871
Microfilms:
Files on legal proceedings against a Jewish inn keeper, 1862–71.
(AP Radom, Rząd Gubernialny, Radom)

ŁUKONICA (pow. Słonim, woj. nowogrodzkie) 1566–1568
Microfilms:
Charters granted to the Jews of Brześć concerning the *arenda* of tolls in Łukonica [Rt], 1566–68.
(RGADA, Moscow, ML)

ŁUKÓW (woj. lubelskie) 1792–1913
Microfilms:
1. Confirmation by King Stanisław August Poniatowski of the charter granted to the Jews [L, P], 1792; a letter of protection by him to a Jew [L], 1792.
(AGAD, Warszawa, Księgi Kanclerskie)
2. Correspondence on the exemption from military service of Rabbinical Seminary graduates, including a list of graduates, 1865–71.
(AGAD, Warszawa, CWW)
3. Certificates and photographs of candidates for the rabbinate [R], 1886–1913.
(AP Białystok, Rząd Gubernialny, Łomża)

ŁUNINIEC (woj. poleskie) 1895
Photocopies:
A plan of a house and a plot designated as a prayer house [R], 1895;
(NIAB, Minsk, Minskoe gubernskoe pravlenie)

ŁYSIEC (pow. Stanisławów, woj. stanisławowskie) 1738–1938
Microfilms:
1. Excerpts from minutes of criminal proceedings against Jews accused of horse theft and burglary in churches of Kołomyja and Łysiec, 1738–50.
(NBANU, L'viv, Arch. Ossolińskich)
2. An inventory of Łysiec and surrounding villages, 1843.
(NBANU, L'viv, Zb. Czołowskiego)
3. Files on confirmation of Jewish community statutes [G, P], 1846–1905.
(TsDIAU, L'viv, Namiestnictwo Galicyjskie)
4. Reports on teaching Jewish religion in elementary schools [G, P], 1882–89.
(TsDIAU, L'viv, Krajowa Rada Szkolna)
5. Files concerning confirmation of statutes of the *Gmilus Chasodim* society, including lists of members [G, P], 1904, 1912–13, 1928–31; files on budget approval and a list of taxpayers, 1938.
(DAIFO, Ivano-Frankivs'k, UW, Stanisławów)
6. Files on assessment of war damages caused to the Jewish community, including plans of synagogues and prayer houses destroyed during World War I, 1922.
(DAIFO, Ivano-Frankivs'k, Powiatowa Komisja Szacunkowa, Bohorodczany)
7. Files on ratifying the budget of the Jewish community, 1922–23; circulars, minutes and correspondence on community elections, including a list of board members [H, P, Y], 1928.
(DAIFO, Ivano-Frankivs'k, Wydział Powiatowy Samorządu, Bohorodczany)

ŁYSOBYKI (pow. Łuków, woj. lubelskie) 1853–1856
Microfilms:
Reports and correspondence on the appointments of rabbis and conflicts between them and the communities, 1853–56.
(AGAD, Warszawa, CWW)

MAGIERÓW (pow. Rawa Ruska, woj. lwowskie) 1703–1937
Microfilms:
1. A complaint against a Jewish *arendar*, 1703.
(TsDIAU, L'viv, Kolektsiia lystiv...)
2. Authorization by the district authorities to collect money for the Polish–Galician Jewish community in Palestine, including a list of donors, 1928–30; a complaint by *Agudas Yisroel* and *Mizrachi* on irregularities in the community elections, 1934–35.
(DALO, L'viv, UW, Lwów)
3. Correspondence about the registration of *Agudas Yisroel*, including a text of the statutes, 1931–37.
(DALO, L'viv, Magistrat, Lwów)

MAGNUSZEW (pow. Kozienice, woj. kieleckie) 1853–1856
Microfilms:
Reports and correspondence of *guberniia* authorities on the appointment of rabbis and litigation between them and the community, as well as a list of rabbis, 1853–56.
(AGAD, Warszawa, CWW)

MAJDAN (pow. Kolbuszowa, woj. lwowskie) 1877–1937
Microfilms:
1. Correspondence with the district authorities regarding *chadorim* and *melamdim*, 1877–1908; correspondence concerning the Jewish community and ratification of statutes, 1895–96.
(DALO, L'viv, Namiestnictwo Galicyjskie)
2. Authorization by the district authorities to collect money for the Polish–Galician Jewish community in Palestine, including a list of donors, 1928–30; files concerning confirmation of a rabbi, 1930; correspondence with the Ministry of Religion about Rabbi T. Horowitz, clippings from various newspapers, 1930–37; correspondence on the community budget, 1932–35.
(DALO, L'viv, UW, Lwów)

MAJDAN SIENIAWSKI (pow. Jarosław, woj. lwowskie) 1628–1759
Microfilms:
Agreements, contracts, accounts and other documents concerning properties of the Sieniawski and Czartoryski families, 1628–1759.
(Bibl. Czartoryskich, Kraków)

MAKÓW MAZOWIECKI (woj. warszawskie) 1566–1915
Microfilms:
1. A *lustracja* of the town, 1566.
(AGAD, Warszawa, ASK)
2. An extract from the *lustracja* of the town, 1775.
(AP Wrocław, Ossolineum)
3. Confirmation by King Stanisław August Poniatowski of a charter granted to the Jews [L, P], 1766.

(AGAD, Warszawa, Księgi Kanclerskie)
4. Records concerning a dispute between the municipality and the Jews, 1839–49.
(AGAD, Warszawa, KRzSW)
5. A file concerning permission to produce non–alcoholic beverages [R], 1909; a file on the closing of a candy factory belonging to a Jew [R], 1909–11; files on illumination of the town and the *arenda* of a bridge [R], 1913–14; files on the arrest and expulsion of Jews suspected of illegal emigrational activity [R], 1913–15; regulations on the dispatch of parcels by Jewish relief comittees [R], 1914–15; letters and reports on community board elections and exemptions from communal taxes for certain members [R], 1914–15; a file on heating and lighting the synagogue [R], 1915.
(AP Białystok, Rząd Gubernialny, Łomża)

MALAWA (pow. Rzeszów, woj. lwowskie) 1819–1881
Microfilms:
Correspondence and legal proceedings concerning *arenda* contracts [G, P], 1819–45, 1865–81; complaints by a Jewish creditor [G, L, P], 1872–80.
(AGAD, Warszawa, Arch. Ostrowskich z Ujazdu)

MARCHWACZ (pow. Kalisz, woj. łódzkie) 1870
Microfilms:
Arenda contract between a nobleman and a Jew concerning alcohol trade, 1870.
(AGAD, Warszawa, Arch. Niemojowskich)

MARGONIN (pow. Chodzież, woj. poznańskie) 1875
Originals:
Memorbuch [H], 1875.

MAŁKINIA (pow. Ostrów, woj. białostockie) 1912–1913
Microfilms:
Files on Jews suspected of clandestine emigration activity [R], 1912–13.
(AP Białystok, Rząd Gubernialny, Łomża)

MAŁY PŁOCK (pow. Łomża, woj. białostockie) 1887–1915
Microfilms:
Correspondence on the construction of a new *mikve* [R], 1887–97; files on the arrest and exile of Jews suspected of spying for the German army [R], 1913–15.
(AP Białystok, Rząd Gubernialny, Łomża)

MARJAMPOL (pow. Stanisławów, woj. stanisławowskie) 1898–1938
Microfilms:
1. Files on community elections, including complaints about the results and lists of voters and community board members [G, P], 1898–1918.
(TsDIAU, L'viv, Ministerium fuer Kultus und Unterricht, Wien)
2. Statutes, minutes and correspondence concerning Jewish associations, 1931–38.
(DAIFO, Ivano-Frankivs'k, UW, Stanisławów)

MARKUSZÓW (pow. Puławy, woj. lubelskie) 1836–1859
Microfilms:
Statistical description of the town, 1836–59.

(AP Lublin, Rząd Gubernialny, Lublin)

MASZKÓW (pow. Miechów, woj. kielecki) 1814–1815
Microfilms:
Minutes in a case of theft and sale of the objects to a Jew, 1814–15.
(NBANU, L'viv, Zb. Goldsteina)

MAZOWIECK – see WYSOKIE MAZOWIECKIE

MCHOWO (pow. Przasnysz, woj. warszawskie) 1913
Microfilms:
Files on illegal border crossings by Jews [R], 1913.
(AP Białystok, Rząd Gubernialny, Łomża)

MEDENICE (pow. Drohobycz, woj. lwowskie) 1895–1896
Microfilms:
Correspondence with the authorities concerning the community and its statutes, 1895–96.
(TsDIAU, L'viv, Namiestnictwo Galicyjskie)

MEDYKA (pow. Przemyśl, woj. lwowskie) 1903–1913
Microfilms:
Files on donations to build a synagogue [G, P], 1903–13.
(TsDIAU, L'viv, Ministerium fuer Kultus und Unterricht, Wien)

MEDYNIA (pow. Łańcut, woj. lwowskie) 1928–1930
Microfilms:
Authorization to collect donations for the Polish–Galician community in Palestine, 1928–30.
(DALO, L'viv, UW, Lwów)

MERECZ (pow. Wilno-Troki, woj. wileńskie) 1792
Copy:
Police report concerning jurisdiction over the Jews of Merecz and construction of a house by a Jew, 1792.

MĘDRZECHÓW (pow. Dąbrowa, woj. krakowskie) 1820–1847
Microfilms:
Documents on *propinacja, arendas* and other economic and legal matters, 1820–47.
(AP Kraków, Arch. Krzeszowickie Potockich)

MĘTKÓW (pow. Chrzanów, woj. krakowskie) 1878
Microfilms:
Files on reorganization of elementary schools attended by Jewish pupils [G, P], 1878.
(TsDIAU, L'viv, Krajowa Rada Szkolna)

MIASTKOWO (pow. Łomża, woj. białostockie) 1913–1915
Microfilms:
Files on the arrest and expulsion of Jews suspected of illegal emigration activity [R], 1913–15.
(AP Białystok, Rząd Gubernialny, Łomża)

MIECHOWICE (pow. Włocławek, woj. warszawskie) 1796–1826
Microfilms:

Files concerning *arenda* contracts, 1796–1826.
(AGAD, Warszawa, Arch. Lubomirskich z Małej Wsi)

MICHAŁOWICE (woj. krakowskie) 1866
Original:
Declaration by a rabbinic assembly against the Reform movement [H], 1866.

MICHÓW (pow. Lubartów, woj. lubelskie)
Microfilms:
Files on the appointments of rabbis and their conflicts with the communities, as well as a list of rabbis, 1853–56.
(AGAD, Warszawa, CWW)

MIECHÓW (woj. kieleckie) 1848–1871
Microfilms:
A project to distribute kosher food to needy Jews and support poor Jewish hospital patients [P, R], 1848–56; correspondence on exempting graduates of the Rabbinical Seminary from conscription, as well as a list of rabbis 1865–71.
(AGAD, Warszawa, CWW)

MIELEC (woj. krakowskie) 1896–1908
Microfilms:
1. A report following inspection of Baron Hirsch Foundation (JCA) schools, 1896–97.
(TsDIAU, L'viv, Krajowa Rada Szkolna)
2. Correspondence on the *Beis Yisroel*, *Adas Yisroel* and *Bnei Emuna* associations, 1908.
(TsDIAU, L'viv, Namiestnictwo Galicyjskie)

MIELNICA (pow. Borszczów, woj. tarnopolskie) 1896–1902
Microfilms:
Correspondence on the election of a rabbi and on the budget [G, P], 1896–1902.
(TsDIAU, L'viv, Namiestnictwo Galicyjskie)

MIĘDZYRZEC PODLASKI (pow. Radzyń, woj. lubelskie) 1686–1864
Microfilms:
1. Records on community income from the manufacture and sale of liquor, 1686–1700.
(AP Kraków, Arch. Krzeszowickie Potockich)
2. Inventories, tax registers, orders of payment and accounts, 1699–1798.
(Bibl. Czartoryskich, Kraków)
3. Confirmation by King August III of the charter granted to the Jews [L], 1736.
(AGAD, Warszawa, MK)
4. A charter granted to the Jews by King August Czartoryski, 1751.
(Arch. PAN, Kraków)
5. Birth, marriage and death records, 1827–35.
(AP Lublin)
6. Files on the donation of a house to the Jewish community, 1855–1864.
(AP Lublin, Rząd Gubernialny, Lublin)

MIĘDZYRZECZ (Korecki) (pow. Równe, woj. wołyńskie) 1605–1939
Original:
A prenuptial agreement [H], 1827; tailors' society record book [H], 1834–59.
Photocopies:
Inventory of the *klucz*, 1736.
(NIAB, Minsk, Arch. Radziwiłłów)
Microfilms:
1. Files on litigation between noblemen, priests and Jewish *arendars*, as well as excerpts from books of the Castle Court in Łuck [Rt], 1605–12.
(AP Kraków, Teki Sanguszków tzw. rzymskie)
2. *Arenda* contracts, 1699–1700; excerpts from the books of the Castle Courts of Łuck and Krzemieniec, files concerning legal proceedings, 1701–49; *supliki* and accounts, 1703; charter by Lubomirski and documents about a meeting of Jews from neigbouring *kahals*, 1721; accounts of Jewish merchants and *arendars* concerning their businesses with noblemen, 1733–50; a register of debts and *supliki* by an *arendar*, 1752; a decree by a tribunal in Łuck concerning Jews from Międzyrzecz and accounts, 18th cent.
(TsDIAU, Kyiv, Arch. Lubomirskich)
3. Regesta, accounts, *uniwersały*, decrees and contracts concerning property of the Sieniawski and Czartoryski families [F, L, P], 1706–85.
(Biblioteka Narodowa, Warszawa)
4. Requests by 88 Jewish merchants from Poland to enter Russia with their merchandise [R], 1739.
(TsDIAU, Kyiv, Kievskaia gubernskaia kantseliariia)
5. Financial register [R], 1816–28; reports and correspondence on the registration and activities of the local branch of the Central Organization of Jewish Craftsmen in Poland, including a list of board members, 1924–34, statutes, minutes, reports and correspondence of *Hechalutz–Pionier* as well as a list of board members, 1926–39.
(DARO, Rivne, Rovenskoe uezdnoe kaznacheistvo)
6. Copies of inscriptions from synagogues and tombstones [R], 1910.
(RGIA, St. Petersburg, Departament dukhovnykh del...)

MIĘDZYRZECZ (Ostrogski) (pow. Zdołbunów, woj. wołyńskie) 1724
Microfilms:
A list of Jews in the community, 1724.
(AP Kraków, Arch. Sanguszków)

MIKOŁAJÓW (pow. Żydaczów, woj. lwowskie) 1709–1939
Microfilms:
1. Accounts of A. M. Sieniawski properties in Mikołajów, 1709–18.
(Bibl. Czartoryskich, Kraków)
2. Confirmation by King Stanisław August of the charter granted to the city by King Zygmunt III, including references to the status of the Jews [L], 1766.
(AGAD, Warszawa, Księgi Kanclerskie)
3. Correspondence with the authorities on *chadorim*, including lists of *melamdim*, 1877–1908.
(TsDIAU, L'viv, Namiestnictwo Galicyjskie)
4. Files on confirming the statutes of the *Bikur Cholim, Gmilus Chasodim* and other associations [G, P], 1871–88, 1904–13, 1921–37.
(DAIFO, Ivano-Frankivs'k, UW, Stanisławów)

5. Correspondence concerning the budget, 1933–36; circulars, reports and correspondence on the election of a rabbi, 1938–39.
(DALO, L'viv, UW, Lwów)

MIKULICZYN (pow. Nadwórna, woj. stanisławowskie) 1922–1930
Microfilms:
Files on confirming the statutes of the *Gmilus Chasodim* association, 1922–30.
(DAIFO, Ivano-Frankivs'k, UW, Stanisławów)

MIKULIŃCE (pow. Tarnopol, woj. tarnopolskie) 1819–1902
Microfilms:
1. Tables citing names of communities and amounts of taxes [G], 1819, 1842–59.
(TsDIAU, L'viv, Namiestnictwo Galicyjskie)
2. Plans of Baron Hirsch Foundation (JCA) schools, 1902.
(TsDIAU, L'viv, Krajowa Rada Szkolna)

MILEJCZYCE (pow. Bielsk, woj. białostockie) 1838–1916
Microfilms:
Documents concerning litigation between Jews and Christians [R], 1838–74, 1889–1916.
(RGIA, St. Petersburg, Obshchestvo polnopraviia…)

MILÓWKA (pow. Żywiec, woj. krakowskie) 1898–1908
Microfilms:
Correspondence between the community and the authorities regarding the statutes, including a list of voters, 1898–1908.
(TsDIAU, L'viv, Namiestnictwo Galicyjskie)

MIŁOSŁAW (pow. Września, woj. poznańskie) 1858–1885
Originals:
Class registers of the Jewish elementary school [G], 1858–1885; *memorbuch* [H], 1882;

MINKOWCE (pow. Dubno, woj. wołyńskie) 1636–1770
Microfilms:
Arenda contracts, 1636, 1770
(AP Kraków, Arch. Sanguszków)

MIR (pow. Stołpce, woj. nowogrodzkie) 1722–1930
Originals:
Receipt for a donation to the Mir *yeshiva*, 1930.
Photocopies:
Inventaries of Mir estates, 1719–20, 1794;
(NIAB, Minsk, Arch. Radziwiłłów)
Microfilms:
1. *Uniwersał* by Anna Sanguszków Radziwiłł given to Jews and Christians from Prussian states, living in Mir, 1722; records of a dispute between Gdal Izakowicz and a Prussian merchant over a confiscated consignment of tobacco [G, P], 1728–29; legal proceedings following damages caused to a Jewish merchant from Mir by a nobleman, 1767.
(AGAD, Warszawa, Arch. Radziwiłłów)

2. Files on the prohibition to import foreign Jewish publications, including books by Yankel Berlin from Mir [R], 1830; denunciations of Jewish publishing houses for publishing books without permission of the censor [R], 1830–32.
(RGIA, St. Petersburg, Glavnoe upravlenie tsenzury)

MIZUŃ (pow. Dolina, woj. stanisławowskie) 1925–1939
Microfilms:
Statutes, minutes and correspondence concerning Jewish associations, 1925–39.
(DAIFO, Ivano-Frankivs'k, UW, Stanisławów)

MŁAWA (woj. warszawskie) 1566–1933
Photocopies:
Community minute book [H], 1925–33.
Microfilms:
1. *Lustracja* of the town, 1566.
(AGAD, Warszawa, ASK)
2. Correspondence on exempting Rabbinical Seminary graduates from military service, 1865–71.
(AGAD, Warszawa, CWW)

MŁYNÓW (pow. Dubno, woj. wołyńskie) 1756–1869
Microfilms:
Accounts for the provision of food (incl. by Jews) to the palace, 1756–1854; records of the *arenda* of fish ponds, 1770–1869; permission by L. Chodkiewiczowa to establish a Jewish school, 1790; records and receipts from a local distillery, 1830; registers of Jewish debts, 1833–51; an application by a Jewish doctor for a passport, 1841; a tax register, 1849–58.
(AP Kraków, Arch. Młynowskie Chodkiewiczów)

MŁYNÓW, surroundings, 1710–1858
Microfilms:
Contracts and accounts of various *arendas*, 1710–1816; a decree issued by the *guberniial* office about the resettlement of countryside Jews in towns, 1832; records of rent and other income from the estates, 1849–58.
(AP Kraków, Arch. Młynowskie Chodkiewiczów)

MODLIBORZYCE (pow. Janów, woj. lubelskie) 1641–1868
Microfilms:
1. Extracts from municipal records and accounts concerning Jews, 1641–1809; *uniwersał* issued by the Royal Treasury Commission, demanding donations for the army, 1788; instructions for a census and the recording of taxes and civil records for Jews, 1790–1808.
(AP Lublin, Księgi Miejskie, Modliborzyce)
2. A statistical description of the town, 1860–61; community accounts, 1868.
(AP Lublin, Rząd Gubernialny, Lublin)

MODRZEJÓW (pow. Będzin, woj. kieleckie) 1842–1911
Microfilms:
1. Records on the construction of a synagogue, 1842–58.
(AP Łódź, Anterioria Rządu Gubernialnego, Piotrków)
2. A request for a tax exemption on spoilt wine, 1864.

(AP Łódź, RSKP)
3. Files on the establishment of an independent community in the town [R], 1885–1911.
(AP Łódź, Rząd Gubernialny, WA, Piotrków)
4. A fine for evading conscription [R], 1897.
(AP Łódź, Rząd Gubernialny, WP, Piotrków)
5. Reports by the border control office [R], 1907.
(AP Łódź, GZŻ, Piotrków)

MODRYCZ (pow. Drohobycz, woj. lwowskie) 1747
Microfilms:
Court decree concerning an inheritance case, 1747.
(TsDIAU, L'viv, Samborska ekonomia)

MOGIELNICA (pow. Grójec, woj. warszawskie) 1777–1918
Microfilms:
1. *Propinacja* contracts, 1777–1845; files on the *kahal* – construction of the synagogue and litigation with the *kahal* in Grójec [H, L, P], 1784–1828; files on contracts and litigation between Jews from Mogielnica and the *kahal* in Nowe Miasto, Łask and Widawa [H, P], 1788–92.
(AGAD, Warszawa, Arch. Lubomirskich z Małej Wsi)
2. Files on the Jewish quarter, 1818–71 and on Jewish refugees, 1917–18.
(AP Warszawa, Magistrat, Piaseczno)
3. Reports and correspondence on the appointment of rabbis and their conflicts with the communities, 1853–56.
(AGAD, Warszawa, CWW)

MOGILANY (pow. Kraków, woj. krakowskie) 1720
Microfilms:
Inquiry into the beating of a Jewish innkeeper by the *starosta* of Mogilany, 1720.
(NBANU, L'viv, Okremi postuplennia)

MOŁCZADŹ (pow. Baranowicze, woj. nowogrodzkie) 1566–1568
Microfilms:
Charters concerning tolls [Rt], 1566–68.
(RGADA, Moscow, ML)

MONASTERZYSKA (pow. Buczacz, woj. tarnopolskie) 1896–1906
Originals:
An appeal for help for fire victims [G], 1903.
Microfilms:
1. Reports from an inspection of Baron Hirsch Foundation (JCA) schools [G, P], 1896–1904.
(TsDIAU, L'viv, Krajowa Rada Szkolna)
2. Correspondence between the community and the authorities about the community budget, including a list of taxpayers, 1897–1906; complaints on the closing of a private *minyan*, 1904–06.
(TsDIAU, L'viv, Namiestnictwo Galicyjskie)

MOSINA (pow. Śrem, woj. poznańskie)
Original:
A prayerbook containing a list of martys and a list of the *Ner Tamid* society members [H], n.d.

MOSTY (pow. Grodno, woj. białostocke) 1673
Photocopies:
Inventory of the *klucz*, 1673.
(NIAB, Minsk, Arch. Radziwiłłów)

MOSTY WIELKIE (pow. Żółkiew, woj. lwowskie) 1640–1938
Microfilms:
1. Inventory of the town, 1640.
(AP Wrocław, Ossolineum)
2. Correspondence with the authorities about *chadorim*, including a list of *melamdim*, 1874–1908; correspondence on the community statutes [G, P], 1897; correspondence with the authorities on community matters, and protests about community elections, 1900–06.
(TsDIAU, L'viv, Namiestnictwo Galicyjskie)
3. Copies of birth and marriage documents, 1901–38.
(DALO, L'viv, Magistrat, Żółkiew)
4. Real estate register and a list of inhabitants, 1913.
(DALO, L'viv, Starostwo Powiatowe, Żółkiew)
5. Correspondence about the *Haor, Hitachdut, Machzikei Hadas* and *Agudas Yisroel* associations, 1923–37.
(DALO, L'viv, Magistrat, Lwów)
6. Correspondence on the community, and its elections, including a budget and list of taxpayers [P, Y], 1931–35.
(DALO, L'viv, UW, Lwów)

MOŚCISKA (woj. lwowskie) 1568–1938
Microfilms:
1. Confirmation by King Zygmunt August of an ancient prohibition for Jews to settle in the town, 1568; documents about the Jewish cemetery and a complaint against the community [G], 18th cent; contracts of land purchase by Jews [G], 1858; lists of eligible voters and community members [G], 1861–70.
(AP Kraków, Teki Schneidra)
2. Correspondence with the authorities on aid to Jews emigrating to new settlements, including a list of names [G], 1789; correspondence with the regional authorities about measures to prevent fires [G, P], 1865–74; correspondence about the *Gmilas Chasodim* society [G, P], 1897–1902.
(TsDIAU, L'viv, Namiestnictwo Galicyjskie)
3. Correspondence about *Agudas Yisroel*, including statutes and registration, 1923–28, 1938.
(DALO, L'viv, Magistrat, Lwów)
4. Correspondence with the authorities on registering a loan society, including statutes and lists of founders and members, 1926–36; correspondence about the *Kultur Liga*, 1926; reports and correspondence on the community board and board elections [P, Y], 1928–30; correspondence about the *Talmud Tora* and the *Nowa Klaus* associations, including statutes, 1928–35; a list of local members of political parties, containing data on political affiliations and nationalities, 1930–31; correspondence with the authorities about the community budget and complaints about unjust increases in taxes, 1932–36; correspondence about community board elections, including a list of board members, citing their ages, professions and political orientations, 1933–38; statistical reports containing names of board members, rabbis and *dayanim*, 1937.
(DALO, L'viv, UW, Lwów)

MSTÓW (pow. Częstochowa, woj. kieleckie) 1887–1892
Microfilms:
The openening of a new Jewish cemetery [R], 1887–92.
(AP Łódź, Rząd Gubernialny, WA, Piotrków)

MSZANA DOLNA (pow. Limanowa, woj. krakowskie) 1897–1908
Microfilms:
Correspondence with the authorities on reorganizing the community, including statutes [G, P], 1897; and on the community elections, 1905–08.
(TsDIAU, L'viv, Namiestnictwo Galicyjskie)

MSZCZONÓW (pow. Błonie, woj. warszawskie) 1778
Photocopy:
An agreement between the community and the municipality, containing a charter for the Jews, 1778
(AGAD, Warszawa, DP)

MURAWICA (pow. Dubno, woj. wołyńskie) 1790–1870
Microfilms:
1. Files on Jews in Murawica [P, R], 1790–1866.
(AP Kraków, Arch. Młynowskie Chodkiewiczów)
2. Correspondence and verdicts on debts of the Jewish community to Polish monasteries [R], 1845–47.
(TsDIAU, Kyiv, Kantseliariia... general-gubernatora)
3. Files on disorders caused by Jews during the collecting of taxes [R], 1867–70.
(DARO, Dubenskii uezdnyi sud)

MUROWANA GOŚLINA (pow. Oborniki, woj. poznańskie) 1811–1879
Originals:
A letter from the rabbi concerning his salary [H], 1828; the record book of a Tora study society [H], 1832–49; the indentures of a tailor's apprentice [G, P], 1833; community statutes [G], 1836; the seating plan of the men's section in the synagogue [H], 1843; the burial society record book [H], 1850–79.
Microfilms:
Community minute book [H], 1811.
(JTS, New York)

MUSZYNA (pow. Nowy Sącz, woj. krakowskie) 1846
Original:
Official instructions concerning the collection of Jewish taxes and the procedure for dealing with Jews residing in the town without permission [G], 1846.

MUŻYŁÓW (pow. Podhajce, woj. tarnopolskie) 1936
Microfilms:
Monographs containing demographic and economic information about Jews, 1936.
(AP Wrocław, Ossolineum, WKNZNP, Lwów)

MYCHÓW (pow. Opatów, woj. kieleckie) 1857–1871
Microfilms:
Files on judicial proceedings against an unauthorized Jewish leaseholder [P, R], 1857–71.
(AP Radom, Rząd Gubernialny, Radom)

MYSŁOWICE (pow. Katowice, woj. śląskie) 1850–1913
Original:
Community statutes, 1850; personal file of Rabbi Dr. Jaffe, 1856–99; the establishment of Katowice as a community independent of Mysłowice, 1861–65; files concerning real estate bought and owned by Jews, 1866–99; disputes over community taxation, 1877–82; files on the sick care and burial societies, 1877–1913; litigation between the community and the police, 1880–1905; the correspondence of the Upper Silesian Comittee of Aid for Russian Jews, 1891–93; financial support for the poor [G], 1901–02.

MYSZ (Nowa Mysz, pow. Baranowicze, woj. nowogródzkie) 1650–1766
Microfilms:
Inventories and accounts, 1650–1730; reports, complaints, accounts and excerpts from books of Castle Courts concerning properties of the Sieniawski family [H, L, P], 1652–1766.
(Bibl. Czartoryskich, Kraków)

MYSZENIEC (Myszyniec, pow. Ostrołęka, woj. białostockie) 1818–1915
Microfilms:
1. Files on synagogues, 1818–60.
(AGAD, Warszawa, CWW)
2. Copies of inscriptions on synagogues and tombstones [H, R], 1910.
(RGIA, St. Petersburg, Departament dukhovnykh del...)
3. Files on the arrest of Jews suspected of illegal activity, including clandestine border crossing [R], 1912–15.
(AP Białystok, Rząd Gubernialny, Łomża)

MYŚLENICE (woj. krakowskie) 1846–1898
Microfilms:
1. Files on confirming the statutes of Jewish communities, 1846–96; correspondence with the *Ahavas Zion* colonization society about emigration to Palestine [G, P], 1898.
(TSDIAU, L'viv, Namiestnictwo Galicyjskie)
2. Report concerning instruction of the Jewish religion [G, P], 1882–89.
(TsDIAU, L'viv, Krajowa Rada Szkolna)

NADARZYN (pow. Błonie, woj. warszawskie) 1848–1869
Microfilms:
Records concerning the community, 1848–69.
(AP Warszawa, Magistrat, Piaseczno)

NADWÓRNA (woj. stanisławowskie) 1792–1939
Microfilms:
1. Refusal of a request for a charter to the Jewish community [G], 1792; files on conscription matters [G, P], 1870; correspondence on elections to the community board, 1895.
(TsDIAU, L'viv, Namiestnictwo Galicyjskie)
2. File on confirming the statutes of the *Ezra* society [G, P], 1871–88, 1921–30; confirmation of *Agudas Yisroel* statutes and a list of members, 1893, 1920–30; statutes, minutes and correspondence on Zionist associations, 1921–30; correspondence concerning activities of the *Bund*, 1923; reports about public meetings organized by *Poalei Zion* and the *Bund*, including statutes, 1926–27; reports and correspondence concerning activities of the Jewish community, including elections, the appointments of rabbis and

dayanim, salaries of rabbis and the finances of the community, including a list of taxpayers, [G, P, Y], 1926–37; reports about activities of the Revisionist Zionists, 1927; reports on public meetings of Jewish parties and associations, 1928; correspondence about *Poalej Zion Lewica*, 1928; reports on the activity of *Hashomer Hatzair*, 1929; reports about Jewish youth movements, 1929–39; registers and lists of Jewish associations, including *Hatzofim Brit Trumpeldor*, 1930–37; a report from conferences of the *Hitachdut* party, 1933; reports about the *Histadrut Hanoar Haivri, Hashomer Hatzair* and *Tzofe* youth movements, and about the *Bund,* 1933; files on protests against British policy in Palestine, 1934; reports and correspondence about activity of *Hitachdut Poalei Zion*, 1935; a statistical description of the district, 1935; a monograph about the political and economic situation of the district, 1936; reports about elections to the community board, including a list of board members, 1938–39; correspondence on the murder of a Jew by a policeman, 1939.
(DAIFO, Ivano-Frankivs'k, UW, Stanisławów)
3. Reports and correspondence on *chadorim* and private Jewish schools [G, P], 1878–81; reports on teaching Jewish religion in elementary schools [G, P], 1882–89.
(TsDIAU, L'viv, Krajowa Rada Szkolna)

NAGÓRZANKA (pow. Buczacz, woj. tarnopolskie) 1902–1910
Microfilms:
Files on teaching Jewish religion in schools, 1902–10.
(TsDIAU, L'viv, Krajowa Rada Szkolna)

NAKŁO (pow. Wyrzysk, woj. poznańskie) 1824–1913
Originals:
A lecture by Jacob Pieczkowski on the Jewish school in Nakło (1824–1913); community records [G], 1835–36.

NAŁĘCZÓW (pow. Puławy, woj. lubelskie) 1772
Microfilms:
Contract between Prince Stanisław Małachowski and a Jew concerning glaziery works in a new palace, 1772.
(AP Lublin, Arch. Małachowskich z Nałęczowa)

NAPRAWA (pow. Myślenice, woj. krakowskie) 1858–1871
Microfilms:
Files on litigation between two Jews, 1858–71.
(AP Radom, Rząd Gubernialny, Radom)

NARAJÓW (pow. Brzeżany, woj. tarnopolskie) 1699–1936
Microfilms:
1. Orders of payment, letters and registers concerning properties of the Sieniawski family [H, P], 1699–1726.
(Bibl. Czartoryskich, Kraków)
2. A *lustracja* of Czartoryski properties, 1766.
(AGAD, Warszawa, Arch. Potockich w Łańcucie)
3. Files on confirmation of Jewish community statutes, 1846–96.
(TsDIAU, L'viv, Namiestnictwo Galicyjskie)
4. Monograph including demographic and economic informationon about the town's Jews, 1936.

(AP Wrocław, Ossolineum, WKNZNP, Lwów)

NAREWKA (pow. Bielsk, woj. białostockie) 19th–20th cent.
Original:
Rabbinical court documents [H], 19th–20th cent.

NAROL (pow. Lubaczów, woj. lwowskie) 1730–1936
Microfilms:
1. Accounts [H, P], 1730–96.
(TsDIAU, Kyiv, Arch. Tarło)
2. Files on the election of rabbis [G, P], 1913–19.
(TsDIAU, L'viv, Ministerium fuer Kultus und Unterricht, Wien)
3. Correspondence on the registration of the *Machzikei Hadas* association, 1932.
(DALO, L'viv, Magistrat, Lwów)
4. Files on an examination in the Polish language for Rabbi Ch. Schapira, 1932; a request by the Jewish community concerning construction of a new prayer house, 1932–33; correspondence on the community budget, 1932–36; correspondence about election of the rabbi, and a request for exemption from the community tax, 1933–35.
(DALO, L'viv, UW, Lwów)

NASIELSK (pow. Pułtusk, woj. warszawskie) 1910
Microfilms:
Copies of inscriptions from synagogues and tombstones [H, R], 1910.
(RGIA, St. Petersburg, Departament dukhovnykh del...)

NAWARJA (pow. Lwów, woj. lwowskie) 1931–1937
Microfilms:
Correspondence with the authorities on registration of the *Machzikei Hadas* association, 1931; correspondence about the community budget and a list of taxpayers, 1933–35; correspondence on the community elections, a list of voters, their professions and places of residence, 1936–37; reports containing names of community board members, rabbis and *dayanim*, 1937.
(DALO, L'viv, UW, Lwów)

NAWOJOWA (pow. Nowy Sącz, woj. krakowskie) 1878
Microfilms:
Reports and correspondence on reorganization of elementary schools attended by Jewish pupils [G, P], 1878.
(TsDIAU, L'viv, Krajowa Rada Szkolna)

NIEBYLEC (pow. Rzeszów, woj. lwowskie) 1897–1935
Microfilms:
1. Statutes of the community, 1897.
(TsDIAU, L'viv, Gmina Żydowska, Lwów)
2. Correspondence concerning community matters, 1898.
(TsDIAU, L'viv, Namiestnictwo Galicyjskie)
3. Correspondence on the community budget, including lists of taxpayers, 1933–35.
(DALO, L'viv, UW, Lwów)

NIEMIRÓW (pow. Rawa Ruska, woj. lwowskie) 1898–1935
Microfilms:
1. Files on activity of the Jewish community and statutes of the community [G, P], 1898–1904.
(TsDIAU, L'viv, Namiestnictwo Galicyjskie)
2. Correspondence about registration of the *Machzikei Hadas* association and a list of board members, 1932–33.
(DALO, L'viv, Magistrat, Lwów)
3. Correspondence about the budget, 1932–35.
(DALO, L'viv, UW, Lwów)

NIEPOŁOMICE (pow. Bochnia, woj. krakowskie) 1732
Microfilms:
A dispute between the municipality and a converted Jewish innkeeper, as well as his complaint to the king, 1732.
(AP Kraków, IT)

NIESUCHOJEŻE (pow. Kowel, woj. wołyńskie) 1834–1876
Microfilms:
Copies of material about *chasidic tzadikim* [R], 1834–76.
(TsDIAU, Kyiv, Dokumenty, sobrannye…)

NIESZAWA (woj. warszawskie) 1869–1870
Originals:
Records concerning citizenship of Jews [R], 1869–70.

NIEŚWIEŻ (woj. nowogródzkie) 1586–1906
Photocopies:
1. Copies of charters for the Jews, 1586, 1589, 1735; excerpts from decrees and contracts concerning the Jews, 1762, 1779; accounts of estates, 1764–68, 1783; contracts and correspondence on renovation of the castle by Jews [P, R], 1832, 1836, 1878–1906;
(NIAB, Minsk, Arch. Radziwiłłów)
2. Register of debts for renovation of the Jewish school, and *arenda* contracts, 1779; excerpts from books of the Castle Court concerning Jews, 1827, 1830.
(NIAB, Minsk, Magistrat, Nieśwież)
3. A file about Leib Dilon from Nieśwież, Russian Jewry's representative to the Tsar [R], 1829, 1831;
(GARF, Moscow, Tret'e otdelenie…)
4. Records about renovation of the castle by Jews [R], 1873–85.
(LCVIA, Vilnius, Radvilu skolu nagrinejimo komisija)
Microfilms:
1. Charters by Polish kings to the city [L, P], 1586–1698; charters by the Radziwiłł family to the Jews, 1589, 1595, 1661, 1670, 1676, 1690; a letter by Mikołaj Krzysztof Radziwiłł, appointing a *wójt* for the Jews, 1595; an *uniwersał* by A. L. Radziwiłł to the Jews [L, P], 1647; a decision of Katarzyna Radziwiłł, sent to the municipality, forbidding Jews to participate in the governing of the town and collecting of taxes during the fair, 1688; a register of real estate and Jews living aroud the main square, 1703; *arenda* contracts, 1703–1826; inquires and other judicial documents concerning inhabitants of the town, 1712–63; an *uniwersał* by Anna z Sanguszków Radziwiłł to Christians and Jews from Germany living in Nieśwież, 1722; files of the governor of Nieśwież, on various economic problems, 1722–50; approbations by M. K.

Radziwiłł and K. S. Radziwiłł given to various Jews to serve as rabbis of the community 1731–63; copies of decrees by MK Radziwiłł concerning various economic and legal matters, *arenda* contracts, accounts [H, P], 1746–51; an *uniwersał* by MK Radziwiłł forbidding Jewish stall-keepers to sell products harmful to health, 1751; a decree after a fire, containing charters to the Jews [L, P], 1758; copies of decrees, registers and a decision of the municipality concerning the Jews [P, R], 1793–95; a copy of a charter given by Radziwiłł to the Jews [L, P], 1804; a register of debts due to the *kahal* [P, R], 1806; copies of proclamations by the Jews [P, R], 1811.
(AGAD, Warszawa, Arch. Radziwiłłów)
2. Instructions by the director of the medical dept. permitting employment of Jewish physicians and veterinarians in the civil service; instructions and requests concerning the rights of Jews to serve as rabbis in various towns of Russia [R], 1883–1903.
(RGIA, St. Petersburg, Departament dukhovnykh del...)
3. Correspondence on elections to the Duma [R], 1905–06.
(RGIA, St. Petersburg, Obshchestvo polnopraviia...)

NISKO (woj. lwowskie) 1846–1937
Microfilms:
1. Files on confirmation of communal statutes, 1846–96; correspondence with the Ministry of the Interior regarding reorganization of the community and the confirmation of its statutes, 1895–96.
(TsDIAU, L'viv, Namiestnictwo Galicyjskie)
2. Correspondence with the authorities on changes in the statutes and raising of taxes, including a list of community board members, 1922; files on elections to the community board, 1928–29; authorization by the authorities to raise funds for the Polish–Galician Jewish community in Palestine, 1928–30; a list of members of the local town council, their nationalities and political affiliations, 1930–31; decrees, reports and correspondence on community elections and budget, including a list of taxpayers, 1933–37.
(DALO, L'viv, UW, Lwów)

NIWKA (pow. Będzin, woj kieleckie) 1911
Microfilms:
A file on the Jewish cemetery [R], 1911.
(AP Łódź, Rząd Gubernialny, WA, Piotrków)

NIŻNIÓW (pow. Tłumacz, woj. stanisławowskie) 1921–1938
Microfilms:
Statutes, minutes and correspondence concerning Zionist associations, 1921–30; complaints by community members about elections and the raising of community taxes [H, P], 1928–37; a list of *Gmilus Chasodim* society members, 1930–31; files on confirming the statutes of various Jewish associations, 1931–32; reports and correspondence about community elections, 1932–36; correspondence with the authorities concerning activity of the Jewish community and about *shechita* of poultry, including a list of community taxpayers 1937–38.
(DAIFO, Ivano-Frankivs'k, UW, Stanisławów)

NOWA GÓRA (pow. Chrzanów, woj. krakowskie) 1652–1822
Microfilms:
1. Investigations, reports, complaints and excerpts from municipal books concerning properties of the Sieniawski family [H, L, P], 1652–1766.
(Bibl. Czartoryskich, Kraków)

2. Registers, accounts, *uniwersały*, decrees and contracts concerning property of the Sieniawski and Czartoryski families [F, L, P], 1706–85.
(Biblioteka Narodowa, Warszawa)
3. An extract from municipal records concerning the sale of land to Jews to build a brewery, 1818–22.
(AP Kraków, IT)

NOWA MYSZ - see MYSZ

NOWE MIASTO (pow. Dobromil, woj. lwowskie) 1659–1939
Photocopies:
A request to release two Jews from prison, 1779.
(AGAD, Warszawa, DP)
Microfilms:
1. *Supliki* to the Sieniawski family from Nowe Miasto, 1659–1711.
(Bibl. Czartoryskich, Kraków)
2. A file concerning confirmation of the Jewish community statutes, 1846–96.
(TsDIAU, L'viv, Namiestnictwo Galicyjskie)
3. Correspondence with the authorities on separating certain neighborhoods from the Jewish community of Chyrów and annexing them to Nowe Miasto, 1928–29; correspondence about the community budget, 1933–36; reports, complaints and correspondence concerning community elections and confirmation of the rabbi, 1933–37; correspondence regarding the budget, institutions, functionaries and administrative structure, including tables with data on rabbis and *dayanim*, 1937–39.
(DALO, L'viv, UW, Lwów)

NOWE MIASTO (pow. Rawa, woj. warszawskie) 1788–1912
Microfilms:
1. Files on agreements and litigation over real estate between Jews from Mogielnica and the *kahal* in Nowe Miasto [H, P], 1788–92.
(AGAD, Warszawa, Arch. Lubomirskich z Małej Wsi)
2. Records of the community and its accounts; files on Jewish purchase of land and building activities, 1820–61.
(AP Łódź, Anterioria Rządu Gubernialnego, Piotrków)
3. Ratification of community accounts and elections; records concerning the upkeep of the *mikve* [R], 1893–1912.
(AP Łódź, Rząd Gubernialny, WA, Piotrków)
4. Fines for evading conscription [R], 1896–98.
(AP Łódź, Rząd Gubernialny, WP, Piotrków)
5. Copies of inscriptions on tombstones and synagogues [H, R], 1910.
(RGIA, St. Petersburg, Departanent dukhovnykh del...)

NOWE MIASTO nad Wartą (pow. Jarocin, woj. poznańskie) 1822–1894
Originals:
Synagogue registers [H], 1822, 1838–44; a draft of the statutes [G], 1834–37; files on: *mazzot,* 1835–59, the Jewish school, 1834–37, the *Chevra Kadisha* [G], 1874–94.
Microfilms:
Community board resolutions [G], 1834.
(Centrum Judaicum, Berlin)

NOWOGRÓD (pow. Łomża, woj. białostockie) 1566–1915
Microfilms:
1. *Lustracje* of the region, 1566.
(AGAD, Warszawa, ASK)
2. Reports, requests and correspondence concerning the division of the community in Nowogród, 1810–12; minutes, reports and correspondence concerning the appointments of rabbis, their education and salaries, 1856–64.
(AGAD, Warszawa, CWW)
3. Birth, marriage and death records (fragmentary), 1826–64.
(AP Łomża)
4. The arrest and expulsion of Jews suspected of spying for the German army [R], 1913–15.
(AP Białystok, Rząd Gubernialny, Łomża)

NOWOGRÓDEK (woj. nowogródzkie) 1563–1893
Photocopies:
1. Charters for the Jews, 1647, 1667, 1724, 1757.
(NIAB, Minsk, Arch. Radziwiłłów)
2. Register of taxes paid by inhabitants of the *jurydyki*, 1759–1859; files on Jewish merchants, 1792–1807, documents on the sale of a plot of land, 1808.
(AGAD, Warszawa, Arch. Radziwiłłów)
3. Information about bookshops and libraries [R], 1886, 1892;
(NIAB, Minsk, Kantseliariia minskogo gubernatora)
4. A request by Jewish merchants for compensation during a cholera epidemic [R], 1848–50.
(GARF, Moscow, Tret'e otdelenie…)
Microfilms:
1. A royal decree concerning the allotment of land to Jews for settlement and construction [Rt], 1563; royal decrees ordering resettlement of Jews in Nowogródek and conferral of nobility and a coat of arms on a Jewish convert to Christianity, as well as a grant of land in the Kiev district [Rt], 1564–65.
(RGADA, Moscow, ML)
2. Records of litigation between Jews, 1832–33.
(AP Wrocław, Ossolineum)
3. Correspondence with the rabbi, regarding marriage certificates [R], 1873–93.
(RGIA, St. Petersburg, Departament dukhovnykh del…)

NOWOSIÓŁKA JAZŁOWIECKA (pow. Buczacz, woj. tarnopolskie) 1936
Microfilms:
A monograph containing demographic and economic data, 1936.
(AP Wrocław, Ossolineum, WKNZNP, Lwów)

NOWOTANIEC (pow. Sanok, woj. lwowskie) 1921–1925
Microfilms:
Correspondence with the authorities on annexation of the Jewish community in Nowotaniec by that of Bukowisko, 1921–25.
(DALO, L'viv, UW, Lwów)

NOWY DWÓR (pow. Sokółka, woj. białostockie) 1566–1913
Photocopies:

Inventories of the town, 1786, 1789;
(NIAB, Minsk, Kollektsia drevnikh inventarei)
Microfilms:
1. Royal charters for the Jews of Grodno concerning *arenda* of beer production and the malt industry in Nowy Dwór [Rt], 1566–68.
(RGADA, Moscow, ML)
2. Certificates and photographs of candidates for the rabbinate [R], 1886–1913.
(AP Białystok, Rząd Gubernialny, Łomża)

NOWY KORCZYN (pow. Stopnica, woj. kieleckie) 1584–1842.
Originals:
A deed to a Jew's house, 1584; regulations concerning Jews residing in the town, 1585.
Microfilms:
1. Financial transaction between the Jewish community and a Catholic order [L,P], 1682–1701
(AP Kraków, Arch. Krzeszowickie Potockich)
2. Letter of protection against the *starosta* granted to the Jewish community by King Stanisław August Poniatowski [L], 1775 and a letter of rebuke from him to the town and the community elders [L], 1776.
(AGAD, Warszawa, Księgi Kanclerskie)
3. Correspondence on extraction of funds from the *kahal* for education, 1829–42.
(AGAD, Warszawa, KRzPiS)

NOWY SĄCZ (woj. krakowskie) 1685–1942
Originals:
Invitation to a wedding [H], 1931
Microfilms:
1. A copy of a royal charter by King Jan III for the Jews [L], 1685; a list of voters and community members [G], 19th cent.
(AP Kraków, Teki Schneidra)
2. Evidence from a criminal case involving a Jew, 1751 .
(AP Kraków, IT)
3. Confirmation by King Stanisław August Poniatowski of a charter granted to the Jews [L, P], 1765.
(AGAD, Warszawa, Księgi Kanclerskie)
4. Records, charters and inventories of the Jews, 1785–87.
(AP Wrocław, Ossolineum)
5. Correspondence with the government concerning *arenda* and financial matters [G, L, P], 1814–18; statutes of the *Talmud Tora* society [G, P], 1891; statutes of the *Gmilus Chasodim* society [G, P], 1893–1912.
(TsDIAU, L'viv, Namiestnictwo Galicyjskie)
6. Proclamations, reports and correspondence concerning *chadorim* and private Jewish schools [G, P], 1878–81.
(TsDIAU, L'viv, Krajowa Rada Szkolna)
7. A list of 156 Jews decorated with a silver medal for the battle near Sącz, 1914.
(NBANU, L'viv, Zb. Goldsteina)
8. Minutes of the Association of Jewish Craftsmen and a register of apprentices, 1925–42.
(AP Kraków, Oddział w Nowym Sączu, Cech Rzemiosł Różnych)

NOWY TARG (woj. krakowskie) 1710–1906
Microfilms:
1. A fragment from village records concerning the Jews, 1710–12.
(AP Wrocław, Ossolineum)
2. Correspondence with the *Ahavas Zion* colonization society [G, P], 1898; correspondence regarding assistance by various societies to school children and students [G, P], 1904–06.
(TsDIAU, L'viv, Namiestnictwo Galicyjskie)

NOWY TOMYŚL (woj. poznańskie) 1881–1906
Originals:
Community records [G, H], 1881–1906.

NUR (pow. Ostrów, woj. białostockie) 1566
Microfilms:
Lustracje, 1566.
(AGAD, Warszawa, ASK)

OBERTYN (pow. Horodenka, woj. stanisławowskie) 1871–1939
Microfilms:
1. Correspondence on confirming the statutes of the *Dorshei Tov* society [G, P], 1871–88, 1921–30; files on confirming the statutes and on the subsequent liquidation of the *Gmilus Chasodim* society, including a membership list [G, P], 1904–13, 1928–31; statutes, minutes and correspondence concerning various associations, 1925, 1931–39; reports on the activities of Zionist parties and associations, 1926; files on the registration of the Jewish Library Association, 1926–34; files on elections to the community board, 1926–37; membership lists of the *Hatzofim Brit Trumpeldor* society, 1930–37; a report on a conference of the *Hitachdut* party, 1933.
(DAIFO, Ivano-Frankivs'k, UW, Stanisławów)
2. Minutes and reports following an inspection of Baron Hirsch Foundation (JCA) schools [G, P], 1896–1904.
(TsDIAU, L'viv, Krajowa Rada Szkolna)
3. Correspondence concerning the community budget [G, P], 1902; correspondence with the district authorities and central government in Vienna concerning protests against results of the community elections [G, P], 1908.
(TsDIAU, L'viv, Namiestnictwo Galicyjskie)
4. Answers to a questionnaire concerning Jews, 1922.
(NBANU, L'viv, Zb. Czołowskiego)

OBORNIKI (woj. poznańskie) 1724–1899
Original:
Translations and confirmation of a charter granted to the Jews [G], 1724, 1754; a file concerning Jewish vagabonds [G], 1834–38; employment of a *shochet* [G], 1834–70; illuminated circumcision register of Yaakov Leib Levenberg [H], 1837–55; account book [G], 1845–47; a monograph by Akiva Posner on the history of the Jewish community and Jewish families in Oborniki [G], 1959;
Microfilms:
1. A decision by King August III, resolving a dispute between the municipality and the *starosta* over Jewish rights in the town and other matters, 1757.
(AP Poznań, Akta miast, woj. poznańskie)

2. Minutes of the community board [G], 1835–99.
(Centrum Judaicum, Berlin)

OBRZYCKO (pow. Szamotuły, woj. poznańskie) 1764–1918
Originals:
Register of community debts and taxes [G], n.d.
Microfilms:
Legal records, 1764–84; community records and files on education, school buildings and teachers' fees [G], 1910–18.
(AP Poznań, Akta miast, woj. poznańskie)

ODOLANÓW (pow. Ostrów, woj. poznańskie) 1814
Microfilms:
Records of Jewish purchase of real estate, 1814.
(AGAD, Warszawa, Komisja Województwa Kaliskiego)

OKRZEJA (pow. Łuków, woj. lubelskie) 1534–1615
Microfilms:
Lustracje, 1534–1615.
(AGAD, Warszawa, ASK)

OLEKSINIEC STARY (pow. Krzemieniec, woj. wołyńskie) 1837–1841
Microfilms:
1. Files on the confiscation of prayer books owned by the rabbi [R], 1837–39.
(TsDIAU, Kyiv, Kantseliariia... general-gubernatora)
2. A list of conscripts in the town [H, R], 1840–41.
(DATO, Ternopil', Magistrat, Krzemieniec)

OLESKO (pow. Złoczów, woj. tarnopolskie) 1756
Microfilms:
A letter by the royal scribe in Warsaw, to the municipality of Lwów concerning Jews from Olesko arrested for minting forged silver coins, 1756.
(TsDIAU, L'viv, Kolektsiia lystiv...)

OLESZYCE and the surroundings (pow. Lubaczów, woj. lwowskie) 1628–1935
Microfilms:
1. Agreements, circulars, decrees, contracts, accounts and other documents concerning properties of the Sieniawski and Czartoryski families in the area [F, L, H, P], 1628–1785.
(Bibl. Czartoryskich, Kraków)
2. Files on elections to the community board, 1928–29, 1934–35.
(DALO, L'viv, UW, Lwów)

OLKUSZ (woj. kieleckie) 1657–1903
Original:
The record book of the burial society [H], 1824–1903.
Microfilms:
1. A decree by King Jan Kazimierz limiting Jewish settlement to five houses in the main square, 1657; a file on a dispute between burghers and Jews, 1776–91.

(AP Kraków, IT)
2. Records of a dispute between burghers and Jews concerning Jewish debts, 1821–50.
(AGAD, Warszawa, KRzSW)
3. Reports and complaints concerning the burial society and burial tarriffs, 1822–59; a project to distribute money to needy Jews and support poor Jewish hospital patients [P, R], 1848–56; reports and correspondence with various government offices concerning appointments of rabbis and litigations between them and community boards, 1853–56; correspondence about the exemption of Rabbinical Seminary graduates from conscription, and lists of rabbis, 1865–71.
(AGAD, Warszawa, CWW)
4. A request by the *kahal* for tax reductions, 1824.
(AGAD, Warszawa, KRzPiS)

5. *Arenda* contracts for the lease of steelworks in Olkusz, and accounts, 1680–81; birth, marriage and death records (fragmentary) [H, P], 1854–70.
(AP Kraków)

OLSZEWO–BORKI (pow. Ostrołęka, woj. białostockie) 1914
Microfilms:
File on exempting a Jewish couple from the passport fee [R], 1914.
(AP Białystok, Rząd Gubernialny, Łomża)

OŁYKA (pow. Łuck, woj. wołyńskie) 1712–1869
Microfilms:
1. Inquires and other judicial documents concerning local inhabitants, 1712–63.
(AGAD, Warszawa, Arch. Radziwiłłów)
2. File on the compulsory sale of a Jew's house for unpaid back taxes [R], 1860–69.
(DARO, Rivne, Dubenskii uezdnyi sud)

OŁYKA, surroundings, 18th cent.
Microfilms:
A list of the Jewish population in the district [H], 18th cent.
(AGAD, Warszawa, Arch. Zamoyskich)

OPALIN (pow. Luboml, woj. wołyńskie) 1779
Microfilms:
Confirmation by King Stanisław August Poniatowski of the charter granted to the town and its Jews, 1779.
(AGAD, Warszawa, Księgi Kanclerskie)

OPATOWIEC (pow. Pińczów, woj. kieleckie) 1800
Microfilms:
A complaint to the municipality about Jewish failure to pay the candle tax, 1800.
(AP Kraków, IT)

OPATÓW (pow. Kępno, woj. poznańskie) 1534–1615
Microfilms:
Inventories and accounts of the Bolesław *starostwo,* 1534–1615.
(AGAD, Warszawa, ASK)

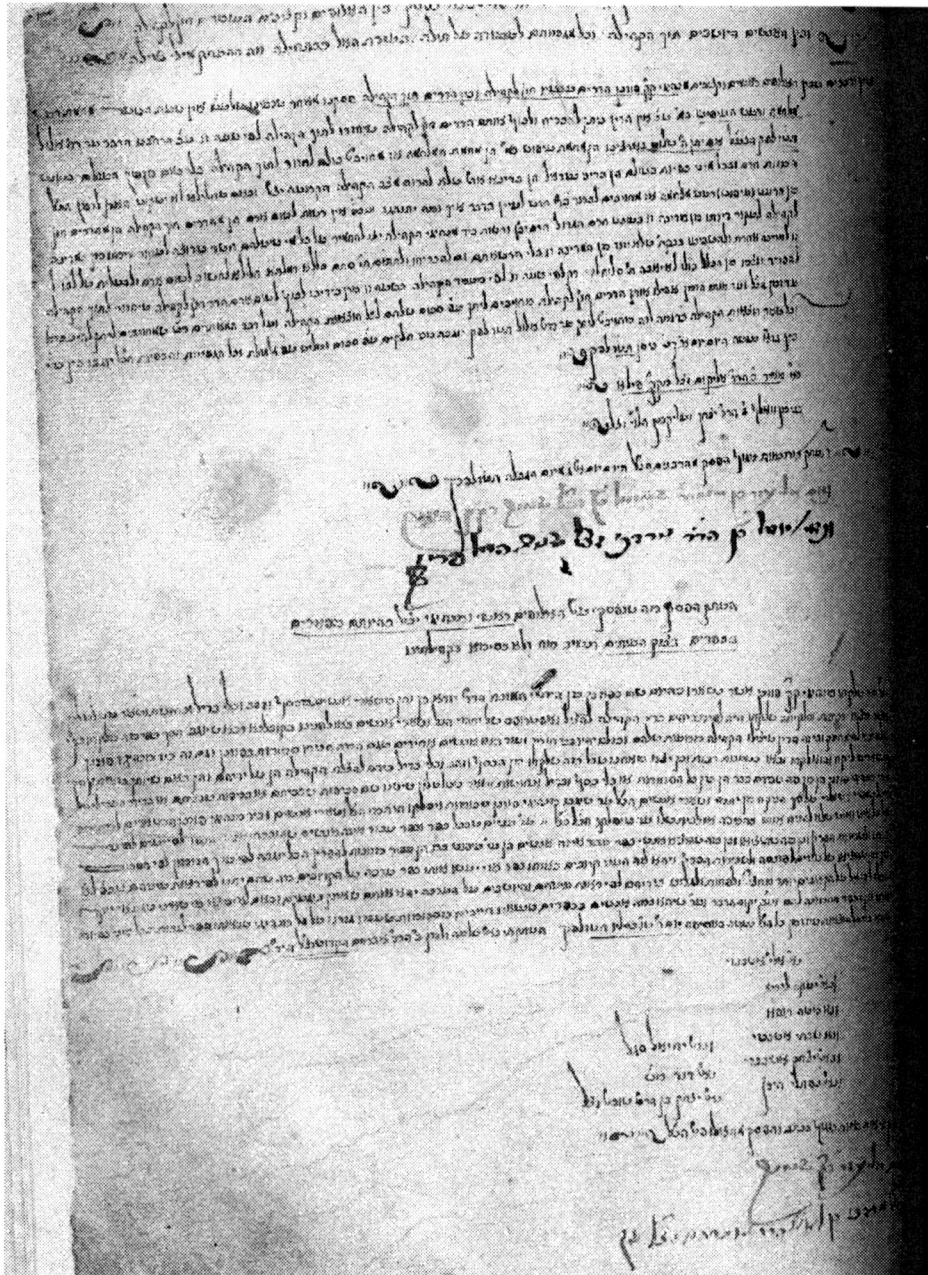

Poznań. Entry from the community minute book. 1655 (Hebrew)

OPATÓW (woj. kieleckie) 1606–1871
Microfilms:
1. Inventories, decrees and proclamations concerning the town and the community, 1606–1788; records on the community (lists, accounts, taxes), 1707–90; files on the settling of Jewish debts, decrees and resolutions concerning administration of the town, 1723–79; accounts of the burial society, 1787–88.
(AGAD, Warszawa, AGWAO)
2. Investigations, reports, complaints and excerpts from municipal books concerning properties of the Sieniawski family [H, L, P], 1652–1766.
(Bibl. Czartoryskich, Kraków)
3. A financial transaction between the Jewish community and a Catholic order [L, P], 1682–1701.
(AP Kraków, Arch. Krzeszowickie Potockich)
4. A file on inheritance, 1714; decrees concerning the Jews, files on Jewish business transactions, records of city income, (incl. from Jews), 1720–29; files on the community [H, L, P], 1721–37; complaints by Christian inhabitants against Jews, 1721–41; a court case concerning a local Jew [L], 1744; minutes on the abduction of a Jew injured near the synagogue, 1744; a loan request [L], 1748.
(AP Kraków, Arch. Sanguszków)
5. A letter on a dispute between the community of Opatów and that of Zamość, 1725.
(AGAD, Warszawa, Arch. Zamoyskich)
6. A request by 88 Jewish merchants from Poland to enter Russia with their merchandise [R], 1739.
(TsDIAU, Kyiv, Kievskaia gubernskaia kantseliariia)
7. A project to distribute kosher food to needy Jews and to support poor Jewish hospital patients [P, R], 1848–56; correspondence concerning exemption from conscription for graduates of the Rabbinical Seminary, including a list of rabbis, 1865–71.
(AGAD, Warszawa, CWW)
8. Files on legal proceedings against local Jews, 1857–66.
(AP Radom, Rząd Gubernialny, Radom)

OPATÓWEK (pow. Kalisz, woj. łódzkie) 1807–1843
Microfilms:
Records concerning the lease of *propinacja* by Jews, 1807–43; files containing descriptions of the town, 1818–26.
(AGAD, Warszawa, Komisja Województwa Kaliskiego)

OPOCZNO (woj. kieleckie) 1534–1931
Original:
A poster announcing community elections [H], 1931.
Microfilms:
1. *Lustracja* of the Sandomierskie *województwo*, 1534–1615.
(AGAD, Warszawa, ASK)
2. Reports and correspondence concerning appointments of rabbis and litigation between them and their communities, including lists of rabbis, 1853–56; correspondence concerning exemptions from conscription for graduates of the Rabbinical Seminary, including a list of rabbis, 1865–71.
(AGAD, Warszawa, CWW)
3. Lists of local Jewish families, 1865–66.
(AP Radom, Rząd Gubernialny, Radom)

OPOLE (pow. Puławy, woj. lubelskie) 1319–1895
Microfilms:
1. Copies of records and charters concerning the town and its Jewish population, 1319–1705; local municipal records (fragmentary), 1510–1811.
(AP Lublin, Księgi Miejskie, Opole)
2. *Arenda* contracts, legal matters, 1796–98; inheritance matters [H, P], 1799–1807; litigation between Jews, 1809; documents concerning a bequest for the construction of a *mikve*, 1855–57.
(AP Lublin, Jurysdykcja dominikalna Józefowa i Opola)
3. A statistical description of the town, 1820–59.
(AP Lublin, Rząd Gubernialny, Lublin)
4. Files on illegal burial societies [R], 1895.
(AP Lublin, Kancelaria Gubernatora Lubelskiego)

ORCHÓWEK (pow. Włodawa, woj. lubelskie) 1867–1875
Microfilms:
Records on *propinacja*, 1867–75.
(AP Lublin, Arch. Zamoyskich z Włodawy)

ORLA (pow. Bielsk Podlaski, woj. białostockie) 1836–1867
Microfilms:
Birth, marriage and death records [P, R], 1836–67.
(AP Białystok)

ORZECHÓWKA (pow. Brzozów, woj. lwowskie) 1936
Microfilms:
Monographs containing demographic and economic information on the Jews, 1936.
(AP Wrocław, Ossolineum, WKNZNP, Lwów)

OSIEK (pow. Jasło, woj. krakowskie) 1875–1877
Microfilms:
Reports containing lists of *chadorim* and teachers [G, P], 1875–77.
(TsDIAU, L'viv, Krajowa Rada Szkolna)

OSIĘCINY (pow. Nieszawa, woj. warszawskie) 1856–1864
Microfilms:
Reports and correspondence on the appointment of rabbis, their education and salaries, 1856–64.
(AGAD, Warszawa, CWW)

OSMOLIN (pow. Gostynin, woj. warszawskie) 1566
Microfilms:
Lustracja of the town, 1566.
(AGAD, Warszawa, ASK)

OSTROŁĘKA (woj. białostockie) 1848–1915
Microfilms:
1. A project to distribute kosher food to needy Jews and support poor Jewish hospital patients [P, R], 1848–56; minutes, reports and correspondence on the appointment of rabbis, their education and salaries, 1856–

64; correspondence on exemption from conscription for graduates of the Rabbinical Seminary, including a list of rabbis, 1865–71.
(AGAD, Warszawa, CWW)
2. Certificates and photographs of candidates for the rabbinate [R], 1886–1913; files on a contract to illuminate the town and for an *arenda* of taxes [R], 1911–13; files on the *arenda* of the ritual slaughter house, incomes from taxes and use of barges on the Narew river [R], 1912–13; documents on permission for a Jewish merchant to work until midnight [R], 1912–14; regulations concerning dispatch of parcels by Jewish relief committees [R], 1914–15.
(AP Białystok, Rząd Gubernialny, Łomża)

OSTROŁĘKA, surroundings, 1914–1915
Microfilms:
File on the arrest and expulsion of Jews suspected of espionage [R], 1914–15.
(AP Białystok, Rząd Gubernialny, Łomża)

OSTROWIEC (pow. Opatów, woj. kieleckie) 1856–1905
Microfilms:
1. Reports and correspondence on the appointment of rabbis, their education and salaries; investigation file against the rabbi, including a list of community members 1856–64.
(AGAD, Warszawa, CWW)
2. Files on pogroms [R], 1903–05.
(GARF, Moscow, Departament politsii…)

OSTROŻEC (pow. Dubno, woj. wołyńskie) 1865–1869
Microfilms:
Files on disorders caused by Jews during the collection of tax debts, and a list of Jewish debtors [R], 1865–69.
(DARO, Rivne, Dubenskii uezdnyi sud)

OSTRÓG (pow. Zdołbunów, woj. wołyńskie) 1616–1914
Photocopies:
A file on the arrest in Omsk of a Jew from Ostróg [R], 1886;
(GAOmO, Omsk, Omskoe gorodskoe politseiskoe upravlenie)
Microfilms:
1. A decree concerning a loan from a Jewish inhabitant, 1616; *arenda* accounts, 1644.
(AP Kraków, Teki Sanguszków, tzw. rzymskie)
2. Files on undue taxation of the Jews, 1617–18.
(TsDIAU, Kyiv, Arch. Zamoyskich)
3. Financial matters between D. Zasławski and a Jew from Ostróg, 1645; decrees concerning taxes, 1655, 1730–46; litigation over financial matters between a nobleman and the *kahal* [L, P], 1719; *supliki* from Jews of Ostróg, 1720–50; *arenda* accounts, inventories and files on the community, 1721–31; a letter from the *Pasha* of Chocim to Prince Sanguszko containing complaints against Jews from Ostróg, 1725; a report of violence against Jews by Jesuit College students [L, P], 1726; a file on litigation between Jesuit College students, Jews and a Tatar commandant, following an assault on Jews by Tatars, 1726–28; files on various legal proceedings, including debts [L, P], 1729–54; litigation between the *kahal* and Franciscans from Międzyrzecz, 1738–46; a document on the appointment of a rabbi, 1777.
(AP Kraków, Teki Sanguszków, tzw. arabskie)

4. Excerpts from municipal books [P, R], 1730, 1762; files on occupation of the synagogue by Russian troops in 1792; copies of documents about *chasidic tzadikim* [R], 1834–76; copies of documents on persecution of the rabbi by the mayor [R], 1849–56; a file on a decision by the community board to celebrate the "miraculous rescue" of the Jews in Ostróg [R], 1906–14.
(TsDIAU, Kyiv, Obshchestvo okhrany pamiatnikov stariny)
5. Accounts, 1736.
(Bibl. Czartoryskich, Kraków)
6. Requests by the *kahal* regarding debt payment, 1779–80.
(RGADA, Moscow, KFE)
7. A decision of the municipal court concerning violation of decrees and nonpayment of penalties by the *kahal*, 1790.
(NBANU, L'viv, Zb. Radzimińskich)
8. A report on fur production [R], 1797–1803.
(RGADA, Moscow, Manufaktur-kollegiia)
9. Files on closing a printing house for printing books without the censor's permission [R], 1828.
(RGIA, St. Petersburg, Peterburgskii tsenzurnyi komitet)
10. Files denouncing printing houses for printing books without the censor's permission [R], 1830–32.
(RGIA, St. Petersburg, Tsentral'noe upravlenie tsenzury)
11. Reports about synagogues, Jewish schools, community employees and Jewish inhabitants [R], 1834; files on the arrest of a Jewish printer for printing a prayerbook without the censor's permission [R], 1837–38; a report about various towns in the area and *propinacja* rights, a register of royal Polish charters and Russian decrees [R], 1849–52; files about the pogroms [R], 1881.
(TsDIAU, Kyiv, Kantseliariia... general-gubernatora)
12. Reports about Jewish schools [R], 1852–58.
(DAKHO, Kamianets'-Podil's'kyi, Direktsiia narodnykh uchilishch...)
13. Files on construction of a Jewish hospital and shelter for the elderly [R], 1863–64.
(RGIA, St. Petersburg, Khoziaistvennyi departament MVD)
14. A report about Jewish community debts [R], 1905–14.
(GARF, Moscow, Bomash)

OSTRÓG, surroundings, 1761–1881
Microfilms:
1. An *arenda* contract for a tavern in the village of Bilczyn, 1761.
(AP Kraków, Archiwum Sanguszków)
2. An inventory of the district, 18th cent.
(AP Wrocław, Ossolineum)
3. A report on honey production [R], 1803.
(RGADA, Moscow, Manufaktur-kollegiia)
4. Reports about synagogues, prayer houses, schools and Jewish inhabitants in various towns of the area [R], 1850.
(TsDIAU, Kyiv, Obshchestvo okhrany pamiatnikov stariny)
5. A statistical report about towns in the district [R], 1871.
(RGIA, St. Petersburg, Khoziaistvennyi departament MVD)
6. Files on leaflets and proclamations instigating pogroms [R], 1881.
(TsDIAU, Kyiv, Kantseliariia... general-gubernatora)

OSTRÓW (pow. Włodawa, woj. lubelskie) 1820–1883
Originals:
Several letters by Rabbi I. M. Freiman [H], 1873–1883.
Microfilms:
Agreements concerning *propinacja,* and *arenda* of inns, flour mills and ponds, 1820–28.
(AP Lublin, Akta gen. Haumana)

OSTRÓW MAZOWIECKA (woj. białostockie) 1647–1923
Originals:
A *ketuba* [H], 1878.
Photocopies:
Charters for the Jews of the town 1647, 1667, 1724, 1757.
(NIAB, Minsk, Arch. Radziwiłłów)
Microfilms:
1. Files on synagogues in the town, 1818–60; reports and correspondence concerning confirmations of rabbis and litigations between them and their communities, 1853–56.
(AGAD, Warszawa, CWW)
2. Certificates and photographs of candidates for the rabbinate [R], 1886–1913; fines for evading conscription [R], 1905; permission to open new businesses, a library and medical services in the town [R], 1905–13; files on *arenda* of municipal incomes and the ritual slaughter house [R], 1911–12; files on the arrest and deportation of Jews for illegal political activity, clandestine border crossing and espionage 1912–15; correspondence on payment for the hospitalization of a Jew from Ostrów in a Jewish hospital in Warsaw [R], 1914.
(AP Białystok, Rząd Gubernialny, Łomża)
3. A list of deportees from the town, 1923.
(DATO, Ternopil', Komenda Powiatowa PP, Trembowla)

OSTRÓW WIELKOPOLSKI (woj. poznańskie) 1724–1875
Originals:
A file on the appointment of a cantor–*shochet* [H]; a plan of the Jewish quarter, 1826; the community budget [G], 1833; the appointment of community employees [G], 1834–47; records on the election of a local committee for liquidating Jewish debts [G], 1835–39; minutes, reports and resolutions of community meetings [G], 1834–65; files on the recruitment tax [G], 1832–46; a register of government taxes, 1835–46; files on income tax [G], 1835–50, and on the appointment of assessors [G], 1857–69; suits by town officials against the community [G], 1841–42, 1873–75; an apprentice's certificate [G], 1852; a file on a Jewish artisans' guild [G], 1858–71.
Microfilms:
1. Copy of the charter granted to the Jews [P,G], 1724.
(AP Poznań, Akta miast, woj. poznańskie)
2. A charter for the Jews, 1783.
(AGAD, Warszawa, Arch. Radziwiłłów)
3. Jewish settlement rights and real estate transactions made by Jews, 1798, 1831.
(AP Poznań, Gmina Żydowska, Ostrów)

OSTRZESZÓW (pow. Kępno, woj. poznańskie) 1790–1882
Originals:

Documents on community debts [G], 1828–29.
Microfilms:
1. Records of the Civil and Military Commission in the district, 1790–91.
(AGAD)
2. Minutes of the community board [G], 1876–82.
(Centrum Judaicum, Berlin)

OŚWIĘCIM (pow. Biała, woj. krakowskie) 1724–1911
Originals:
A letter of recommendation for a teacher from the *Talmud Tora* society [G], 1911.
Microfilms:
1. Records of litigation between the municipality and the community; complaints regarding a trading partnership between a Jew and a non Jew; records of various *arendas* (incl. *propinacja*), 1724–95.
(AP Kraków, IT)
2. Confirmation by King Stanisław August Poniatowski of the charter granted to the Jews [L], 1766.
(AGAD, Warszawa, Księgi Kanclerskie)
3. Requests by Jews to acquire real estate [G], 1805, 1806; lists of eligible voters [G], 1867, 1870.
(AP Kraków, Teki Schneidra)
4. Material on the community statutes [G, P], 1846–99; correspondence with the authorities on complaints against community elections, the community statutes and the rabbi of the community [G, P], 1899–1908.
(TsDIAU, L'viv, Namiestnictwo Galicyjskie)

OTTYNIA (pow. Tłumacz, woj. stanisławowskie) 1704–1939
Microfilms:
1. Minutes on criminal proceedings in Stanisławów for assaults against Jews in Ottynia, 1704–21.
(NBANU, L'viv, Arch. Ossolińskich)
2. Statutes, minutes, correspondence, reports and membership lists of Jewish associations [G, P], 1894–99, 1921–38; reports concerning burial charges [G, P], 1921–35; files on the *Gmilus Chasodim* society, including membership lists, 1922–31; files on community board elections, 1926–39; statutes and reports on activities of Jewish youth movements, 1929–30; files on *Hatzofim Brit Trumpeldor*, 1930–37; minutes, reports and correspondence on salaries of rabbis and assistant rabbis, 1932–35; reports concerning elections of delegates to the 18th Zionist Congress [P, Y], 1933; reports on the local committees of the OŻPP, *Histadrut Hanoar Haivri*, *Hashomer Hatzair* and *Tzofe* societies, 1933.
(DAIFO, Ivano-Frankivs'k, UW, Stanisławów)
3. Minute book of the community board, 1925–28.
(DAIFO, Ivano-Frankivs'k, Gmina Żydowska, Ottynia)

OZIERANY (pow. Nowogródek, woj. nowogródzkie) 1863–1864
Microfilms:
Reports on the organization of Jewish hospitals and shelters for the elderly [R], 1863–64.
(RGIA, St. Petersburg, Khoziaistvennyi departament MVD)

OZORKÓW (pow. Łęczyca, woj. łódzkie) 1869–1913
Originals:
Documents certifying the citizenship of Jewish emigrants from the town [R], 1869–70.
Microfilms:

1. A file on a Jew accused of attempting to forge letters of credit [R], 1886; the registration of a philanthropic society [R], 1909–13.
(AP Łódź, Kancelaria Gubernatora Kaliskiego)
2. A file on a Jewish private school, 1906–09.
(AP Łódź, Dyrekcja Szkolna, Łódź)

OŻARÓW (MAZOWIECKI) (pow. Warszawa, woj. warszawskie) 1853–1856
Microfilms:
Reports and correspondence on the confirmation of rabbis and litigations between them and their communities, 1853–56.
(AGAD, Warszawa, CWW)

PABIANICE (pow. Łask, woj. łódzkie) 1836–1914
Microfilms:
1. Records concerning the community and its accounts, 1836–66; files on Jewish residents, 1855–62.
(AP Łódź, Anterioria Rządu Gubernialnego, Piotrków)
2. Financial records concerning Jewish schools [R], 1889–1909.
(AP Łódź, Dyrekcja Szkolna, Łódź)
3. Fines for evading conscription [R], 1893–1902.
(AP Łódź, Rząd Gubernialny, WP, Piotrków)
4. The *arenda* of the *mikve* [R], 1900–06; ratification of community accounts and elections [R], 1901–13; records concerning Jewish charitable and educational activity [R], 1901–13; files on reconstruction of the synagogue [R], 1902–09.
(AP Łódź, Rząd Gubernialny, WA, Piotrków)
5. Documents concerning various Jewish societies and schools [R], 1901–02, 1910–12; investigations of Jews [R], 1910.
(AP Łódź, Policmajster m. Pabianic)
6. Records of Jews arrested for the possession of illegal political literature [R], 1905–06.
(AP Łódź, GZŻ, Piotrków)
7. Requests to register various philanthropic and cultural societies (*Talmud–Tora*, *Gmilus Chasodim*, etc.) [R], 1909–14.
(AP Łódź, Rząd Gubernialny, KP, Piotrków)

PAJĘCZNO (pow. Radomsko, woj. łódzkie) 1822–1913
Microfilms:
1. Records on the community and its accounts, 1822–62.
(AP Łódź, Anterioria Rządu Gubernialnego, Piotrków)
2. A complaint against members of the community; fines for evading conscription [R], 1887–1902.
(AP Łódź, Rząd Gubernialny, WP, Piotrków)
3. Ratification of community elections and accounts [R], 1903–13.
(AP Łódź, Rząd Gubernialny, WA, Piotrków)

PARCZEW (pow. Włodawa, woj. lubelskie) 1570–1766
Microfilms:
1. An extract from the *lustracja* of the Lublin *województwo*, 1570.
(AP Lublin, Księgi Miejskie, Lublin)
2. Extracts from local court records concerning Jews, 1591–1604.

(AP Lublin, Księgi Miejskie, Parczew)
3. Confirmations by Kings Zygmunt III and Stanisław August Poniatowski of the charter granted to the town (incl. definitions of Jewish rights) [L, P], 1623, 1766.
(AGAD, Warszawa, Księgi Kanclerskie)
4. Evidence concerning the burning down of Jewish schools and private houses [L], 1630.
(AP Lublin, Księgi Grodzkie Lubelskie)
5. A file about an assault on a Jew [L, P], 1759.
(AP Kraków, Arch. Sanguszków, teki tzw. arabskie)

PARSZEWICZE (pow. Pińsk, woj. poleskie) 1855–1892
Photocopies:
Investigation file about unauthorized Jewish teachers [R], 1855–92.
(NIAB, Minsk, Minskii okruzhnoi sud)

PARYSÓW (pow. Garwolin, woj. lubelskie) 1856–1864
Microfilms:
Minutes, reports and correspondence concerning the appointment of rabbis, their education and salaries, 1856–64.
(AGAD, Warszawa, CWW)

PARZĘCZÓW (pow. Łęczyca, woj. łódzkie) 1909–1910
Originals:
Drawing of a wooden synagouge, n.d.
(IKG Wien - Juedisches Museum)
Microfilms:
1. Appointment of a rabbi [R], 1909.
(AP Łódź, Rząd Gubernialny, WA, Kalisz)
2. Copies of inscriptions on tombstones and synagogues [H, P, R], 1910.
(RGIA, St. Petersburg, Departament dukhovnykh del…)

PAWŁOWICE (pow. Garwolin, woj. lubelskie) 1895–1896
Microfilms:
File on the annexation of the Jewish community in Pawłowice to that of Garwolin [R], 1895–96.
(AP Lublin, Rząd Gubernialny, Lublin)

PECZENIŻYN (pow. Kołomyja, woj. stanisławowskie) 1893–1939
Microfilms:
1. Files on confirmation of the *Mizrachi* and *Gmilus Chasodim* society statutes, including membership lists [G, P], 1893, 1920–31; reports on *Poalei Zion*, 1920–21; statutes, minutes and correspondence concerning Jewish associations, 1921–30; correspondence with the authorities on the *Bund*, 1923; files on activity of the *Poalei Zion–Lewica* party and lists of the central committees of *Poalei Zion–Lewica* and *Poalei Zion–Prawica*, 1924–25; a report on collecting money for Jews in Palestine, 1926; correspondence on supervision of Jewish communities in the region, complaints against the community board, budget ratifications, changes of statutes and taxes on *shechita*, 1926–35; reports on the Revisionist Zionist party, 1927, and on *Hashomer Hatzair*, 1929; reports and board membership lists of the local branch of the OŻPP, 1933; correspondence with the authorities regarding complaints of community employees about non

payment of salaries, and dismissals, 1936; files on salaries for rabbis and *dayanim,* 1936; files on the community budget and a list of tax payers, 1938.
(DAIFO, Ivano-Frankivs'k, UW, Stanisławów)
2. Decrees and correspondence about military service, including a list of persons assigned to military works, 1920; a list of members of the local relief committee, 1920; circulars and correspondence on the activities of the *Bund* and *Poalei Zion* in the district, 1920–22.
(DAIFO, Ivano-Frankivs'k, Starostwo Powiatowe, Peczeneżyn)
3. Files on the *Bikur Cholim* society, including a text of the statutes, 1930–34; files on the *Hatzefira* and *Gmilus Chasodim* associations, including lists of board members, 1931–36; files on the *Agudas Achim* craftsmen association, including a list of board members, 1931–39; files on *Brit Trumpeldor, Hechalutz* and *Achva,* including statutes and lists of board members.
(DAIFO, Ivano-Frankivs'k, Starostwo Powiatowe, Kołomyja)

PEREHIŃSKO (pow. Dolina, woj. stanisławowskie) 1924–1938
Microfilms:
Files on Jewish societies, 1924–37; documents on founding the *Gmilus Chasodim* society, 1936–38.
(DAIFO, Ivano-Frankivs'k, UW, Stanisławów)

PIASECZNO (pow. Warszawa, woj. warszawskie) 1689–1871
Microfilms:
1. Economic records concerning Jews in the *starostwo,* 1689–1739.
(Bibl. Czartoryskich, Kraków)
2. Files on the Jewish population, 1808–71; records of the Jewish community and its possessions, 1818–48; the expulsion of non resident Jews, 1844–54; regulations on Jewish dress, 1846–71; files on the community and its accounts, 1848–71; files on income from taxes on kosher meat, 1855–62.
(AP Warszawa, Magistrat, Piaseczno)
3. A request by an *arendar* for financial aid, 1864.
(AGAD, Warszawa, RSKP)

PIASKI (pow. Lublin, woj. lubelskie) 1858–1936
Originals:
Birth, marriage and death register [P, R], 1858–59, 1879, 1888; a bachelor certificate, 1936.
Microfilms:
Description of towns in the Lublin region, 1860–61; correspondence about the bequest of a Jew from Piaski [R], 1875–76.
(AP Lublin, Rząd Gubernialny, Lublin)

PIASKI (Piaseczna Góra, pow. Gostyń, woj. poznańskie) 1837–1896
Originals:
Correspondence with the authorities [G], 1837–88; community statutes [G], 1896.

PIĄTEK (pow. Łęczyca, woj. łódzkie) 1901–1910
Microfilms:
1. Records on a Jew under police observation [R], 1901–04.
(AP Łódź, Kancelaria Gubernatora Kaliskiego)
2. Copies of inscriptions on tombstones and synagogues [H, P, R], 1910.
(RGIA, St. Petersburg, Departament dukhovnykh del...)

PIERZCHNICA (pow. Stopnica, woj. kieleckie) 1850–1868
Microfilms:
Files on *arenda* and *propinacja* [P, R], 1850–68.
(AGAD, Warszawa, KRzPiS)

PILICA (pow. Olkusz, woj. kieleckie) 1792–1910
Originals:
Drawing of a wooden synagogue, n.d.
(IKG Wien - Juedisches Museum)
Microfilms:
1. Records of the municipal court in a case involving a Jew, 1792.
(AP Kraków, IT)
2. Reports and drafts of the community budget [H, P, R], 1820–63; reports and correspondence about ratification of rabbinical appointments and litigations between rabbis and communities, 1853–56; a project to distribute kosher food to needy Jews and support poor Jewish hospital patients [P, R], 1848–56.
(AGAD, Warszawa, CWW)
3. Community records, a list of community members and complaints about taxes, 1840–41.
(AGAD, Warszawa, KRzPiS)
4. Birth, marriage and death records [P, R], 1858–70.
(AP Chrzanów)
5. Copies of inscriptions on tombstones and synagogues [H, P, R], 1910.
(RGIA, St. Petersburg, Departament dukhovnykh del...)

PILICA, surroundings, 1800–1817
Microfilms:
Decree by Friedrich Wilhelm, King of Prussia, concerning organization of the Jewish communities in the districts of Pilica and Siewierz [G, P], 1800; files on taxes from Jews in these districts [G, P], 1810–17.
(AGAD, Warszawa, KRzPiS)

PILZNO (pow. Ropczyce, woj. krakowskie) 1539–1649
Photocopies:
Confirmation by King Jan Kazimierz of charters issued by Kings Zygmunt (1539), Zygmunt August (1566) and Stefan Batory (1576–77) concerning jurisdiction, *propinacja* and the expulsion of the Jews, 1649.
(AP Kraków, DP)

PIŃCZÓW (woj. kieleckie) 1632–1867
Microfilms:
1. Fragments of the community minute book [H], 1632–1740.
(YIVO, New York)
2. A complaint by the *kahal* about the attitude of Lutherans and Calvinists towards the Jews, 1767.
(NBANU, L'viv, Arch. Ossolińskich)
3. Files on taxes for military expenses, requests for exemption and correspondence between the community and the Highest Provisional Board of the Duchy of Warsaw, 1813–22; files on financial obligations of the local *kahal* to the church in Jędrzejów and correspondence concerning payments to the Cracow Academy [L, P], 1836–48.
(AGAD, Warszawa, KRzPiS)

4. Records on the Jewish community: correspondence, tax matters, accounts, 1820–67; reports, minutes and complaints concerning burial societies, 1822–50.
(AGAD, Warszawa, CWW)

PIŃSK (woj. poleskie) 1566–2001
Originals:
A copy of the minute book and correspondence of the *Safa Brura,* Hebrew language society [H], 1890; documents, publications, newspaper clippings, copies and notes concerning the Jews [G, H, P, Y], 19th–20th cent.; the program of the *Machzikei Hadas* society [H], 1912; report of the Jewish Hospital Commission [H, Y], 1930; copies of birth, marriage and death records (fragmentary) [H, P], 1927–35.
Correspondence, maps, minutes and video recordings [H, Y], 1919, 1928–2001.
(Archives of the Landsmannschaft of Pińsk, Karlin, Janów and surroundings)
Photocopies:
1. Excerpts from records concerning real estate and litigation among Jews, 1743–49; excerpts from registers of legal proceedings between Jews from Pińsk and Karlin and noblemen, concerning property and financial matters, 1782–94; records concerning criminal and financial matters, 1787–94; excerpts from municipal minutes concerning the Jews, 1791–95.
(NIAB, Minsk, Pinskaia Magdeburgia)
2. Investigation file about unauthorized Jewish teachers [R], 1855–92.
(NIAB, Minsk, Minskii okruzhnoi sud)
3. Information about bookshops and libraries [R], 1886, 1892.
(NIAB, Minsk, Kantseliaria minskogo gubernatora)
4. Statistical report about industrial plants in the surroundings [R], 1882–85.
(NIAB, Minsk, Minskii gubernskii statisticheskii komitet)
5. Minutes of the construction office about permits for construction and renovation of community buildings in the surroundings [R], 1898, 1902.
(NIAB, Minsk, Minskoe gubernskoe pravlenie)
6. Register of Jewish school owners in the area [R], 19th cent.
(NIAB, Minsk, Direktsiia narodnykh uchilishch)
7. A file on reopening synagogues [R], 1946–59.
(NIAB, Minsk, Sovet po delam religioznykh kul'tov)
8. Register of Jewish entrepreneurs [R], n.d.
(NIAB, Pinskaia kazennaia palata)
Microfilms:
1. Royal charters for *arenda* of taxes [Rt], 1566–68; royal charters about exemptions from taxes and customs for the Jews [Rt], 1558–61.
(RGADA, Moscow, ML)
2. Confirmation by King Jan III Sobieski of charters for the Jews, 1669; a letter by a community official requesting Jews to volunteer information on rebel peasants, 1769.
(AGAD, Warszawa, Arch. Radziwiłłów)
3. Economic records concerning Jews and Christians [P, B], 1676–77; an inventory of the Jews living in the town [P, Y], 1738; a list of documents concerning the community [P, Y], 1741; two inventories of the town, 1764, 1778; records of the *arendas* of local taverns, 1789.
(Bibl. PAN, Kraków)
4. A copy of a charter from 1533 permitting construction of a synagogue, 1780.

(AP Kraków, Arch. Sanguszków, teki tzw. rzymskie)

5. Excerpts from municipal books concerning financial matters between the Jews and the Jesuit College, 1699, 1716; requests (*memoriały*) from the *kahal*, 1786.

(RGADA, Moscow, KFE)

6. Reports by the governor of Minsk about complaints by Christians against a Jewish *arendar* from Pinsk [R], 1804–05.

(TsDIAU, Kyiv, Kievskii voennyi gubernator)

7. Litigation over financial matters between the Carmelites and the Jews [R], 1840.

(RGIA, St. Petersburg, Rimsko-katolicheskaia kollegiia...)

8. File on clandestine Jewish organizations [R], 1899; files on the pogroms [R], 1903–06; a file on *Hatchiya* [R], 1909; correspondence with the local committee of the Society for the Spread of Enlightenment among the Jews of Russia [R], 1914.

(GARF, Moscow, Departament politsii...)

9. Copies of inscriptions on tombstones and synagogues [R, H], 1910.

(RGIA, St. Petersburg, Departament dukhovnykh del...)

10. A report on the transport of deportees towards the interior of Russia [R], 1915.

(RGVIA, Moscow, Kantseliariia nachal'nika shtaba...)

PIOTRKÓW KUJAWSKI (pow. Nieszawa, woj. poznańskie) 1793–1800
Microfilms:
The file of the community's lawyer, in a suit against the *starosta* [G], 1793–1800.

(ŻIH, Warszawa)

PIOTRKÓW TRYBUNALSKI (woj. łódzkie) 1775–1936
Originals:
Documents regarding marriages of Jews from Koło, Przedecz and Piotrków, 1854.
Microfilms:
1. A moratorium granted to a Jewish merchant by King Stanisław August Poniatowski [L], 1775; confirmation by him of the charter granted to the Jews, 1778 and a decree by him, settling a dispute between a Jewish merchant and his creditors, 1792.

(AGAD, Warszawa, Księgi Kanclerskie)

2. Records concerning the community and its accounts, 1822–66; records of a local commission dealing with the finances of the community, 1828–69; files on Jewish hospitals, 1845–66.

(AP Łódź, Anterioria Rządu Gubernialnego, Piotrków)

3. Files on Jewish hospitals, orphanages, shelters and other charitable institutions, financial matters, bequests and donations for Jewish hospitals, as well as files on physicians [P, R], 1844–1913.

(AP Łódź, Rząd Gubernialny, RO, Piotrków)

4. A project to distribute kosher food to needy Jews and support poor Jewish hospital patients [P, R], 1848–56.

(AGAD, Warszawa, CWW)

5. Files on the community and its accounts, 1859–65; Jewish schools, 1859–65.

(AP Łódź, Rząd Gubernialny, NP, Piotrków)

6. Records and correspondence concerning Jewish schools and *chadorim* [P, R], 1859–1913.

(AP Łódź, Dyrekcja Szkolna, Łódź)

7. Files on donations for the Jewish hospital, 1860–61.

(AP Łódź, Akta Magistratu, Piotrków)

8. Files on the ritual slaughter house and the *krupka* [R], 1868, 1871, 1909–10; a file on organization of the Jewish quarter and *jurydyki* [R], 1869; financial matters, loans and real estates [R], 1869–1911; licenses for the establishment of Jewish business enterprises [R], 1879, 1909; the construction and renovation of the synagogue, *mikve* and school and the *arenda* of the *mikve* [R], 1879–93, 1900–12; ratification of community accounts and elections [R], 1879–93, 1899–1913; payments for the medical treatment of poor Jews [R], 1893–1904; the administration of the Jewish quarter; records concerning the construction of a road leading to the Jewish quarter and the cemetery [R], 1900–03; appointment of a rabbi [R], 1900–12; requests to establish and register prayer–houses and cultural and charitable societies [R], 1904–13; files concerning donations and bequests to the community and the Jewish hospital [R], 1904–13.
(AP Łódź, Rząd Gubernialny, WA, Piotrków)
9. Financial complaints concerning Jews [R], 1899–1911.
(AP Łódź, Rząd Gubernialny, WP, Piotrków)
10. Requests to register cultural societies [R], 1907–14.
(AP Łódź, Rząd Gubernialny, KP, Piotrków)
11. Investigations of Jews suspected of involvement in the *Bund* and other illegal political organizations [R], 1904–08; a report on the distribution of proclamations published by the Central Committee of the *Bund*, including texts of the proclamations [R], 1912.
(AP Łódź, GZŻ, Piotrków)
12. Copies of letters by Rabbi Meir Shapira to the local Jewish community concerning community matters, *Agudas Yisroel* and *Yeshivas Chachmei Lublin* [H], 1929–36.
(AP Lublin, Gmina Żydowska, Lublin)

PIOTRKÓW TRYBUNALSKI, surroundings, 1835–1914
Microfilms:
1. Records concerning the establishment of Jewish schools and *chadorim* [P, R], 1835–38, 1866–1914; a report on the number of children in the district [P, R], 1898; 1882–1914.
(AP Łódź, Dyrekcja Szkolna, Łódź)
2. Files regarding the tax on Jewish dress, 1846–58.
(AP Łódź, Anterioria Rządu Gubernialnego, Piotrków)
3. Records concerning Jewish inhabitants of agricultural districts [P, R], 1864–1914; files on the expulsion of Jews from the countryside [P, R], 1883–1914.
(AP Łódź, Rząd Gubernialny, Komisarz do spraw włościańskich pow. piotrkowskiego, Piotrków)
4. Files on Jewish education [R], 1871; records concerning burial taxes [R], 1878; a file on the demarcation of community borders in the Kalisz and Piotrków areas [R], 1884–97; expenses for the needy [R], 1911; community tax for Jewish industrialists [R], 1893–94; examinations for the rabbinate [R], 1893–95, 1904–12; records concerning the elections and finances of various communities [R], 1893–95, 1905–13; requests to convert to Christianity [R], 1893–94, 1901–14; files concerning civil records [R], 1894–1908; complaints against community officials [R], 1899–1911; requests to establish prayer–houses [R], 1899–1914; records concerning government income from "Jewish" taxes [R], 1900–04; requests by Jews to open businesses [R], 1900–06; requests to enlarge the number of community officials [R], 1902–03; a file on charity for unemployed workers during the recession caused by the the Russo-Japanese war [R], 1904–06; files on the appointment and dismissal of rabbis, and on the appointment of community board members [R], 1904–07; on payment for medical treatment of poor Jews [R], 1905–14; complaints against the amount of community tax [R], 1906–14; on vacations for rabbis and community officials [R], 1908–11; a file on the Rabbinical Commission of the Ministry of Interior [R], 1908–13; files on *shechita* [R], 1910

(AP Łódź, Rząd Gubernialny, WA, Piotrków)

5. Files on Jewish dress [R], 1871–72, 1899–1905; records of measures taken against anti-Jewish outbursts (incl. in the wake of the Beilis affair) [R], 1900–01, 1913; a file on immigrants to the area [R], 1902–03; reports on the Zionist movement and the activities of the *Bund* [R], 1903; fines for unauthorized political activity [R], 1906; requests to establish Jewish schools and *chadorim* [R], 1911; documents and regulations concerning permission for foreign Jews to enter Russia [R], 1912; records concerning various communities and rabbis [R], 1913; complaints of Jews against agitation by Catholic priests for a boycott of Jewish commerce [R], 1913–14; a file on the decision to distribute various Jewish journals abroad [R], 1913–14.

(AP Łódź, Kancelaria Gubernatora Piotrkowskiego)

6. Fines for evading conscription [R], 1888–1910; reports on foreign Jews in the district [R], 1889–1901; requests for exemptions from taxes [R], 1901–05.

(AP Łódź, Rząd Gubernialny, WP, Piotrków)

7. Files and financial reports concerning Jewish hospitals and charitable institutions [R], 1902–08.

(AP Łódź, Rząd Gubernialny, RO, Piotrków)

8. Secret correspondence concerning revolutionary activities [R], 1904–08; files on Jewish education [R], 1905; reports concerning disturbances on the 1st and 3rd of May 1903 [R], 1905; complaints and informers' reports concerning Jews [R], 1905–06; fines for misdemeanours [R], 1905–07; reports on strikes and other illegal political activities [R], 1905–08; files on Jews forbidden to enter the Russian Empire [R], 1905–08; records of searches and arrests of Jews involved in illegal political activity and the possession and distribution of illegal publications [P, R], 1905–10; a file on various societies and organizations [R], 1906; files and correspondence concerning Jews sent into exile [R], 1906–10; files on the loyalty of various personalities [R], 1906–13; correspondence on those involved in helping Jews emigrate illegally [R], 1907–09; records on Jews sentenced to death, hard labour, or exile [R], 1909–11.

(AP Łódź, GZŻ, Piotrków)

9. Files on Jews sent into exile [R], 1907–08.

(AP Łódź, Kancelaria Gubernatora Kaliskiego)

10. Files on Jewish territorialists [R], 1907–09, on the Hebrew Language Society [R], 1908 and on the Society for the Spread of Enlightenment among the Jews of Russia [R], 1913–14.

(AP Łódź, Rząd Gubernialny, KP, Piotrków)

11. Statistical data concerning synagogues and rabbis [R], 1908.

(RGIA, St. Petersburg, Khoziaistvennyi departament MVD)

PISTYŃ (pow. Kosów, woj. stanisławowskie) 1877–1938
Microfilms:
1. Correspondence with the authorities regarding *chadorim,* and a list of *melamdim,* 1877–1908.

(TsDIAU, L'viv, Namiestnictwo Galicyjskie)

2. Files on confirming the statutes of various Jewish associations, 1923–34; files on community board elections, 1926–37; lists of *Gmilus Chasodim* society board members, 1930–31; files on Jewish associations, containing lists of board members, 1930–37; files on a Jewish agricultural society, 1933–38.

(DAIFO, Ivano-Frankivs'k, UW, Stanisławów)

3. A report from the local police station concerning anti-Jewish leaflets, 1938.

(DAIFO, Ivano-Frankivs'k, Prokuratura Sądu Okręgowego, Kołomyja)

PLESZEW (pow. Jarocin, woj. poznańskie) 1834–1885
Originals:

Minutes of community meetings and resolutions [G], 1834–62; files on community elections and cases of corruption among community officials [G], 1834–62; records concerning community functionaries and administrative matters (incl. civil registration and the holding of services only in authorized synagogues) [G], 1834–44; files on the construction of a building at the cemetery and a study–house [G], 1834–49; community accounts and taxation records [G], 1834–37, 1847–71; official regulations concerning the naturalization of Jews [G], 1834–45; files on education [G], 1836–44; instructions and memoranda from the local authorities [G], 1842–53; files on a project to found Jewish colonies in the Grand Duchy of Posen [G], 1846; donations by Jews from Pleszew living in New York to construct a fence around the cemetery [G, H], 1882; a letter by Rabbi Dr. Feilchenfeld from Poznań on raising funds to construct a prayer house [G, H], 1885.

Microfilms:
Documents and decisions of the community board [G], 1834–36; instructions concerning the registration of marriage announcements [G], 1834–37; files on vocational education [G], 1834–40; records of the community administration and decisions of the community board [G], 1836–70.
(Centrum Judaicum, Berlin)

PŁAWNO (pow. Radomsko, woj. łódzkie) 1822–1914
Microfilms:
1. Records concerning the community and its accounts, 1822–66.
(AP Łódź, Anterioria Rządu Gubernialnego, Piotrków)
2. Reports and correspondence concerning appointments of rabbis and litigation between them and their communities, 1853–56.
(AGAD, Warszawa, CWW)
3. A list of Jews aged 20 to 24, 1867–73.
(AP Łódź, Radomszczański Urząd Powiatowy)
4. Fines for evading conscription [R], 1897–99.
(AP Łódź, Rząd Gubernialny, WP, Piotrków)
5. Ratification of community elections, accounts and appointments of rabbis [R], 1899–1914.
(AP Łódź, Rząd Gubernialny, WA, Piotrków)

PŁOCK (woj. warszawskie) 1521–1910
Photocopies:
Charters granted to townsmen by King Zygmunt I forbidding Jews to engage in retail trade [L], 1521, 1523; six documents concerning Jewish life in the town [L, P], 1523–1723; a decree issued by a Royal Commission settling a dispute between the municipality and the community over trading rights [L], 1540; confirmation by King August II of a charter concerning tax payments by Jews [L, P], 1723; confirmation by King Stanisław August Poniatowski of the charter granted to the Jews [L, P], 1770.
(AGAD, Warszawa, DP)
Microfilms:
1. A fragment of a *lustracja*, 1580; An inventory of the town, 18th cent.
(AP Wrocław, Ossolineum)
2. Reports, minutes and complaints concerning burial societies, 1822–50; reports and correspondence on the appointment of the rabbi and ligitation with the community, 1853–56.
(AGAD, Warszawa, CWW)
4. Records of litigation between the municipality and Jews over the ownership of land, 1824–55.
(AGAD, Warszawa, KRzSW)

5. A file on the opening of the *Ezra* society [R], 1910.
(AP Łódź, Rząd Gubernialny, WA, Piotrków)

PŁOCK, surroundings, 1566–1908
Microfilms:
1. A *lustracja* of the *województwo*, 1566.
(AGAD, Warszawa, ASK)
2. Files on the setting up an *eruv* in the Jewish quarter and reports on ensuing conflicts between Christians and Jews, 1818–71; files on financial corruption in the area [P, R], 1848–56; reports and correspondence concerning appointments of rabbis and examinations for the rabbinate, as well as lists of rabbis and *dayanim* of the Rabbinical Seminary, 1823–53; correspondence concerning exemption from military service of graduates of the Rabbinical Seminary, including lists of rabbis, 1865–71.
(AGAD, Warszawa, CWW)
3. Statistical data about synagogues and rabbis in various towns of the area [R], 1908.
(RGIA, St. Petersburg, Khoziaistvennyi departament MVD)

PŁOCK MAŁY, see MAŁY PŁOCK

PŁOŃSK (woj. warszawskie) 1566–1785
Microfilms:
1. A *lustracja* of the *województwo*, 1566.
(AGAD, Warszawa, ASK)
2. Charters to the Jews by King Michał Korybut [L, P], 1652, 1677.
(AGAD, Warszawa, Księgi Grodzkie Wyszogródzkie)
3. Confirmation by King August III of the charter granted to the Jews [L, P]; confirmation by him of an agreement between the community and the municipal and guild authorities [L, P]; confirmation by King Stanisław August Poniatowski of an agreement concerning *propinacja,* 1720–85.
(AGAD, Warszawa, DP)
4. Confirmation by King Stanisław August Poniatowski of the charter to the Jews [L, P], 1766.
(AGAD, Warszawa, Księgi Kanclerskie)

PNIEWO (pow. Łomża, woj. białostockie) 1913–1915
Microfilms:
Files on the arrest and exile of Jews suspected of assisting other Jews to cross the border illegally [R], 1913–15.
(AP Białystok, Rząd Gubernialny, Łomża)

PNIEWY (pow. Szamotuły, woj. poznańskie) 1834–1858
Originals:
Community debts [G], 1834–58; litigation between the Church in Brody and the local community [G], 1836–37; a history of the Jewish community by Akiva Posner [G], correspondence [G, Y], n.d.

POBEREŻE (pow. Stanisławów, woj. stanisławowskie) 1930
Microfilms:
Reports by directors of public schools in the Stanisławów district on social, national, cultural and economic relations [P, U], 1930.
(DAIFO, Ivano-Frankivs'k, Inspektorat Szkolny, Stanisławów)

POBIEDZISKA (pow. Poznań, woj. poznańskie) 1845
Originals:
A confirmation by the rabbi of marriage banns [G], 1845.

POCZAJÓW NOWY (pow. Krzemieniec, woj. wołyńskie) 1724–1928
Originals:
Confirmation by the rabbinical court of Lwów of a verdict by the rabbinical court of Drohobycz in matters of jurisdiction [H], 1724.
Photocopies:
Correspondence of Baron David Ginzburg regarding the Jews of the town [R], 1890–1905;
(RNB, St. Petersburg, Ginzburg)
Microfilms:
1. A report on the confiscation of illegally printed prayerbooks [R], 1837–39.
(TsDIAU, Kyiv, Kantseliariia... general-gubernatora)
2. Requests, reports and correspondence on the violation of rules for the conscription of Jews, including a list of Jewish recruits [H, R], 1840–41.
(DATO, Ternopil', Magistrat, Krzemieniec)
3. Budget of the Society for the Care of Jewish Orphans in Volhynia for the maintenace of orphans in the Krzemieniec district for the year 1928, including a list of the orphans, 1928.
(DATO, Ternopil', Urząd Powiatowy, Krzemieniec)

PODBEREŹCE (pow. Zborów, woj. tarnopolskie) 1838–1848
Microfilms:
1. A file on the expulsion of a Jew arrested for smuggling goods [R], 1838–42.
(TsDIAU, Kyiv, Kantseliariia... general-gubernatora)
2. Lists of Jewish inhabitants, drawn up for tax purposes [R], 1847–48.
(DATO, Ternopil', Magistrat, Krzemieniec)

PODGÓRZE (pow. Ostrołęka, woj. białostockie) 1909–1912
Microfilms:
A file on the license for producing soda water [R], 1909–12.
(AP Białystok, Rząd Gubernialny, Łomża)

PODGÓRZE (woj. krakowskie) 1878–1937
Microfilms:
1. Reports and correspondence on the reorganization of elementary schools attended by Jews, including a list of girls [G, P], 1878.
(TsDIAU, L'viv, Krajowa Rada Szkolna)
2. Correspondence on registration of the *Talmud Tora*, 1937.
(DALO, L'viv, UW, Lwów)

PODHAJCE (woj. tarnopolskie) 1750–1911
Microfilms:
1. A *supliki* made by Jewish *arendars,* 1750.
(AP Kraków, Zb. Rusieckich)
2. Complaints regarding tax payments [G], 1775; lists of eligible voters, 1870.
(AP Kraków, Teki Schneidra)

3. Correspondence with the Ministry of Religion on changes in the community statutes [G, P], 1875–77; correspondence about the Jewish Library Society, 1895–1911.
(TsDIAU, L'viv, Namiestnictwo Galicyjskie)

PODHORODCE (pow. Stryj, woj. stanisławowskie) 1930
Microfilms:
Board membership lists of the *Hechalutz* movement, 1930.
(DAIFO, Ivano-Frankivs'k, UW, Stanisławów)

PODKAMIEŃ (pow. Brody, woj. tarnopolskie) 1877–1908
Microfilms:
Correspondence between the community and the district authorities regarding *chadorim*, including a list of *melamdim* in the area [G, P], 1877–1908.
(TsDIAU, L'viv, Namiestnictwo Galicyjskie)

PODWOŁOCZYSKA (pow. Skałat, woj. tarnopolskie) 1895–1906
Microfilms:
Correspondence with the district authorities concerning ratification of the community statutes, 1895–96; correspondence about the *Achva* society [G, P], 1906.
(TsDIAU, L'viv, Namiestnictwo Galicyjskie)

POLANKA (pow. Równe, woj. wołyńskie) 1915
Microfilms:
Permission for a Jew to produce paper products [R], 1915.
(RGIVA, Moscow, Shtab Kievskogo voennogo okruga)

POŁAJEWO (pow. Oborniki, woj. poznańskie) 1854
Originals:
Application for a cantor's position [H], 1854.

POŁANIEC (pow. Sandomierz, woj. kieleckie) 1765–20th cent.
Originals:
A drawing of a wooden synagouge, n.d.
(IKG Wien - Juedisches Museum)
Microfilms:
1. Confirmation by King Stanisław August Poniatowski of the charter granted to the Jews [L, P], 1765.
(AGAD, Warszawa, Księgi Kanclerskie)
2. Reports and correspondence concerning appointment of the rabbi and his relations with the community, 1853–56.
(AGAD, Warszawa, CWW)

POMORZANY (pow. Zborów, woj. tarnopolskie) 1682–1895
Photocopies:
Inventory of the town and the surroundings, 1682, 1689, 1703, 1719, 1720–24.
(NIAB, Minsk, Arch. Radziwiłłów)
Microfilms:
1. Copies of legal and economic decisions by Prince Radziwiłł and *arenda* contracts with local Jews, 1746–47.

(AGAD, Warszawa, Arch. Radziwiłłów)
2. Correspondence on the vacant position of a rabbi, 1895.
(TsDIAU, L'viv, Namiestnictwo Galicyjskie)

POPOWICE (pow. Grojec, woj. warszawskie) 1796–1826
Microfilms:
Files on *arenda* of property, 1796–1826.
(AGAD, Warszawa, Arch. Lubomirskich z Małej Wsi)

POROZÓW (pow. Wołkowysk, woj. białostockie) 1886–1913
Originals:
A drawing of a wooden synagouge, n.d.
(IKG Wien - Juedisches Museum)
Microfilms:
Certificates, identity cards and photographs of candidates for the rabbinate [R], 1886–1913.
(AP Białystok, Rząd Gubernialny, Łomża)

PORYCK (pow. Włodzimierz, woj. wołyńskie) 1863–1864
Microfilms:
Files on construction of a Jewish hospital and home for the aged [R], 1863–64.
(RGIA, St. Petersburg, Khoziaistvennyi departament MVD)

PORYTE (pow. Łomża, woj. białostockie) 1912–1915
Microfilms:
Files on the arrest of Jews suspected of illegal political activity [R], 1912–15.
(AP Białystok, Rząd Gubernialny, Łomża)

POSUCHÓW (pow. Brzeżany, woj. tarnopolskie) 1700–1738
Microfilms:
Accounts, registers, inventories and tax registers, 1700–38.
(Bibl. Czartoryskich, Kraków)

POTYLICZ (pow. Rawa Ruska, woj. lwowskie) 1523–1584
Microfilms:
Confirmation by King Zygmunt III of a charter given to the city in 1523 by King Zygmunt I, 1584.
(AP Kraków, Teki Schneidra)

POZNAŃ (woj. poznańskie) 1528–1936
Originals:
Sefer Hazichronot (community minute book) [H, Y], 1592–1689; *Pinkas Haksherim* (record book of the "electors") [H, Y], 1621–1831; the record book (fragmentary) and other documents of the burial society [H], 1690–1912; registers of debts owed to the Christian clergy and noblemen [H], 1772–1842; a register of *ketubot*, including a list of rabbis [H], 1784–1876; the record book of the *gabbaim* of the synagogue [H], 1785–1800; the *memorbuch* of the *Geulat Nefesh* society [H], 18th cent.; an edict forbidding the sale of houses owned by Christians to Jews [G], 1806; a notebook containing drafts of articles by David Caro [H], 1812; statutes and minutes of the *Chevrat Bachurim* society [H], 1815–39; government confirmations of the elections of Rabbi Akiva Eger and Rabbi Salomon Eger [G], 1815, 1839; a *memorbuch* [H], 1817; the record book of the rabbinical court [H], 1818–34; the record and account books of a *Tora* study society [H],

1819–33; documents on a cholera epidemic and measures taken against it [G], 1831; statutes and reports of the Jewish orphanage [G], 1838–1917; personal material of Rabbi Dr. Wolf Feilchenfeld [G, L], 1848–99; a letter by Rabbi Mendel Loewenstamm against religious reform [G], 1856; community statutes [G], 1872; correspondence, notes and documents of Rabbi Dr. Bloch [G], 1883–1913; statutes of the *Turnverein* [G], 1906; files on community elections [G], 1910–13; material relating to the general elections [G], 1918–20 financial records of the Heimann Trade School [G], 1922–25; a copy of the *pinkas* of the "new" synagogue [H, Y], 1929.

Photographs:

Photograph of the old *Beit Midrash*, 1907;

Microfilms:

1. Confirmation by King Zygmunt III of the charter granted to the Jews, 1593; an agreement between the municipality and the Jews, 1614; a decree of King August III concerning Jewish debts, and decisions concerning delineation of the Jewish quarter [L, P], 1756; confirmation by King Stanisław August Poniatowski of the charters granted to the Jews by Kings Michał Korybut, Jan III and August II [L], 1765.
(AGAD, Warszawa, Księgi Kanclerskie)

2. Records concerning Jews [L, P], 16th–18th cent.
(AP Poznań, Akta Grodzkie)

3. Extracts from official court records relating to Jews, conflicts with the Polish inhabitants, contracts and charters, 1604–88; register of debts by the Jewish community to nobilty and clergy, 1755; excerpts from municipal court records, 1767–86.
(AP Poznań, Księgi Grodzkie Poznańskie)

4. Registers of the Jewish population and taxes, 1705–08.
(Bibl. Czartoryskich, Kraków)

5. Proclamations of the General Crown Confederation concerning the liquidation of Jewish debts, 1776.
(AP Lublin, Księgi Grodzkie i Ziemskie Lubelskie)

6. Copies of charters and other documents (from 1528–63) concerning Jews [L, P], 1779.
(AP Poznań, Księgi Miejskie, Poznań)

7. Confirmation of debt payments by the Jewish community, 1779–80.
(RGADA, Moscow, KFE)

8. The ratification of an agreement between the community and the Justice Commission [G], 1796.
(Deutsches Zentralarchiv, Merseburg)

9. Files on the supervision of circumcisions and burials, 1825–1902; care for strangers and other community functions and local organizations [G], 1825–1919; records of the institute for Jewish orphans [G], 1841–1916; matters concerning foreign Jews [G], 1847–1915; files on Jewish associations [G], 1847–1919; records of a new Jewish association for medical care and burial in Poznań [G], 1873–1905; files on the Jewish cemetery [G], 1876–92; Association for Promotion of Crafts under the auspices of the Jewish Loan Society [G], 1889–92; records of the Association for Promotion of Jewish Interests [G], 1907–11; foundation of a new Jewish cemetery [G], 1910–15; files on a professional (trade) union of Orthodox Jews [G], 1917–18.
(AP Poznań, Polizei–Praesidium Posen)

10. Legal documents and the statutes of the community [G], 1903–04.
(AP Poznań, Akta miast,woj. poznańskie)

11. Files on the Association of Liberal Jews [G], 1909–20; records concerning various Jewish organizations; files (incl. lists) on Jewish and German residents in the city [G], 1909–36; register of Germans and Jews in Poznań, 1920–24.

(AP Poznań, Starostwo Grodzkie)
12. A membership list of the *Amicitia* humanitarian society, 1935–36.
(DAIFO, Ivano-Frankivs'k, Towarzystwo *Achduth Bnai Brith,* Stanisławów)

POZNAŃ, surroundings, 1534–1921
Originals:
Two official letters to the leaders of the Jews in the Grand Duchy of Posen concerning their civil status, 1818; a list of the naturalized Jews in the Grand Duchy in 1834; statutes and annual reports of the Society for the Promotion of Agriculture and Handcrafts among the Jews, 1895, 1909–11; statutes of the society of Jewish teachers [G], n.d.
Microfilms:
1. Records of the hearth tax paid by Jews, 1611.
(AP Wrocław, Ossolineum)
2. Excerpts from court minutes concerning legal proceedings between Christians and Jews, and appeals concerning verdicts of Jewish courts [L, P], 1659–1723; *uniwersał* concerning pledging objects and its appropriate registration [L, P], 1703.
(AP Poznań, Księgi Wojewodzińskie Poznańskie)
3. Files on trades practiced by Jews; the legal status of Jews; files on Jewish migration; government reports on Jewish religious practices and education [G], 1823–47.
(Deutsches Zentralarchiv, Merseburg)

PRASZKA (pow. Wieluń, woj. łódzkie) 1818–1875
Microfilms:
1. Descriptions of the town, 1818–26.
(AGAD, Warszawa, Komisja Województwa Kaliskiego)
2. Records concerning the opening of a shelter for poor and aged Jews [R], 1870–75.
(AP Łódź, ROGK)

PROBUŻNA (pow. Kopyczyńce, woj. tarnopolskie) 1895–1908
Microfilms:
Correspondence with the district authorities about community matters and confirmation of the statutes, 1895–96; complaints about the community elections [G, P], 1905–08.
(TsDIAU, L'viv, Namiestnictwo Galicyjskie)

PROSZOWICE (pow. Miechów, woj. kieleckie) 1757–1759
Microfilms:
Various local records concerning Jews, 1757–59.
(AP Kraków, IT)

PRUCHNIK (pow. Jarosław, woj. lwowskie) 1895–1936
Microfilms:
1. Correspondence concerning a vacant rabbinical position [G, P], 1895–96.
(TsDIAU, L'viv, Namiestnictwo Galicyjskie)
2. Correspondence with the district authorities about the *Kultur Liga*, 1926; files on community elections, 1928–29; correspondence on the community budget, including a list of taxpayers, 1933–36.
(DALO, L'viv, UW, Lwów)
3. Corespondence about registration of *Machzikei Hadas* and *Agudas Yisroel*, 1933–34.

(DALO, L'viv, Magistrat, Lwów)
4. Monographs containing demographical and economical data, 1936.
(AP Wrocław, Ossolineum, WKNZNP)

PRUSKI (pow. Zdołbunów, woj. wołyńskie) 1730
Microfilms:
Money order given by an *arendar*, 1730.
(AP Lublin, Akta dóbr Andronów i Buchowicze)

PRUŻANA (woj. poleskie) 1863–1906
Microfilms:
1. Files on the organization of Jewish hospitals and shelters [R], 1863–64.
(RGIA, St. Petersburg, Khoziaistvennyi departament MVD)
2. Correspondence concerning elections to the Duma [R], 1906.
(RGIA, St. Petersburg, Obshchestvo polnopraviia...)

PRZASNYSZ (woj. warszawskie) 1566–1910
Microfilms:
1. A *lustracja*, 1566.
(AGAD, Warszawa, ASK)
2. Records of litigation between a Jew and the mayor, 1811–12.
(AGAD, Warszawa, RSiRMKW)
3. Records concerning synagogues, 1818–60; correspondence on exemption from military service for graduates of the Rabbinical Seminary, and a list of rabbis, 1865–71.
(AGAD, Warszawa, CWW)
4. Copies of inscriptions on tombstones and synagogues [H, P, R], 1910.
(RGIA, St. Petersburg, Departament dukhovnykh del...)

PRZEDBÓRZ (pow. Końskie, woj. kieleckie) 1765–1873
Microfilms:
1. Confirmation by King Stanisław August Poniatowski of the charter granted to the Jews [L, P], 1765; a letter of protection granted by him to a Jewish trader [L], 1792.
(AGAD, Warszawa, Księgi Kanclerskie)
2. Files on legal proceedings against Jews, 1858–73.
(AP Radom, Rząd Gubernialny, Radom)

PRZEDECZ (pow. Włocławek, woj. warszawskie) 1847–1910
Original:
Birth, marriage and death records (fragmentary) [P, R], 1847–55, 1870.
Microfilms:
Copies of inscriptions on tombstones and synagogues [H, P, R], 1910.
(RGIA, St. Petersburg, Departament dokhovnykh del...)

PRZEDMIEŚCIE DYNOWSKIE (pow. Brzozów, woj. lwowskie) 1936
Microfilms:
Monographs containing demographical and economical data, 1936.
(AP Wrocław, Ossolineum, WKNZNP, Lwów)

PRZEMYŚL (woj. lwowskie) 1550–1938

Originals:

Promissory note issued by the community to the Dominican Seminary [H, P], 1700; reports of the *Bikur Cholim* Society [P, Y], 1871–74; a speech by Rabbi Gedaliah Schmelkes at a protest meeting against the Beilis trial [G], 1913.

Microfilms:

1. Various documents on conflicts between the Jewish community and the town [L, P], 1550–1649; confirmations of royal charters to the Jews of the town [L], 1559–78, 1633, 1649; a complaint against the mayor for selling land near the synagogue to the Jews [L], 1595; a decision of the town council against a Jewish *arenda* of mead production [L], 1646; files on litigation between Jews and non–Jews, including a list of Jewish merchants in the town [L, P], 1652–92, 1707–47; a list of Jewish houses, n.d. (1650–70)
(AP Przemyśl, DP)

2. Records of conflicts and legal proceedings between Jews and the furriers' guild [L, P], 1589–1691; records of bakers' guild, complaints against Jews, n.d. (about 1590); a book of charters of the Jews from Przemyśl 16th–17th cent.; a court decision concerning Jewish disrespect for the Christian Sabbath and non payment of taxes [L], 1659; a complaint to the royal tribunal regarding secret agreements between Jews and municipal councilors, 1664; a decree by royal commissioners about the production of mead, 1685; a *lustracja* of the Jewish street and a description of its houses, 1692; records concerning litigation between Jews and guilds [L, P], 1698, 1783; a charter by August II from 1710 abolishing an exemption for the Jews of Przemyśl from taxes on the production of beer and other beverages [L], 1711; records of the butchers' guild containing protests by the community board about a breach of contract, 1736; [L, P], 1774; records of the tailors' guild, including an agreement with Jewish tailors and a list of Jewish boys who completed their apprenticeship [G, P], 1786–1858.
(AP Przemyśl, Akta m. Przemyśla)

3. Confirmation by King Zygmunt III of a charter granted to the Jews [L], 1592.
(AGAD, Warszawa, MK)

4. Court records (fragmentary) concerning cases between Jews and non-Jews [P, L], 1595–1790.
(AP Wrocław, Ossolineum, Acta Castri Premisliensis)

5. A letter by the *wojewoda* of Ruthenia concerning taxes paid by the *kahal*, 1701; decrees, complaints and accusations concerning non payment of debts by the *kahal* to a monastery [L, P], 1703–78.
(TsDIAU, L'viv, Kolektsiia lystiv...)

6. A letter by King Zygmunt III to the *wojewoda*, requesting just treatment for the Jews of Przemyśl, 1612.
(AP Kraków, Teki Sanguszków tzw. rzymskie)

7. Private agreements, accounts, contracts concerning properties of the Sieniawski and Czartoryski families, (including a register of Jewish population and taxes, 1705–08) ,1628–1763;.
(Bibl. Czartoryskich, Kraków)

8. Files concerning debts of the Council of Four Lands and the Jewish community in Przemyśl to the Jesuit order in Jaroslaw [H, L, G], (1664) 1740–55; the *krupka* tax and records concerning liquidation of the kahal's debts [G, L, P], (1670) 1777–83; a report about litigation between Jews and Christians concerning *propinacja* [G], 1781.
(AP Kraków, Teki Schneidra)

9. Charters and *arenda* contracts concerning Jews in Przemyśl [G, H, L, P, Y], 1686–1805.
(AP Lublin, Zb. Czołowskiego)

10. A *suplika* by *arendars* from Przemyśl, 1748.
(TsDIAU, Kyiv, Arch. Potockich z Tulczyna)

11. A decree concerning payment of taxes for army maintenance, 1753–67.
(TsDIAU, L'viv, Arch. Lanckorońskich)
12. Confirmation by Stanisław August Poniatowski of a charter granted to the Jews [L, P], 1765.
(AGAD, Warszawa, Księgi Kanclerskie)
13. Correspondence with the provincial authorities about elections for the community and the rabbinate, including documents relating to Rabbi Jacob Orenstein and to *chasidim* [G], 1819–23; material on *shechita*, 1894–97; correspondence about various societies assisting children and students [G, P], 1904–06; statutes of the *Linas Hazedek* and *Machzikei Tora* societies, 1907; statutes of a society for economic reforms among politically independent Jews, 1908.
(TsDIAU, L'viv, Namiestnictwo Galicyjskie)
14. Reports on teaching Jewish religion in elementary schools [G, P], 1882–89.
(TsDIAU, L'viv, Krajowa Rada Szkolna)
15. Statutes of the Jewish community [G, P], 1891–1914.
(TsDIAU, L'viv, Gmina Żydowska, Lwów)
16. Correspondence with the district authorities about ratifying the statutes of the *Żydowska Scena Robotnicza im. Jakuba Gordina* association, 1921–22, and concerning permission for a Jewish performance, *"Wielka szopa przemyska"*, 1926; correspondence about the *Kultur Liga*, 1926; minutes and reports concerning community board elections, budget and other matters, including a list of taxpayers,1926–38; correspondence about the Herzl Society, 1929–30; correspondence with the authorities about exemptions from customs for parcels sent from abroad, 1930; a report about a conference of the *Tarbut* society, attended by Chaim Nachman Bialik, 1930–31; lists of members of local town councils, citing their nationalities and political affiliations, 1930–31; materials on a conference of *Gordonia*, 1930–31; correspondence about *Hitachdut* delegates to the Zionist Congress, 1930–31; correspondence about a Jewish boycott of a German antisemitic film, 1936; correspondence with the district authorities concerning the liquidation of the *Linas Hatzedek* association, 1936; correspondence with the district authorities about a play in Yiddish by the E. R. Kamińska Dramatical Circle, 1936.
(DALO, L'viv, UW, Lwów)
17. Reports about the activities of *Bnai Brith,* 1928–29.
(DAIFO, Ivano-Frankivs'k, Towarzystwo *Achduth Bnai Brith,* Stanisławów)
18. Reports on the activity of the *Ogólno-Żydowska Partia Pracy (OŻPP)*, including a list of the local committee members, 1933.
(DAIFO, Ivano-Frankivs'k, UW, Stanisławów)

PRZEMYŚL, surroundings, 1734–1881
Microfilms:
1. Excerpts from municipal books and court records concerning taxes paid by Jews from Przemyśl and the surroundings [L, P], 1734–72.
(TsDIAU, L'viv, Samborska ekonomia)
2. *Arenda* contracts of villages in the area between noblemen and the *wojewoda* of Podolia, 1752–79.
(TsDIAU, L'viv, Arch. Lanckorońskich)
3. Translated excerpts from minutes of the Four Lands Council about conflicts between the communities of Mościska and Przemyśl concerning synagogues and cemeteries, and correspondence concening Karaites [G, H, L, P], 1775–80; correspondence with the district authorities about assistance for Jews in new settlements, including a list of names [G], 1789; a register of taxes paid by various communities [G], 1819;

correspondence with the provincial authorities about places of residence for Jews and about taxes [G], 1820–21.
(TsDIAU, L'viv, Namiestnictwo Galicyjskie)
4. Material about *chadorim* and private Jewish schools in the district [G, P], 1878–81.
(TsDIAU, L'viv, Krajowa Rada Szkolna)

PRZEMYŚLANY (woj. tarnopolskie) 1766–1927
Microfilms:
1. A *lustracja* of the poll–tax in Czartoryski properties, 1766.
(AGAD, Warszawa, Arch. Potockich w Łańcucie)
2. Correspondence with the provincial authorities concerning measures against fire [G, P], 1865–74; reports concerning *chadorim* in the district, including a list of *chadorim* and pupils [G, P], 1877–1908; minutes and correspondence concerning ratification of the community statutes, 1897–1905; reports and correspondence regarding complaints against Jewish community officials [G, P], 1902.
(TsDIAU, L'viv, Namiestnictwo Galicyjskie)
3. Corespondence on ratifying the statutes of *Agudas Yisroel*, 1895, 1920–27.
(DAIFO, Ivano-Frankivs'k, UW, Stanisławów)

PRZEWORSK (woj. lwowskie) 1749–1938
Microfilms:
1. Accounts and receipts of the *kahal* [G, P], 1749, 1758.
(NBANU, L'viv, Zb. Goldsteina)
2. *Arenda* contract of flour mills in the Lubomirski *klucz*, 1782.
(AP Kraków, Teki Schneidra)
3. Correspondence with the district authorities regarding *chadorim*, including a list of *melamdim*, 1874–1908.
(TsDIAU, L'viv, Namiestnictwo Galicyjskie)
4. Files on elections to the community board, 1928–38; lists of members of local town councils, citing their nationalities and political affiliations, 1930–31; a list of members of the Zionist organization in Przeworsk, 1931; correspondence on the community budget, including a list of taxpayers, 1933–35; reports containing names of community board members, rabbi and *dayan* of the community, 1937.
(DALO, L'viv, UW, Lwów)
5. Correspondence about the registration of *Agudas* Yi*sroel* and *Machzikei Hadas*, 1935.
(DALO, L'viv, Magistrat, Lwów)

PRZYRÓW (pow. Częstochowa, woj. kieleckie) 1822–1913
Microfilms:
1. Records concerning the community and its accounts 1822–1867; the establishment of a Jewish hospital 1839.
(AP Łódź, Anterioria Rządu Gubernialnego, Piotrków)
2. Fines for evading conscription [R], 1898.
(AP Łódź, Rząd Gubernialny, WP, Piotrków)
3. Ratification of community elections and accounts [R], 1900–13; the appointment of a new rabbi [R], 1906; the rebuilding of a prayer–house after a fire [R], 1907–08.
(AP Łódź, Rząd Gubernialny, WA, Piotrków)

PRZYSUCHA (pow. Opoczno, woj. kieleckie) 1853–1860
Microfilms:
1. Reports and correspondence concerning appointment of rabbis and their relations with the communities, 1853–56.
(AGAD, Warszawa, CWW)
2. A list of Jewish families, 1860.
(AP Radom, Rząd Gubernialny, Radom)

PRZYTYK (pow. Radom, woj. kieleckie) 1844–1871
Microfilms:
Records of the Jewish community [P, R], 1844–71.
(AGAD, Warszawa, CWW)

PSZCZYNA (woj. śląskie) 1832–1847
Originals:
Letters and other documents concerning the Jews [H], 1832–1847.

PUKASOWCE (pow. Stanisławów, woj. stanisławowskie) 1930
Microfilms:
Reports by directors of public schools in the Stanisławowski *powiat* containing descriptions of various localities and their social, national and cultural relations as well as economic and sanitary conditions [P, U], 1930.
(DAIFO, Ivano-Frankivs'k, Inspektorat Szkolny, Stanisławów)

PUŁAWY (woj. lubelskie) 1706–1851
Microfilms:
1. Registers, accounts, *uniwersały*, decrees and contracts concerning properties of the Sieniawski and Czartoryski families [F, L, P], 1706–85.
(Biblioteka Narodowa, Warszawa)
2. Letters to E. Sieniawska and accounts regarding properties in Puławy, 1707–09, 1716–22, 1736.
(Bibl. Czartoryskich, Kraków)
3. Files on financial aid granted to the community by Prince Czartoryski, 1832–51.
(AGAD, Warszawa, KRzSW)

PUŁTUSK (woj. warszawskie) 1818–1915
Microfilms:
1. Files on permission to set up an *eruv* in the Jewish quarter and ensuing conflicts with Christians, 1818–71; correspondence about draft exemptions for graduates of the Rabbinical Seminary in Warsaw, including a list of rabbis, 1865–71.
(AGAD, Warszawa, CWW)
2. File on renovation and *arenda* of the *mikve*, including a list of the renovation committee members [R], 1887–97; file on accusation of a prison guard responsible for the escape from arrest of Jewish inhabitants of Pułtusk [R], 1893–94; a file on the arrest and exile of Jews suspected of assisting illegal emigration [R], 1913–15.
(AP Białystok, Rząd Gubernialny, Łomża)
3. Copies of inscriptions on tombstones and synagogues [H, P, R], 1910.
(RGIA, St. Petersburg, Departament dukhovnykh del...)

PUŃSK (pow. Suwałki, woj. białostockie) 1831–1937
Photocopies:
Correspondence with the authorities about the community budget, 1936–37;
(AP Suwałki, Starostwo Powiatowe Suwalskie)
Microfilms:
Complaints concerning damages caused by soldiers and Jews to a Catholic priest [R], 1831.
(RGIA, St. Peterburg, Rimsko-katolicheskaia kollegiia…)

PYZDRY (pow. Konin, woj. łódzkie) 1765–1799
Microfilms:
1. Confirmation by King Stanisław August Poniatowski of the charter to the Jews [L, P], 1765.
(AGAD, Warszawa, Księgi Kanclerskie)
2. Minutes of the Civil Court, 1791–92; account books of the community [H, P], 1791–99.
(AP Poznań, Akta miast, woj. poznańskie)

RACHMANÓW (pow. Krzemieniec, woj. wołyńskie) 1847–1848
Microfilms:
Records containing names of Jewish inhabitants for tax purposes [R], 1847–48.
(DATO, Ternopil', Magistrat, Krzemieniec)

RADCZA (pow. Stanisławów, woj. stanisławowskie) 1923–1930
Microfilms:
1. Data concerning the Jewish population, 1923–24.
(DAIFO, Ivano-Frankivs'k, Starostwo Powiatowe, Stanisławów)
2. Reports by directors of public schools describing the localities and their social, national and cultural relations, as well as economic and sanitary conditions [P, U], 1930.
(DAIFO, Ivano-Frankivs'k, Inspektorat Szkolny, Stanisławów)

RADOGOSZCZ (pow. Łódź, woj. łódzkie) 1887–1910
Microfilms:
1. Administrative matters [R], 1887; financial matters of a printing house [R], 1889–91; correspondence about settling soldiers in the area, following their army service [R], 1892; insurance of various houses [R], 1892; issuing of passports [R], 1893.
(AP Łódź, Urząd Gminy Radogoszcz)
2. Request to establish a *Bikur Cholim* society [R], 1910.
(AP Łódź, Rząd Gubernialny, KP, Piotrków)

RADOM (woj. kieleckie) 1534–1948
Originals:
Posters and announcements, 1931–32.
Microfilms:
1. *Lustracje*, 1534–1615.
(AGAD, Warszawa, ASK)
2. The oath taken by Jewish merchants in the local court, 1721.
(AGAD, Warszawa, Księgi Grodzkie Wieluńskie)
3. Files on Jewish settlement in the city, 1811–55.

Raduń. Letter from the Chafetz Chaim yeshiva, 1933 (Hebrew)

(AGAD, Warszawa, KRzSW)

4. Municipal records and correspondence concerning the community (incl. decrees of the Tsar on Jewish matters); files on community functionaries; records concerning community elections (incl. lists of those eligible to vote); records concerning the finances of the community; material on the collection of community taxes; contributions and other funds for the support of Jewish schools, synagogues etc.; assistance for the poor; files on the leasing of various taxes; material on the *arenda* of income from the *mikve*, the sale of kosher meat and the sale of seats in the synagogue; files on rabbis in Radom; Jewish schools and *chadorim*; requests to establish new schools; fines for illegal teaching; files on Jewish hospitals; loans for a Jewish hospital from a municipal fund; files on *propinacja, arendas* and taverns; documents relating to a Jewish settlement in the town; houses and other properties owned by Jews; files on the sale of real estate; the construction of houses and loans for the purpose; requests for the construction of new community buildings; records concerning the enlargement of the Jewish cemetery; requests to establish a candle factory; files on the destruction of Jewish property by fire; records on the Merchants' Society (incl. lists of Jewish merchants); material on the restriction of Jewish participation in the Loan and Savings Society; correspondence on civil registration and fines for failure to register; files on the adoption of family names by Jews; records concerning Jewish dress and fines for failure to comply with the law; correspondence on the translation of documents from Yiddish to Russian; files of personal requests and complaints; records on the recruitment of Jews (incl. lists of Jewish recruits); correspondence on assistance for the families of recruits; fines for evading conscription [P, R], 1813–1917.

(AP Radom, Akta Magistratu, Radom)

5. Files on the Jewish community, election rules, accounts, community taxes, drafts of forms [P, R, Y], 1818–45; information concerning civil register, fines for failure to register births, marriages and deaths, statements by Jews explaining the reasons of non registration of births, 1846–50; files on Jews converting to Christianity, correspondence with the diocese of Sandomierz and Kielce–Kraków containing information about converted Jews, 1846–66; correspondence about traditional Jewish dress and lists of Jews allowed to dress traditionally, 1850–57.

(AP Radom, Rząd Gubernialny, Radom)

6. Reports and correspondence on ratifying elections of rabbis, exams for the rabbinate, tuition exemption, lists of rabbis and *dayanim*, 1823–56; a project to distribute kosher food to needy Jews and to support poor Jewish hospital patients [P, R], 1848–56; correspondence on exemption from military service of Warsaw Rabbinical Seminary graduates, 1865–71.

(AGAD, Warszawa, CWW)

7. Material on persecution of Jews in military zones during WW I [R], 1914–15.

(GARF, Moscow, Katsenel'son)

8. Correspondence between the state administration and the school council on registering *chadorim*, a request for permission to open a *cheder* and personal documents of teachers, 1920–21; a request for permission to open a private Hebrew school; certificates and other documents of Jewish students of the coeducational high school of the *Towarzystwo Przyjaciół Wiedzy* [Friends of Knowledge Society], 1924–25.

(AP Radom, Rada Szkolna miasta Radomia)

9. Correspondence with the Central Jewish Committee in Warsaw and the Jewish Committee in Kielce concerning repatriation of Jews from the Soviet Union, their settlement in Western Poland and a list of Jews returning from concentration camps, a list of Jews registered with the committee in Radom; various forms of aid for needy Jews; information about antisemitic incidents; decisions concerning Jewish community property and the Jewish cemetery, 1945–48.

(AP Radom, Okręgowy Komitet Żydowski, Radom)

RADOM, surroundings, 1766–1915
Microfilms:
1. A letter by Rabbi Isaac of Lubartów, instructing how to collect taxes for Jewish debts in the area of Lublin and Radom, 1766.
(AP Lublin, Castr.)
2. Information about corruption in the Radom *guberniia* [P, R], 1848–56; files on division of the *guberniia* into Jewish communities, a list of the towns and villages and respective communities, 1853–57.
(AGAD, Warszawa, CWW)
3. Lists of communities and localities, rabbis and *melamdim*, salaries of rabbis and various communal taxes, 1851–58; a file on a court case about unauthorized *propinacja*, 1858–1871; a list of community councils in various towns, accounts and payments to the Jewish hospital in Radom, 1859–66; a list of synagogues and prayer houses in the *guberniia*, 1860; a petition concerning the Society for the Spread of Enlightenment among the Jews of Russia and the status of a similar association in Radom [R], 1907–14.
(AP Radom, Rząd Gubernialny, Radom)
4. Lists of Jews living in various communities [R], 1887–98; files on community elections, including lists of voters in various communities [R], 1896–1904; information on synagogues and prayer houses [R], 1904–08; a conference of a rabbinical commission and a conference of delegates of Jewish communities, a list of distinguished personalities and electors from the Radom *guberniia* [R], 1910–11.
(AP Radom, Akta Magistratu, Radom)
5. Statistical data about synagogues and rabbis in various towns of the Radom *guberniia* [R], 1908.
(RGIA, St. Petersburg, Departament dukhovnykh del...)
6. Information about the pro–German orientation of Jews, correspondence about release of Jews from arrest and abolition of other repressive measures [R], 1914–15.
(RGVIA, Moscow, Shtab...)

RADOMSKO (woj. łódzkie) 1818–1913
Microfilms:
1. Files on permission to set up an *eruv* in the Jewish quarter and conflicts with Christians, 1818–71.
(AGAD, Warszawa, CWW)
2. Community records and accounts, 1822–66.
(AP Łódź, Anterioria Rządu Gubernialnego, Piotrków)
3. Requests for permission to construct new houses [R], 1869–91; records on the sale of land to the community to extend the cemetery [R], 1873–75; ratification of community accounts and elections [R], 1900–10; the appointment of a new rabbi and a new cantor, requests to increase the salaries of community employees and the number of positions available [R], 1901–04; files on the *shochet* and the income from the sale of kosher meat [R], 1904–06; files on the *arenda* of the *mikve* [R], 1904–09; three requests to open kerosene stores [R], 1895, 1908–10; records of two bequests to the community [R], 1913.
(AP Łódź, Rząd Gubernialny, WA, Piotrków)
4. Fines for evading conscription [R], 1891–1902.
(AP Łódź, Rząd Gubernialny, WP, Piotrków)
5. Files on private Jewish schools [R], 1902–03, 1907–08.
(AP Łódź, Dyrekcja Szkolna, Łódź)
6. Police investigations of Jews [R], 1905–06.
(AP Łódź, GZŻ, Piotrków)

7. Request to register charitable and cultural societies (*Linas Hatzedek, Talmud Tora, Hazamir*) [R], 1908–13.

(AP Łódź, Rząd Gubernialny, KP, Piotrków)

RADOMSKO, surroundings, 1866–1914
Microfilms:
1. Files on the ownership of agricultural settlements other than by peasants [P, R], 1866–1914

(AP Łódź, Rząd Gubernialny, Komisarz do spraw włościańskich pow. noworadomskiego, Piotrków)
2. Records about enforcing the legislation on Jewish dress [R], 1871–82.

(AP Łódź, Radomszczański Urząd Powiatowy)
3. Files on *chadorim* [R], 1891–99.

(AP Łódź, Dyrekcja Szkolna, Łódź)
4. Fines for evading conscription [R], 1892–1902.

(AP Łódź, Rząd Gubernialny, WP, Piotrków)
5. Requests to open businesses [R], 1908–09.

(AP Łódź, Rząd Gubernialny, WA, Piotrków)

RADOMYŚL (pow. Tarnobrzeg, woj. lwowskie) 18th cent–1939
Microfilms:
1. Municipal records, *propinacja* agreements, accounts and charters, 18th cent.

(AP Wrocław, Ossolineum)
2. Statute of a tailors' society [G, P, Y], 1901–06; correspondence about the *Shnos Chaim* society, including a text of the statutes, 1908.

(TsDIAU, L'viv, Namiestnictwo Galicyjskie)
3. Correspondence on community matters, among them, community institutions, elections, budget and functionaries, including lists of tax payers, board members (citing their ages, professions and political affiliations) rabbis and *dayanim*, 1933–39.

(DALO, L'viv, UW, Lwów)

RADOSZYCE (pow. Końskie, woj. kieleckie) 1534–1856
Microfilms:
1. *Lustracje* of the Sandomierz *województwo,* containing data on Radoszyce, 1534–1615.

(AGAD, Warszawa, ASK)
2. Reports and correspondence on the appointment of rabbis and their relations with the community, 1853–56.

(AGAD, Warszawa, CWW)

RADUŃ (pow. Lida, woj. nowogrodzkie) 1931–1933
Originals:
Letters issued by the *Chafetz Chaim yeshiva*, soliciting financial support [H], 1931–33.

RADYMNO (pow. Jarosław, woj. lwowskie) 1929–1939
Microfilms:
Election of a rabbi, 1929–38; reports and correspondence about corruption of the community board, 1931; and about community elections, including a list of board members, 1938–39.

(DALO, L'viv, UW, Lwów)

RADZANÓW (pow. Mława, woj. warszawskie) 1856–1864
Microfilms:
Reports and correspondence concerning appointment of rabbis, their education and salaries, including a list of graduates from the Rabbinical Seminary in Warsaw, 1856–64.
(AGAD, Warszawa, CWW)

RADZIECHÓW (woj. tarnopolskie) 1791–1939
Photocopies:
Register of merchants, entrepreneurs and owners of houses [R], 1939.
(DALO, L'viv, L'vovskii obkom…)
Microfilms:
1. Memorandum of the district authorities on the burning down of a tavern run by a Jew, 1791.
(AP Kraków, IT)
2. A register of Jewish businesses in the district [U], 1939.
(DALO, L'viv, L'vovskii obkom…)

RADZIŁÓW (pow. Szczuczyn, woj. białostockie) 1886–1913
Microfilms:
Certificates and photos of candidates for the rabbinate [R], 1886–1913.
(AP Białystok, Rząd Gubernialny, Łomża)

RADZIEJÓW (pow. Nieszawa, woj. warszawskie) 1826–1910
Microfilms:
1. A request by a Jew to nullify a fine [R], 1826–27.
(AGAD, Warszawa, SSKP)
2. Copies of inscriptions on tombstones and synagogues [H, P, R], 1910.
(RGIA, St. Petersburg, Departament dukhovnykh del…)

RADZIWIŁŁÓW (pow. Dubno, woj. wołyńskie) 1801–1936
Microfilms:
1. Correspondence of the governor of Volhynia concerning a tobacco factory [R], 1801–02.
(RGADA, Moscow, Manufaktur-kollegiia)
2. Investigations of false certificates issued by *kahal* employees in order to obtain passports [R], 1822–23; investigation concerning misuse of community registration forms [R], 1825–27; decrees, requests and reports concerning leadership of the community, illegal fines and punishments imposed on members of the community [R], 1826–28; investigation file on alleged abuse of power by the leadership of the community [H, R], 1833–34; file on a *cherem* forbidding Jews to buy vodka from a Jewish innkeeper [H, P, R], 1843–45, 1853; file on an accusation of members of the community of evading conscription, including a list of persons involved [R], 1853–57.
(DATO, Ternopil', Magistrat, Krzemieniec)
3. Investigation about tax collection irregularities in the town [R], 1826–33.
(GARF, Moscow, Tret'e otdelenie…)
4. File on Jewish participation in commerce of smuggled goods [R], 1833–36; file on *chasidic tzadikim* in various towns of the area (including a text by M. Kalisher about them) [R], 1834–76; file on measures against Jews evading conscription [R], 1841–43; a complaint by a Jewish merchant concerning confiscation of books [R], 1842–43; information about synagogues, prayer houses, Jewish schools and Jews in the town

[R], 1850; reports, appeals and correspondence about anti–government agitation, anti-Jewish disturbances, pogroms and measures against them [G, R], 1905–07.
(TsDIAU, Kyiv, Kantseliariia... general-gubernatora)
5. File on Jewish books sent to the Volhynian governor's offices for approval [R], 1841.
(TsDIAU, Kyiv, Kievskii tsenzurnyi komitet)
6. File on organization of Jewish hospitals and charitable institutions [R], 1853–64.
(RGIA, St. Petersburg, Khoziaistvennyi departament MVD)
7. Instruction concerning the employment of Jewish physicians and veterinarians, decrees, instructions and requests concerning necessary qualifications and rights of Jews to become rabbis [R], 1883–1903.
(RGIA, St. Petersburg, Departament dukhovnykh del...)
8. Monographs containing demographic and economic information about inhabitants in various towns of the region, 1936.
(AP Wrocław, Ossolineum, WKNZNP, Lwów)

RADZYŃ (woj. lubelskie) 1742–1871
Microfilms:
1. Inventory of the town and its inhabitants, 1742.
(AP Lublin, Księgi Miejskie, Radzyń)
2. A file concerning the financial matters of a Jew who left the Jewish community after his conversion, 1763–68.
(AP Kraków, Arch. Sanguszków, teki tzw. arabskie)
3. Extracts from municipal and court records concerning Jews, 1786–93.
(AP Wrocław, Ossolineum)
4. Correspondence concerning the appointment of a rabbi and the exemption from conscription of the graduates of the Rabbinical Seminary in Warsaw, 1865–71.
(AGAD, Warszawa, CWW)

RAFAŁOWKA (pow. Sarny, woj. wołyńskie) 1834–1876
Microfilms:
File on *chasidic tzadikim* in various towns of the area (including a text by M. Kalisher) [R], 1834–76.
(TsDIAU, Kyiv, Dokumenty, sobrannye...)

RAJGRÓD (pow. Szczuczyn, woj. białostockie) 1905–1915
Microfilms:
Fines for evading conscription [R], 1905; a file on the arrest and expulsion of Jews suspected of clandestine border crossing [R], 1913–15.
(AP Białystok, Rząd Gubernialny, Łomża)

RAKONIEWICE (pow. Wolsztyn, woj. poznańskie) 1662
Microfilms:
A charter granted to the town, containing the right *de non tolerandis Judeais* [L, P], 1622.
(AP Poznań, Akta miast, woj. poznańskie)

RAKOWCZYK (pow. Kołomyja, woj. stanisławowskie) 1931–1938
Microfilms:
Files on the activity of *Żydowskie Towarzystwo Rolnicze* (Jewish Agricultural Society) including the statutes, 1931–38.

(DAIFO, Ivano-Frankivs'k, Starostwo Powiatowe, Kołomyja)

RAKOWIEC (pow. Horodenka, woj. stanisławowskie) 1930–1937
Microfilms:
Card file of *Achva* society members, 1930–37.
(DAIFO, Ivano-Frankivs'k, UW, Stanisławów)

RAKÓW (pow. Mołodeczno, woj. wilenskie) 1776–1945
Originals:
Pinkas of a *Tora* study society [H], 1810–1915, 1945.
Photocopies:
An agreement between the Basilian monastery and the Jewish community regarding theft in the church, 1776.
(NIAB, Minsk, Minskii zemskii sud)
Microfilms:
Two inventories of the town, 1756–63.
(AP Wrocław, Ossolineum)

RANIŻÓW (pow. Kolbuszowa, woj. lwowskie) 1877–1929
Microfilms:
1. Correspondence with the authorities about *chadorim*, and a list of *melamdim*, 1877–1908.
(TsDIAU, L'viv, Namiestnictwo Galicyjskie)
2. Reports and minutes on the creation of a separate Jewish community in the town, correspondence about elections to the community board, 1924–29.
(DALO, L'viv, UW, Lwów)

RASZKÓW (pow. Ostrów, woj. poznańskie) 1896–1904
Originals:
Congratulatory letters and New Year's greetings from Rabbi M. Landau [G], 1896–1904.

RAWA MAZOWIECKA (woj. warszawskie) 1566–1914
Microfilms:
1. A *lustracja* of the rawskie, płockie and mazowieckie *województwo*, containing information on the population of Rawa Mazowiecka, 1566, 1570.
(AGAD, Warszawa, ASK)
2. Records concerning the community and the elections, 1822–66.
(AP Łódź, Anterioria Rządu Gubernialnego, Piotrków)
3. Files on Jewish teachers and schools [P, R], 1836–1913.
(AP Łódź, Dyrekcja Szkolna, Łódź)
4. Files on the Jewish quarter, 1851–59.
(AGAD, Warszawa, KRzSW)
5. Fines for evading conscription [R], 1888–1902.
(AP Łódź, Rząd Gubernialny, WP, Piotrków)
6. Ratification of community accounts and elections [R], 1893–1911; donations to the community [R], 1900–01; material on the renovation of the *mikve* and on income from the *arenda* of it [R], 1900–13; requests to open businesses [R], 1909.
(AP Łódź, Rząd Gubernialny, WA, Piotrków)

7. A request to register a charitable society [R], 1913–14.
(AP Łódź, Rząd Gubernialny, KP, Piotrków)

RAWA, surroundings, 1765–1915
Microfilms:
1. List of debts of communities in the district to be liquidated according to the instructions of the Crown Treasury Commission, 1765.
(AP Lublin, Castr.)
2. A decree of the local *sejmik* forbidding the lease of *propinacja* to Jews, 1785.
(AGAD, Warszawa, Księgi Grodzkie Sieradzkie)
3. Files on taxes paid for the right to wear traditional Jewish dress, 1846–57.
(AP Łódź, Anterioria Rządu Gubernialnego, Piotrków)
4. Correspondence concerning the exemption from conscription of graduates from the Rabbinical Seminary in Warsaw, including a list of rabbis, 1865–71.
(AGAD, Warszawa, CWW)
5. Records concerning *chadorim* [R], 1893–98.
(AP Łódź, Dyrekcja Szkolna, Łódź)
6. Fines for evading conscription [R], 1897–1902.
(AP Łódź, Rząd Gubernialny, WP, Piotrków)
7. Records about a society to support the Jewish hospital [R], 1913–15.
(GARF, Moscow, Departament politsii…)

RAWA RUSKA (woj. lwowskie) 1812–1939
Photocopies:
Last will of Rabbi Chaim Yehuda Federbusch [H], 1859.
(Rabbi A. Hollender, New York)
Microfilms:
1. Inventory of Rawa Ruska, containing a register of Jewish inhabitants, 1812; answers to a questionnaire concerning the Jews, 1922.
(NBANU, L'viv, Zb. Czołowskiego)
2. Correspondence and reports about *chadorim* and Jewish private schools [G, P], 1878–81; reports from an inspection of Baron Hirsch Foundation (JCA) schools, including personal files of teachers [G, P], 1896–1904.
(TsDIAU, L'viv, Krajowa Rada Szkolna)
3. Correspondence concerning communal taxes and ratification of statutes, 1895–97; correspondence about community elections [G, P], 1902–08; complaints by community members about illegal collection of taxes for *shechita*, 1906–07.
(TsDIAU, L'viv, Namiestnictwo Galicyjskie)
4. Correspondence about the following societies: *Postęp*, 1921–39; *Yad Charutzim*, including a text of the statutes [G, P], 1923–39; *Kultur Liga*, reports and correspondence with the authorities about opening a course in Hebrew, 1926; *Agudas Yisroel*, including a text of the statutes, 1927–34; authorization by the district authorities to collect funds for the Polish–Galician Jewish community in Palestine, including a list of donors, 1928–30; *Gmilus Chasodim*, 1928–36; *Hapoel*, including statutes, 1929–36; *Machzikei Limud*, 1931–32; *Gordonia*, 1931–36; *Hatikva*, including statutes, 1931–39; *Machzikei Hadas*, including a list of board members, 1932–33. Reports and correspondence on community elections, including a list of council members, their ages, professions and political affiliations, 1928–38; correspondence with the district

authorities about the rabbi's, salary 1929; a list of members of the local selfgovernment, their nationalities and political affiliations, 1930–31; correspondence about the community budget, including a list of taxpayers, 1933–34; reports containing lists of council members, rabbis and *dayanim* of the community, 1937; correspondence between the authorities and the community regarding the community organization (budget, institutions, functionnaries), rabbis and *dayanim*, 1937–39; reports and correspondence about Polish language exams for rabbis and *dayanim*, 1938–39.
(DALO, L'viv, UW, Lwów)

RAWA RUSKA, surroundings, 1877–1907
Microfilms:
A report about *chadorim* in the district, including a list of *chadorim*, 1877–1907; reports and correspondence concerning reorganization of the Jewish communities in the district [G, P], 1897–1903.
(TsDIAU, L'viv, Namiestnictwo Galicyjskie)

RAWICZ (woj. poznańskie) 1645–1920
Originals:
Confirmation of community elections and receipts for the repayment of loans to the church [G, H, L, P], 1705–1858; records of the rabbinical court, letters and bills of sale of synagogue seats [H], 1718–1835; files on real estate owned by the community , 1784–1877; community accounts, 1794–1839, 1877–94; files on taxes paid by Jews [G, H], 1806–87; records of community elections, resolutions and announcements [G, Y], 1819–87; renovation of the synagogue [G], 1824–1889; files on the Jewish hospital and the care of the sick [G], 1825–78; file on debts to the Catholic church in Kobierno and Pakosław [G], 1830–1850; government supervision of the community administration [G], 1833–87; community statutes [G], 1834; marriage agreements [G], 1835, 1839–45; records concerning prayer–houses, the *mikve* and the supply of *matzot* at Passover time [G, H], 1835–57; acounts of the Jewish school [G], 1836; official instructions concerning Jewish education and the maintenance of the Jewish school [G], 1846–71; synagogue accounts [G], 1865–87
Photocopies:
Jahrzeit register [H], 1842–1920.
(Private collection, London)
Microfilms:
1. Charters granted to the burghers defining Jewish economic rights and duties, 1645; documents regulating relations between Jews and burghers, 1648; charters granting rights to two Jews to live and trade in the town, 1692; records of litigation over economic matters, 1713–44, 1775; synagogue record book [G, H], 1835–88.
(AP Poznań, Akta miast, woj. poznańskie)
2. Registers, accounts, decrees and contracts concerning properties and inhabitants on the properties of the Sieniawski–Czartoryski families [F, L, P], 1706–85.
(Biblioteka Narodowa, Warszawa)
3. Minutes and decisions of the community council [G], 1834–86; correspondence between the community and the authorities concerning community matters [G], 1838–39.
(Centrum Judaicum, Berlin)

REJOWIEC (pow. Chełm, woj. lubelskie) 1853–1856
Microfilms:

Correspondence about appointments of rabbis, and their relations with the communities, including a list of rabbis, 1853–56.
(AGAD, Warszawa, CWW)

REMBERTÓW (woj. warszawskie) 1933–1934
Photocopies:
A file of *Kibbutz "Bruria"* of *Hapoel Hamizrachi* [H], 1933–34.

ROGOŹNO (pow. Oborniki, woj. poznańskie) 1778–1857
Originals:
An agreement concerning Jewish commerce [G], 1778; a register of the recruiting tax paid by Jews, 1829–34; the election of community officials, 1833–42; the appeal of a nearby community for assistance in building a synagogue, 1835; Jewish education, 1835–57; correspondence of the Jewish tailors' guild with the authorities [G], 1843–47; statutes of the *Talmud Tora* society [G], 1892.

ROHATYN (woj. stanisławowskie) 1663–1939
Microfilms:
1. Circular letters, accounts, decrees and *uniwersały* concerning inhabitants and properties of M. Sapieha, St. Siemieński, M. i A. Sieniawski and A. Czartoryski, 1663–1765.
(Bibl. Czartoryskich, Kraków)
2. Confirmation by King Jan Kazimierz of a charter granted to the Jews by King Władysław IV, 1663; confirmation by King Michał Korybut Wiśniowiecki of the charter granted by King Władysław IV (27.03.1633) to the Jews in Rohatyn, 1669; lists of voters [G, P], 1865–70.
(AP Kraków, Teki Schneidra, DP)
3. Reports about Jewish schools [G], 1788; correspondence about support for Jewish schools [G, P], 1880; correspondence with the district authorities about complaints against various communities in the district, 1882–83; correspondence about the *Zion* and *Postęp* (*Haskalah*) societies, text of statutes [G, P], 1894; correspondence with the *Ahavas Zion* society about emigration to Palestine [G, P], 1898.
(TsDIAU, L'viv, Namiestnictwo Galicyjskie)
4. Reports concerning *chadorim* and teachers [G, P], 1875–77.
(TsDIAU, L'viv, Krajowa Rada Szkolna)
5. Materials on confirming the statutes of the *Talmud Tora* and *Emuna* societies, 1893, 1920–30; statutes, minutes and correspondence concerning Zionist organizations, 1921–30; a file on the closing of the Jewish cemetery. [G, P], 1921–35; a register of associations in the district [P, U], 1922–23; materials on confirming the statutes of the *Gmilus Chasodim* society, 1922–30; correspondence with the district authorities about the activities of the *Bund*, 1923; records concerning civil registry and population statisics, 1923–24; reports and correspondence on registration and statutes of charity institutions for helping children and youth, 1923–28; a register of Jewish associations and material on some of them, 1924–38; reports and correspondence on the registration, activity and liquidation of the *Żydowski Dom Narodowy*, *Żydowski Klub Towarzyski* and *Żydowski Klub Makabi* societies, statutes and membership list of *Makabi*, 1924–38; a report about the collection of money for Jews in Palestine, 1926; reports about the following societies: Revisionist Zionists, 1927; *Hashomer–Hatzair*, 1929–37; various Jewish youth organizations, including statutes, 1929–30; *Żydowska Rada Sieroca i Ochrona Młodzieży*, *Hitachdut* and *Hechalutz*, including lists of board members 1930; *Gmilus Chasodim*, 1930–36; *Towarzystwo Opieki nad Halucami i Emigrantami Palestyńskimi "Ezra"*, 1930–35; *Opieka nad Żydowską Młodzieżą "Gordonia"*, 1930–36; various Jewish societies, including lists of board members 1930–37; *Hatzofim Brit Trumpeldor* and *Achva* 1930–37;

reports and correspondence concerning the activities of the Jewish community [G, P, Y], 1931–36; records of Jewish sport clubs, 1931–36; records of *Stowarzyszenie Opieki nad Młodzieżą Żydowską* and files on the liquidation of the *Sholem Aleichem* society, 1931–38; reports and statutes of *Ogólno-Żydowska Partia Pracy*, 1932–33; reports concerning the associations: *Histadrut Hanoar Haivri*, and *Tzofe*, 1933; correspondence concerning board members of *Żydowskie Stowarzyszenie Rolnicze* and their political affiliations, 1933; records of *Hanoar Hatziyoni*, 1933–34; records of *Yad Charutzim*, 1933–37; a monograph on the district, 1934; files on protests against British policy in Palestine, 1934; records of *Żydowskie Towarzystwo Kulturalno-Oświatowe "Tarbut"*, 1934–38; decrees, reports and correspondence about the activity of the *Hitachdut Poalei Zion* party, 1935; a report about the distribution of anti-Jewish publications, 1936; records of the *Związek Opieki nad Sierotami i Młodzieżą Żydowską* and WIZO societies, 1937–38.
(DAIFO, Ivano-Frankivs'k, UW, Stanisławów)
6. Documents concerning appointment of rabbis [G, P], 1913–19.
(TsDIAU, L'viv, Ministerium fuer Kultus und Unterricht, Wien)
7. Statutes of the *Towarzystwo Spożywcze, Rzemieślników, Kupców i Wykonujących Wolne Zawody Wyznania Mojżeszowego w Rohatyniu*, 1919; reports and correspondence concerning popular meetings organized by Jewish, Polish and Ukrainian associations, a register of them, 1919–21.
(DAIFO, Ivano-Frankivs'k, Starostwo Powiatowe, Rohatyn)
8. Reports about elementary schools, students and teachers in the district, 1921–22; statistical reports about children in elementary schools according to their nationality and religion, 1923.
(DAIFO, Ivano-Frankivs'k, Rada Szkolna, Rohatyn)
9. District records of the general census from, 1931; population statistics, 1938.
(DAIFO, Ivano-Frankivs'k, UW, Stanisławów)
10. Monthly police reports concerning activity of political parties and associations, 1930–32; political and social monograph on the district, 1935; reports concerning the activities of Zionist associations, 1935–36; reports and correspondence about anti-Jewish actions organized by Ukrainian nationalists, 1936–37.
(DAIFO, Ivano-Frankivs'k, Komenda Wojewódzka PP, Stanisławów)
11. Reports and correspondence on the legalization of *chadorim* and other Jewish religious schools and cultural institutions, including a list of *chadorim* and Hebrew courses organized by *Tarbut*, 1934–36.
(DAIFO, Ivano-Frankivs'k, Inspektorat Szkolny, Stanisławów)
12. Payroll sheets of Jewish community employees, 1937–39.
(DAIFO, Ivano-Frankivs'k, Wojewódzkie Biuro Funduszu Pracy, Stanisławów)

ROKITNO (pow. Sarny, woj wołyńskie) 1883–1936
Microfilms:
1. Instructions regarding the employment of Jewish physicians and veterinarians; decrees, instructions and requests concerning necessary qualifications and rights for Jews to become rabbis in Russia [R], 1883–1903.
(RGIA, St. Petersburg, Departament dukhovnykh del...)
2. Reports and correspondence about disorders, strikes and pogroms in various towns [R], 1905.
(TsDIAU, Kyiv, Kantseliariia... general-gubernatora)
3. A monograph containing demographic and economic information about inhabitants in various towns of the region, 1936.
(AP Wrocław, Ossolineum, WKNZNP, Lwów)

ROPCZYCE (woj. krakowskie) 1740–1896
Microfilms:
1. *Suplika* by the mayor and population of Ropczyce, 1740.
(TsDIAU, Kyiv, Arch. Potockich z Tulczyna)
2. An inventory of the *starostwo*, 1760.
(AP Wrocław, Ossolineum)
3. A report on teaching Jewish religion in elementary schools [G, P], 1882–89.
(TsDIAU, L'viv, Krajowa Rada Szkolna)
4. Correspondence about the *Zion* society, including statutes [G, P], 1894; correspondence with the district authorities about confirmation of community statutes, 1895–96.
(TsDIAU, L'viv, Namiestnictwo Galicyjskie)

ROSSOSZ (pow. Biała Podlaska, woj. lubelskie) 1729–1759
Microfilms:
A charter granted to the town by Prince Karol Sapieha, 1729–59.
(NBANU, L'viv, Arch. Sapiehów)

ROZDÓŁ (pow. Żydaczów, woj. stanisławowskie) 1720–1938
Microfilms:
1. Orders, complaints and registers concerning the payment of military taxes by the Jews of Rozdół and Chodorów, 1720–56; *arenda* contracts from Rozdół and the surrounding villages, 1731–77; testimonies and other material concerning the murder of the rabbi's daughter [L, P], 1766–67; a file on legal proceedings against a Jew. [L, P], 1766–67; a list of Jews and Christians, by street, for tax purposes, 1772–1826; inventory of the town and its suburbs, 1792–93; a list of taverns in Rozdół and Chodorów, 18th cent.; a list of Jews in Rozdół, 1801; a file on *propinacja*, and a list of Jews, 1812–83; a list of Jews and non Jews, arranged by occupation and tax levels, 1820; excerpts from a register of penalties concerning the violation of commerce regulations by a Jewish innkeeper, 1867; a list of poor Jews and Catholics in Rozdół, 1930; a register of craftsmen, 1933.
(TsDIAU, L'viv, Arch. Lanckorońskich)
2. Files on debts of the Jewish community [H, L, P], 1767–70.
(TsDIAU, L'viv, Kolektsiia dokumentiv…)
3. Reports on Jewish schools [G], 1788; correspondence with the district authorities regarding *chadorim*, including a list of *melamdim*, 1877–1908.
(TsDIAU, L'viv, Namiestnictwo Galicyjskie)
4. *Sumariusz* of inhabitants living in the *rozdolski klucz*, 1827.
(TsDIAU, L'viv, Arch. Lanckorońskich)
5. A list of voters [G], 1868.
(AP Kraków, Teki Schneidra)
6. Files concerning registration of *Ezra,* 1871–88, 1921–30, *Mizrachi, Merkaz Ruchani* and *Agudas Yisroel,* 1895, 1920–27; records concerning the civil register, 1823–24; correspondence concerning budget, *shechita* and *lustracja* of the Jewish community, 1926–35; statutes, minutes and correspondence concerning Jewish associations, 1931–38; reports and correspondence concerning community elections, 1932–36; directory and board of: the *Chevra Kadisha,* 1933–36, *Żydowskie Towarzystwo Szkoły Ludowej i Średniej,* 1933–37 and *Yad Charutzim,* 1933–37; election and confirmation of a rabbi and a *dayan,* 1935–36; material on an examination of proficiency in the Polish language for rabbinical candidates, 1936; correspondence with the district authorities about the functioning of the community, 1937–38

DAIFO, Ivano-Frankivs'k, UW, Stanisławów)

ROZPRZA (pow. Piotrków, woj. łódzkie) 1822–1913
Microfilms:
1. Records concerning the community and its accounts, 1822–66.
(AP Łódź, Anterioria Rządu Gubernialnego, Piotrków)
2. Correspondence concerning *chadorim,* 1890–99.
(AP Łódź, Dyrekcja Szkolna, Łódź)
3. Fines for evading conscription [R], 1891–96.
(AP Łódź, Rząd Gubernialny, WP, Piotrków)
4. Ratification of community elections and accounts [R], 1893–1913; a file on the rabbi's salary [R], 1901; a request to open a business [R], 1909.
(AP Łódź, Rząd Gubernialny, WA, Piotrków)

ROZWADÓW (pow. Tarnobrzeg, woj. lwowskie) 1758–1939
Microfilms:
1. Decisions of the Council of Four Lands regulating relations between the *kahals* of Busk, Rozwadów and Siemiatycze [L, P], 1758.
(NBANU, L'viv, Arch. Radzimińskiego)
2. Reports on the inspection of Baron Hirsch Foundation (JCA) schools, and teachers' personal files, 1896–97.
(TsDIAU, L'viv, Krajowa Rada Szkolna)
3. Authorization by the district authorities to collect donations for the Polish–Galician Jewish community in Palestine, including a list of donors, 1928–30; circular letters, reports and correspondence about the community council elections, including a list of council members, 1928–39; correspondence about the *Yad Charutzim*, workers' society, 1938.
(DALO, L'viv, UW, Lwów)
4. Correspondence on the registration of the *Mizrachi*, including statutes and a list of members, 1932.
(DALO, L'viv, Magistrat, Lwów)

ROŻAN (pow. Maków Mazowiecki, woj. warszawskie) 1566–1915
Microfilms:
1. *Lustracja*, 1566.
(AGAD, Warszawa, ASK)
2. A letter concerning Jews, 1694.
(AP Wrocław, Ossolineum)
3. Records of litigation between a Jewish innkeeper and the owner of a nearby village, 1788.
(AGAD, Warszawa, Księgi Grodzkie Różanskie)
4. A letter of rebuke from King Stanisław August Poniatowski to the municipality regarding the breach of an agreement with the community, 1792.
(AGAD, Warszawa, Księgi Kanclerskie)
5. A file on confiscation of dye in a shop belonging to a Jew [R], 1909–10; a request to open a book store [R], 1911–12; exemption from passport fees for an inhabitant of Rożan [R], 1914–15; a file concerning payment for construction of bridges to a Jewish entrepreneur [R], 1914–15; file on the arrest and expulsion to the eastern provinces of Russia of Jews suspected of espionage [R], 1915.
(AP Białystok, Rząd Gubernialny, Łomża)

ROŻAN, surroundings, 1790
Microfilms:
Instructions of the local nobility to their representatives at the *Sejm* concerning the resettlement of Jews from villages to towns, 1790.
(AGAD, Warszawa, Księgi Grodzkie Różanskie)

ROŻNIATÓW (pow. Dolina, woj. stanisławowskie) 1898–1937
Microfilms:
1. Correspondence between the community and the district authorities about community statutes, the community's rabbi, Isaac Hirsch Hamerling and community elections [G, P], 1898–1908;
(TsDIAU, L'viv, Namiestnictwo Galicyjskie)
2. Reports on the arrest of Jews suspected of sabotage [R], 1915–16.
(DAIFO, Ivano-Frankivs'k, Nachal'nik Dolinskogo uezda…)
3. Statutes, minutes and correspondence concerning Jewish associations and Zionist organizations, 1921–38; directory and board members of *Yad Charutzim*, 1923, 1929–32; decrees, minutes and correspondence about confirmation of the community statutes, 1923–24; files on registration of *Hashomer Hatzair* and *Agudas Yisroel*, including texts of statutes, 1927–37; directory and board members of *Hertzlia*, 1930; index card and board members of *Achva*, 1930–37; reports and correspondence concerning the activity of the Jewish community. [G, P, Y], 1931–35; reports and correspondence about community elections, 1932–36; a report about a meeting of the *Mizrachi*, 1932; reports about the *Histadrut Hanoar Haivri*, *Hashomer Hatzair* and *Tzofe* Jewish youth associations, 1933; correspondence with the district authorities about the statute and the registration of *Kupat Gmilus Chasodim*, text of the statutes and a list of members, 1934; records conerning salaries of rabbis and their assistants, complaints by rabbis and other employees of the community concerning salaries and dismissals, 1936.
(DAIFO, Ivano-Frankivs'k, UW, Stanisławów)

ROŻNÓW (pow. Kosów, woj. stanisławowskie) 1922–1938
Microfilms:
Files on confirmation of the *Gmilus Chasodim* statutes, 1922–31; a list of Jewish associations, 1924–37; lists of board members of Jewish agricultural associations, 1933–38.
(DAIFO, Ivano-Frankivs'k, UW, Stanisławów)

ROŻYSZCZE (pow. Łuck, woj. wołyńskie) 1905
Microfilms:
Reports and correspondence concerning the political situation, pogroms and measures to prevent them [G, R], 1905.
(TsDIAU, Kyiv, Kantseliariia… general-gubernatora)

RÓWNE (woj. wołyńskie) 1540–1939
Microfilms:
1. Royal decrees acquitting the Jews of Lithuania of accusations regarding an alleged circumcision of Christian boys; acquittal of Jews, accused of trading in stolen objects [R], 1540–41.
(RGADA, Moscow, ML)
2. Confirmation of payment, 1721.
(AP Kraków, Arch. Podhoreckie Potockich)
3. Records on payment of debts by a rabbi, 1767.
(TsDIAU, Kyiv, Arch. Zamoyskich)

4. A file on Jewish books sent to the Volhynia governor's offices for inspection [R], 1841.
(TsDIAU, Kyiv, Kievskii tsenzurnyi komitet)

5. File about the expulsion of Jewish innkeepers for supposed connections with criminals [R], 1841; a file on the forgery of documents in an investigation of a Jewish woman's suicide [R], 1841–44; file on the rights of settlement in the town and on the rights of Jews living there to trade in alcoholic beverages, a list of charters by Polish Kings and decrees by the Russian authorities [R], 1849–52; information about synagogues, prayer houses, Jewish schools and the Jewish population in the town [R], 1850; correspondence about pogroms and files on legal proceedings against participants, including lists of arrested suspects and of victims [R], 1881; a file on establising a Jewish night guard [R], 1881; files on demonstrations by Jews, and investigation files of arrested Jews [R], 1905; reports and correspondence about disorders, strikes, pogroms and measures to prevent them [R], 1905.
(TsDIAU, Kyiv, Kantseliariia... general-gubernatora)

6. *Revizskie skazki* [R], 1858–60.
(DARO, Rivne, Rovenskoe uezdnoe kaznacheistvo)

7. File on the organization of Jewish hospitals and charitable institutions [R], 1863–64.
(RGIA, St. Petersburg, Khoziaistvennyi departament MVD)

8. Files of the Society for the Spread of Enlightenment among the Jews of Russia, a list of towns where books and financial support were sent, lists of books and names of donors [R], 1888–99.
(GARF, Moscow, Departament politsii...)

9. Report on a school for Jewish women, 1898–1900.
(RGIA, St.Petersburg, OPE)

10. Correspondence of the community with the Alliance Israélite Universelle [F, H], 19th–20th cent.
(AIU, Paris)

11. Statutes, reports and correspondence about the registration and activities of: the local branch of *Związek Zawodowy Nauczycieli Szkół Żydowskich w Polsce*, including a list of members, 1920–38; *Linas Hatzedek*, including a list of board members, 1922–38; *Towarzystwo Szerzenia Pracy Zawodowej i Rolnej wśród Żydów* (ORT), including a list of members and board members, 1922–39; *Towarzystwo Ochrony Zdrowia Ludności Żydowskiej w Polsce* (TOZ), including a list of members and board members, 1923–38; *Żydowski Klub Sportowy Hasmoneja*, including a list of board members, 1923–39; *Hachnasas Orchim*, including a list of board members and those who received loans, 1924–39; *Towarzystwo Opieki nad Sierotami Żydowskimi*, including a list of the Central Council and members of the local branch, 1930–39; *Igud shel Hatzohar*, including a list of board members, 1933–36; *Brit Hechayal*, including a list of members and board members, 1934–38; *Kultur Liga*, including a list of members and board members, 1939.
(DARO, Rivne, Starostwo Powiatowe, Równe)

12. Budget, community tax register and complaints, 1934–38; minutes of the community council and of the comission for community taxes, including a list of tax payers, 1935–38.
(DARO, Rivne, Gmina Żydowska, Równe)

RÓWNE, surroundings, 1766–1834
Microfilms:
1. *Arenda* contracts, 1766–67.
(TsDIAU, Kyiv, Arch. Lubomirskich)

2. A report about *kahals*, synagogues, Jewish schools, functionaries of various communal institutions and the Jewish population [R], 1834.
(TsDIAU, Kyiv, Kantseliariia... general-gubernatora)

RÓŻANKA (pow. Stryj, woj. stanisławowskie) 1936–1937
Microfilms:
Reports and correspondence concerning anti-Jewish actions by Ukrainian nationalists, 1936–37.
(DAIFO, Ivano-Frankivs'k, Komenda Wojewódzka PP, Stanisławów)

RÓŻANKA (pow. Szczuczyn, woj. nowogródzkie) 1804
Microfilms:
A file of the Supreme Tribunal of Lithuania and Grodno on legal proceedings between a Catholic priest, Duke Sapieha and the Jewish community [R], 1804.
(RGIA, St. Petersburg, Rimsko-katolicheskaia kollegiia…)

RUDA (pow. Żydaczów, woj. stanisławowskie) 1621
Microfilms:
Documents concerning *arenda* of the village, 1621.
(AP Kraków, Arch. Sanguszków, Teki tzw. rzymskie)

RUDKI (woj. lwowskie) 1628–1937
Microfilms:
1. Private agreements, accounts and contracts concerning properties of the Sieniawski and Czartoryski families, 1628–1759.
(Bibl. Czartoryskich, Kraków)
2. A letter by a parish priest to the *wojewoda* of the Ruthenian lands about litigation with Jews, 1701.
(TsDIAU, L'viv, Kolektsiia lystiv…)
3. Proclamations, reports and correspondence concerning *chadorim* and Jewish private schools [G, P], 1878–1881; reports about teaching Jewish religion in elementary schools [G, P], 1882–89.
(TsDIAU, L'viv, Krajowa Rada Szkolna)
4. Correspondence with the district authorities about citation of citizenship in the civil register, 1891–92; correspondence about vacant positions in the rabbinate, 1895; correspondence with the district authorities about the Jewish community and confirmation of community statutes, 1895–96; correspondence about the appointment of a rabbi [G, Hung., P], 1896; correspondence about the *Yad Charutzim* society, 1904.
(TsDIAU, L'viv, Namiestnictwo Galicyjskie)
5. A list of candidates for the community board, citing their political affiliations, 1922–26; correspondence regarding community matters, 1922–26; correspondence about the *Kultur Liga*, 1926; lists of town council members, their nationalities and political affiliations, 1930–31; reports and correspondence about the community budget, including a list of tax payers, 1932–37; decrees, complaints and correspondence about elections of the community board, council and rabbi 1933–37. (DALO, L'viv, UW, Lwów)
6. Correspondence about registration of the *Machzikei Hadas* society, including a list of board members, 1930, and about the registration of *Agudas Yisroel*, 1931–35.
(DALO, L'viv, Magistrat, Lwów)

RUDNIK (pow. Nisko, woj. lwowskie) 1925–1939
Microfilms:
1. Correspondence with the district authorities about the registration and liquidation of the *Oddział Związku Robotników Drzewnych* association, 1925–32; correspondence about community matters – elections, budget, rabbinate, a list of tax payers and the *Yad Charutzim* society, 1929–39.
(DALO, L'viv, UW, Lwów)
2. Correspondence about the registration of *Agudas Yisroel*, 1925–33.

(DALO, L'viv, Magistrat, Lwów)

RUTKI (pow. Łomża, woj. białostockie) 1850–1909
Microfilms:
1. Birth, marriage and death records (fragmentary), 1850–60.
(AP Łomża)
2. A file on illegal commerce in pharmaceutical products by Jews, 1909.
(AP Białystok, Rząd Gubernialny, Łomża)

RYBNIK (woj. śląskie) 1766–1916
Originals:
Papers of the Haase family (incl. a list of the Jews in the town), 1766–1916; a register of taxes paid to the government, 1847–64; records of the inauguration and jubilee celebrations of the synagogue, 1848, 1898; files on the Jewish elementary school, 1881–97; budgets of the community, 1887–90.

RYBNO (pow. Stanisławów, woj. stanisławowskie) 1930
Microfilms:
Reports by directors of public schools about social, national, cultural, economical and sanitary conditions in the town [P, U], 1930.
(DAIFO, Ivano-Frankivs'k, Inspektorat Szkolny, Stanisławów)

RYBOTYCZE (pow. Dobromil, woj. lwowskie) 1846–1935
Microfilms:
1. Files about confirmation of Jewish community statutes, 1846–96.
(TsDIAU, L'viv, Namiestnictwo Galicyjskie)
2. Authorization by the district authorities to collect donations for the Polish–Galician Jewish community in Palestine, and a list of donors, 1928–30; correspondence about the community budget, and a list of tax payers, 1933–35.
(DALO, L'viv, UW, Lwów)

RYCZYWÓŁ (pow. Kozienice, woj kieleckie) 1534–1778
Microfilms:
1. A *lustracja* of the Sandomierz *województwo*, 1534–1615.
(AGAD, Warszawa, ASK)
2. Confirmation by King Stanisław August Poniatowski of a charter granted to the Jews [L, P], 1778.
(AGAD, Warszawa, MK)
3. Two petitions by the community to the owner of the town, 18th cent.
(Bibl. im. Łopacińskiego, Lublin)

RYCZYWÓŁ (pow. Oborniki, woj. poznańskie) 1891
Originals:
Inauguration program of a new synagogue [G], 1891.

RYDZYNA (pow. Leszno, woj. poznańskie) 18th–19th cent.
Originals:
A notebook of a *maskil* containing poems, letters, translations and other texts [G, H], 19th cent.
Microfilms:
Official orders concerning obligations and taxes to be paid by the Jews, 18th cent.

(AP Poznań, Akta miast, woj. poznańskie)

RYMANÓW (pow. Sanok, woj. lwowskie) 1686–1939
Microfilms:
1. Charters, memoranda, requests, *arenda* contracts and other materials concerning Jews [G, H, L, P, Y], 1686–1805.
(AP Lublin, Zb. Czołowskiego)
2. An agreement between the community in Rymanów and municipal authorities in Krosno permitting Jews to participate in fairs in exchange for a tribute to the mayor and municipal board, 1776.
(AP Kraków, Teki Schneidra)
3. Files on confirmation of Jewish community statutes, 1846–96.
(TsDIAU, L'viv, Namiestnictwo Galicyjskie)
4. Records concerning elections of the community council and the rabbinate, as well as protests regarding irregularities, 1928–37; authorization by the district authorities to collect donations for the Polish–Galician Jewish community in Palestine, and a list of donors, 1928–30; correspondence with the district authorities and the Ministry of Religion about the community budget, correspondence with Rabbi Hirsch Horowitz about his salary [P, Y], 1934–35; correspondence about the *Yad Charutzim* society, 1938; reports and correspondence about Polish language examinations for rabbis and *dayanim*, 1938–39.
(DALO, L'viv, UW, Lwów)
5. Correspondence about the registration of *Agudas Yisroel*, 1932.
(DALO, L'viv, Magistrat, Lwów)

RYPIN (woj. warszawskie) 1825
Original:
Records of Jewish births (fragmentary), 1825.

RYTWIANY (pow. Sandomierz, woj. kieleckie) 1652–1766
Microfilms:
1. Reports, letters, complaints and excerpts from municipal books concerning properties of the Sieniawski and Czartoryski families [H, L, P], 1652–1766.
(Bibl. Czartoryskich, Kraków)
2. Accounts concerning Rytwiany, 1708–29; inventory of the Rytwiany *klucz*, 1733.
(AP Kraków, Arch. Krzeszowickie Potockich)

RZECZYCA (pow. Sieradz, woj. łódzkie) 1899
Microfilms:
Ratification of community elections [R], 1899.
(AP Łódź, Rząd Gubernialny, WA, Piotrków)

RZECZYCA (pow. Tarnobrzeg, woj. lwowskie) 1755–1769
Microfilms:
Contracts involving Jews, 1755–60; an inventory of the *starostwo*, 1769.
(AP Wrocław, Ossolineum)

RZESZÓW (woj. rzeszowskie) 1705–1939
Microfilms:
1. Files and inventories of the Jewish population and taxes, 1705–08.
(Bibl. Czartoryskich, Kraków)

2. A letter on the payment of a debt by the community, 1713.
(TsDIAU, L'viv, Kolektsiia dokumentiv…)

3. Correspondence with the provincial authorities concerning taxes, synagogues and *minyanim* in private houses [G, L], 1819–26; complaints and requests concerning the right of residence [G], 1822–29; tax register [G], 1842–59; files regarding community statutes [G, P], 1846–1904; correspondence with the district authorities concerning *chadorim*, and a list of *melamdim*, 1877–1908; correspondence about the level of communal taxes, 1888–90; statutes of the *Dorshei Tov* society [G, P], 1888–1912; correspondence with the district authorities about citation of citizenship in civil registers, 1891–92; correspondence about the *Gmilus Chasodim* society [G, P], 1897; complaints about the community elections, 1902–07; complaints and correspondence about the election and appointment of Rabbi Nathan Lewin from Rohatyn as the rabbi of Rzeszów [G, P], 1904–05; records on foundation of the *Safa Berura* society, including a text of the statutes [G, P], 1910–12.
(TsDIAU, L'viv, Namiestnictwo Galicyjskie)

4. Reports about teaching Jewish religion in elementary schools [G, P], 1882–89.
(TsDIAU, L'viv, Krajowa Rada Szkolna)

5. Statutes of the Jewish community, 1897, 1901; a report about the activities of the temporary community council for the period 1904–07.
(TsDIAU, L'viv, Gmina Żydowska, Lwów)

6. Correspondence about the celebration honoring the inauguration of the Hebrew University in Jerusalem, 1924–25; correspondence about the *Kultur Liga*, 1926; material concerning elections to the community council, 1928–29; lists of the town council members, their nationalities and political affiliations, 1930; a list of Zionist Organization members in Rzeszów, 1931; reports and correspondence about community elections, including a list of the board members, 1933–39; correspondence about the community budget, and a list of taxpayers, 1933–34; reports containing names of board members, rabbis and *dayanim*, 1937.
(DALO, L'viv, UW, Lwów)

7. Correspondence about the registration of *Agudat Hanoar Haivri*, a text of the statutes and a list of board members, 1928–39; correspondence about *Machzike Hadas*, 1930–38.
(DALO, L'viv, Magistrat, Lwów)

8. Reports concerning the activity and list of local committees of *Ogólno-Żydowska Partia Pracy* (OŻPP), 1933.
(DAIFO, Ivano-Frankivs'k, UW, Stanisławów)

RZGÓW (pow. Łódź, woj. łódzkie) 1896–1898
Microfilms:
Fines for evading conscription [R], 1896–98.
(AP Łódź, Rząd Gubernialny, WP, Piotrków)

SAMBOR (woj. lwowskie) 1716–1938
Microfilms:
1. *Supliki* by Jews from Sambor, 1716–18.
(Bibl. Czartoryskich, Kraków)

2. Complaints by inhabitants of Sambor against the municipality for violation of their charters [L, P], 1732; excerpts from municipal records concerning construction of a synagogue in Sambor [L, P], 1732; a protest against the verdict of a municipal court concerning debts of a merchant from Gdańsk to a merchant from Sambor [L], 1755; decrees and protests concerning claims by creditors against a merchant from Sambor [H, L, P], 1755–69; a protest of the community against the baptism of an *arendar* from Sambor [L], 1758;

interrogation of a merchant in a matter of fraud, 1759; accusation of merchants from Sambor of the inappropriate division of an inheritance, 1763; decrees concernig debts [L], 1767.
(TsDIAU, L'viv, Ekonomia Samborska)

3. Agreements between burghers of the town and merchants, and court verdicts, 1743; 1782; records concerning debts of the *kahal* to the Jesuit order [G], 1786; correspondence regarding a petition of the town citizens against construction of a house by Jews [G], 1802; A complaint of the affiliated communities regarding high taxes, 1839–1841; a list of voters to the *Sejm*, 1870.
(AP Kraków, Teki Schneidra)

4. Confirmation by King Stanisław August Poniatowski of the charter granted to Jews, permitting them to settle in a suburb of the town [L, P], 1765.
(AP Wrocław, Ossolineum)

5. Correspondence about Jews living in the Jewish quarter [G], 1795–1818; files concerning the community statutes [G, P], 1846–96; records and statute of the *Dorshei Tov* society [G, P, Y], 1872–1911; correspondence about the *Zion* society, including a text of the statutes [G, P], 1894; a file on shechita, 1894–97; correspondence with the Interior Ministry concerning reorganization of the community, 1895; correspondence about the *Chevre Mikre* society, including a text of the statutes, 1902; correspondence on election of a rabbi [G, P], 1902–04.
(TsDIAU, L'viv, Namiestnictwo Galicyjskie)

6. Reports about teaching Jewish religion in elementary schools [G, P], 1822–89; statutes, reports and lists of students at a private Jewish school for commerce, established and maintained by O. Gotthelf [G, P], 1886–1920.
(TsDIAU, L'viv, Krajowa Rada Szkolna)

7. Documents about the arrest of a Russian Jew [R], 1841.
(TsDIAU, Kyiv, Kantseliariia... general-gubernatora)

8. Complaints by community members against the amount of taxes [G, P], 1911–14.
(TsDIAU, L'viv, Ministerium fuer Kultus und Unterricht, Wien)

9. Correspondence about registration of *Agudas Yisroel*, a text of the statutes and a list of members, 1922–23; register of Jewish debtors from Sambor, owning real estate in Lwów, 1929–31; correspondence about the registration of *Machzike Hadas*, 1933.
(DALO, L'viv, Magistrat, Lwów)

10. Correspondence about the election of the civil registry maintenance committee, 1923–24; correspondence with the police regarding a prohibition to use theYiddish language at meetings of the community board, 1924; correspondence about a celebration honoring the inauguration of the Hebrew University in Jerusalem, 1924–25; correspondence about the *Kultur Liga*, 1926; documents concerning elections to the community board and council, 1928–29; lists of town council members, their nationalities and political affiliations, 1930–31; correspondence with the district authorities about registration of *Związek Regionalny Przemysłowców i Kupców Drzewnych Okręgu Samborskiego*, including a text of the statutes, 1931–33; correspondence about community matters: budgets, elections, taxes and lists of the community taxpayers, 1932–34; Statistical reports containing lists of board members, rabbis and *dayanim*, 1937; correspondence about the *Yad Charutzim* society, 1938.
(DALO, L'viv, UW, Lwów)

11. Reports on the activity of the *Ogólno-Żydowska Partia Pracy* (OŻPP), 1933.
(DAIFO, Ivano-Frankivs'k, UW, Stanisławów)

SAMBOR, surroundings, 1709–1908
Microfilms:
1. An inventory of the Sambor district (1563), a copy from 1785.
(TsDIAU, L'viv, Ekonomia Samborska)
2. Accounts concerning properties of A. M. Sieniawski, 1709–18.
(Bibl. Czartoryskich, Kraków)
3. An extract from the inventory of the royal estates in the district, 1760.
(AP Wrocław, Ossolineum)
4. Files concerning *arenda* in towns and villages of the Sambor *ekonomia* [G, L, P], 1772–73.
(TsDIAU, L'viv, Arch. Lanckorońskich)
5. Correspondencee with the regional authorities about financial matters and *arenda*, lists of names and an investigation of a conflict between Rabbi Jacob Ornstein and Chaim Ber Modlinger over the rabbinate [G, L, P], 1814–18; tables of taxes paid by various communities [G], 1819; correspondence with the regional authorities about *arenda* [G], 1819–22; correspondence about requests concerning rights of residence [G, P], 1822–29; community elections and complaints [G], 1823–25; reports concerning *chadorim* in the district of Sambor and a list of *chadorim*, 1877–1908.
(TsDIAU, L'viv, Namiestnictwo Galicyjskie)
6. Protests by small communities concerning increases in taxes [G], 1839–41.
(AP Kraków, Teki Schneidra)

SANDOMIERZ (woj. kieleckie) 1640–1866
Photocopy:
A verdict in the case of a nobleman accused of murdering four Jews, 1792.
(AGAD, Warszawa, DP)
Microfilms:
1. Two inventories of the town, 1640, 1753.
(AP Wrocław, Ossolineum)
2. Registers of the Jewish population and amounts of taxes, 1705–08.
(Bibl. Czartoryskich, Kraków)
3. Confirmation by King Stanisław August Poniatowski of the charter granted to the Jews [L, P], 1765; two letters of protection granted by him to Jewish merchants [L, P], 1775, 1792.
(AGAD, Warszawa, Księgi Kanclerskie)
4. Demands for the payment of taxes from the community, 1824–27.
(AGAD, Warszawa, KRzSW)
5. Files on the expulsion of a Jewish innkeeper from the town, 1831.
(AGAD, Warszawa, WCPL)
6. Reports, complaints and other materials concerning burial societies, 1822–50; a project for the distribution of kosher food to poor Jews and for the support of poor Jewish hospital patients [P, R], 1848–56.
(AGAD, Warszawa, CWW)
7. Files on Jews converting to Catholicism, 1846–66.
(AP Radom, Rząd Gubernialny, Radom)

SANDOMIERZ, surroundings, 1682–1810
Microfilms:

1. File on financial matters between Jews and noblemen [L, P], 1682–1701; an inventory of the district and its inhabitants, 1704; an inventory of Sandomierz estates, 1757–72; financial records from the Potocki estates, 1759–60.
(AP Kraków, Arch. Krzeszowickie Potockich)
2. *Lustracja* of the district, 1765.
(AGAD, Warszawa, ASK)
3. A court case between Jewish *arendars* of the Sandomierz *ekonomia* and the community of Ulanów concerning the poll tax, including data on the population [L, P], 1747–56.
(AGAD, Warszawa, Arch. Kameralne)
4. Records of the debts of the Jewish communities in the *województwo*, 1765.
(AP Lublin, Księgi Grodzkie i Ziemskie Lubelskie)
5. Files on organization of *kahals* in the *województwo*, financial problems related to the partitions of Poland and collecting of taxes [H, P], 1810.
(AGAD, Warszawa, CWW)

SANOK (woj. lwowskie) 1707–1938
Originals:
A poster, 1928.
Microfilms:
1. Extracts from official records concerning Jews, 1707–12; tax records, 1735.
(AP Wrocław, Ossolineum)
2. Accounts and revenues from Sanok estates, 1731–63.
(Bibl. Czartoryskich, Kraków)
3. Correspondence with the district authorities concerning assistance to Jews relocated to new settlements, including a list of names [G], 1789; correspondence with the regional authorities about *arenda*, terrain and houses [G], 1819–22; correspondence with the district authorities about village inns on land belonging to Christians [G], 1853; correspondence on vacant positions for the rabbinate, 1895; correspondence regarding various communal matters [G, P], 1895, 1898; correspondence about the *Bund* [G, P], 1906–12.
(TsDIAU, L'viv, Namiestnictwo Galicyjskie)
4. Minutes of an investigation concerning the theft and sale of goods to a Jew, 1814–15.
(NBANU, L'viv, Zb. Goldsteina)
5. Decrees, reports and correspondence concerning the closing of *chadorim* [G, P], 1868–74.
(TsDIAU, L'viv, Krajowa Rada Szkolna)
6. Reports and correspondence concerning activities of the community – statutes, elections, budget, including lists of tax payers, board members, rabbis and dayanim, 1921–38; reports and correspondence about the *Talmud Tora*, 1927; an authorization by the district authorities to collect donations for the Polish–Galician Jewish community in Palestine, including a list of donors, 1928–30; lists of self-government members, their nationalities and political affiliations, 1930–31; a list of Zionist Organization members in Sanok, 1931; correspondence with the district authorities and the Ministry of Interior regarding a dispute about Tobias Horowitz, a candidate for the rabbinate, 1930–38; correspondence about the *Yad Charutzim* society, 1938.
(DALO, L'viv, UW, Lwów)
7. Correspondence about registration of the *Mizrachi*, statutes and a list of members, 1927.
(DALO, L'viv, Magistrat, Lwów)

SARNAKI (pow. Siedlce, woj. lubelskie) 1758–1864
Microfilms:
1. Decisions of the Council of Four Lands regulating the relationship between the *kahals* of Busk, Rozwadów, Sarnaki and Siemiatycze [L, P], 1758.
(NBANU, L'viv, Arch. Radzimińskiego)
2. A file on synagogues in the Lublin *guberniia*, 1818–60; minutes and correspondence concerning appointments of rabbis, their education and salaries, including a list of graduates of the Rabbinical Seminary in Warsaw, 1856–64.
(AGAD, Warszawa, CWW)

SARNKI GÓRNE (pow. Rohatyn, woj. stanisławowskie) 1933–1938
Microfilms:
Lists of board members of Jewish agricultural societies, 1933–38.
(DAIFO, Ivano-Frankivs'k, UW, Stanisławów)

SARNOWA (pow. Rawicz, woj. poznańskie) 1818–1877
Originals:
Lists of the Jewish population of the town [G], 1818–43; records of taxes paid by Jews [G], 1828–54; government regulations concerning Jewish burial [G], 1830–40; reports on the education of Jewish orphans [G], 1832–72; files on Jewish migration [G], 1834–44; minutes of community meetings [G], 1834–45; files on individuals joining or leaving the community [G], 1834–69; records of annual payments to a Catholic priest [G], 1834–54; proceedings of the debt cancellation committee [G], 1834–45; the repayment of debts to a priest [G], 1876–77.

SASÓW (pow. Złoczów, woj. tarnopolskie) 1682–1932
Photocopies:
Inventories of Sasów, 1682, 1689, 1703, 1719–24;
(NIAB, Minsk, Arch. Radziwiłłów)
Microfilms:
1. Correspondence between the community, the district authorities and the Ministry of Religion concerning the rabbinate [G, P], 1897–1908.
(TsDIAU, L'viv, Namiestnictwo Galicyjskie)
2. Material about an examination in the Polish language for Rabbi Spira of Sasów, 1931–32.
(DALO, L'viv, UW, Lwów)

SĄDOWA WISZNIA (pow. Mościska, woj. lwowskie) 1787–1935
Photocopies:
Correspondence concerning community elections, 1922.
(DALO, L'viv, UW, Lwów)
Microfilms:
1. Correspondence with the regional authorities concerning financial matters and *arenda* [G, L, P], 1787–93.
(TsDIAU, L'viv, Namiestnictwo Galicyjskie)
2. Correspondence with the district authorities about establishing a temporary community board, (including a list of board members elected in 1910), 1922; material on community elections, 1923–33; correspondence with the district authorities about Hebrew lessons, 1924–26; community matters (budget, lists of community tax payers) [P, Y], 1931–35.

(DALO, L'viv, UW, Lwów)

3. Correspondence about the registration of *Machzikei Hadas*, 1932.

(DALO, L'viv, Magistrat, Lwów)

SECEMIN (pow. Włoszczowa, woj. kieleckie) 1816–1836
Microfilms:
An investigation of corruption on the part of the mayor, and complaints by Jews, 1816–36.
(AGAD, Warszawa, KRzPiS)

SEJNY (pow. Suwałki, woj. białostockie) 1850–1937
Photocopies:
1. Decrees and information concerning conscription of Jews, and lists of conscripts, 1850–52.
(AP Suwałki, Akta m. Suwałki)
2. Orders requiring an examination in the Polish language for rabbis, and regarding community taxes and budget, 1931–37.
(AP Suwałki, Starostwo Powiatowe Suwalskie)
Microfilms:
1. Reports and correspondence concerning appointments of rabbis and their relations with the communities, including a list of rabbis, 1853–56; correspondence on exemptions from conscription for graduates of the Rabbinical Seminary in Warsaw, and a list of rabbis, 1865–71.
(AGAD, Warszawa, CWW)
2. Copies of inscriptions on tombstones and synagogues [H, P, R], 1910.
(RGIA, St. Petersburg, Departament dukhovnykh del…)
3. A list of persons expelled from Sejny, 1923.
(DATO, Ternopil', PKPP, Trembowla)

SEMENÓWKA (pow. Horodenka, woj. stanisławowskie) 1932–1938
Microfilms:
A list of the board members of *Hatchiya*, 1932–38.
(DAIFO, Ivano-Frankivs'k, UW, Stanisławów)

SEROCK (pow. Pułtusk, woj. warszawskie) 1775–1910
Originals:
Copies of local records concerning Jews, 1775, 1837–59; birth, marriage and death records (fragmentary), 1808–22.
Microfilms:
Copies of inscriptions on tombstones and synagogues [H, P, R], 1910.
(RGIA, St. Petersburg, Departament dukhovnykh del…)

SEROCZYN (pow. Ostrołęka, woj. białostockie) 1566
Microfilms:
Lustracje of Seroczyn, 1566.
(AGAD, Warszawa, ASK)

SĘDZISZÓW (pow. Ropczyce, woj. krakowskie) 1753–1919
Microfilms:
1. *Arenda* contracts, 1753–54.
(AP Kraków, Arch. Sanguszków)

2. Correspondence, about the *Chevra Kadisha* and *Bikur Cholim* societies, 1895–1913.
(TsDIAU, L'viv, Namiestnictwo Galicyjskie)
3. Documents concerning the rabbi [G, P], 1913–19.
(TsDIAU, L'viv, Ministerium fuer Kultus und Unterricht, Wien)

SĘPOLNO (woj. pomorskie) 1813–1884
Originals:
A promissory note of the community [G], 1813; ligitation between the Catholic Church and the Jewish community over financial matters [G], 1842–43; a reference letter by the rabbi [H], 1884.

SIEDLCE (woj. lubelskie) 1790–1930
Originals:
Photographs of pogroms by the Russian Army, 1906. A receipt for a donation to the *Beis Yosef yeshiva* in Siedlice, 1930.
Microfilms:
1. Records of litigation involving a Jewish *arendar*, 1790.
(AP Wrocław, Ossolineum)
2. A project to distribute kosher food to poor Jews and to support poor Jewish hospital patients [P, R], 1848–56; reports and correspondence concerning appointments of rabbis and their relations with the communities, a list of rabbis, 1853–56; correspondence concerning exemptions from conscription for graduates of the Rabbinical Seminary in Warsaw, and a list of rabbis, 1865–71.
(AGAD, Warszawa, CWW)
3. Documents concerning pogroms [R], 1891.
(RGIA, St. Petersburg, Obshchestvo polnopraviia...)

SIEDLCE, surroundings, 1908
Microfilms:
Records on synagogues and rabbis in the towns of the Siedlce *guberniia* [R], 1908.
(RGIA, St. Petersburg, Departament dukhovnykh del...)

SIEDLISKA (pow. Tarnów, woj. krakowskie) 18th cent.–1936
Microfilms:
1. Records on the interrogation of a Jew in a suit involving a nobleman, 18th cent.
(AP Kraków, IT)
2. Monographs containing demographic and economic information about the inhabitants, 1936.
(AP Wrocław, Ossolineum, WKNZNP, Lwów)

SIEDLISZCZE (pow. Chełm, woj. lubelskie) 1783–1874
Microfilms:
1. A monetary demand by the National Education Commission from the community, 1783.
(AP Lublin, Księgi Grodzkie Chełmskie)
2. Correspondence about the establishment of a new Jewish community, including a list of voters and council members [R], 1869–74.
(AP Lublin, Rząd Gubernialny, Lublin)

SIEMIANOWICE ŚLĄSKIE (pow. Katowice, woj. śląskie) 1913
Originals:
Records on the founding of the *Jüdischer Frauenverein* [G], 1913.

SIEMIATYCZE (pow. Bielsk, woj. białostockie) 1676–1883
Microfilms:
1. Records on debts of the community to the Jesuit order in Drohiczyn [L, P], 1676–1775.
(RGADA, Moscow, KFE)
2. A letter concerning the arrest of Jews, 1743; decisions of the Council of Four Lands in Jarosław regulating the relationship between the *kahals* of Busk, Rozwadów, Sarnaki and Siemiatycze [L, P], 1758.
(NBANU, L'viv, Arch. Sapiehów)
3. Identity documents and letters of protection for Jews from Siemiatycze, 1807, 1809; a register of Jews for tax purposes [R], 1861.
(AP Białystok, Rząd Gubernialny, Łomża)
4. Correspondence with a school in Siematycze [R], 1878–83.
(RGIA, St. Petersburg, OPE)

SIENIAWA (pow. Jarosław, woj. lwowskie) 1628–1937
Microfilms:
1. Private agreements, accounts, contracts and other documents concerning estates of the Sieniawski and Czartoryski families [H, L, P], 1628–1766; registers and commercial accounts concerning trade between Sieniawa and Gdańsk [H, P], 1682–1740; inventories, *arenda* accounts, contracts, *supliki*, *uniwersały*, decrees, circular letters and registers of inhabitants in the town and *klucz* of Sieniawa [H, L, P], 1695–1765.
(Bibl. Czartoryskich, Kraków)
2. Registers, accounts, *uniwersały*, decrees and contracts concerning estates and inhabitants of Sieniawa [F, L, P], 1706–85.
(Biblioteka Narodowa, Warszawa)
3. Accounts, orders of payments and debts of the Jewish community [L, P], 1748–56.
(TsDIAU, L'viv, Koleksiia dokumentiv…)
4. *Lustracja* of Czartoryski estates, 1766.
(AGAD, Warszawa, Arch. Potockich w Łańcucie)
5. Documents concerning election to the community board and council, 1928–29; correspondence concerning the budget and the rabbinate, including a list of tax payers, 1932–37, reports, complaints and correspondence on the election of the rabbi and community council, 1935–37.
(DALO, L'viv, UW, Lwów)

SIENKIEWICZE (pow, Horochów, woj. wołyńskie) 1936
Microfilms:
Monographs containing demographic and economic information about inhabitants, 1936.
(AP Wrocław, Ossolineum, WKNZNP, Lwów)

SIERADZ (woj. łódzkie) 1792–1914
Microfilms:
1. The establishment of a commission by King Stanisław August Poniatowski to settle the financial affairs of a Jewish merchant, 1792.
(AGAD, Warszawa, Księgi Kanclerskie)
2. Files on the Jewish quarter, 1820–62.
(AGAD, Warszawa, Komisja Województwa Kaliskiego)
3. Correspondence concerning exemptions from conscription for graduates of the Rabbinical Seminary in Warsaw, including a list of rabbis, 1865–71.
(AGAD, Warszawa, CWW)

4. Ratification of community accounts and elections [R], 1895, 1913–14; various requests to the community [R], 1896–1900, 1910–13.
(AP Łódź, Rząd Gubernialny, WA, Piotrków)
5. Correspondence concerning organization of elections to the *Duma* [R], 1906.
(RGIA, St. Petersburg, Obshchestvo polnopraviia…)
6. A request to open a shelter for Jewish children [R], 1908.
(AP Łódź, Kancelaria Gubernatora Kaliskiego)

SIERADZ, surroundings, 1661–1897
Microfilms:
1. Three *lustracje* of the *wojewodztwo*, 1661, 1765, 1789.
(AGAD, Warszawa, ASK)
2. A file on the conversion of a Jew to Christianity [R], 1897.
(AP Łódź, Rząd Gubernialny, WA, Kalisz)

SIERAKÓW (pow. Międzychód, woj. poznańskie) 1848–1902
Originals:
Minutes of the community council [G], 1848–1919; community accounts [G], 1852–1902; acquisition of plots by the *Chevra Kadisha* in order to enlarge the cemetery [G], 1867.

SIETESZ (pow. Przeworsk, woj. lwowskie) 1878
Microfilms:
Reports and correspondence on the reorganization of elementary schools attended by Jewish children [G, P], 1878.
(TsDIAU, L'viv, Krajowa Rada Szkolna)

SIEWIERZ (pow. Zawiercie, woj. kieleckie) 1897
Microfilms:
Fines for evading conscription [R], 1897.
(AP Łódź, Rząd Gubernialny, WP, Piotrków)

SKAŁA (pow. Borszczów, woj. tarnopolskie) 1891–1908
Original:
Correspondence of a Jewish merchant with his sons in New York [H, Y], 1891–1908.
Microfilms:
Correspondence concerning community matters and ratification of the statutes, 1895–96.
(TsDIAU, L'viv, Namiestnictwo Galicyjskie)

SKAŁAT (woj. tarnopolskie) 1876–1926
Microfilms:
1. Correspondence about aid for Jewish schools [G, P], 1876–77; correspondence with the district authorities about citation of citizenship in civil registers, 1891–92.
(TsDIAU, L'viv, Namiestnictwo Galicyjskie)
2. Reports and correspondence on the reorganization of elementary schools attended by Jewish children [G, P], 1878.
(TsDIAU, L'viv, Krajowa Rada Szkolna)
3. Correspondence about permitting Jews exiled to Skałat to return to Śniatyn [R], 1917.
(DAIFO, Ivano-Frankivs'k, Chief of the Śniatyn district)
4. Answers to a questionnaire concerning Jews in Skałat, 1922.

(NBANU, L'viv, Zb. Czołowskiego)
5. Reports about collecting money for Jews in Palestine, 1926.
(DAIFO, Ivano-Frankivs'k, UW, Stanisławów)

SKIDEL (pow. Grodno, woj. białostockie) 1849
Original:
A copy of a tailors' society record book [H], 1849.

SKOLE (pow. Stryj, woj. stanisławowskie) 1652–1939
Microfilms:
1. Reports, complaints and excerpts from municipal books concerning estates of the Sieniawski and Czartoryski families [H, L, P], 1652–1766.
(Bibl. Czartoryskich, Kraków)
2. A *lustracja* of Czartoryski estates, 1766.
(AGAD, Warszawa, Arch. Potockich w Łańcucie)
3. Records concerning the registration and ratification of statutes of: *Poalei Tzedek, Safa Berura, Agudas Yisroel*, 1893, 1920–30; statutes, minutes and correspondence concerning various Jewish associations [G, P], 1894, 1899, 1924–39; statutes, reports and correspondence concerning Zionist parties and associations, 1921–30; reports and correspondence concerning confirmation of the statutes of *Żydowskie Towarzystwo Gimnastyczno–Sportowe Dror*, 1921–30; records of: *Yad Charutzim*, 1921–38; *Gmilus Chasodim* and *Keren Kayemet*, 1922–31; correspondence with the district authorities concerning the *Bund*, 1923; statistics concerning the Jewish population, 1923–24; records concerning civil records, 1923–24; reports and correspondence about confirmation of statutes and registration of Jewish charitable associations aiding children and youth, 1923–28; reports about collecting funds for Jews in Palestine, 1926; a report about activities of Jewish youth organizations, 1929–30; records of *Hechalutz*, 1930; records of *Towarzystwo Ochrony Zdrowia Ludności Żydowskiej 'TOZ'*, 1930–34; records of *Towarzystwo Opieki nad Halucami i Emigrantami 'Ezra'*, 1930–35; materials of the second general census in the district 1931; records of: *Achva, Hatzofim Brit Trumpeldor*, 1930–37; of sport associations, 1931–36; of *Hashomer Hatzair*, 1931–37; of the academic association, *Emuna*, 1932–35; reports and correspondence concerning community elections, 1932–36; records and lists of *Chevra Kadisha* board members, 1933–36; records of *Żydowski Związek Inwalidów, Wdów i Sierot Wojennych*, 1933–37; records of the *Liga Pomocy Pracującym w Palestynie, Hitachdut*, 1933–37.
(DAIFO, Ivano-Frankivs'k, UW, Stanisławów)
4. Correspondence about a vacant position of the rabbinate [G, Hung., P], 1896.
(TsDIAU, L'viv, Namiestnictwo Galicyjskie)
5. A list of community tax payers and their professions, 1935.
(DALO, L'viv, UW, Lwów)
6. Reports and correspondence concerning anti-Jewish actions by Ukrainian nationalists, 1936–37.
(DAIFO, Ivano-Frankivs'k, Komenda Wojewódzka PP, Stanisławów)

SKULIN (pow. Kowel, woj. wołyńskie) 1652–1766
Microfilms:
Supliki, decrees and excerpts from municipal books concerning inhabitants and estates of the Sieniawski and Czartoryski families [H, L, P], 1652–1766.
(Bibl. Czartoryskich, Kraków)

SKULSK (pow. Konin, woj. łódzkie) 1937–1938
Microfilms:
The community budget, 1937–38.

חברה מדעית עברית, וילנה.

Jüdische wissenschaftliche Gesellschaft.

Abteilung für die Wissenschaft des Judentums.
" " Sprachwissenschaft, Literatur u. Kunst.
" " Anthropologie, Psychologie u. Pädagogik.
" " Philosophie.
" " Rechtswissenschaft.
" " Geschichte.
" " Medizin u. Naturwissenschaft.

מחלקה לחכמת ישראל.
· לבלשנות, ספרות ואמנות.
· לאנתרופולוגיה, פסיכולוגיה ופדגוגיה.
· לפילוסופיה.
· לתורת המשפטים.
· להסטוריה.
· למדעי הרפואה והטבע.

Wilno, _____ וילנה, _____ Nr. _____

בוילנה נוסדה חברה מדעית עברית. החברה שייה לה למטרה לאסוף וללכד

את כל אנשי המדע העברים לעבודה

העבודה המדעית העברית א

מכונים וחברות מדע שונות, העוסק

בין עבידתם ואין להם תכנית עבודה

אנשי המדע היחידים ואת חברות הע

ארץ צריכות להוסד חברות מדע עב

חברות המדע העוסקות בענף-מדע יד

מרכזית (אולי בקשר עם האוניברסי

פי תכנית שטחית רחבה. על=ידי הה

מאורגנת שטחית. החברה המרכזית ו

עברים וכו' ותארגן את העבודה המד

מצרפים אנו למכתב זה תקנ

להודיע לנו על עמדתכם בדבר נחי

רחבים. מבקשים אנו ג"כ להודיע ל

בחשבון בשביל עבודה בעלת=ערך לא

בבקשה לשלח לנו ג"כ את ה

את כתבי החברה בוילנה.

יש לכתב על · פי הכתבת: Poland

תקנון

החברה המדעית העברית

בוילנה.

פרק א.

שם. מקום ומטרת החברה.

§ 1. על יסוד תקנון זה נוסדת חברה בשם „חברה מדעית עברית" עם מקום מושבה הקבוע בוילנה.

§ 2. מטרת החברה היא כהתפתחות המדעים, הספרות ות אמנות בחוד חקירת דברי ימי ישראל, הפילולוגיה והספרות העברית, משפטים ופילוסופיה.

§ 3. להגשמת מטרותיה החברה:

א. מארגנת ישיבות מדעיות של חבריה;

ב. מוציאה לאור כתבים מדעיים (ספרים וכתבי-עת);

ג. יוצרת תנאים, שהחברים יוכלו לעסק בעבודתם המדעית;

ד. מארגנת בקורים מדעיים ותערוכות.

ה. עורכת התחרויות מדעיות וניועת פרסים בער העבידות המדעיות הכי-טובות;

ו. מארגנת הרצאות פומביות;

ז. מארגנת את העבודה המדעית במחלקות (§ 4);

1

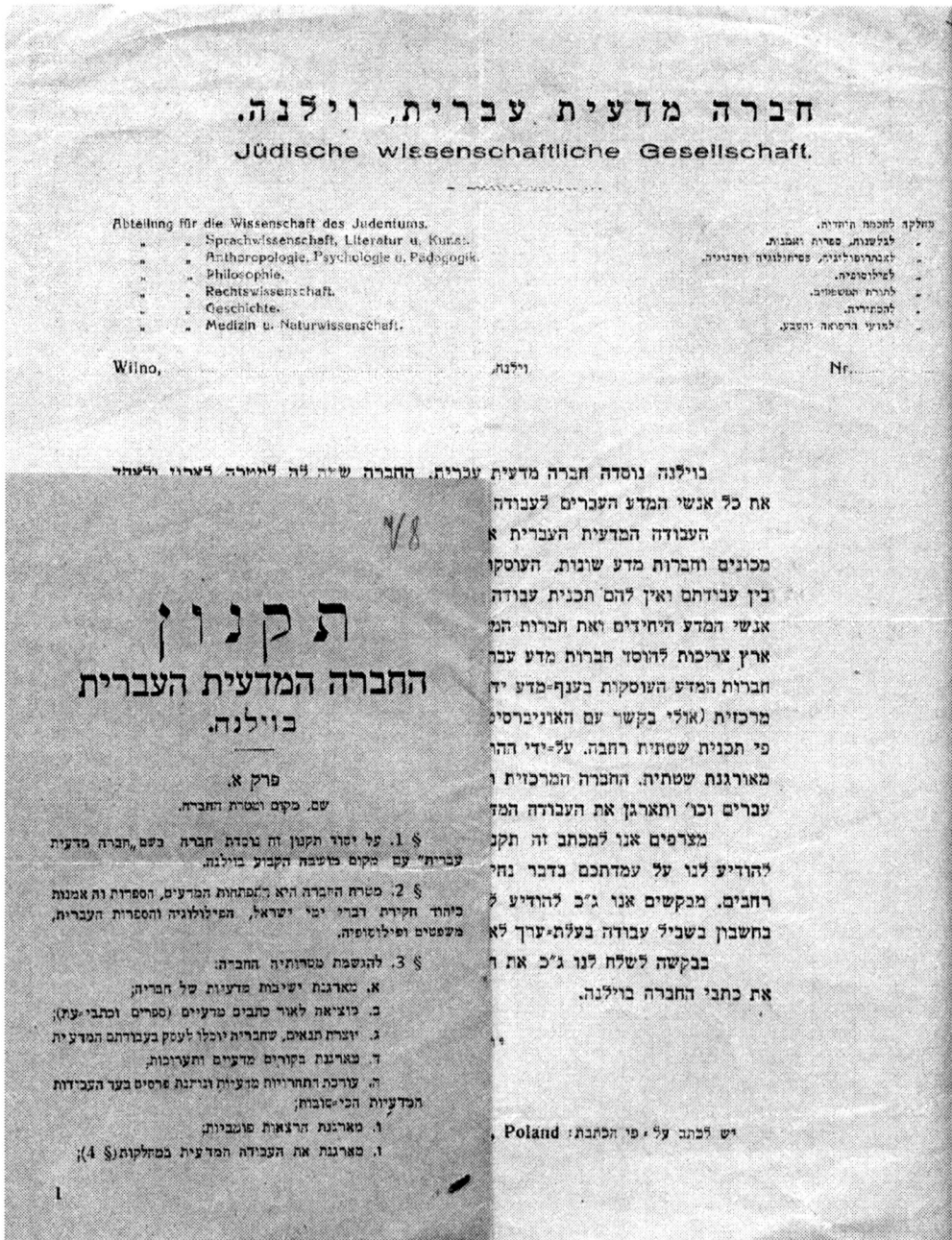

Wilno. Statutes and proclamation of the Hebrew Scientific Society, 1920s (Hebrew)

(AP Poznań, Gmina Żydowska, Skulsk)

SŁABOSZEWICE (woj. kieleckie, pow. Sandomierz) 1652–1766
Microfilms:
Supliki, decrees and excerpts from municipal books concerning inhabitants and estates of the Sieniawski and Czartoryski families [H, L, P], 1652–1766.
(Bibl. Czartoryskich, Kraków)

SŁOBÓDKA LEŚNA (pow. Kołomyja, woj. stanisławowskie) 1935–1938
Microfilms:
A report about an agricultural school, established by the Baron Hirsch Foundation (JCA), 1935–38.
(DAIFO, Ivano-Frankivs'k, Gmina Żydowska, Kołomyja)

SŁONIM (woj. nowogrodzkie) 1558–1916
Originals:
Proclamations issued by the German army, regulating Jewish life [G, P, R, Y], 1916.
Photocopies:
1. A letter of reference, written by Rabbi Mordechai Hoffman [H], 1890.
2. Excerpts from records of the Castle Court in Słonim concerning Jews [Rt], 1560–61, 1569–74.
(NIAB, Minsk, Slonimski grodskii sud)
Microfilms:
1. Royal charter for a Jew from Brześć concerning *arendas* and taxes in Słonim [Rt], 1558–68.
(RGADA, Moscow, ML)
2. Real estate transactions [Rt, P], 1613–23.
(RGADA, Moscow, KFE)
3. *Supliki*, decrees, accounts, circular letters, *uniwersały* and excerpts from municipal books concerning inhabitants and estates of the Sieniawski and Czartoryski families [H, L, P], 1652–1766.
(Bibl. Czartoryskich, Kraków)
4. Various *arenda* contracts [G, H, P, Y, Byelorussian], 1763–97; records on the arrest and trial of a Jew, files on legal proceedings [H, P, Y], 1780–86.
(Bibl. PAN, Kraków)
5. Files on organization of the community and charitable institutions [R], 1863–64.
(RGIA, St. Petersburg, Khoziaistvennyi departament MVD)
6. Correspondence concerning elections to the *Duma* [R], 1905–06.
(RGIA, St. Petersburg, Obshchestvo polnopraviia…)
7. A request for a license to produce wine [R], 1914–15.
(RGIA, St. Petersburg, Glavnoe upravlenie neokladnykh sborov…)

SŁUPIEC (pow. Stopnica, woj. kieleckie) 1895–1914
Microfilms:
Ratification of community elections and accounts, 1895–1914.
(AP Łódź, Rząd Gubernialny, WA, Kalisz)

SMOLEŃ (pow. Olkusz, woj. kieleckie) 1739
Microfilms:
A decree concerning debts, 1739.
(AP Kraków, Arch. Sanguszków)

SMORZE (pow. Stryj, woj. stanisławowskie) 1921–1937
Microfilms:
Statutes, minutes and correspondence concerning Jewish associations, 1921–30; records and board member lists of the *Achva* society, 1930–37; records of the *Hatikva* society, 1932–36.
(DAIFO, Ivano-Frankivs'k, UW, Stanisławów)

SOBKÓW (pow. Jędrzejów, woj. kieleckie) 17th cent.–1850
Microfilms:
1. Minutes of an accusation against a Jew from Sobków for theft, 17th cent.
(TsDIAU, L'viv, Arch. Lanckorońskich)
2. A request for a remission of debts (taxes), 1816.
(AGAD, Warszawa, KRzPiS)
3. Reports, complaints and other materials concerning the burial society, 1822–50.
(AGAD, Warszawa, CWW)

SOCHACZEW (woj. warszawskie) 1556–1856
Original:
Copy of a verdict by King Zygmunt III in the case of a child allegedly murdered by Jews, 1617.
Photocopies:
Three confirmations (Kings August II, August III and Stanisław August Poniatowski) of the charter granted to Jews in 1633 [L], 1725–65.
(AGAD, Warszawa, DP)
Microfilms:
1. Records of the case of an alleged host desecration [L, P], 1556.
(Bibl. PAN, Kraków)
2. *Lustracje* of the rawskie, płockie and mazowieckie *województwa*, containing data on the Jewish population, 1566, 1570.
(AGAD, Warszawa, ASK)
3. Evidence given in the case of an attack against a Jew, 1738.
(AP Kraków, Zb. Rusieckich)
4. Confirmation by King Stanisław August Poniatowski of the charter granted to Jews [L], 1765; letters of protection granted by him to Jewish merchants [L], 1792;
(AGAD, Warszawa, Księgi Kanclerskie)
5. Records of a dispute involving a Jew, 1811–12.
(AGAD, Warszawa, RSiRMKW)
6. A project to distribute kosher food to poor Jews and to support poor Jewish hospital patients [P, R], 1848–56.
(AGAD, Warszawa, CWW)

SOCHOCIN (pow. Płońsk, woj. warszawskie) 1886–1913
Microfilms:
Certificates and photographs of rabbinical candidates [R], 1886–1913.
(AP Białystok, Rząd Gubernialny, Łomża)

SOKAL (woj. lwowskie) 1524–1939
Microfilms:

1. A charter by King Zygmunt I concerning *propinacja*, 1524; a confirmation by King Zygmunt III of a decree stating that the Christians should sell real estate exclusively to Christians, 1597–98; files on *propinacja* [G], 1769–81; confirmation by King Stanisław August Poniatowski of all charters granted to the Jews of Sokal by his predecessors [L, P], 1778; lists of voters to the community board [G], 1863.
(AP Kraków, Teki Schneidra)

2. Accounts, real estate transactions, testimonies in the rabbinical court, obligations, *ketubot*, and other documents from various towns in Poland and Russia [H, Y], 1711–1845.
(TsDIAU, Kyiv, Arch. Potockich z Tulczyna)

3. Accounts, bills and debts of the community, 1738.
(TsDIAU, L'viv, Kolektsiia dokumentiv…)

4. Confirmation by King Stanisław August Poniatowski of the charter granted to the Jews [L, P], 1765.
(AGAD, Warszawa, Księgi Kanclerskie)

5. Legal records concerning Jews (fragmentary), 1635–45; municipal records, 1768–72.
(AP Wrocław, Ossolineum)

6. Receipt from the *kahal*, 1786.
(NBANU, L'viv, Zb. Goldsteina)

7. Correspondence with the district authorities concerning the community and ratification of statutes, 1895–96; correspondence about a society of merchants and industrialists, 1905–11; correspondence about the *Allgemeiner Juedischer Arbeiterverband Oesterreiches* [G, P], 1907–12.
(TsDIAU, L'viv, Namiestnictwo Galicyjskie)

8. Answers to a questionnaire concerning the Jews, 1922.
(NBANU, L'viv, Zb. Czołowskiego)

9. Reports and correspondence about construction in the Jewish cemetery, 1922–26; correspondence about the *Kultur Liga*, 1926; community matters (budget, a list of taxpayers), 1927, 1933–36; elections to the community council, 1928–29, 1933; authorization by the district authorities to collect donations for the Polish–Galician Jewish community in Palestine, including a list of donors, 1928–30; reports about a congress of *Hitachdut* in Sokal, and a list of delegates to the Zionist Congress, 1930–31; reports containing names of community council and board members, rabbis and *dayanim*, 1937.
(DALO, L'viv, UW, Lwów)

10. Correspondence about the registration of the *Mizrachi*, a text of the statutes and a list of members, 1922; correspondence about the registration of *Agudas Yisroel*, 1930–39.
(DALO, L'viv, Magistrat, Lwów)

SOKAL, surroundings, 1748–1931
Microfilms:
1. *Arenda* contracts of villages in the Sokal district, 1748; files on debts of the Jewish community to the St. Brigide order [L], 1767–84.
(TsDIAU, L'viv, Kolektsiia dokumentiv pro katolyts'ki monastyri…)
2. Reports concerning the activity of *Poalei Zion* in the district, 1929–31.
(DALO, L'viv, UW, Lwów)
3. Reports and correspondence concerning *chadorim* and Jewish private schools in the Sokal district [G, P], 1878–81.
(TsDIAU, L'viv, Krajowa Rada Szkolna)

SOKOŁÓW (pow. Kolbuszowa, woj. lwowskie) 1777–1939
Microfilms:

1. Instructions of the town's owner to the community in an economic matter; a file on the *krupka*; a contract concerning the *arenda* of income from the sale of meat, 1777–87.
(AP Kraków, IT)

2. Correspondence with the district authorities regarding *chadorim* in the area, and a list of *melamdim*, 1877–1908; correspondence about the *Zion* society, including a text of the statutes [G, P], 1894.
(TsDIAU, L'viv, Namiestnictwo Galicyjskie)

3. Correspondence about communal matters, e.g. taxes, communal institutions, the rabbinate and elections, including a list of board members, 1925, 1932–39; correspondence about registration of the *Mizrachi*, and a text of the statutes, 1928; authorization by the district authorities to collect donations for the Polish–Galician Jewish community in Palestine, including a list of donors, 1928–30.
(DALO, L'viv, UW, Lwów)

4. Correspondence about the registration of *Agudas Yisroel*, 1934.
(DALO, L'viv, Magistrat, Lwów)

SOKOŁÓW (pow. Stryj, woj. stanislawowskie) 1920–1938
Microfilms:
Records on confirming the statutes of *Agudas Yisroel*, 1920–30; statutes, minutes and correspondence regarding Zionist associations, 1921–30; lists of the board members of *Achva*, 1930–37; and the *Liga Pomocy Pracującym w Palestynie, Hitachdut*, 1933–37; a report on the election of a rabbi, 1934–38.
(DAIFO, Ivano-Frankivs'k, UW, Stanisławów)

SOKOŁÓW PODLASKI (pow. Sokołów, woj. lubelskie) 1853–1930
Originals:
Minutes of a *yeshiva* student council, including a list of fifty *yeshiva* students [H], 1918; receipts for money donated to the *yeshiva*, 1930.
Microfilms:
1. Reports and correspondence concerning the appointments of rabbis, their salary and education, a list of graduates of the Rabbinical Seminary in Warsaw and a list of rabbis, 1853–64.
(AGAD, Warszawa, CWW)
2. Requests and permits for the production and sale of wine, and a plan of the factory [R], 1914–15.
(RGIA, St. Petersburg, Glavnoe upravlenie neokladnykh sborov…)

SOKOŁÓWKA (pow. Złoczów, woj. tarnopolskie) 1877–1908
Microfilms:
Correspondence between the community and the district authorities regarding *chadorim*, including a list of *melamdim* [G, P], 1877–1908.
(TsDIAU, L'viv, Namiestnictwo Galicyjskie)

SOKOŁY (pow. Wysokie Mazowieckie, woj. białostockie) 1826–1930
Originals:
Birth, marriage and death records (fragmentary) [P, R], 1852–1930.
Microfilms:
Birth, marriage and death records (fragmentary) [P, R], 1826–78.
(AP Białystok)

SOKÓŁKA (woj. białostockie) 1797–1923
Photocopies:

Inventories of estates, 1786; *summariusz* of the *ekonomia* of Sokólka, 1786, 1789.
(NIAB, Minsk, Kollektsiia drevnikh inventarei)
Microfilms:
1. A letter concerning real estate, 1797.
(AP Białystok, Rząd Gubernialny, Łomża)
2. A list of persons exiled from the town, 1923.
(DATO, Ternopil', Komenda Powiatowa PP, Trembowla)

SOKUL (pow. Łuck, woj. wołyńskie) 1883
Microfilms:
File on damages to the Jews caused by fire [R], 1883.
(TsDIAU, Kyiv, Kantseliariia... general-gubernatora)

SOLEC (pow. Iłża, woj. kieleckie) 1534–1615
Microfilms:
Lustracja of the sandomierskie voivodship containing statistical data on inhabitants (fragmentary), 1534–1615.
(AGAD, Warszawa, ASK)

SOLEC (pow. Drohobycz, woj. lwowskie) 1936
Microfilms:
Monographs containing demographic and economic information about the inhabitants, 1936.
(AP Wrocław, Ossolineum, WKNZNP, Lwów)

SOLECZNIKI, see WIELKIE SOLECZNIKI

SOŁOTWINA (pow. Nadwórna, woj. stanisławowskie) 1780–1960
Photocopies:
Reports and correspondence on the liquidation of the Jewish cemetery. [R], 1946, 1957, 1960.
(DAIFO, Ivano-Frankivs'k, Upolnomochennyi Sovieta...)
Microfilms:
1. Correspondence concerning *arenda* and taxes [G], 1780–81; correspondence with the authorities about ratification of the statutes, complaints about community elections, administration and the election of a rabbi [G, P], 1884–1907.
(TsDIAU, L'viv, Namiestnictwo Galicyjskie)
2. Records on ratification of the *Chevra Kadisha* statutes, 1871–88, 1921–30; records concerning civil registration, 1923–24; reports and correspondence about confirmation of statutes and registration of charity associations aiding children and youth, 1923–28; a list of the *Yad Charutzim* board members and statutes; 1923, 1933–37; reports and correspondence concerning community elections, including complaints about them, and the raising the salaries of the council members [H, P], 1928–39; correspondence regarding the election of rabbis and *dayanim*, 1934–37; files on ratification of the community budget, including a list of tax payers, 1938.
(DAIFO, Ivano-Frankivs'k, UW, Stanisławów)
3. Answers to a questionnaire concerning Jews, 1922.
(LNBANU, L'viv, Zb. Czołowskiego)

4. Documents concerning ratification of the community budget, 1922–23; files on ratifying the statutes of the *Chevra Kadisha* and *Nos'ei Hamita* societies [G, P], 1922–23; minutes and correspondence on community council elections, including a list of council members [H, P, Y], 1928.
(DAIFO, Ivano-Frankivs'k, Starostwo Powiatowe, Bohorodczany)

SOMPOLNO (pow. Koło, woj. łódzkie) 1853–1864
Microfilms:
Reports and correspondence concerning appointments of rabbis and their relations with the communities, and lists of rabbis and members of the rabbinicale examination commission, 1853–64.
(AGAD, Warszawa, CWW)

SOSNOWIEC (woj. kieleckie) 1862–1931
Original and Photocopies:
Family documents, rabbinic correspondence and manuscripts of Rabbi Avraham Meir Gittler, the community's rabbi [H, Y], 1862–1925; a proclamation concerning community elections, 1931.
Microfilms:
1. Files on Jewish schools and teachers [R], 1890–1913.
(AP Łódź, Dyrekcja Szkolna, Łódź)
2. A complaint by two Jews concerning a Cossack troop [R], 1895–99; a request to establish an association of metalworkers [R], 1896–1903; a complaint against watchmen for concealing a theft [R], 1901;a fine for evading conscription [R], 1902.
(AP Łódź, Rząd Gubernialny, WP, Piotrków)
3. Files on the Jewish cemetery [R], 1896–1909; ratification of community accounts and elections [R], 1899–1913; the appointment of religious officials [R], 1901–02; a license to collect charity [R], 1901; request to open businesses and lease factories [R], 1908; expenses for medical services for the poor [R], 1909; a Jewess' conversion to Catholicism [R], 1910; a request by a Jew to open a *mikve*, and reports about it [R], 1912–13.
(AP Łódź, Rząd Gubernialny, WA, Piotrków)
4. Records concerning donations to the community and proposals for their use [R], 1902–13.
(AP Łódź, Rząd Gubernialny, RO, Piotrków)
5. Police reports on Jews suspected of belonging to illegal political organizations [R], 1906; possession and distribution of illegal literature [R], 1906; crossing the border illegally [R], 1910–12.
(AP Łódź, GZŻ, Piotrków)
6. Requests to register charitable, educational and cultural societies; registration of the *Linas Hatzedek* society [R], 1907; records concerning the *Hazamir* society [R] and the *Talmud Tora*, 1908–11.
(AP Łódź, Rząd Gubernialny, KP, Piotrków)
7. An order to exile a Jew, 1908.
(AP Łódź, Kancelaria Gubernatora Kaliskiego)

SOŚNICA (pow. Jarosław, woj. lwowskie) 1895–1896
Microfilms:
Correspondence with the district authorities concerning ratification of community statutes, 1895–96.
(TsDIAU, L'viv, Namiestnictwo Galicyjskie)

SPAS (pow. Turka, woj. lwowskie) 1937–1938
Microfilms:

Correspondence with the authorities concerning registration of the *Towarzystwo Domu Modlitwy* (prayer house), 1937–38.
(DALO, L'viv, UW, Lwów)

STANISŁAWCZYK (pow. Brody, woj. tarnopolskie) 1895–1896
Microfilms:
Correspondence with the district authorities concerning ratification of the statutes, 1895–96.
(TsDIAU, L'viv, Namiestnictwo Galicyjskie)

STANISŁAWÓW (pow. Mińsk Mazowiecki, woj. warszawskie) 1865–1871
Microfilms:
Correspondence concerning exemptions from conscription for graduates of the Rabbinical Seminary in Warsaw, including a list of rabbis, 1865–71.
(AGAD, Warszawa, CWW)

STANISŁAWÓW (woj. stanisławowskie) 1685–1962
Originals:
A poster announcing the performance, *Dos Leben in Stanislavov* [Y], 1931;
Photocopies:
Correspondence and reports about the situation of synagogues and prayer houses, including photographs of synagogues [R], 1946, 1957, 1960.
(DAIFO, Ivano-Frankivs'k, Upolnomochennyi Soveta …)
Microfilms:
1. Letter by a merchant from Stanisławów to a merchant from Kraków, 1685–86.
(TsDIAU, L'viv, Kolektsiia lystiv…)
2. Excerpts from Armenian books concerning *arenda*, loans and commerce with Jews, 1703–09, inventory of Stanisławów, 1770.
(NBANU, L'viv, Arch. Ossolińskich)
3. A collection of documents, accounts, real estate transactions, testimonies before rabbinical courts, obligations, *ketubot* and letters from various towns in Poland and Russia, among them Stanisławów [H, Y], 1711–1845.
(TsDIAU, Kyiv, Arch. Potockich z Tulczyna)
4. Correspondence with the provincial authorities concerning residence rights[G], 1806–26, 1829–35; correspondence about taxes [G], 1820–41; correspondence with the regional authorities about *arenda* of taverns and transferrals of Jews from one area to another [G], 1834–37; proposed statutes of the community [G], 1853–54; records concerning propaganda among Jewish youth to join the military [G, P], 1870; correspondence about *Czytelnia Izraelicka*, statutes of *Hizaharu Bivnei Aniyim* society, a statute of *Agudas Achim – Brueder Bund*, statute of *Agudas Yeshurim* [G, P], 1871; statutes of *Dorshei Tov Vachesed*, statute of *Gomel Chesed*, statutes of *Beis Lechem* and others [G, P], 1872; records concerning ritual slaughter, 1894–97; correspondence with the *Ahavas Zion* society about emigration to Palestine [G, P], 1898; statutes of the *Tzeirei Yisroel* society [G, P], 1907; correspondence about the *Ognisko* society aiding school children and *Ochronka Żydowska*, providing shelter for children learning trade; correspondence about other societies aiding school children, sick people and Tora study, 1908.
(TsDIAU, L'viv, Namiestnictwo Galicyjskie)
5. Census of inhabitants and domestic animals [G, P], 1857; reports and correspondence concerning allotment of land for construction of a synagogue, 1872–94; reports and correspondence about subvention

for *Linas Hatzedek*, 1899–1914; reports and correspondence concerning subvention for a Jewish association donating fire-wood for poor Jews, a list of donors, 1902–14; register of *chadorim*, 1903–07; reports and correspondence about subvention for the *Bratnia Pomoc* society, 1903–13; reports and correspondence concerning establishment of a new Jewish cemetery, 1909–26; financial report of the *Praca Kobiet* society, a list of members, 1913; reports and correspondence concerning construction of the *Or Tora yeshiva* [P, U], 1928–32; monograph about culture and economy in the 1920's; correspondence with Rada Szkolna and Czacki School on leasing a gymnasium to the *Makabi* sport association, 1933–36; a report about activity of *Towarzystwo Ochrony Zdrowia Ludności Żydowskiej w Polsce*, 1934–35; monograph of Stanisławów, a list of municipal council members, 1939.

(DAIFO, Ivano-Frankivs'k, Magistrat, Stanisławów)

6. Decrees, reports and correspondence on closing of *chadorim* [G, P], 1868–74; proposition of a statute for the Jewish school [G, P], 1868–74; proclamations, reports and correspondence concerning *chadorim* and private Jewish schools [G, P], 1878–81; reports about teaching Jewish religion in elementary schools [G, P], 1882–89; reports concerning the S. Weinberg Jewish school of commerce, a list of students [G, P], 1918.

(TsDIAU, L'viv, Krajowa Rada Szkolna)

7. <u>Records on registration, statutes and/or activities of the following:</u> *Tomchei Nistarim, Hachnasas Kala, Dorshei Tov* [G, P], 1871–88, 1921–30; *Mizrachi*, 1919–21; *Związek Żydowski Inwalidów, Wdów i Sierot Wojennych*, Jewish libraries (including a list of founding members), 1921–30; *Towarzystwo Pań ku Wspieraniu Biednych Żydowskich Położnic* and *Keren Kayemet*, 1922–30; *Żydowska Kuchnia Ludowa*, including a membership list, 1925–30; various Zionist associations, 1925–33; the religious associations: *Kehilas Yisroel, Beis Hatfitza, Kehilas Yaakov, Beis Avruhem*, including lists of founders and members, 1925–39; *Związek Przemysłowców i Kupców Drzewnych*, 1929–35; Revisionist Zionists, 1927–28, 1939; *Okręgowa Żydowska Rada Sieroca*, 1928; *Hashomer Hatzair* and other youth organizations, 1929–30; *Żydowska Rada Sieroca i Ochrona Młodzieży*, 1930; the Jewish youth association, *Giskala*, 1930; *Linas Hatzedek*, 1930–37; Jewish musical, dramatical and literary associations, 1930–37; *Hatzofim Brit Trumpeldor*, 1930–37; various Jewish scouts organizations, 1930–37; *Achva*, 1930–37; *Związek Obywatelski Kobiet Żydowskich*, 1931; various sport associations, 1931–36; *Hashomer Hatzair*, 1931–37; *Bikur Cholim*, 1931–37; *Żydowska Partia Pracy*, 1932–33; *Brit Trumpeldor*, 1933; local committees of *Ogólno-Żydowska Parti Pracy* (OŻPP), 1933; the youth organizations, *Histadrut Hanoar Haivri* and *Tzofe*, 1933; *Żydowskie Towarzystwo Rolnicze*, 1933; *Stowarzyszenie Pań ku Wspieraniu Położnic Żydowskich*, 1933–34; *Towarzystwo ku Wspieraniu Zubożałych Kupców Żydowskich*, statute, 1933–35; *Achdut*, 1933–36; *Żydowskie Towarzystwo Szkoły Ludowej i Średniej*, 1933–37; *Hakoach, Beis Yehuda Dom Żydowski, Shivat Zion* and *Stowarzyszenie Pomocy Żydowskim Ofiarom Wojennym, Inwalidom, Wdowom i Sierotom*, 1933–37; Jewish economic organizations, 1934; *Żydowskie Towarzystwo Kulturalno–Oświatowe 'Tarbut'*, 1934–38; *Hitachduth – Poalei Zion*, 1935, 1939; *Marbitzei Tora* and *Kehilas Jakob*, 1935–36; *Okręgowa Żydowska Rada Sieroca*, 1935–37; *Stowarzyszenie Kobiet Żydowskich 'Samopomoc'* and *Gordonia*, 1936; <u>Board and membership lists of:</u> *Yad Charutzim*, 1930–31; *Żydowskie Towarzystwo Ochrony Zdrowia Ludności Żydowskiej 'TOZ'*, 1930–34; *Opieka nad Dzieckiem Żydowskim*, 1930–34; *Towarzystwo Opieki nad Halucami i Emigrantami Palestyńskimi 'Ezra'*, 1930–35; charitable societies helping Jewish orphans, 1930–35; *Opieka nad Żydowską Młodzieżą, Gordonia*, 1930–36; *Żydowskie Stowarzyszenie Kulturalno–Oświatowe 'Hatzefira'*. 1930–37;

<u>The Jewish community:</u> reports and correspondence concerning finance and administration of the community, 1921–25; reports on renovating a synagogue and closing a *mikve* [G, P], 1921–30; records concerning civil registration and statistical data on Jewish inhabitants, 1923–24; complaints concerning

Jewish cemeteries, 1925–39; reports on raising funds for Jews in Palestine, 1926; reports and correspondence concerning the activity of the Jewish community. [G, P, Y], 1931–38;

Reports about: celebrations honoring the inauguration of the Hebrew University in Jerusalem, 1925; activities of Jewish political parties, 1925–26; public meetings and conferences of *Poalei Zion* and the *Bund*, 1926–28; a meeting regarding the struggle to promote use of the Yiddish language and against Zionists promoting Hebrew, 1926; a meeting of the district committee of the *Bund* and a lecture organized by the committee of *Poalei Zion Prawica*, 1932; a meeting of *Liga dla Pracującej Palestyny*. 1932; conferences of *Agudas Yisroel* and *Talmud Tora*, 1932–33; meetings of the *Bund*, 1932–33; elections of delegates to the XVIII Zionist Congress, and establishment of *Mifal Arlozorov*, 1933; a conference of the *Hitachdut* Party attended by David Ben Gurion, 1933; meetings of Zionist associations, 1935–36; congresses of *Żydowskie Towarzystwo Rolnicze*, 1935;

General: files on confiscation of the newspaper, *Der Morgen*; a statute of *Żydowska Rada* [P, U, Y], 1926–27; materials from the second general census 1931; correspondence concerning Communist activity at the Leib Peretz Association, 1932–33; a decree against anti-Jewish violence, 1934; files on permission to use banners and badges by various Jewish associations, among them the Jewish sports organization, *Menora*, 1937–39; a statistical report about the population, 1938; correspondence about the liquidation of *Samopomoc dla Żydów Akademików*, 1939; reports by informers concerning activities of the *Bund*, 1939.

(DAIFO, Ivano-Frankivs'k, UW, Stanisławów)

8. New statutes of the community [G], 1878.

(TsDIAU, L'viv, Gmina Żydowska, Lwów)

9. Files on publishing the *Stanislauer Glocke* [G, P, Y], 1913–18.

(DAIFO, Ivano-Frankivs'k, Prokuratura Państwowa, Stanisławów)

10. Community budget 1919, 1930; minutes and correspondence concerning the community elections, and statutes, 1925–26; records on the establishment of a new Jewish cemetery [G, H, P], 1926–29; correspondence with Jewish associations regarding subventions by the community [H, P, Y], 1927–28.

(DAIFO, Ivano-Frankivs'k, Gmina Żydowska, Stanisławów)

11. A file on war damages caused to the *Chaskiel Heiss* synagogue, 1921–22.

(DAIFO, Ivano-Frankivs'k, Miejscowa Komisja Szacunkowa, Stanisławów)

12. The Jewish community: Reports and correspondence concerning: ratification of the community statutes and budget [G, P], 1919–20; the slaughter–house, 1922–25; a list of *chadorim* and teachers, 1928–35; community elections, rabbinate and budget and list of tax payers, 1934–35;

Registration, statutes and activities of: *Yeshivas Or Tora, Chaverim Kol Israel, Mitet, Mizrachi, Agudas Yisroel, Templum, Merkaz Ruchani* [G, P], 1919–39; *Hachnasas Orchim, Ner Tamid* and *Żydowski Dom Sierot Wojennych*, including lists of members, 1922–27; *Żydowska Rada Sieroca i Ochrona Młodzieży*, including lists of members, 1922–28; *Żydowskie Towarzystwo Szkoły Ludowej i Średniej*, 1923–24; *Cech Rzeźników*, 1923–29; *Związek Rzemieślników Żydowskich 'Yad Charutzim'*, 1923–39; the Jewish sports club, *Jutrzenka*, 1924; *Towarzystwo Opieki nad Chalucami i Emigrantami palestyńskimi 'Ezra'*, including membership list, 1925; associations of women and charity, 1925–39; Jewish agricultural associations, including member lists,1928–39; Zionist organizations, 1929–34; a list of the local committee members of *Hitachdut*, 1933; public meetings organized by *Hitachdut Poalei Zion*, 1934; *Żydowskie Towarzystwo Szkoły Ludowej i Średniej, Mizrachi, Keren Hayesod, Hitachadut Poalei Zion, Keren Kayemet Le-Israel*, Związek *"Wuzet"*, Revisionist Zionists; May 3rd celebrations, 1936;

Police reports concerning: public meetings of Jewish, Zionist and Ukrainian associations [P, U], 1922–29; Communist youth organizations, a leaflet of the *Bund* [P, Y], 1925; *Ogólno-Żydowska Partia Pracy*. [P, Y], 1932–33; popular meetings organized by the *Mizrachi*, 1933; the womens' group of *Agudas Yisroel*, 1933;

activities of Zionists and Revisionist Zionists, 1933; the establishment of *Stronnictwo Państwa Żydowskiego w Polsce*, including a list of committee members, 1934–37; board members of *Hitachdut Poalei Zion*, 1936–37; establishment and activities of the Jewish *Klub Młodych Inteligentów*, 1936–38; activities of *Hashomer Hazair*, 1937;

Varia: a register of Jewish children in public schools,and a list of teachers, 1922–26; documents concerning confiscation of *Der Morgen* No 7 and *Jugend Beilage* [P, U, Y], 1927–29; description of the periodicals *Komunikaty Żydowskiego Towarzystwa Gimnastycznego 'Hakoach' i 'Sztegem'.*, 1931–32; materials concerning a license for publication of *Die Woche*, 1934–36; materials on issuing the weekly, *Dus Wort*, 1937–38.

(DAIFO, Ivano-Frankivs'k, Starostwo Powiatowe, Stanisławów)

13. A schedule of classes at the Baron Hirsch Foundation (JCA) school, 1923; correspondence about teaching Jewish religion in public schools, 1926–29; statistical data about Jewish students in public schools and a list of students at the Kazimierz Wielki school, 1928; reports and correspondence concerning legalization of *chadorim* and other Jewish religious and non–religious schools, a list of *chadorim*, statutes of *Talmud Tora, Yeshivas Or Tora*, Hebrew courses organized by the *Safa Berura* society, 1934–36; correspondence about confirming the statutes of a private kindergarten, 1938–39.

(DAIFO, Ivano-Frankivs'k, Inspektorat Szkolny, Stanisławów)

14. Records concerning the establishment and activities of *Achdut Bnai Brit*, statutes, registers, founding committee, board and members [G, P], 1927–32; correspondence with Jewish associations about subventions and activity of *Achdut Bnai Brit*, 1934–36; a folder 'Bnei Brit Palestine House–Building Fund Ltd in Jerusalem' [E, G, H, P], 1935–36.

(DAIFO, Ivano-Frankivs'k, *Bnai Brit,* Stanisławów)

15. Reports and correspondence concerning renovation of the main synagogue, 1929–30.

(DALO, L'viv, UW, Lwów)

16. A monthly report by the district police concerning the activities of political parties and associations, 1930–32; reports concerning activities of Zionist associations, 1935–36; reports and correspondence concerning anti-Jewish actions by Ukrainian nationalists, 1936–37; police reports containing lists of board members of *Klub Młodych Inteligentów* and *Związek Pracowników Handlowych i Biurowych w Polsce*, 1937; reports concerning conferences and meetings organized by Jewish associations, 1938–39; secret information concerning activities of the *Bund.*, 1938–39.

(DAIFO, Ivano-Frankivs'k, Komenda Wojewódzka PP, Stanisławów)

17. Police reports concerning: the "balance of political and national forces" in the district self government council., including lists of members, 1930–34; materials about the activity of *Powszechny Związek Zawodowy Pracowników Handlowych i Biurowych w Polsce*, 1931–34; the activity of Leib Peretz Association, 1932–34; lists of members and boards of Jewish religious, Zionist, youth, cultural, educational, sports and professional associations, 1933–36; member lists of the sports club, *Admira*, 1935; the activity of the Jewish dramatical association, *Scena*, including a list of members, 1935–37.

(DAIFO, Ivano-Frankivs'k, Komenda Powiatowa PP, Stanisławów)

18. Correspondence about emigration to Palestine, 1931–39.

(DAIFO, Ivano-Frankivs'k, Oddz. Syndykatu Emigracyjnego, Stanisławów)

19. Files concerning corrupt practices by N. Seibald, president of the Jewish community council, 1935; a report by the district police concerning activities of the *Bund*, 1939.

(DAIFO, Ivano-Frankivs'k, Prokuratura Sądu Okręgowego, Stanisławów)

20. Reports and correspondence on legal proceedings against *'Słowo' – Żydowski tygodnik polityczno-społeczny* because of articles calling for a boycott of the newspaper *Kurier Stanisławowski*, 1936–38.

(DAIFO, Ivano-Frankivs'k, Sąd Okręgowy, Stanisławów)

21. A list of Jewish community employees, 1936–39; pay–sheet of *Marbitzei Tora* and statutes, 1937–38.

(DAIFO, Ivano-Frankivs'k, Wojewódzkie Biuro Funduszu Pracy, Stanisławów)

22. Decrees of the Council for Religious Affairs concerning taxes for religious functionnaries and registration of the Jewish community [R], 1946–47; reports about functioning prayer houses and their officials and a list of synagogues and prayer houses [R], 1947; files on utilization of synagogue buildings [R], 1947–57; decrees concerning distribution of *matzot* among Jews and the prohibition to sell seats in synagogues [R], 1950; reports concerning registration of Jewish communities and prayer houses [R], 1954–62.

(DAIFO, Ivano-Frankivs'k, Upolnomochennyi Soveta…)

STANISŁAWÓW (woj. stanisławowskie), surroundings, 1704–1959

Microfilms:

1. Excerpts from court books concerning assaults on Jews and thefts in various localities of the region, 1704–23.

(NBANU, L'viv, Arch. Ossolinskich)

2. A map of the district, n.d.

Files on: ratifying the statutes of various Jewish associations in the *województwo* [G, P, Ukr], 1871, 1877, 1888, 1893–95, 1920–30; registration of the *Mizrachi*, including its statutes for Galicia [G, P], 1912, 1919–21; registration and ratifying the statutes of Jewish libraries, including lists of founders, 1921–30; a decree concerning supervision of the Jewish organization, *Pomoc ofiarom pogromów w Polsce* [Aid for Victims of Pogroms in Poland], 1922; reports about political movements, 1922–23; a list of associations in various districts of the *województwo* [P, U], 1922–23; reports and correspondence on raising funds for the Polish–Galician community in Palestine, 1922–29; reports and correspondence on permission to organize meetings and speeches in Yiddish [P, Y], 1922–30; instructions regulating civil registers and prohibiting the use of Hebrew, 1923–24; reports and correspondence with district authorities about activities of the *Bund* and *Poalei Zion*, 1923–26; police reports concerning the political situation, 1925–38; instructions by the Ministry of the Interior concerning the policy towards national minorities, 1926; correspondence about supervising Jewish communities, 1926–35; reports by district offices concerning data on Jewish, Polish and Ukrainian associations and professional organizations, 1926–28; complaints about community elections in various communities [H, P], 1928–37; maps and lists of Jewish communities, 1929; correspondence concerning elections of councils and rabbis in Jewish communities, 1930–32;

results of the second general census in various localities, 1931; material on the registration and activities of *Juna Esperantisto, Towarzystwo dla Żydowskiej Młodzieży Szkolnej 'Samopomoc', Herzliyah, Tzofe, Poalei Tzedek* and other associations in the district, including membership lists, 1931–39; files on legislation relating to Jewish communities and state loan among members of Jewish communities [P, Y], 1932–33; a list of *Yad Charutzim* branches; protests and resolutions against anti–Jewish speeches in the Reichstag, 1932; correspondence and reports about the activities of *Hitachadut* and other Zionist parties, 1932; among them, *Poalei Zion Lewica*, 1933; complaints against Jewish community leaders in economic matters, 1933–36; instructions to the *wojewoda* about supervising public speeches by *Poalei Zion Lewica* leaders before municipal elections, 1934; instructions on preventing anti-Jewish disturbances, 1934; statistical descriptions of various districts, 1935; correspondence with Jewish communities about communal taxes, 1935–39; a report about political forces in selfgovernmental institutions, and a list of political parties, 1936; reports about demonstrations and public meetings relating to anti-Jewish speeches and Jewish emigration from Poland, 1936; circulars, reports and correspondence concerning Jewish, Polish and Ukrainian professional organizations, 1936; reports and correspondence concerning popular meetings organized by Zionist parties and associations [P, Y], 1936–37; materials concerning exams in the Polish language for rabbinical candidates, 1936–37; information about Jewish political organizations [P, Y], 1937–38; an investigation of the activities of Jewish organizations in the region [P, Y], 1937–39; report about the activity of *Hitachdut Poalei–Zion*, 1938; material on ratification of community budgets in the region, 1938; material concerning the policy of polonization in politics and economics, 1939.

(DAIFO, Ivano-Frankivs'k, UW, Stanisławów)

3. Reports on teaching Jewish religion in elementary schools, 1895–97.

(TsDIAU, L'viv, Krajowa Rada Szkolna)

4. Reports and correspondence concerning registering and ratifying the statutes of: *Samopomoc dla Żydowskiej Młodzieży Szkolnej, Żydowski Związek Pracy Społecznej Kobiet, Żydowskie Stowarzyszenie Wzajemnej Pomocy 'Braterstwo'*, TOZ, *Związek Żydowski Inwalidów, Wdów i Sierot Wojennych*, WIZO, *Gomlei Chesed* and various Jewish youth movements [G, P], 1919–39; statistical data on the inhabitants, 1923–24; reports by the district police on the activity of *Poalei Zion Prawica, Hitachadut* and *Bund*, including leaflets of *Hitachdut* in Polish and Yiddish [P, Y], 1926; a statistical report about the number of communities and community members in the district, 1927; correspondence with Jewish communities and parish congregations about the celebration of May 3rd, 1927–29; reports by the district police about activities of Jewish, Polish, Ukrainian and Zionist associations in the district, 1931–34; a conference of rabbis in the region, 1936; a list of German, Jewish and Ukrainian community centers, 1937; a monograph on the economic and political situation, 1930s.

(DAIFO, Ivano-Frankivs'k, Starostwo Powiatowe, Stanisławów)

5. A register of Jewish communities in the region, 1922; correspondence about statutes of Jewish communities, 1922–24.

(DALO, L'viv, UW, Lwów)

6. Circulars about elections and *lustracja* of Jewish communities, 1928–32.

(DAIFO, Ivano-Frankivs'k, Starostwo Powiatowe, Śniatyn)

7. Descriptions of the political situation in the district, 1928, 1932; a register of Jewish, Polish and Ukrainian associations, including lists of board members [P, U, Y], 1928–36; police reports on activities of Jewish, Polish and Ukrainian political parties in the district, 1932–33; reports on the activities of Jewish political parties and associations, including lists of members - *Samopomoc, Yad Charutzim, Hitachatut Poalei Zion*, Revisionist Zionists, *Mizrachi, Agudas Yisroel, Ogólno-Żydowska Partia Pracy* (OŻPP), 1933–34; records concerning Jewish religious, Zionist, youth, cultural, educationa, athletic and professional associations, 1933–36; correspondence with police stations about weapons held by emigrants to Palestine, 1935; a register of Jewish, Polish and Ukrainian periodical subscriptions, 1937.

(DAIFO, Ivano-Frankivs'k, Komenda Powiatowa PP, Stanisławów)

8. Reports by directors of public schools concerning social, national, cultural, economic and sanitary conditions in the respective administrative units [P, U], 1930; reports and correspondence on the legalization of *chadorim* and other Jewish religious and secular schools, 1934–36.

(DAIFO, Ivano-Frankivs'k, Inspektorat Szkolny, Stanisławów)

9. Socio–political monographs about various districts, 1935; reports and correspondence on anti–Jewish actions organized by Ukrainian nationalists in various localities of the region, 1936–37; reports by police district headquarters concerning activity of Jewish members of the Communist Party, in the area 1937; proclamation by *Rada Krajowa Klasowych Związków Zawodowych* and *Komitet Pomocy Ofiarom Pogromu w Brześciu* and reports by district police headquarters on raising funds for victims of the pogrom in Brześć, 1937; correspondence with the district police headquarters about creation of *Blok Mniejszości*

Narodowych w Polsce [G, P, Y], 1937–38; material on anti-Jewish actions and activities of Jewish selfdefence fighting squads, including list of localities where anti-Jewish actions took place, 1937–38; secret investigations regarding the activities of German, Jewish and Ukrainian political associations [P, Y], 1937–39.
(DAIFO, Ivano-Frankivs'k, Komenda Wojewódzka PP, Stanisławów)
10. Correspondence concerning emigration to the USA, a list of emigrants, 1932; lists of emigrants to Palestine, 1935–37.
(DAIFO, Ivano-Frankivs'k, Oddz. Syndykatu Emigracyjnego, Stanisławów)
11. Information about prayer houses and lists of functionaries [R], 1944–47; instructions of the Council for Religious Affaires concerning closing of Jewish cemeteries and synagogues, taxes for religious functionaries and registration of the Jewish community [R], 1946–47; files on utilization of synagogue buildings [R], 1947–57; reports concerning registration of Jewish communities, list of prayer houses and community functionaries [R], 1959.
(DAIFO, Ivano-Frankivs'k, Upolnomochennyi Soveta…)

STARA SŁUPIA (pow. Opatów, woj. kieleckie) 1794
Microfilms:
Investigation of the murder of a Jew, 1794.
(AP Kraków, IT)

STARA SÓL (pow. Sambor, woj. lwowskie) 1615
Microfilms:
A decree by King Zygmunt III prohibiting Jews from joining guilds, settling in the town or dealing with commerce, crafts and *propinacja*, 1615.
(AP Kraków, Teki Schneidra)

STARE MIASTO (pow. Łańcut, woj. lwowskie) 1895
Microfilms:
Correspondence concerning vacant rabbinical positions, 1895.
(TsDIAU, L'viv, Namiestnictwo Galicyjskie)

STARE SIOŁO (pow. Bóbrka, woj. lwowskie) 1716–1935
Microfilms:
1. Private agreements, receipts, contracts, and other documents regarding estates of the Sieniawski and Czartoryski families, 1628–1759.
(Bibl. Czartoryskich, Kraków)
2. Authorization by the district authorities to collect money for the Polish–Galician Jewish community in Palestine, including a list of donors, 1928–30; correspondence on the community budget, and a list of tax payers, 1933–35.
(DALO, L'viv, UW, Lwów)

STAROGARD (GDAŃSKI) (woj. pomorskie) 1838–1895
Originals:
Register of the income of the Burial Society [Y], 1838–65; minutes and correspondence of the Jewish Womens's Society [G], 1855–1920; community statutes [G], 1857; files on taxes paid by Jews [G], 1857–87; records of community meetings [G], 1880–86; laws, commercial regulations and parliamentary rules [G], 1890; appointment of a rabbi [G], 1895.

Microfilms:
Minutes and decisions of the community council [G], 1854–56.
(Centrum Judaicum, Berlin)

STARY SAMBOR (pow. Sambor, woj. lwowskie) 1761–1939
Microfilms:
1. Testimonies concerning an illegal Jewish brewery [L], 1761.
(TsDIAU, L'viv, Ekonomia Samborska)
2. Reports and correspondence on ratification of the community statutes [G, P], 1894–98.
(TsDIAU, L'viv, Namiestnictwo Galicyjskie)
3. Correspondence about the registration of *Agudas Yisroel*, statutes and a list of members, 1922; correspondence about registration of the *Machzikei Hadas* society, 1932.
(DALO, L'viv, Magistrat, Lwów)
4. Records concerning the community council, 1928–30; correspondence about the community budget, including a list of tax payers, 1931–36; reports, complaints and correspondence concerning community elections, 1936–39.
(DALO, L'viv, UW, Lwów)

STARY SAMBOR, surroundings, 1900–1908
Microfilms:
Reports concerning *chadorim*, including a list of *chadorim*, 1900–08.
(TsDIAU, L'viv, Namiestnictwo Galicyjskie)

STARUNIA (pow. Nadworna, woj. lwowskie) 1925–1939
Microfilms:
Statutes, minutes and correspondence concerning Jewish associations, 1925–39.
(DAIFO, Ivano-Frankivs'k, UW, Stanisławów)

STASZÓW (pow. Sandomierz, woj. kieleckie) 1652–1871
Microfilms:
1. Reports and excerpts from municipal books concerning estates of the Sieniawski and Czartoryski families [H, L, P], 1652–1766.
(Bibl. Czartoryskich, Kraków)
2. Registers, accounts, *uniwersały*, instructions and contracts concerning inhabitants and estates of the Sieniawski and Czartoryski families, 1706–85.
(Biblioteka Narodowa, Warszawa)
3. Inventory of estates, 1760–70; real estate contracts, 1761–76; *arenda* contracts for inns and flour mills, 1795–96; accounts regarding *propinacja*, 1815–24; inventory of *arenda*, inns, flour mills and other revenues in the Staszów estates, 1822.
(AP Kraków, Arch. Krzeszowickie Potockich)
4. *Lustracja* of poll–tax in the estates of August Aleksander Czartoryski, 1766.
(AGAD, Warszawa, Arch. Potockich w Łańcucie)
5. Legal proceedings against a Jew, dealing with *propinacja*, 1858–71.
(AP Radom, Rząd Gubernialny, Radom)

STAWISKI (pow. Łomża, woj. białostockie) 1910
Microfilms:

Copies of inscriptions on Jewish tombstones and synagogues [H, P, R], 1910.
(RGIA, St. Petersburg, Departament dukhovnykh del...)

STAWISZYN (pow. Kalisz, woj. łódzkie) 1820–1910
Microfilms:
1. Files containing a description of the town, 1820–22.
(AGAD, Warszawa, Komisja Województwa Kaliskiego)
2. Copies of inscriptions on Jewish tombstones and synagogues [H, P, R], 1910.
(RGIA, St. Petersburg, Departament dukhovnykh del...)

STECOWA (pow. Śniatyn, woj. stanisławowskie) 1933–1938
Microfilms:
Records of the *Hitachdut* society and of Jewish agricultural associations, 1933–38.
(DAIFO, Ivano-Frankivs'k, UW, Stanisławów)

STEPAŃ (pow. Kostopol, woj. wołyńskie) 1677–1828
Microfilms:
1. Complaints against Jews, 1677.
(AP Kraków, Teki Sanguszków t. zw. rzymskie)
2. Inspection reports [R], 1816–28.
(DARO, Rivne, Rovenskoe uezdnoe kaznacheistvo)

STĘŻYCA (pow. Garwolin, woj. lubelskie) 1534–1766
Microfilms:
1. *Lustracja* of the sandomierz *województwo,* containing data on Stężyca, 1534–1615.
(AGAD, Warszawa, ASK)
2. Investigations, reports, complaints and excerpts from municipal books concerning properties of the Sieniawski family [H, L, P], 1652–1766.
(Bibl. Czartoryskich, Kraków)

STĘSZEW (pow. Poznań, woj. poznańskie) 1847
Originals:
Drawing of a new *mikve*, 1874.

STOLIN (woj. poleskie) 1886–1964
Photocopies:
A file about a Jewish prayer house [R], 1886–88.
(NIAB, Minsk, Minskoie gubernskoie pravlenie)
A letter by Dr. Z. Rabinovich from Haifa about archives of *tzadikim* [R], 1964.
(NARB, Minsk, Sovet po delam religioznykh kul'tov)

STOŁPIN (pow. Radziechów, woj. tarnopolskie) 1699–1720
Microfilms:
Inventories, tax registers, *asygnacje* and accounts, 1699–1720.
(Bibl. Czartoryskich, Kraków)

STOPNICA (woj. kieleckie) 1690–1871
Microfilms:
1. Documents on litigation between the town council and the parish priest, involving Jews, 1690.

(TsDIAU, L'viv, Arch. Lubomirskich)

2. Documents regarding taxes paid by Jews for maintenance of the army [L, P], 1816.

(TsDIAU, L'viv, Arch. Lanckorońskich)

3. Correspondence concerning exemptions from conscription for graduates of the Rabbinical Seminary in Warsaw, including a list of graduates, 1865–71.

(AGAD, Warszawa, CWW)

STRATYŃ (pow. Rohatyn, woj. stanisławowskie) 1928–1937

Microfilms:

1. Complaints by members of the community concerning elections and administrative problems [H, P], 1928–37.

(DAIFO, Ivano-Frankivs'k, UW, Stanisławów)

2. Reports and correspondence concerning legalization of *chadorim* and religious and secular Jewish schools, including a list of *chadorim* and their owners, 1934–36.

(DAIFO, Ivano-Frankivs'k, Inspektorat Szkolny, Stanisławów)

STRYJ (woj. stanisławowskie) 1663–1939

Originals:

Letter of protection [G], 1794; legal proceedings regarding debts [G], 1832; documents regarding tobacco commerce [G], 1844.

Microfilms:

1. Circulars, accounts, decrees and *uniwersały* concerning inhabitants and estates belonging to M. i A. Sieniawski and A. Czartoryski., 1663–1765.

(Bibl. Czartoryskich, Kraków)

2. Receipts of the *kahal* (fragmentary) [G, H, P], 1738–86; a letter by I. Glass concerning acquisition of books [H], 1897.

(NBANU, L'viv, Zb. Goldsteina)

3. Confirmation by King Stanisław August Poniatowski of charters regulating Jewish settlement [L, P], 1766.

(AGAD, Warszawa, Księgi Kanclerskie)

4. Correspondence with the regional authorities concerning *arenda*, financial matters, taxes and customs [G, L, P], 1787–95, 1814–25; correspondence about synagogues and *minyanim* in private houses [G, L], 1819–26; correspondence with the regional authorities about permission of marriages, register of marriages, 1820–23; correspondence regarding place of residence for Jews [G], 1820–21; tax register of the district [G], 1842–59; files on the closing of a Jewish cemetery and a plan of the cemetery [G, P], 1865–74; correspondence about the *Zion* society, statute [G, P], 1890–1902; materials concerning ritual slaughter, 1894–97; correspondence concerning various associations for support of merchants [G, P], 1897; correspondence with *Ahavas Zion* about emigration to Palestine [G, P], 1898; correspondence regarding *Poalei Zion* [G, P], 1904; correspondence about *Bursa Żydowska* for school boys and students of a gymnasium, 1904–07; statute of *Chevra Kadisha Halvayas Hames* [G, P], 1907–12; correspondence about *Kaufmannische Verein Osei Tov* and *Dorshei Tov* [G, P], 1908.

(TsDIAU, L'viv, Namiestnictwo Galicyjskie)

5. Reports and correspondence concerning closing of *chadorim* [G, P], 1868–74; reports on teaching of the Jewish religion in elementary schools [G, P], 1882–89.

(TsDIAU, L'viv, Krajowa Rada Szkolna)

6. Statutes, minutes and correspondence concerning Jewish associations [G, P], 1894, 1899, 1921–37; materials and statutes of *Merkaz Ruchani* [G, P], 1920–30; reports and correspondence concerning registration and activities of *Towarzystwo Dramatyczno–Muzyczne im. A. Goldfadena, Robotniczy Klub Sportowy, Klub Towarzyski im. Szaloma Asza* and *Żydowski Klub Przyjaciół Literatury i Sztuki im. Pereca*, 1921–30; reports concerning prayer houses [G, P], 1921–35; minutes, register of associations in Stryj district [P, U], 1922–23; records concerning registration of *Gmilus Chesed, Keren Kayemet* and WIZO, 1922–30; correspondence concerning the *Bund*, 1923; statistical data on Jews, 1923–24; files on Jewish civil registration, 1923–24; reports and correspondence concerning ratification of statutes of Jewish associations helping children and youth, 1923–28; reports by the authorities concerning activities of Jewish associations, 1925–26; records concerning registration of *Żydowski Dom Ludowy Beth–Am*, statutes and a list of the founding committee, 1925–30; reports about the activities of Zionist parties and associations, 1926; reports about raising funds for Jewish settlements in Palestine, 1926; reports concerning popular meetings organized by *Poalei Zion* and *Bund*, inauguration of a branch of *Towarzystwo Uniwersytetu Robotniczego*, statute, 1926–27; records of *Żydowskie Towarzystwo Szkoły Ludowej i Średniej*, 1926–30; correspondence concerning inspection and supervision of Jewish communities, community budget, change of statute and ritual slaughter, 1926–35; reports about the activities of Revisionist Zionists and a meeting of *Hitachadut*, 1927; report about the district conference of the *Bund*, 1928; complaints against community elections [H, P], 1928–37; reports about the activities of *Hashomer Hatzair* and a conference of *Achva*, 1929; reports about activities of Jewish youth movements, 1929–30; records of *Hechalutz*, 1930; records of *Yad Charutzim* and *TOZ*, 1930–34; records *of Towarzystwo Opieki nad Halucami i Emigrantami Palestyńskimi 'Ezra'*, 1930–35; records of charity societies, 1930–35; records *of Opieka nad Młodzieżą Żydowską 'Gordonia'*, 1930–36; records of literary, dramatical and musical associations, 1930–37; records of *Hatzofim Brit Trumpeldor*, 1930–37; records of Jewish associations, statutes, liquidation, 1930–39; records of the second census (on December, 1931), 1931; reports and correspondence concerning the activities of the Jewish community. [G, P, Y], 1931–35; records of Jewish sport associations, 1931–36; records of *Hashomer Hatzair*, 1931–37; records of *Żydowski Dom Przytułków*, 1931–39; records of *Związek Kupców Żydowskich* and *Żydowskie Zrzeszenie Gospodarcze* [P, U], 1931–39; reports and correspondence concerning salaries of rabbis and *dayanim*, 1932–35; records of *Stowarzyszenie Akademickie 'Emuna'* and *Hebronia*, 1932–35; reports and correspondence concerning activities of the Jewish community and community elections, 1932–36; records of *Hatikva*, 1932–36; reports by the district authorities about the acivities of Zionist associations [P, Y], 1933; report and correspondence about a conference of *Agudas Yisroel.*, 1933; reports concening elections of delegates for the 18th Zionist Congress, establishment of a committee, *Mifal Arlozorov*, 1933; records concerning OŻPP, 1933; reports from a conference of *Hitachdut*, 1933; reports concerning *Histadrut Hanoar Haivri, Hashomer Hatzair* and *Tzofe*, 1933; reports concerning *Brit Trumpeldor*, 1933–34; records of *Chevra Kadisha*, 1933–36; correspondence about registration of *Żydowski Związek Inwalidów, Wdów i Sierot Wojennych*, statutes, 1933–37; records of *Hitachadut*, 1933–37; reports concerning meetings organized by Jewish parties, decrees concernig prevention of anti-Jewish disorders, 1934; statistical reports about the population, 1938.
(DAIFO, Ivano-Frankivs'k, UW, Stanisławów)
7. Answers for questionnaire concerning Jews, 1922.
(NBANU, L'viv, Zb. Czołowskiego)
8. Report about a conference of Revisionist Zionists, 1930–31; records of *Gmilus Chasodim*, 1930–31; records concernig exams of proficiency in Polish for R. Rathaus, candidate for a rabbinical position in Lutowisko, 1932–35.
(DALO, L'viv, UW, Lwów)

9. Monthly reports by the district police headquarters about activities of Jewish associations and parties, 1930–32; reports about activities of Zionist oragnizations, 1935–36; a monograph dealing with political–social aspects, 1935; statistical description of the district of Stryj, 1935; reports about distribution of an anti–Jewish booklet by *Stronnictwo Narodowe*, 1936; reports and correspondence concerning anti–Jewish actions by Ukrainian nationalists, 1936–37.
(DAIFO, Ivano-Frankivs'k, Komenda Wojewódzka PP, Stanisławów)
10. Reports and correspondence concerning insurance for a case of unemployment of workers in a ritual slaughter–house, 1936–39.
(DAIFO, Ivano-Frankivs'k, Wojewódzkie Biuro Funduszu Pracy, Stanisławów)

STRYKÓW (pow. Brzeziny, woj. łódzkie) 1821–1914
Microfilms:
1. Various land registry records including Jewish property, 1821–66; records concerning community elections and accounts, 1822–66; complaints to the municipal and communal authorities, 1840–54.
(AP Łódź, Anterioria Rządu Gubernialnego, Piotrków)
2. Files on community income from the sale of imported liquor [R], 1870–71; ratification of community elections and accounts [R], 1893–1914; a license for the rabbi to wear traditional dress [R], 1893.
(AP Łódź, Rząd Gubernialny, WA, Piotrków)
3. Two requests to register charitable societies (*Linas Hatzedek, Gmilus Chasodim*) [R], 1907–13.
(AP Łódź, Rząd Gubernialny, KP, Piotrków)
4. Fines for evading conscription [R], 1899.
(AP Łódź, Rząd Gubernialny, WP, Piotrków)

STRZELISKA NOWE (pow. Bóbrka, woj. lwowskie) 1877–1935
Originals:
A drawing of a wooden synagouge, n.d.
(IKG Wien, Juedisches Museum)
Photocopies:
Community budget and a list of taxpayers, 1933–1935;
(DALO, L'viv, UW, Lwów)
Microfilms:
1. Correspondence with the district authorities about *chadorim* and a list of *melamdim*, 1877–1908; correspondence concerning community statutes, 1898.
(TsDIAU, L'viv, Namiestnictwo Galicyjskie)
2. Authorization by the district authorities to collect money for the Polish–Galician Jewish community in Palestine, including a list of donors, 1928–30; correspondence about community matters, budget and taxes, including a list of taxpayers [P, Y], 1931–35.
(DALO, L'viv, UW, Lwów)

STRZELNO (pow. Mogilno, woj. poznańskie) 1860–1861
Microfilms:
A file on special payments required from members leaving the community, 1860–61.
(AP Bydgoszcz, Kgl. Reg. Bromberg, Abt. D. Intern)

STRZYŁKI (pow. Turka, woj. lwowskie) 1928
Microfilms:
Circulars, reports and correspondence concerning community elections, 1928.

(DALO, L'viv, UW, Lwów)

STRZYŻÓW (pow. Rzeszów, woj. lwowskie) 1895–1931
Microfilms:
1. Correspondence with the Ministry of Interior about reorganizing the community, 1895; correspondence regarding the *Zion* and *Postęp (Haskalah), Chevra Kadisha* and *Gmilus Chasodim* societies , including statutes [G, H, P], 1895–1914.
(TsDIAU, L'viv, Namiestnictwo Galicyjskie)
2. Correspondence about the registration of *Czytelnia Żydowska*, 1924–25; correspondence about the *Kultur Liga*, 1926; correspondence on the antagonism between the Orthodox and Zionists, 1927–28; material concerning community elections, 1928–30; correspondence about rabbinical positions, and an election poster in Yiddish [P, Y], 1928–32; lists of town council members, their nationalities and political affiliations, 1930; correspondence concerning ratification of preliminary community budgets, 1930–31.
(DALO, L'viv, UW, Lwów)

SUCHA (pow. Zywiec, woj. krakowskie) 1894–1918
Originals:
School certificates, 1894–1895, 1927; register of Jewish children taking private lessons on religious subjects, 1910–1913, 1918.

SUCHA RZECZKA (pow. Augustów, woj. białostockie) 1915
Microfilms:
Files of EKOPO about the condition of Jews, a list of women who were raped and a list of missing Jews [R], 1915.
(GARF, Moscow, Bomash)

SUCHOSTAW (pow. Kopyczyńce, woj. tarnopolskie) 1846–1896
Microfilms:
Files on ratification of community statutes, 1846–96.
(TsDIAU, L'viv, Namiestnictwo Galicyjskie)

SUCHOWOLA (pow. Sokółka, woj. białostockie) 1786–1789
Photocopies:
Inventories of estates, containing lists of Jewish inhabitants, 1786, 1789.
(NIAB, Minsk, Kollektsia drevnikh inventarei)

SULEJÓW (pow. Piotrków, woj. łódzkie) 1864–1913
Microfilms:
1. Records concerning the community, 1864–66.
(AP Łódź, Anterioria Rządu Gubernialnego, Piotrków)
2. Files on Jewish primary schools [R], 1875–97.
(AP Łódź, Dyrekcja Szkolna, Łódź)
3. Ratification of community elections and accounts [R], 1899–1913; files on acquisition of a plot of land [R], 1900; files on the *arenda* of the *mikve* and on the synagogue [R], 1904–11; requests for a license to open a ritual slaughter house [R], 1909.
(AP Łódź, Rząd Gubernialny, WA, Piotrków)
4. Fines for evading conscription [R], 1902.
(AP Łódź, Rząd Gubernialny, WP, Piotrków)

SULMIERZYCE (pow. Radomsko, woj. lódzkie) 1845–1914
Microfilms:
1. Files on the community, 1845–66.
(AP Łódź, Anterioria Rządu Gubernialnego, Piotrków)
2. Fines for evading conscription [R], 1902.
(AP Łódź, Rząd Gubernialny, WP, Piotrków)
3. Ratification of community elections and accounts [R], 1902–14.
(AP Łódź, Rząd Gubernialny, WA, Piotrków)

SURAŻ (pow. Białystok, woj. białostockie) 1507–1911
Originals:
Marriage records (fragmentary) [R], 1885–1911.
Microfilms:
Charters and decrees concerning the town [L, P], 1507–1778.
(TsDIAU, L'viv, Arch. Lubomirskich)

SUWAŁKI (woj. białostockie) 1808–1939
Photocopies:
1. A list of farmers, including Jews, 1808; Files concerning *propinacja* taxes, 1808–1819; lists of traders and manufacturers, 1809–12, 1833–50, 1863–64, 1884, 1886, 1894 ; lists of tax payers, 1810–13, 1851; a list of brewery proprietors, alcohol distilleries etc., 1816–91; correspondence with the authorities concerning requests to open enterprises, 1820–86; historical and statistical descriptions of Suwałki, 1820–29; correspondence with authorities about the prohibition for Jews to work and trade on Sundays, 1830–59; community budget and lists of tax payers, 1842–98; reports of financial-economic activities of the community [P, R], 1842–78; reports concerning schools, synagogues and the community employees, 1850–51; files concerning conscription, 1850–52; a list of home owners, 1843–54, 1888–89; a list of Jews permitted to dress traditionally without paying a fine, 1846–49; files concerning elections to the community council [R], 1849–52, 1873; files concerning elections to the guild board, 1854–66, 1871; reports and statistics concerning Suwalki, including data on the Jewish community, 1856–90; files on enlarging the Jewish cemetery and on exemptions for the Jews from taxes to the Catholic Church, 1860–61; files concerning streets where the Jews may or may not reside, 1860–66; reports concerning the Jewish hospital, including statistics, 1863–69 ; lists of factories, manufacturers, and products, 1864–68, 1897; files on the opening of a Jewish school for boys, 1865–68; demographic data, 1866–85; a list of salt traders, 1867; a list of *melamdim* [R], 1870–71; statistical reports concerning the Jewish population, schools, synagogues, rabbis and other data [R], 1871; files on the elections of a rabbi [R], 1874–76; statistical data concerning births, marriages and deaths among Jews [R], 1874–84; a request for a license to open an enterprise [R], 1876; files on taxes for the Jewish school [R], 1877–95; lists of jewellers and watch-makers [R], 1878–1900; a request to open a prayer house in a private home [R], 1871; requests for money from the city council for maintenance of a Jewish school [R], 1871, 1888–89; a list of proprietors of inns and shops [R], 1871; correspondence concerning repairs of a burnt prayer-house [R], 1887; files concerning elections of deputees for trade matters at the city council, including a list of candidates [R], 1887–1911; lists of town-councillors [R], 1888; a list of poor Jews who received financial help [R], 1892; a list of schools and data about teachers [R], 1893; a list of Jewish coachmen [R], 1897.
(AP Suwałki, Akta Miasta Suwałk)
2. A list of the citizens who deposited money in the local bank, 1851–76.
(AP Suwałki, Suwalska Kasa Oszczędności)

3. Files concerning the Jewish hospital, 1863–70.
(AP Suwałki, Rada Opiekuńcza Zakładów Dobroczynnych pow. suwalskiego)
4. Complaints of the Jews about violations of rights during elections to the *Duma* [R], 1906.
(AP Suwałki, Komisja Powiatowa Suwalska do Spraw Wyborów do Dumy Państwowej)
5. Files concerning insurance of Jewish community real estate [R], 1912–13.
(AP Suwałki, Inspektor Ubezpieczeniowy Powiatu Suwalskiego)
6. Lists of Jews and non-Jews exempted from army service [R], 1914–15.
(AP Suwałki, Urząd Powiatowy Suwalski do Spraw Powinności Wojskowych m. Suwałki)
7. Lists of traders permitted to practice their professions [R], 1912–14.
(AP Suwałki, Kasa Powiatowa Suwalska)
8. Files concerning activities of *Tymczasowa Rada* and *Rada Ludowa,* 1918–20.
(AP Suwałki, Tymczasowa Rada Obywatelska Okręgu Suwalskiego i Zarząd Rady Ludowej Okręgu Suwalskiego)
9. Correspondence between the Jewish community and the *starostwo* concerning budget, taxes, *Talmud Tora* school, editing of Jewish newspapers; lists of: tax payers, *lustracja* of the community, proprietors of mills and windmills, syndicates, physicians, proprietors of enterprises, etc., 1921–39.
(AP Suwałki, Starostwo Powiatowe Suwalskie)

Microfilms:
1. Records concerning the setting up of an *eruv* in the Jewish quarter and conflicts with Christians, 1818–71; decrees, minutes and correspondence concerning order of prayers, territorial division of *kahals*, marriages, burial societies, a list of prayer houses, 1821–71; reports and correspondence concerning ratification of the elections of rabbis and internal conflicts between them and their communities, including a list of rabbis, 1853–64.
(AGAD, Warszawa, CWW)
2. Investigation files concerning a Jew from Suwałki, 1831.
(AGAD, Warszawa, WCPL)
3. Decrees, circulars and reports on the prohibition to conduct prayers during Sabbath and festivals in private houses, including a list of house owners [R], 1853–83; a request by a charitable society to open a shelter for the elderly, including statutes and a list of members [R], 1907; records regarding the Jewish hospital [R], 1910–14; a request for financial aid [R], 1915.
(AP Białystok, Rząd Gubernialny, Łomża)
4. Records on the Jewish hospital [R], 1870–1915.
(AP Białystok, Rada Opieki Społecznej)
5. Copies of inscriptions on synagogues and tombstones [H, P, R], 1910.
(RGIA, St. Petersburg, Departament dukhovnykh del...)

SUWAŁKI, surroundings, 1908–1939
Photocopies:
Files concerning distribution of the Jewish press, 1932–35; a list of people suspected of Communist agitation, and of people worthy of special attention; files concerning emigration to Palestine, 1931–39.
(AP Suwałki, Starostwo Powiatowe Suwalskie)
Microfilms:
1. A report on synagogues and rabbis in the *guberniia* Suwałki [R], 1908.
(RGIA, St. Petersburg, Departament dukhovnykh del...)

2. Correspondence concerning expulsion of untrustworthy Jews, and a prohibition to sell alcohol [R], 1915–16.
(RGVIA, Moscow, Shtab Dvinskogo voennogo okruga)
3. A list of people expelled from the district, 1923.
(DATO, Ternopil', Komenda Powiatowa PP, Trembowla)

SWARZĘDZ (pow. Poznań, woj. poznańskie) 1646–1900
Originals:
Copies of charters granted to Jews [G, P], 1646, 1758, 1847; *pinkas* and account books of the burial society [G, H], 1694–1850; files concerning the synagogue, financial matters and sales of seats [G, H], 1730–1864; *pinkas hakahal* (community record book) [H], 1758–1828; records of community accounts [G, H], 1771–1899; tax registers [G, H], 1777–1872; records of the repayment of debts to a local church [G], 1793–1804; records of disputes with the community of Poznań [G], 18th-19th cent.; several documents of the rabbinate [H], 1806–41; litigation between the community and the brewers' guild, 1808–34; various requests concerning taxes [G, H], 1811; community minute book [G], 1812–39; files and registers of correspondence [G], 1812–79; accounts regarding burial in the cemetery [G], 1818–50; documents on inheritances [G], 1818–60; records concerning litigation between a parish priest and the community [G, P], 1819–22; records of the Jewish school [G, H], 1819–67; a file on hospitalization costs [G], 1820–28; files on the naturalization of Jews [G], 1833–47; complaints [G], 1834–41; register of *shechita* [H], 1835–37; penalties [G], 1835–72; community elections [G], 1837–40; records of the sick care society [G, H], 1845–1900; charters and other rights [G], 1847; files on members leaving the community [G], 1853, 1860–67; files on aid for the poor [G], 1846–47.
Microfilms:
1. *Pinkas hakahal* [H], 1698–1758.
(JTS, New York)
2. *Pinkassim* and account books of the community and the synagogue [G, H], 1734–1823.
(AP Poznań, Gmina Żydowska, Swarzędz)
3. Rental payments by the community to the Church in Siedlec [G, P], 1735, 1772, 1794–1817; *arenda* contracts and other financial agreements [G, H], 1792–1838; correspondence concerning an agreement between communities of Swarzędz and Poznań [G], 1805, 1819, 1834; minutes of community council meetings [G], 1834–35.
(Centrum Judaicum, Berlin)
4. Register of levies to the Church [G], 1781–1846.
(ŻIH, Warszawa)

SYNOWÓDZKO WYŻNE (pow. Stryj, woj. stanisławowskie) 1921–1937
Microfilms:
Statutes, minutes and correspondence of Zionist associations, 1921–30; records of Jewish associations, 1924–37; correspondence concerning registration and statutes of the *Czytelnia Młodzieży Żydowskiej*, 1930–32; records of the *Achva* society, 1930–37.
(DAIFO, Ivano-Frankivs'k, UW, Stanisławów)

SZAMOCIN (pow. Chodzież, woj. poznańskie) 1818–1847
Originals:
Pinkas of the burial society [H], 1818–35; payment records of various taxes [G], 1827–43; files on community debts [G], 1835–36, 1841, 1846; a demand for rent by the owner of the town [G], 1836; records

of community administration [G], 1837–38; community accounts [G], 1847; accounts of the Jewish school [G], 1847.

Microfilms:
Pinkas of the Burial and Sick Care Society [H], 1818.
(YIVO, New York)

SZAMOTUŁY (woj. poznańskie) 1834–1905
Originals:
Files on community debts [G], 1835–37, 1846; an appeal printed after a fire in the synagogue [G], 1852; the sale of seats in the synagogue [G], 1859, 1905; community taxes [G], 1869–70; the plan of a *mikve* [G], 19th–20th cent.
Microfilms:
Minutes of community council meetings [G], 1834–63; supervision of peddlars [G], 1834.
(Centrum Judaicum, Berlin)

SZCZAWNICA (pow. Nowy Targ, woj. krakowskie)
Originals:
Brochure of the *Tikva* society for sick and poor school children and students, n.d.

SZCZEBRZESZYN (pow. Zamość, woj. lubelskie) 1653–1859
Microfilms:
1. An extract from legal records concerning Jews, 1653.
(Bibl. im. Łopacińskiego, Lublin)
2. Copies of inscriptions on tombstones [H, R], 17th–18th cent.
(TsGIASP, St. Petersburg, "Evreiskaia Starina")
3. Records of the community's debts to the Church in Zamość, 1750–86.
(AP Lublin, Kolegiata w Zamościu)
4. Statistical description, 1832–59.
(AP Lublin, Rząd Gubernialny, Lublin)
5. Reports, minutes and complaints concerning the burial society, 1822–50; a project to donate kosher meet to the poor and support poor Jewish hospital patients [P, R], 1848–56.
(AGAD, Warszawa, CWW)

SZCZEKOCINY (pow. Włoszczowa, woj. kieleckie) 1792–1812
Microfilms:
1. A letter of protection granted to a Jewish couple by King Stanisław August Poniatowski [L], 1792.
(AGAD, Warszawa, Księgi Kanclerskie)
2. Records and concerning taxes for kosher meat, 1812.
(AGAD, Warszawa, KRzPiS)

SZCZERCÓW (pow. Łask, woj. łódzkie) 1898–1912
Microfilms:
1. Ratification of community accounts and elections [R], 1901–12.
(AP Łódź, Rząd Gubernialny, WA, Piotrków)
2. Fines for evading conscription [R], 1898.
(AP Łódź, Rząd Gubernialny, WP, Piotrków)

SZCZERZEC (pow. Lwów, woj. lwowskie) 1878–1936
Microfilms:
1. Reports and correspondence concerning reorganization of elementary schools attended by Jewish pupils [G, P], 1878–89.
(TsDIAU, L'viv, Krajowa Rada Szkolna)
2. Correspondence with the district authorities concerning the Jewish community and ratification of statutes, 1895–96.
(TsDIAU, L'viv, Namiestnictwo Galicyjskie)
3. Answers to a questionnaire concerning the Jews, 1922.
(NBANU, L'viv, Zb. Czołowskiego)
4. Reports and correspondence about an increase in taxes for ritual slaughter, community elections and the budget, including a list of tax payers, 1931–35; reports containing names of community council members, rabbis and *dayanim*, 1937.
(DALO, L'viv, UW, Lwów)
5. Monograph containing demographical and economic data, 1936.
(AP Wrocław, Ossolineum, WKNZNP, Lwów)

SZCZUCIN (pow. Dabrowa, woj. krakowskie) 1889
Original:
Copy of the record book of a *Mishna* study society [H], 1889.

SZCZUCZYN (woj. białostockie) 1826–1923
Microfilms:
1. A file on the confiscation of a plot of land from a Jew [R], 1859–60.
(AGAD, Warszawa, SSKP)
2. Birth, marriage and death records (fragmentary), 1865.
(AP Ełk)
3. Files concerning permission to open a dentist's surgery and midwife's facility [R], 1907, 1909–13; a file concerning *arenda* of street lighting [R], 1909–13; records concerning execution of fine payments [R], 1911–14; file on the *arenda* of various taxes [R], 1912–13; a request for exemption from quartering soldiers and a list of home owners [R], 1912–13.
(AP Białystok, Rząd Gubernialny, Łomża)
4. A list of persons evicted from the district, 1923.
(DATO, Ternopil', Komenda Powiatowa PP, Trembowla)

SZCZUROWICE (pow. Radziechów, woj. tarnopolskie) 1877–1908
Microfilms:
Correspondence between the community and the district authorities regarding *chadorim*, including a list of *melamdim* [G, P], 1877–08; correspondence about community statutes, 1898; correspondence regarding community elections, 1898–08; correspondence between the community and the authorities regarding complaints by the rabbi about his salary [G, P], 1903–08; correspondence regarding alleged misdeeds of the community council, 1906–08.
(TsDIAU, L'viv, Namiestnictwo Galicyjskie)

SZERSZÓW (pow. Prużana, woj. poleskie) 1558–1561
Microfilms:
Charters concerning *arenda* contracts, 1558–61.

(RGADA, Moscow, ML)

SZTABIN (pow. Augustów, woj. białostockie) 1853–1856
Microfilms:
Reports and correspondence by government offices on the appointment of rabbis and on other communal matters, including a list of rabbis, 1853–56.
(AGAD, Warszawa, CWW)

SZUBSK (pow. Kutno, woj. warszawskie) 1847
Originals:
Documents regarding marriage banns, 1847.

SZUMSK (pow. Krzemieniec, woj. wołyńskie) 1746–1935
Microfilms:
1. Copies of decrees and *arenda* contracts, 1746–47.
(AGAD, Warszawa, Arch. Radziwiłłów)
2. A complaint by the town administrator against Jews for bringing vodka to the town illegally [R], 1821.
(DATO, Ternopil', Kremenetskii povetovyi khorunzhyi)
3. Files on confiscation of prayer books possessed by a rabbi [R], 1837–39.
(TsDIAU, Kyiv, Kantseliariia... general-gubernatora)
4. Register of Jews for tax purpose [R], 1847–48.
(DATO, Ternopil', Magistrat, Krzemieniec)
5. Reports, syllabus, budget and correspondence concerning the *Talmud Tora*, as well as a list of students [H, P], 1922–25, 1930; register of teachers in Jewish schools, 1931–35.
(DATO, Ternopil', Inspektorat Szkolny, Krzemieniec)

SZYBALIN (pow. Brzeżany, woj. tarnopolskie) 1700–1738
Microfilms:
Accounts, inventories and tax registers, 1700–38.
(Bibl. Czartoryskich, Kraków)

SZYDŁOWIEC (pow. Końskie, woj. kieleckie) 1853–1945
Microfilms:
1. Reports and correspondence concerning appointments of rabbis and their relationship with the communities, including lists of rabbis, 1853–56.
(AGAD, Warszawa, CWW)
2. A report about the tragic fate of 105 Jewish inhabitants, citing their professions and other personal data, 1945.
(AP Radom, Okręgowy Komitet Żydowski, Radom)

SZYDŁÓW (pow. Stopnica, woj. kieleckie) 1682–1910
Microfilms:
1. A file concerning financial matters [L, P], 1682–1701.
(AP Kraków, AKPot)
2. Registers, accounts, *uniwersały*, decrees and contracts concerning estates of the Sieniawski and Czartoryski families [F, L, P], 1706–85.
(Biblioteka Narodowa, Warszawa)
3. A letter of protection granted to a Jewish couple by Stanisław August Poniatowski [L], 1792.
(AGAD, Warszawa, Księgi Kanclerskie)

Szkoła ludowa _2_ klasowa _mieszana pospol._ w _Zembrzycach_

L. katalogu głównego _42_ Stopień _drugi_ Rok nauki _drugi_

ZAWIADOMIENIE SZKOLNE.

Imię i nazwisko ucznia (uczenicy): _Henryk Saustrom_

urodzony dnia _29. stycznia_ 1890 w _Zembrzycach_

w _Galicyi_, religii _Mojżesz._ obrządku

Rok szkolny 1897/8	I. półrocze:	II. półrocze:
Obyczaje :	dość dobre	naganne !
Pilność:	dobra	dobra
w nauce religii :		
w czytaniu :	bardzo dobry	dobry
w pisaniu :	dostateczny	dostateczny
w języku polskim :	dostateczny	dobry
w języku ruskim :		
w języku niemieckim :		
w rachunkach w połączeniu z nauką o formach geometrycznych :	dobry	dobry
w wiadomościach z dziejów i przyrody :		
w rysunkach :	dostateczny	dostateczny
w śpiewie :	dostateczny	dostateczny
w robotach ręcznych :		
w gimnastyce :	dobry	dobry
Postęp ogólny :	dostateczny	dostateczny
Porządek zewnętrzny :	niejednostajny	niejednostajny
Liczba opuszczonych godzin szkolnych :	usprawiedliwionych 720 nieusprawiedliwionych .—	usprawiedliwionych .— nieusprawiedliwionych .—
Uwagi nauczyciela klasy :		
Podpis ojca, matki lub opiekuna :	Moritz Saustrom	

w _Zembrzycach_ dnia _29. stycznia_ 1898.

Zembrzyce. School certificate, 1898 (Polish)

4. Reports and complaints concerning burial societies, 1822–50.
(AGAD, Warszawa, CWW)
5. Copies of inscriptions on tombstones and synagogues [H, P, R], 1910.
(RGIA, St. Peterburg, Departament dukhovnykh del...)

ŚNIADOWO (pow. Łomża, woj. białostockie) 1807–1915
Microfilms:
1. Identity documents and letters of protection, 1807, 1809; a complaint by a Jew against illegal actions of the *wójt* [R], 1907–08; a file on the arrest and expulsion to the Irkutsk *guberniia* of Jews suspected of espionage [R], 1915.
(AP Białystok, Rząd Gubernialny, Łomża)
2. Reports and correspondence concerning the separation of the communities: Śniadowo, Łomża and Nowogród, 1810–12.
(AGAD, Warszawa, CWW)
3. Birth, marriage and death records (fragmentary), 1827–64.
(AP Łomża)

ŚNIATYN (woj. stanisławowskie) 1581–1938
Microfilms:
1. Charters granted to Jews by King Stefan Batory [L], 1581, 1588; *arenda* agreement for collecting municipal taxes, 1780; community voting lists [G], 1818; voters' list for parliamentary elections, 1870; a list of Jewish house owners [G], 19th cent.
(AP Kraków, Teki Schneidra)
2. Excerps from Armenian files in Stanisławów concerning Jewish commerce, loans and *arenda,* 1703–09.
(NBANU, L'viv, Arch. Ossolińskich)
3. Reports on teaching Jewish religion in elementary schools [G, P], 1882–89; inspection reports of Baron Hirsch Foundation (JCA) schools [G, P], 1896–1904.
(TsDIAU, L'viv, Krajowa Rada Szkolna)
4. Records on ratifying statutes of the *Beis Abraham, Talmud Tora, Mizrachi* and *Merkaz Ruchani* societies, 1893, 1920–30; statutes, minutes and correspondence about Zionist organizations, 1921–30; reports concerning *chadorim* [G, P], 1921–35; records of the *Yad Charutzim* society*,* 1921–38; statistical data concerning the inhabitants, 1923–24; records concerning civil registry offices, 1923–24; records on the *starosta*'s prohibition to hold conferences in Hebrew, 1923–25; reports and correspondence concerning statutes and registration of charitable societies, 1923–35; records on Jewish associations, 1924–39; reports by the district police about activities of Jewish associations and political parties, 1925–26; a report on collecting money for Jews in Palestine, 1926; correspondence about supervision of Jewish communities and complaints against the community council, 1926–35; reports about public meetings organized by Jewish parties and associations, 1926–28; report about activities of *Hashomer Hatzair, Hechalutz,* and other youth movements, 1929–37; records of: *Żydowskie Koło Akademickie,* 1930, *Żydowska Rada Sieroca i Ochrona Młodzieży,* 1930, *Gmilas Chesed,* 1930–31, *Towarzystwo Opieki nad Halucami i Emigrantami 'Ezra',* 1930–35, *Gordonia,* 1930–36, *HaTzofim Brit Trumpeldor,* 1930–37 and *Achva,* 1930–37; records of the second general census, reports containing data on communities, nationalities, religions, businesses, political parties and relationships between national minorities, 1931; reports and correspondence concerning activities of the Jewish community. [P, Y], 1931–35; records of Jewish sport associations, 1931–38; files about: *Ogólno-Żydowska Partia Pracy (OŻPP),* 1932–33, *Hatchiya,* 1932–38, *Brit*

Trumpeldor, 1933, *Histadrut Hanoar Haivri* and T*zofe*, 1933, *Tarbut*, 1934–38, *Hitachdut Poalei Zion*, 1935, *Związek Opieki nad Sierotami i Młodzieżą Żydowską* and WIZO, 1937–38.
(DAIFO, Ivano-Frankivs'k, UW, Stanisławów)
5. Records concerning ritual slaughter, 1894–97; correspondence with the Ministry of Interior regarding various requests and communal taxes [G, P], 1895; correspondence about societies supporting sick children, students and Tora study, 1908.
(TsDIAU, L'viv, Namiestnictwo Galicyjskie)
6.Correspondence with the government about permission for Jews deported from Śniatyn to return home, including a list of names [R], 1916.
(DAIFO, Ivano-Frankivs'k, Nachal'nik Sniatinskogo uezda)
7. Monthly reports by the district police about activities of Jewish parties and associations, 1930–32, 1935–36; files on Ch. Trepper and M. Czerner–Rosenbaum, members of *OŻPP*, 1932–33; a monograph on the district, 1935; reports and correspondence concerning anti-Jewish actions by Ukrainian nationalists, 1936–37.
(DAIFO, Ivano-Frankivs'k, Komenda Wojewódzka PP, Stanisławów)
8. Report concerning activities of the *Bund* and *OŻPP*, including list of OŻPP board members, 1933; reports about activities of Revisionist Zionists, *Poalei Zion Lewica, Hitachdut Poalei Zion, Hechalutz, Hakoach* and *Yad Charutzim*, 1935.
(DAIFO, Ivano-Frankivs'k, Posterunek Policji Państwowej, Śniatyn)
9. Birth registry index, 1937; reports and correspondence concerning the community budget, 1938.
(DAIFO, Ivano-Frankivs'k, Starostwo Powiatowe, Śniatyn)

ŚNIATYN, surroundings, 1922–38
Microfilms:
A register of associations [P, U], 1922–23; correspondence with district authorities about activities of the *Bund*, 1923; circulars by the authorities in Stanisławów and reports about elections and inspections of Jewish communities, 1928–36; a statistical description of the district, 1935; information regarding distribution of anti-Jewish brochures, 1936; statistics concerning the population, 1938.
(DAIFO, Ivano-Frankivs'k, UW, Stanisławów)

ŚREM (woj. poznańskie) 1609–1902
Originals:
Statutes of the burial society [H], 1808–52, 1872–73; files on the payment of taxes by Jews [G], 1835–48; financial records of the community [G], 1843–71; litigation between the community and a neighbouring parish [G], 1843–1900; *pinkas* of the study house [H], 1853–95; minutes of community meetings [G], 1854–1902; application for the position of rabbi [G], 1877.
Microfilms:
Confirmation by King Zygmunt III of a municipal order confiscating all income from the sale of houses to Jews [L], 1609.
(AP Poznań, Akta miast,woj. poznańskie)

ŚRODA (woj. poznańskie) 1654–1885
Originals:
Records of the burial society [G], 1816–70; financial records of the community [G], 1833–85; the renovation of the synagogue [G], 1833–62; a file on Jewish education [G], 1834–35; the appointment of a cantor and a *shochet* [G], 1835–45; a register of community correspondence [G], 1837–44; correspondence

with local and national authorities [G], 1837–80; a file on the distribution of *matzot* for Passover time [G], 1839–52; assistance for the poor [G], 1840–54; files on the payment of taxes [G], 1846–82.
Microfilms:
1. A resolution of the *sejmik* imposing a tax on a Christian and on Jewish *arendars* for the redeeming of captives, 1654–55.
(AP Poznań, Księgi Grodzkie Kaliskie)
2. The register of a community tax [G], 1830–35.
(ŻIH, Warszawa, Prow. Poznań)
3. Minutes of community board meetings [G], 1839–54.
(Centrum Judaicum, Berlin)

ŚWIERCZYŃSKO (pow. Piotrków, woj. łódzkie) 1829–1832
Microfilms:
Files on taxes imposed on the *kahal* for educational purposes, 1829–32.
(AGAD, Warszawa, KRzPiS)

ŚWIERZE (pow. Chełm, woj. lubelskie) 1783–1870
Microfilms:
1. Correspondence on payments from the community to the National Education Commission, 1783–86.
(AP Lublin, Księgi Grodzkie Chełmskie)
2. A file on the release of a local rabbi from rabbinical duties [R], 1869–70.
(AP Lublin, Rząd Gubernialny, Lublin)

ŚWIERŻEŃ (pow. Stołpce, woj. nowogrodzkie) 1722–1747
Microfilms:
An *uniwersał* by Princess Anna Radziwiłł granted to Christians and Jews from German lands living in the town, 1722; copies of economic and legal regulations by M. K. Radziwiłł and *arenda* contracts with Jews, 1746–47.
(AGAD, Warszawa, Arch. Radziwiłłów)

ŚWIĘCIANY (woj. wileńskie) 1886–1904
Microfilms:
1. Report about a *Talmud Tora* [R], 1886.
(RGIA, St. Petersburg, OPE)
2. Reports about secret Jewish organizations, including lists of suspects and arrested persons [R], 1900–04.
(GARF, Moscow, Departament politsii…)

TARCZYN (pow. Grójec, woj. warszawskie) 1910
Microfilms:
Copies of inscriptions on tombstones and synagogues [H, P, R], 1910.
(RGIA, St. Petersburg, Departament dukhovnykh del…)

TARŁÓW (pow. Iłża, woj. kieleckie) 1747–1856
Microfilms:
1. Court case concerning Jews [L], 1747.
(AP Kraków, Arch. Sanguszków, teki tzw. arabskie)
2. Reports and correspondence about the rabbinate, conflicts between rabbis and communities and lists of rabbis, 1853–56.

(AGAD, Warszawa, CWW)

TARNOBRZEG (woj. lwowskie) 1695–1939
Microfilms:
1. Extracts from municipal records concerning Jews [L, P], 1695–1830.
(AP Kraków, IT)
2. Reports and correspondence concerning *chadorim* and Jewish private schools [G, P], 1878–81.
(TsDIAU, L'viv, Krajowa Rada Szkolna)
3. Correspondence about community elections and statutes, 1895–96; correspondence about the *Zion Hametzuyenet* association, including statutes, 1904.
(TsDIAU, L'viv, Namiestnictwo Galicyjskie)
4. Correspondence about celebrations honoring the inauguration of the Hebrew University, 1924–25; correspondence concerning the *Kultur Liga*, 1926; reports and correspondence concerning community elections, including lists of council members, their ages, professions and political affiliations, 1928–38; a list of Zionist Organization members in Tarnobrzeg, 1931; reports and correspondence concerning the community budget; files on termination of a contract between Rabbi A. Horowitz and the Jewish community, 1935–39; reports containing lists of council members, rabbis and *dayanim* of the community, 1937–39; correspondence about the *Yad Charutzim* association, 1938.
(DALO, L'viv, UW, Lwów)
5. Correspondence about registration of *Mizrachi* and *Tzeirei Mizrachi*, including statutes and lists of members, 1931–36.
(DALO, L'viv, Magistrat, Lwów)

TARNOBRZEG, surroundings, 18th cent.–1930
Microfilms:
1. Various contracts and other records concerning *arendas,* a list of Jewish tax payers; a grant of permission for Jews to establish a craft guild, a bill of sale of a plot of land to a Jew. 18th–19th cent.
(AP Kraków, Arch. Dzikowskie Tarnowskich)
2. Lists of members of local town council, their nationalities and political affiliations, 1930.
(DALO, L'viv, UW, Lwów)

TARNOGRÓD (pow. Biłgoraj, woj. lubelskie) 1628–1837
Microfilms:
1. Private agreements, accounts, contracts and other documents concerning estates and properties of the Sieniawski and Czartoryski families, 1628–1759.
(Bibl. Czartoryskich, Kraków)
2. Records of the community's debts to the Church in Zamość [H, L, P], 1649–1826.
(AP Lublin, Kolegiata w Zamościu)
3. Debts of the Jewish community to a monastery in Biłgoraj [G, H, P], 1667, 1728, 1783.
(TsDIAU, L'viv, Kolektsiia dokumentiv…)
4. A statistical description of the town, 1819–59.
(AP Lublin, Rząd Gubernialny, Lublin)
5. Correspondence with the authorities about *arenda* of taverns and displacement of Jews from one place to another, 1834–37.
(TsDIAU, L'viv, Namiestnictwo Galicyjskie)

TARNOPOL (woj. tarnopolskie) 1686–1939
Microfilms:
1. Charters, requests, *supliki*, *arenda* contracts, tax registers [G, H, L, P, Y], 1686–1805.
(AP Lublin, Zb. Czołowskiego)
2. Correspondence with the provincial authorities about the Jewish school, and about government permission for Jews to leave the country, including lists of people obligated to return and pay their debts [G], 1817–38; tables of taxes [G], 1842–59; correspondence on supporting the Jewish school, including a history of it [G, P], 1876–77; correspondence about the *Zion* society, including statutes [G, P], 1894; files on ritual slaughter 1894–97; community elections, 1894; correspondence with the Ministry of Religion about education requirements for rabbinical candidates, and about vacant rabbinical positions [G, Hung., P], 1896; correspondence about the *Bursa Izraelicka* society, including statutes, 1897; correspondence with *Ahavas Zion* about emigration to Palestine [G, P], 1898; correspondence about the *Kimcha Depischa* society, including statutes [G, P], 1898–1914.
(TsDIAU, L'viv, Namiestnictwo Galicyjskie)
3. Minutes and inventories regarding the sale of Jewish property for debts, 1819, 1842.
(TsDIAU, L'viv, Kolektsiia dokumentiv…)
4. Reports from inspections of Jewish schools, 1872–73.
(TsDIAU, L'viv, Krajowa Rada Szkolna)
5. Correspondence and reports concerning financial matters of the main Jewish schools for boys and girls in Tarnopol, including lists of teachers [G, P], 1873–92; correspondence of a Jewish school in the Mikulinieckie suburb about financial aid for poor students, listed in the files, 1877–93; correspondence and reports about financing the construction of a new hospital, including a register of the Jewish businesses which financed the building, 1892–96; instructions, reports and correspondence about the closing of *chadorim* for sanitary reasons, 1893–94; correspondence between the district authorities and the community about the Jewish cemetery, including a plan of it and a list of synagogues, 1906–17, 1931–35; correspondence concerning subvention for the Jewish sports club *Yehuda*, 1913–14; reports, statutes and correspondence on the financial and economic activity of the Jewish hospital, including lists of employees, 1929–39; correspondence with the authorities about opening courses for nurses, 1937.
(DATO, Ternopil', Gmina Żydowska, Tarnopol)
6. Documents on the election of a rabbi [G, P], 1910–13; budget report of a fund for Jewish schools in Lwów, Brody and Tarnopol, 1915–18.
(TsDIAU, L'viv, Ministerium fuer Kultus und Unterricht, Wien)
7. Documents of the *Żydowski Komitet Obywatelski*, 1919–20.
(DALO, L'viv, Magistrat, Lwów)
8. Instructions regarding supervision of the activities of *Nasze Dzieci*, 1921; a register of staff, children and youth under the care of Jewish, Polish and Ukrainian associations, 1923; authorization to raise funds for Jewish educational and cultural associations, 1925–39; correspondence with the district police about boycott of Jewish commerce by Ukrainians, 1926; authorization by the district authorities for activities of the Jewish associations: *Tzdaka Vachesed*, *Jezierna Klaus Haszow Hatzadik*, *Mitet* and *Chevra Kadisha*, 1929; register of Jewish schools, 1929; decrees by the district authorities suspending the activity of *Yad Charutzim* and *Osei Chesed*, 1931; reports about elections of delegates to the 18th Zionist Congress [P, Y], 1933; membership lists of *Aliyat Hashachar*, *Agudas Achim*, *Bikur Cholim*, *Hechalutz – Pionier*, *Żydowski Robotniczy Klub Sportowy 'Hapoel'*, *Masada*, *Toszbit*, work group *Busleja Gordonia*, 1934; material about the liquidation of *Towarzystwo Opieki nad Sierotami Żydowskimi*, 1934; correspondence with the district authorities about the registration of *Brit Yehuda*, *Bikur Cholim–Chesed*, *Haoved*, *Hanoar Haivri*,

Hashomer Hatzair and *Gush Avoda*, including board and membership lists, 1935; a register of Jewish, Polish and Ukrainian associations and political organizations, 1938; reports about activities and members of the following societies: *Związek Syjonistów, Związek Żydowski Urzędników Prywatnych, Hashachar Haovdim*, the carpenters' association- *'Zjednoczenie', Żydowski Robotniczy Klub Sportowy, Brit Hechayal, Agudas Achim, Bikur Cholim*, 1939.

(DATO, Ternopil', Komisariat Policji Państwowej, Tarnopol)

9. Answers to questionnaires concerning Jews, 1922.

(NBANU, L'viv, Zb. Czołowskiego)

10. A list of participants in a summer camp for Jewish youth, 1933.

(DATO, Ternopil', Komenda Powiatowa PP, Trembowla)

11. Report about activities of *Brit Trumpeldor*, 1933.

(DAIFO, Ivano-Frankivs'k, UW, Stanisławów)

TARNOPOL, surroundings, 1785–1938
Microfilms:

1. Register of *chadorim*, 1878; reports concerning a program for teaching Jewish religion in elementary schools, 1895–97; a project to set up Jewish schools by the Baron Hirsch Foundation (JCA), 1902.

(TsDIAU, L'viv, Krajowa Rada Szkolna)

2. Statistical and financial reports of the Jewish Committee for Aid to War Victims concerning aid for war victims, including lists of victims [R], 1916–17.

(DATO, Ternopil', Komitet pomoshchi...)

3. Instructions by the regional police headquarter in Lwów concerning forced displacement from the *województwo*, of Jewish immigrants from Russia, 1921.

(DATO, Ternopil', Komenda Powiatowa PP, Trembowla)

4. List of communities and their budgets, 1922, 1935; correspondence about statutes of Jewish communities, 1922–24.

(DALO, L'viv, UW, Lwów)

5. A letter by the authorities about inspecting the missionary activities of the London Society for Promotion of Christianity among Jews, 1924.

(DATO, Ternopil', Komenda Powiatowa PP, Tarnopol)

6. A report about the political and criminal situation in the district, 1933; correspondence with police headquarters about distribution of anti-Jewish leaflets, 1936–37; register of Jewish, Polish and Ukrainian associations and political organizations, 1938.

(DATO, Ternopil', Komisariat Policji Państwowej, Tarnopol)

TARNORUDA (pow. Skałat, woj. tarnopolskie) 1714–1766
Microfilms:

1. Correspondence with Prince A. Czartoryski, accounts and *arenda* contracts, 1714–45; orders of payment, accounts, contracts and reports concerning estates of the Sieniawski family, 1720–28; reports and accounts of the Tarnoruda *klucz*, 1742.

(Bibl. Czartoryskich, Kraków)

2. *Lustarcja* of the poll tax on Czartoryski estates, 1766.

(AGAD, Warszawa, Arch. Potockich w Łańcucie)

TARNÓW (woj. krakowskie) 1639–1920
Originals:

An account of a blood libel [H], 1839; statutes and report of the society of Tarnów Jews in Vienna [G], 1909.

Microfilms:

1. A document concerning a debt to a Jewish leaseholder, 1639; a license for Jews to buy houses from Christians, 1736; records of various *arendas*, 1738, 1744; a letter by Gdal Ickowicz to the rabbi of Tarnów [L, P], 1742; records of the rabbinical and the Commissar's courts, 1750, 1752; *supliki* by the *kahal* concerning *propinacja* and *arenda* contracts, 1752, 1759; various documents regarding *propinacja*, 1771–85; a complaint against the rabbi, 18th cent.

(AP Kraków, Teki sanguszkowskie tzw. rzymskie)

2. Financial documents of the community (fragmentary) [G, H, P], 1738–86.

(NBANU, L'viv, Zb. Goldsteina)

3. The will of an *arendar*, 1760, 1767; a complaint against a Jew. 1767.

(AP Kraków, IT)

4. Documents concerning debts of the Jewish community [H, L, P], 1772.

(TsDIAU, L'viv, Kolektsiia dokumentiv...)

5. Reports about Jewish schools [G], 1788; correspondence with the regional authorities about *arendas*, houses and land ownership [G], 1819–22; correspondence about community elections, and the rabbinate, including complaints about the elections [G], 1819–23; correspondence about *propinacja* and taxes, statistical tables and reports about activities of *chasidim* [G], 1820–41; correspondence about marriage authorizations [G], 1823–24; tax tables [G], 1842–59; correspondence about conducting religious celebrations [G], 1845; correspondence about the *Tempelverein* society [G, P], 1874–1912; statutes of the *Menachem Avelim* society [G, P], 1891–1909; correspondence with the district authorities about citation of citizenship in the civil register, 1891–92; files on *shechita*, 1894–97; correspondence with the Ministry of Interior and the Ministry of Religion about community matters [G, P], 1895; correspondence about vacant rabbinical positions [G, Hung., P], 1896; correspondence regarding various societies for aid to school children and students [G, P], 1904–06.

(TsDIAU, L'viv, Namiestnictwo Galicyjskie)

6. Birth and death records [G], 1808–55.

(AP Kraków)

7. Instructions, reports and correspondence on the closing of *chadorim* [G, P], 1868–74; reports about teaching Jewish religion in elementary schools [G, P], 1882–89; statutes of *Izraelicko–Polska Szkoła Ludowa* w Tarnowie, 1890–91; reports about inspections of Baron Hirsch Foundation (JCA) schools, 1896–97; reports and lists of students in the commercial school [G, P], 1915–20.

(TsDIAU, L'viv, Krajowa Rada Szkolna)

TARNÓW, surroundings, 1738–85.

Microfilms:

1. Records of various *arendas*, 1738–85.

(AP Kraków, IT)

2. *Arenda* contracts for inns and flour mills, second half of 18th cent.

(AP Kraków, Arch. Sanguszków)

TARTAKÓW (pow. Sokal, woj. lwowskie) 1927–1936

Microfilms:

1. Correspondence with the district authorities about various community matters and the statutes, budget, community matters and lists of community tax payers, 1927–36.

(DALO, L'viv, UW, Lwów)
2. Authorization by the district authorities to collect money for the Polish–Galician Jewish community in Palestine, including a list of donors, 1928–30.
(DALO, L'viv, UW, Lwów)
3. Correspondence concerning the registration of *Machzikei Hadas*, 1932.
(DALO, L'viv, Magistrat, Lwów)

TATARÓW (pow. Nadwórna, woj. stanisławowskie) 1934–1936
Microfilms:
A file on an exam in the Polish language taken by Rabbi H. M. Fischer, 1934–35; material about elections of a rabbi and *dayanim*, 1935–36.
(DAIFO, Ivano-Frankivs'k, UW, Stanisławów)

TEKUCZA (pow. Kołomyja, woj. stanisławowskie) 1920
Microfilms:
Instructions, circulars and correspondence concerning appeals to the Ukrainian and Jewish populations in Eastern Galicia to contribute to the military effort, including lists of persons chosen for the work, 1920.
(DAIFO, Ivano-Frankivs'k, Starostwo Powiatowe, Peczeniżyn)

TELECHANY (pow. Iwacewicze, woj. poleskie) 1855–92
Photocopies:
A file on an unauthorized Jewish school [R], 1855–92.
(NIAB, Minsk, Minsky okruzhnoy sud)

TERESPOL (pow. Biała, woj. lubelskie) 1818–1860
Microfilms:
Material concerning synagogues, 1818–60; reports and correspondence of government offices about rabbis and conflicts between them and the communities, including lists of rabbis, 1853–56.
(AGAD, Warszawa, CWW)

TĘCZYN (pow. Chrzanów, woj. krakowskie) 1652–1766
Microfilms:
1. Decrees, requests, complaints and excerpts from municipal books concerning estates of the Sieniawski and Czartoryski families [H, L, P], 1652–1766.
(Bibl. Czartoryskich, Kraków)
2. Inventory of inhabitants, properties and real estate in the *klucz*, 1705, 1706–12.
(AP Kraków, Arch. Krzeszowickie Potockich)

TŁUMACZ (woj. stanisławowskie) 1846–1949
Microfilms:
1. Files concerning ratification of Jewish community statutes, 1846–96; propaganda urging Jewish youth to enlist in the military [G, P], 1870; correspondence with the Ministry of Religion about changes in the community statues [G, P], 1875–77.
(TsDIAU, L'viv, Namiestnictwo Galicyjskie)
2. Material about ratifying the statutes of *Agudas Yisroel, Poalei Tzedek* and *Safa Brura*, 1893, 1920–30; reports concerning the activities of *Poalei Zion, Hashomer Hatzair, Histadrut Hanoar Haivri, Tzofe, Hatzofim Brit Trumpeldor* and other Jewish youth movements [P, U], 1920–37; records concerning *Gmilus Chasodim*, 1922–31; statistical data regarding Jewish inhabitants, 1923–24, reports and correspondence

concerning statutes and registration of Jewish charity societies for aid to children and youth, 1923–28; reports by the district police about the activities of Jewish political parties, 1925–26; reports about meetings organized by *Poalei Zion*, the *Bund* and other Jewish associations and political parties, 1926–28; correspondence about the Jewish community: ratification of the budget, changes in the statutes, taxes on kosher meat, elections, allegations of corruption etc., 1926–36; report about activities of the Revisionist Zionists, 1927; correspondence with the district authorities about liquidation of the Jewish library, 1928– 35; records of: *Żydowska Rada Sieroca i Ochrona Mlodziezy*, 1930, *Kadima*, 1930, *Linas Hatzedek*, 1930– 37 and other Jewish cultural, sports and Zionist associations [P, Y], 1930–37; records of the second general census, 1931; circulars, reports and statutes of OŻPP, 1932–33; a report about elections of delegates to the 18th Zionist Congress [P, Y], 1933; protests against British policy in Palestine, 1934; decrees, reports and correspondence regarding activities of *Hitachdut Poalei Zion*, 1935; records of *Yad Charutzim*, 1936; statistical data concerning the population, 1938.
(DAIFO, Ivano-Frankivs'k, UW, Stanisławów)
3. Answers to a questionnaire on Jews, 1922.
(NBANU, L'viv, Zb. Czołowskiego)
4. Monthly reports by district police headquarters about the activities of Jewish associations and political parties, 1930–32.
(DAIFO, Ivano-Frankivs'k, Komenda Powiatowa PP, Tłumacz)
5. Budget of the community and a list of community taxpayers, 1932–36.
(DAIFO, Ivano-Frankivs'k, Gmina Żydowska, Tłumacz)
6. Investigation files of irregularities during community elections, and alleged misappropriation of community funds by the head of the council, 1933–35.
(DAIFO, Ivano-Frankivs'k, Prokuratura Sądu Okregowego, Stanisławów)
7. Circulars, reports and correspondence about legalizing *chadorim* and other Jewish religious and secular schools, including a list of *chadorim* and their owners, 1934–36.
(DAIFO, Ivano-Frankivs'k, Inspektorat Szkolny, Stanisławów)
8. Reports by district police headquarters concerning activities of Zionist associations, 1935–36.
(DAIFO, Ivano-Frankivs'k, Komenda Wojewódzka PP, Stanisławów)
9. A report on prayer houses, synagogues and a synagogue being used as a warehouse [R], 1949.
(DAIFO, Ivano-Frankivs'k, Upolnomochennyi Soveta…)

TŁUMACZ, surroundings, 1923–1936
Microfilms:
1. Correspondence with the district authorities about activities of the *Bund* in the district, 1923; a monograph and a statistical description of the district, 1934–35; information concerning the distribution of antisemitic brochures, 1936.
(DAIFO, Ivano-Frankivs'k, UW, Stanisławów)
2. Reports concerning children studying in public schools, 1926–28.
(DAIFO, Ivano-Frankivs'k, Powiatowa Rada Szkolna, Tłumacz)
3. A monograph dealing with political and social aspects, 1935.
(DAIFO, Ivano-Frankivs'k, Komenda Wojewódzka PP, Stanisławów)

TŁUMACZYK (pow. Kołomyja, woj. stanisławowskie) 1921–1936
Microfilms:
1. Statutes, minutes and correspondence concerning Jewish associations, 1921–30; records of the *Hatikva,* educational association, 1932–36.

(DAIFO, Ivano-Frankivs'k, UW, Stanisławów)

2. Records on activities of the *Hatikva* association, including statutes and a list of members, 1929–35.

(DAIFO, Ivano-Frankivs'k, Starostwo Powiatowe, Kołomyja)

TŁUSTE (pow. Zaleszczyki, woj. tarnopolskie) 1811–1904

Original:

An appeal for financial aid to Jewish victims of a cholera epidemic [G], 1894.

Microfilms:

1. Copy of a charter for Jews by the owner of the town, 1811.

(NBANU, L'viv, Zb. Baworowskich)

2. Instructions concerning taxes paid by inn keepers, 1894.

(NBANU, L'viv, Zb. Goldsteina)

3. Correspondence with the district authorities regarding *chadorim* in the area, including a list of *melamdim*, 1874–1908; reports and correspondence on the reorganization of the Jewish community and its statutes [G, P], 1890–98.

(TsDIAU, L'viv, Namiestnictwo Galicyjskie)

4. Reports of inspections of the Baron Hirsch Foundation (JCA) schools, including personal documents of teachers [G, P], 1896–1904.

(TsDIAU, L'viv, Krajowa Rada Szkolna)

TOMASZÓW LUBELSKI (woj. lubelskie) 1647–1861

Microfilms:

1. Records of the community's debts to the church in Zamość, 1647–1796.

(AP Lublin, Kolegiata w Zamościu)

2. A letter by J. Branicki (who was attacked by the Jews of the town) to Prince Zamoyski, 1716.

(AGAD, Warszawa, Arch. Zamoyskich)

3. Reports and correspondence about: confirming elections of rabbis, fee exemptions and exams of the Rabbinical Seminary in Warsaw, lists of rabbis and *dayanim*, relations between rabbis and communities, 1823–56.

(AGAD, Warszawa, CWW)

4. Statistical description, 1860–61.

(AP Lublin, Rząd Gubernialny, Lublin)

TOMASZÓW MAZOWIECKI (pow. Brzeziny, woj. łódzkie) 1825–1931

Original:

A proclamation concerning community elections [Y], 1931.

Microfilms:

1. Records concerning the community, 1825–66.

(AP Łódź, Anterioria Rządu Gubernialnego, Piotrków)

2. Records concerning imported wool, 1826; records of taxes paid by Jews [P, R], 1826–62; files on Jewish residence rights, 1828–59; files on Hebrew books, 1828–62; a register of correspondence with the magistrate, 1828–34; 1863; community accounts [P, R], 1829–1914; files on the conversion of Jews and activities of the London Missionary Society [R], 1833–98; authorization given to Jews to work during Christian festivals, 1835; records concerning the conscription of Jews (lists, exemptions, fines for evasion etc.) [P, R], 1840–1905; files on the civil registration of Jews [P, R], 1842–67, 1871–72, 1886–89; register of merchandise taxed by the authorities, 1845; a register of home owners proprietors, 1849–52; files on various legal proceedings, 1856–61; illegal *shechita*, 1857; accounts of the magistrate [P, R], 1860–64,

1897; donations for the Jewish hospital, 1861; a list of Jews for recruitment purpose, 1862–66; Jewish schools and *chadorim* [R], 1871–1912; the administration of the *mikve* and prayer–houses [R], 1871–1913; files about the legislation on Jewish dress and its enforcement [R], 1871–98; hospitalization expenses [R], 1875–76; requests by merchants for various business licenses [R], 1880, 1887; files on the appointments of rabbis and other community officials [R], 1882–1902; files on Jewish property matters [R], 1883–84, 1889; records of the burial society [R], 1886–87; the arrest of two Jews [R], 1887; decoration of Jewish merchants with silver medals [R], 1887; information about foreign Jews [R], 1887–90; an assault on the rabbis' house [R], 1889; records on temporary Jewish residents in the town, dealing with commerce and businesses [R], 1887–90; records concerning emigration of Jews from Russian territories with the aid of a colonization society [R], 1892; files on charitable activities of the community [R], 1892–94; community board [R], 1894–95; donation of a plot for construction of a Jewish school, 1897; a request to include the Jews of Strażyce in the community of Tomaszòw [R], 1899; community elections [R], 1900–12; donation of a plot to the Jewish community [R], 1906;
(AP Łódź, Magistrat, Tomaszów)
3. Files on Jewish schools and their finances [R], 1868–1914.
(AP Łódź, Dyrekcja Szkolna, Łódź)
4. Records of houses built by Jews without authorization [R], 1876–82; a file on the conversion of a Jew to Christianity [R], 1877; files concerning Jewish businesses [R], 1889; ratification of community accounts and elections [R], 1893–1916; records on the sale of a plot of land by the community [R], 1900–01; request by a Jew to sell his land to his son [R], 1901; the appointment of a religious official [R], 1902–04; permission to open a provident fund '*Svad'ba*' (Wedding) [R], 1903–06; files concerning the Jewish cemetery [R], 1904–07; a request to open a kerosene store [R], 1909.
(AP Łódź, Rząd Gubernialny, WA, Piotrków)
5. Fines for evading conscription,1890–1910 [R]; a request to open a paper factory [R], 1896; correspondence and litigation between the municipality and various Jews [R], 1901–10.
(AP Łódź, Rząd Gubernialny, WP, Piotrków)
6. Request to open a Jewish ward in the hospital [R], 1896–1909; requests to register Jewish charity societies [R], 1903, 1909; file on registration of the Jewish cultural society, *Hazamir* [R], 1908–11.
(AP Łódź, Rząd Gubernialny, KP, Piotrków)
7. Police investigations of Jews suspected of political offences [R], 1905–07.
(AP Łódź, GZŻ, Piotrków)
8. An order to exile a Jew [R], 1907.
(AP Łódź, Kancelaria Gubernatora Kaliskiego)

TOPORÓW (pow. Radziechów, woj. tarnopolskie) 1699–1912
Microfilms:
1. Inventories, tax registers, orders of payments and accounts, 1699–1720.
(Bibl. Czartoryskich, Kraków)
2. Correspondence between the community and the district authorities about *chadorim*, including a list of *melamdim* [G, P], 1877–1908; a report about the Jewish community [G, P], 1890; statutes of the *Tikvat Zion* society [G, P], 1907–12.
(TsDIAU, L'viv, Namiestnictwo Galicyjskie)

TORCZYN (pow. Łuck, woj. wołyńskie) 1834–1895
Microfilms:
1. Copies of documents about *tzadikim* in various towns [R], 1834–76.

(TsDIAU, Kyiv, Dokumenty, sobrannye)

2. File about support of rabbis with the *korobka* tax [R], 1877–81; reports and requests concerning Jewish schools, salaries for rabbis, community accounts and lists of rabbis in the Volhynia and Podolia *guberniias* [R], 1881–95.

(RGIA, St. Petersburg, Departament dukhovnykh del...)

TORUŃ (woj. pomorskie) 1566–1939
Originals:

A letter empowering a Jew to represent the community before the Prussian authorities [G], 1799; community statutes [G], 1822–89; petitions of the community [G], 1850–94; official instructions concerning the payment of community taxes [G], 1852–92; minutes and resolutions of community meetings [G], 1857–95; records of the Central Committee for the Support of Russian Jews and Russian Jewish Emigration [G], 1882–91.

Microfilms:

1. A *lustracja* of the area, 1566.

(AGAD, Warszawa, ASK)

2. Files concerning Toruń, 1862–1939.

(AIU, Paris, Comités locaux et comunautés)

TOUSTE (pow. Skałat, woj. tarnopolskie) 1663–1894
Originals:

An appeal to help Jews suffering from cholera [G], 1894.

Microfilms:

Circular letters, accounts and decrees by M. Sapieha, St. Siemieński, M. and A. Sieniawski and A. Czartoryski concerning their estates and inhabitants, 1663–1765.

(Bibl. Czartoryskich, Kraków)

TRABY (pow. Wołożyn, woj. nowogródzkie)
Original:

Birth certificate [H], 1876.

TREMBOWLA (woj. tarnopolskie) 1576–1933
Microfilms:

1. Confirmation by King Stefan Batory of an agreement between the *starosta* and a Jewish *arendar* of tolls and mills, 1576; confirmation by him of the furriers' guild statutes, forbidding Jewish participation, 1578; confirmation by King Stanisław August Poniatowski of the charter granted to Jews [L], 1765.

(AGAD, Warszawa, Księgi Kanclerskie)

2. Extracts from official records concerning Jews, 1626, 1726–29; a *lustracja* of the *starostwo*, 1661–64; an inventory of the *starostwo* and its inhabitants, 1778.

(AP Wrocław, Ossolineum)

3. Receipts issued by the *kahal* to the Carmelite monastery [L, P], 1735–83.

(TsDIAU, L'viv, Kolektsiia dokumentiv pro katolyts'ki monastyri...)

4. Inventory of the *starostwo* of Trembowla, 1762.

(TsDIAU, Kyiv, Arch. Potockich z Tulczyna)

5. Correspondence with the provincial authorities concerning authorization of marriages [G], 1809–19; tax tables [G], 1842–59; correspondence about the *Zion* and *Postęp* societies and statutes [G, P], 1895.

(TsDIAU, L'viv, Namiestnictwo Galicyjskie)

6. A report about activities of political parties and associations in the district, 1925; requests by police authorities for reports about Zionist organizations, 1926; reports about social and economical life in the district, 1927; circulars and reports about activities of OŻPP; 1932–33.
(DATO, Ternopil', Komenda Powiatowa PP, Trembowla)

TROKI (pow. Wilno–Troki, woj. wileńskie) 1839–1908
Photocopies:
Rights for Karaites to have a separate community and for Jews to sojourn in Troki during the fairs [R], 1611, 1714, 1720, 1761.
(RGIA, St. Petersburg, Departament dukhovnykh del...)
Microfilms:
A file regarding monetary claims by priests from the Benedictine monastery against a Jewish *arendar* [R], 1839; statistical data concerning Karaite prayer houses and religious functionaries [R], 1908.
(RGIA, St. Petersburg, Rimsko-katolicheskaia kollegiia...)

TROKI, surroundings, 1807
Microfilms:
Complaints by a Jew against Mariawitki nuns from Wilno for attempting to convert his son by force [R], 1807.
(RGIA, St. Petersburg, Rimsko-katolicheskaia kollegiia...)

TRUSKOLASY (pow. Częstochowa, woj. kieleckie) 1901
Microfilms:
Fines for evading conscription [R], 1901.
(AP Łódź, Rząd Gubernialny, WP, Piotrków)

TRYŃCZA (pow. Przeworsk, woj. lwowskie) 18th cent.
Microfilms:
Complaint against a Jew, 18th cent.
(TsDIAU, Kyiv, Arch. Lubomirskich)

TRZCINIEC (pow. Lubartów, woj. lubelskie) 1936
Microfilms:
Monographs containing demographic and economic data, 1936.
(AP Wrocław, Ossolineum, WKNZNP, Lwów)

TRZEMESZNO (pow. Mogilno, woj. poznańskie)
Originals:
Text of a speech by Rabbi J.J. Abraham on June 18, 1871, celebrating the Prussian victory [G], 1871; records and statutes of burial societies and care for the sick [G], 1873; copy of a *memorbuch* of the community, burnt in 1885 [G], 1885.

TUCHLA (pow. Stryj, woj. stanisławowskie) 1930–1937
Microfilms:
1. Records of the *Hitachdut* society, 1930.
(DAIFO, Ivano-Frankivs'k, UW, Stanisławów)
2. Material concerning antisemitic actions by Ukrainian nationalists, 1936–37;
(DAIFO, Ivano-Frankivs'k, Komenda Wojewódzka PP, Stanisławów)

TUCHOLKA (pow. Stryj, woj. stanisławowskie) 1925–1939
Microfilms:
Statutes, minutes and correspondence about Jewish associations, 1925–39.
(DAIFO, Ivano-Frankivs'k, UW, Stanisławów)

TUCZYN (pow. Równe, woj. wołyńskie) 1652–1934
Microfilms:
1. Requests, complaints, decrees and excerpts from municipal books regarding estates of the Sieniawski and Czartoryski families [H, L, P], 1652–1766.
(Bibl. Czartoryskich, Kraków)
2. Report about a tannery [R], 1801.
(RGADA, Moscow, Manufaktur-kollegiia)
3. Copies of inscriptions on synagogues and tombstons [H, R], 1910.
(RGIA, St. Petersburg, Departament dukhovnykh del…)
4. Inspection reports [R], 1816–28; excerpts from minutes, statutes and correspondence about the founding of *Stowarzyszenie Kulturalno–Oświatowe, 'Freiheit'*, including a list of the founding committee, 1931–34.
(DARO, Rivne, Rovenskoe uezdnoe kaznacheistvo)

TULIGŁOWY (pow. Rudki, woj. lwowskie) 1878
Microfilms:
Material about reorganization of elementary schools attended by Jewish pupils [G, P], 1878.
(TsDIAU, L'viv, Krajowa Rada Szkolna)

TULISZKÓW (pow. Konin, woj. łódzkie) 1905
Microfilms:
Records concerning the establishment of a new community in the town [R], 1905.
(AP Łódź, Rząd Gubernialny, WA, Kalisz)

TUREK (woj. łódzkie) 1817–1910
Microfilms:
1. Files containing a description of the town, 1817–21.
(AGAD, Warszawa, Komisja Województwa Kaliskiego)
2. A request to convert to Christianity [R], 1895; ratification of community elections [R], 1895–96.
(AP Łódź, Rząd Gubernialny, WA, Kalisz)
3. Files on Jews sent into exile [R], 1908–09.
(AP Łódź, Kancelaria Gubernatora Kaliskiego)
4. Copies of inscriptions on synagogues and tombstons [H, R], 1910.
(RGIA, St. Petersburg, Departament dukhovnykh del…)

TUREK, surroundings, 1913–1914
Microfilms:
Ratification of the accounts of various communities [R], 1913–14.
(AP Łódź, Rząd Gubernialny, WA, Kalisz)

TURKA (woj. lwowskie) 1904–1938
Microfilms:
1. Files concerning ratification of statutes and liquidation of the *Gmilus Chesed* society[G, P], 1904–30; statutes, minutes and correspondence about Jewish associations, 1921–30; statistical data concerning the

Jewish population, 1923–24; correspondence concerning the statutes and registration of *Hitachdut*, 1923–30; reports and correspondence concerning speculations during the implementation of land reform in the district, 1924; reports about the activities of: Revisionist Zionists, 1927, *Hashomer Hatzair* and other youth movements, 1929–30, the local committees of OŻPP, 1933.
(DAIFO, Ivano-Frankivs'k, UW, Stanisławów)
2. Correspondence about the registration of *Agudas Yisroel*, including a list of names, 1928–33, and of *Machzike Hadas*, 1932.
(DALO, L'viv, Magistrat, Lwów)
3. Community voters' list, 1930.
(DALO, L'viv, Starostwo Powiatowe, Turka)
4. Monthly reports by district police about the activities of political parties and associations, 1930–32.
(DAIFO, Ivano-Frankivs'k, Komenda Wojewódzka PP, Stanisławów)
5. Correspondence about community matters, among them: budget and legal matters, including legal matters lists of tax payers, of community council members, rabbis and *dayanim* [R, U], 1931–37; correspondence about supervision of the workers' associations (*Yad Charutzim*), 1938.
(DALO, L'viv, UW, Lwów)

TURKA, surroundings, 1922–1923
Microfilms:
A register of associations in the district [P, U], 1922–23.
(DAIFO, Ivano-Frankivs'k, UW, Stanisławów)

TUROBIN (pow. Krasnystaw, woj. lubelskie) 1667–1797
Microfilms:
1. Records of the community's debts to the church in Zamość, 1667–1773.
(AP Lublin, Kolegiata w Zamościu)
2. A contract for the *arenda* of community taxes, 1797.
(AP Kraków, IT)
3. A list of houses destroyed during the fire of 1769 and an estimation of rebuilding costs, 1770; an accusation by the Żółkiew community that the Turobin community held a census of Jews outside its area of jurisdiction, 1775.
(AP Lublin, Księgi Grodzkie Krasnostawskie)

TUROBIN, surroundings, 1765–1855
Microfilms:
Financial and legal records concerning Jews, 1765–1855.
(AP Kraków, Arch. Młynowskie Chodkiewiczów)

TUROŚL (pow. Ostrołęka, woj. białostockie) 1913–1915
Microfilms:
A file on the arrest and expulsion from the *guberniia* of Jewish inhabitants suspected of espionage [R], 1913–15.
(AP Białystok, Rząd Gubernialny, Łomża)

TURZA WIELKA (pow. Dolina, woj. stanisławowskie) 1932–1936
Microfilms:
Records of the *Hatikva* association, 1932–36.
(DAIFO, Ivano-Frankivs'k, UW, Stanisławów)

TURZEC (pow. Stołpce, woj. nowogrodzkie) 1765–1855
Microfilms:
Contract for the town's *arenda*, 1765–82; general *arenda* of the county, 1800–55.
(AP Kraków, Arch. Młynowskie Chodkiewiczów)

TURZYSK (pow. Kowel, woj. wołyńskie) 1834–1876
Microfilms:
Copies of documents concerning *chasidic* leaders in various towns [R], 1834–76.
(TsDIAU, Kyiv, Dokumenty, sobrannye…)

TUSZYN (pow. Łódź, woj. łódzkie) 1890–1913
Microfilms:
1. A fine for evading conscription [R], 1890.
(AP Łódź, Rząd Gubernialny, WP, Piotrków)
2. Ratification of community elections and accounts [R], 1901–13; the appointment of a new rabbi [R], 1906–07.
(AP Łódź, Rząd Gubernialny, WA, Piotrków)

TYCZYN (pow. Rzeszów, woj. lwowskie) 1846–1938
Microfilms:
1. Files on organization of Jewish communities and ratification of statutes, 1846–96; correspondence with the district authorities and complaints against communities in the district, 1882–83; correspondence concerning vacant rabbinical positions, 1895; correspondence regarding various societies to help school children and Torah students, including statutes, 1908.
(TsDIAU, L'viv, Namiestnictwo Galicyjskie)
2. Correspondence about the community budget, 1932–36; correspondence with the district authorities regarding community elections, and a list of council members, their ages, professions and political orientations, 1933–38.
(DALO, L'viv, UW, Lwów)

TYKOCIN (pow. Wysokie Mazowieckie, woj. białostockie) 1705–1935
Originals:
Birth, marriage and death records (fragmentary) [P, R], 1844–1935; marriage certificate, 1872.
Microfilms:
1. Register of the Jewish population and taxes paid by them, 1705–08.
(Bibl. Czartoryskich, Kraków)
2. *Uniwersał* by Princess Anna Sanguszko–Radziwiłł granted to Christians and Jews from Germany living in Tykocin and other towns, 1722.
(AGAD, Warszawa, Arch. Radziwiłłów)
3. A letter concerning the communities of Tykocin and Białystok and the local *arendas*, 1750.
(AGAD, Warszawa, Arch. Roskie)
4. Birth, marriage and death records (fragmentary) [P, R], 1826–76.
(AP Białystok)
5. File on issuing a certificate as a surgeon's assistant to a Jew [R], 1893–1913; fines for evading conscription [R], 1905; file on permission for a Jew to be apothecary's apprentice [R], 1905–08; licence for production of soda water [R], 1908–12; establishment of a Jewish cemetery [R], 1909; minutes and correspondence about enlarging the Jewish cemetery [R], 1912; *arenda* contracts [R], 1912–13.

(AP Białystok, Rząd Gubernialny, Łomża)

TYRAWA WOŁOSKA (pow. Sanok, woj. lwowskie) 1928–1938
Microfilms:
Authorization by the district authorities to collect money for the Polish–Galician, Jewish community in Palestine, including a list of donors, 1928–30; reports concerning community elections, 1929–38.
(DALO, L'viv, UW, Lwów)

TYSZKOWCE (pow. Horodenka, woj. stanisławowskie) 1930–1937
Microfilms:
Records of various Jewish associations, 1930–37.
(DAIFO, Ivano-Frankivs'k, UW, Stanisławów)

TYSZOWCE (pow. Tomaszów, woj. lubelskie) 1786–1860
Original:
A promissory note issued by the community to the village of Klątew [H, P], 1786.
Microfilms:
Statistical description of the town (1827–1859), 1860.
(AP Lublin, Rząd Gubernialny, Lublin)

TYŚMIENICA (pow. Tłumacz, woj. stanisławowskie) 1703–1936
Microfilms:
1. Excerpts from Armenian files of Stanisławów concerning loans, *arenda*s and commerce with Jews from Tyśmienica, 1703–09; excerpts from court minutes concerning assaults on Jews, 1704–21.
(NBANU, L'viv, Arch. Ossolińskich)
2. Correspondence with the authorities about financial matters and taxes [G, P], 1793–95; correspondence concerning complaints by Jews against residence restrictions [G], 1819–20.
(TsDIAU, L'viv, Namiestnictwo Galicyjskie)
3. Reports about teaching Jewish religion in elementary schools [G, P], 1882–89.
(TsDIAU, L'viv, Krajowa Rada Szkolna)
4. Files on ratifying the statutes of *Agudas Yisroel* and *Talmud Tora Haklali*, 1893, 1920–30; statutes, minutes and correspondence concerning Zionist organizations, 1921–30; records of *Gmilus Chesed*, 1922–31; reports and correspondence about ratifying the statutes of Jewish charity associations, 1923–28; records and statutes of *Yad Charutzim*, 1926, 1936; records of *Gordonia*, 1930–36; reports and correspondence concerning community elections, 1932–36; reports about elections of delegates to the 18th Zionist Congress, 1933.
(DAIFO, Ivano-Frankivs'k, UW, Stanisławów)

TYŚMIENICZANY (pow. Stanisławów, woj. stanisławowskie) 1930
Microfilms:
Reports by directors of public schools containing descriptions of social, national, cultural, economic and hygienic conditions [P, U], 1930.
(DAIFO, Ivano-Frankivs'k, Inspektorat Szkolny, Stanisławów)

UCHANIE (pow. Hrubieszów, woj. lubelskie) 1860
Microfilms:
A statistical description of the town, 1860.
(AP Lublin, Rząd Gubernialny, Lublin)

UHNÓW (pow. Rawa Ruska, woj. lwowskie) 1933–1935
Microfilms:
A list of the board members of *Hatikva*, 1933; correspondence regarding the budget and a list of community tax payers, 1933–35; correspondence about *Agudas Yisroel*, 1934.
(DALO, L'viv, UW, Lwów)

UHRYNÓW DOLNY (pow. Stanisławów, woj. stanisławowskie) 1930
Microfilms:
Reports by directors of public schools containing descriptions of social, national, cultural, economic and hygienic conditions [P, U], 1930.
(DAIFO, Ivano-Frankivs'k, Inspektorat Szkolny, Stanisławów)

UJAZD (pow. Brzeziny, woj. łódzkie) 1825–1912
Microfilms:
1. Community elections and other matters, 1825–66.
(AP Łódź, Anterioria Rządu Gubernialnego, Piotrków)
2. Community accounts [R], 1901–12; ratification of community elections [R], 1904–05, 1911; files concerning the rabbi's salary [R], 1911.
(AP Łódź, Rząd Gubernialny, WA, Piotrków)

ULANÓW (pow. Nisko, woj. lwowskie) 1747–1934
Microfilms:
1. Court case between Jewish *arendars* of the Sandomierz *ekonomia* and the Ulanów community concerning poll tax, and data on the population [L, P], 1747–56.
(AGAD, Warszawa, Arch. Kameralne)
2. Tables of taxes [G], 1819; correspondence about the community and ratification of statutes, 1895–96.
(TsDIAU, L'viv, Namiestnictwo Galicyjskie)
3. Correspondence concerning changes of the Jewish community statutes, 1922; authorization by the district authorities to collect money for the Polish–Galician Jewish community in Palestine, including a list of donors, 1928–30; correspondence about community matters, budget and a list of community tax payers, 1933–34.
(DALO, L'viv, UW, Lwów)
4. Correspondence on registration of *Agudas Yisroel* and the *Yesodei Hatora* school, 1931.
(DALO, L'viv, Magistrat, Lwów)

ULICKO ZARĘBANE (pow. Rawa Ruska, woj. lwowskie) 1936
Microfilms:
Monographs containing demographic and economic information, 1936.
(AP Wrocław, Ossolineum, WKNZNP, Lwów)

ULUCZ (pow. Brzozów, woj. lwowskie) 1938
Microfilms:
Correspondence on registration of the *Mizrachi*, 1938.
(DALO, L'viv, Magistrat, Lwów)

UŁASZKOWCE (pow. Czortków, woj. tarnopolskie) 1784–1925
Microfilms:

A list of inn keepers [G, P], 1784, 1810, 1839–41; files on investigation of a robbery and murder of a Jew, 1790; files on the material situation of the *kahal* and its members, a list of Jewish inhabitants [G, H, P], 1797–1851; file on accusation of theft by two Jews during the fair [G, H, P], 1803; litigation between two Jews [G, H, P], 1806–18; complaint by the *kahal* in Jagielnica against the *kahal* in Ułaszkowce about unpaid taxes, 1812–13; inquiry about a dispute between merchants from Buczacz and Ułaszkowce, 1821; *arenda* contract of a flour mill [P, R], 1914–25.
(TsDIAU, L'viv, Arch. Lanckorońskich)

UNIEJÓW, surroundings, (pow. Turek, woj. łódzkie) 1886–1888
Microfilms:
A request by local peasants to expel a Jew from the district [R], 1886–88.
(AP Łódź, Kancelaria Gubernatora Kaliskiego)

URYCZ (pow. Stryj, woj. stanisławowskie) 1933–1937
Microfilms:
Records of the *Liga Pomocy Pracującym w Palestynie 'Hitachdut'*, 1933–37.
(DAIFO, Ivano-Frankivs'k, UW, Stanisławów)

URZĘDÓW (pow. Janów, woj. lubelskie) 1626–1777
Microfilms:
1. Records of taxes paid by Jews, 1626, 1668.
(AP Wrocław, Ossolineum)
2. A complaint about Jewish *arendars*, 1777.
(Bibl. im. Łopacińskiego, Lublin)

URZĘDÓW, surroundings, 1762–1861
Microfilms:
1. Excerpts from municipal books of Modliborzyce regarding taxes and a register of inhabitants, 1762–1809; instructions on the regulation of taxes and the holding of a census, 1790.
(AP Lublin, Księgi Miejskie, Modliborzyce)
2. A statistical description of the town (1849–59), 1860–61.
(AP Lublin, Rząd Gubernialny, Lublin)

USTRZYKI DOLNE (pow. Lesko, woj. lwowskie) 1898–1939
Microfilms:
1. Correspondence with the district authorities about the community statutes, 1898–1901; correspondence regarding a petition by several Jews not to include their illegal children in the community civil register, 1900–05; correspondence about community elections [G, P], 1903–06.
(TsDIAU, L'viv, Namiestnictwo Galicyjskie)
2. Correspondence with the district authorities and police on the refusal of a request to register the *Klub Dramatyczny im. An-skiego* due to the communist activity and arrest of several club members, including statutes and lists of founders and members, 1928–30; correspondence about election of a rabbi, 1932–36; correspondence about the community budget and a list of tax payers, 1933–35; circulars, reports and correspondence concerning community elections, including a list of community council members, 1933, 1938–39.
(DALO, L'viv, UW, Lwów)
3. Correspondence about the registration of *Machzikei Hadas* and a list of board members, 1932.
(DALO, L'viv, Magistrat, Lwów)

UŚCIE ZIELONE (pow. Buczacz, woj. tarnopolskie) 1897–1936
Microfilms:
1. Correspondence on community matters, 1897, and about complaints concerning Rabbi E. Horowitz, 1901–05.
(TsDIAU, L'viv, Namiestnictwo Galicyjskie)
2. Indictment against two Jews for disrespect of a religious procession, 1898.
(DAIFO, Ivano-Frankivs'k, Prokuratura Państwowa, Stanisławów)
3. Monographs containing demographic and economic data concerning Jews, 1936.
(AP Wrocław, Ossolineum, WKNZNP, Lwów)

UŚCIMÓW (pow. Włodawa, woj. lubelskie) 1820–1828
Microfilms:
Arenda contracts, 1820–28.
(AP Lublin, Akta gen. Haumana, dzierżawcy dóbr rządowych Uścimów i Jedlanka)

UŚCIECZKO (pow. Zaleszczyki, woj. tarnopolskie) 1890–1904
Microfilms:
1. Reports and correspondence about reorganizing the Jewish community [G, P], 1890.
(TsDIAU, L'viv, Namiestnictwo Galicyjskie)
2. Reports from inspections of Baron Hirsch Foundation (JCA) schools [G, P], 1896–1904.
(TsDIAU, L'viv, Krajowa Rada Szkolna)

UZIN (pow. Stanisławów, woj. stanisławowskie) 1923–1924
Microfilms:
Information regarding the number of inhabitants in the area of the civil registry office, 1923–24.
(DAIFO, Ivano-Frankivs'k, Starostwo Powiatowe, Stanisławów)

WADOWICE (woj. krakowskie) 1820–1910
Microfilms:
1. Correspondence with the provincial authorities about residence permits [G], 1820–29; files on ratification of community statutes, 1846–96; statutes of the *Stowarzyszenie Żydowskie dla Poparcia Starców*, 1910.
(TsDIAU, L'viv, Namiestnictwo Galicyjskie)
2. Material on the closing of *chadorim* [G, P], 1868–74.
(TsDIAU, L'viv, Krajowa Rada Szkolna)

WARĘŻ (pow. Sokal, woj. lwowskie) 1928–1935
Microfilms:
1. Authorization by the district authorities to collect funds for the Polish–Galician Jewish community in Palestine, including a list of donors, 1928–30.
(DALO, L'viv, UW, Lwów)
2. Correspondence on the registration of: *Machzike Hadas*, including statutes and a list of board members, 1932 and of *Agudas Yisroel*, 1934; correspondence on the community budget, 1935.
(DALO, L'viv, Magistrat, Lwów)

WARKA (pow. Grójec, woj. warszawski) 1566
Microfilms:
Lustracja, 1566.

(AGAD, Warszawa, ASK)

WARKOWICZE (pow. Dubno, woj. wołyńskie) 1869–1870
Microfilms:
A file on disorders caused by Jews during the collection of taxes [R], 1869–70.
(DARO, Rivne, Dubenskii uezdnyi sud)

WARSZAWA (woj. warszawskie) 1483–1950
Originals:
Pinkas of the *Chevra Kadisha* (printed in 1911), 1785–1870; papers of Jacob Tugendhold, government censor of Jewish literature 1828–50; a file of Matthias Bersohn, the art collector and historian, containing certificates, diplomas and letters, 1845–1908; a certificate signed by rabbis from Warsaw that M. Zajdel of Łódź is qualified to serve as a rabbi, 1865; *pinkas* of the burial society (fragmentary) [H], 1875–1905; telegrams to P. Rabinowicz on the occasion of his 50th birthday and the 25th anniversary of his literary activity [H] , 1895; album of photographs given to the community secretary, J. L. Grossglik on the 25th anniversary of his activity, 1899; a poster announcing the appearance of *Der Weg* [Y], 1905; statutes and posters of the *Towarzystwo Niesienia Pomocy Żydom Ofiarom Wojny*, WW I; minutes of a meeting of the Jewish Merchants' Guild [Y], 1914; two appeals to Jewish girls and women by a committee for the modesty of Jewish maidens, 1918, 1939; invitation of a sanitary comission of the community [H], n.d; a letter of protest against antisemitism by a students' association, 1920; a letter of the *Żydowska Strzecha Akademicka* association denying accusations of Bolshevism, 1920; a letter by an association to aid the deaf and dumb to the JDC representative in Switzerland, 1923; invitation to the graduation ceremony of a nursing course at the Jewish hospital, 1925; a letter concerning the publication of the booklet, "List of Hebrew Names", 1928; proclamations issued by various parties and factions during community elections [P, Y], 1931; program of the 75th anniversary of the January, 1863 uprising, 1938; announcement of a concert of the Jewish Symphonic Orchestra, 1939; the telephone book of Warsaw, 1939; school certificates [Y], n.d.; congratulations on the 70th birthday of Shaul Pinchas Rabinovitz; musical notes of the Jewish national guard march, n.d.;
Photocopies:
1. An order by King Zygmunt I to A. Goliński, settling litigation between Christians and Jews, 1527; confirmation by King Zygmunt August of previous charters, 1570; charter given to the town by King Stefan Batory, forbidding Jews to dwell in Warsaw, 1580; excerpts from municipal books regarding a complaint against Jews, 1580; letter of protection given by King Władysław IV to a Jew, 1646; charter given by King Władysław IV to the city of Warsaw against the Jews, 1648; verdicts of a tribunal in litigation between the municipality and the Jews, 1648; confirmation by King Jan Kazimierz of previous charters, 1650; a charter by King Jan III Sobieski, 1678; summons of a Jew by the *wójt's* tribunal, 1795.
(AGAD, Warszawa, DP)
2. A decree limiting the sojourn of Jews in Warsaw during sessions of the *Sejm*, 1781.
(Bibl. im Łopacińskiego, Lublin)
3. Reports about the capture of Warsaw and the participation of Jews in its defence [R], 1794.
(RGVIA, Moscow, Voenno-uchenyi arkhiv…)
Microfilms:
1. Copies of charters granted to the city against Jews [L, P], 1483–1730; *lustracje*, 1566.
(AGAD, Warszawa, ASK)
2. A letter of King Zygmunt I to the *starosta* concerning the rights of those living in the city (incl. Jews), 1527; the charter *de non tolerandis Judaeis* granted to the city by King Zygmunt I [L], 1527; confirmations

of this charter by Kings Zygmunt II, Stefan Batory, Jan Kazimierz, Władysław IV and Jan Sobieski [L], 1570–1678; a letter of King Stefan Batory concerning litigation between the municipal authorities and the Jews, 1580; letter of King Władysław IV granting a Jewish family the right to own a tavern in the city, 1646; records concerning litigation between a Christian and a Jew, 1795.
(AGAD, Warszawa, DP)

3. Private agreements, reports, correspondence, receipts, contracts, accounts concerning estates and businesses of the Sieniawski and Czartoryski families, 1628–1759.
(Bibl. Czartoryskich, Kraków)

4. A letter by King August III to the administrator of royal estates criticizing the leasing of certain estates to the Jews, 1762; charter by King Stanisław August Poniatowski, granting a Jew the right to supply jewellery to the court, 1767.
(AGAD, Warszawa, Księgi Kanclerskie)

5. Files on financial agreements and legal proceedings between a nobleman and a Jew, 1781–1809.
(AGAD, Warszawa, Arch. Przeździeckich)

6. Contracts, receipts, court decisions and other materials concerning the *Bracia Roesler* merchant's society and the Hartig Company [F, G, L, P], 1790–1817.
(TsDIAU, L'viv, Arch. Lubomirskich)

7. Descriptions of streets in Warsaw, end 18th cent.
(Bibl. Uniwersytetu Warszawskiego, Zb. Banku Polskiego)

8. Identity cards for Jews, 1804–62; files on taxes and other payments made by Jews, 1808, 1845; prohibition of Jewish residence in the city center, 1809–61; regulations of the number of Jews entering the city, 1816–63; files on Jacob Epstein, 1817–52; registers of the Jewish residents in the city and taxes paid by them, 1822–42; records concerning kosher meat, 1824–64; a request by a Jew for exemption from the residence tax, 1832–33; files on the purchase of houses by Jews, 1835–53; files on synagogues in Warsaw, 1842; changes in the regulations concerning the purchase of real estate by Jews, 1858–60; files on the community, 1867.
(AGAD, Warszawa, KRzSW)

9. Files concerning excomunication, 1817–58; files about the activities of a Jewish "healer", exploiting naive people, 1818–19; files on synagogues, 1818–60; reports and complaints about burial societies, including inventories of them, 1822–50; reports and correspondence on confirmation of elections for the rabbinate, exams at the Rabbinical Seminary, fee exemptions and lists of rabbis, 1823–53; files about nutrition for Jews in prisons, 1824–25; files on the Jewish hospital, reports by the community concerning the hospital's administration and finances, 1824–38; files on the *Komitet Starozakonnych*, a decree by Tsar Nikolas I, liquidating the committee, financial matters, tax registers and documents regarding the Rabbinical Seminary [P, R], 1837–48; files on rules of *shechita*, corruption in the sale of kosher meat by the Jewish community and police investigations [H, P, R], 1839–49, rulings concerning taxes for kosher meat and requests for exemptions from Jews not consuming kosher meat [P, R], 1857–60; a file on Jewish hospitals, and the support for them required of Jews, including lists of Jews who purchased kosher meat, Jews who purchased non-kosher meat and Jews who converted to Christianity [P, R], 1848–56; reports and correspondence concerning appointments of rabbis, their education and salaries, their relationships with the communities, expansion of the Rabbinical Seminary, exemption from conscription for graduates of the Rabbinical Seminary, and lists of rabbis and Seminary graduates, 1853–71; minutes and correspondence concerning the arrival in Warsaw of a Protestant pastor and the expulsion of English missionaries [F, G, P, R], 1855–69; a file on the appointment of Rabbi Jacob Gesundheit as Chief Rabbi and the opposition of *chasidim* [R], 1870–71.

(AGAD, Warszawa, CWW)

10. File on the establishment of a Jewish high school, 1818.

(AGAD, Warszawa, RSKP)

11. Records of the taxes paid by Jews entering the city, 1822–42; files on the transfer of Jews from houses in the centre of the city, 1824–49; purchase of houses in the town by Jews, 1825–41; regulations on limiting the number of Jews entering the city, 1829–31; a file on a Jewish elementary school, 1831.

(AGAD, Warszawa, KRzSW)

12. Records on the participation of Jews in the City Guard, 1831; a file on the residence permit, 1831.

(AGAD, Warszawa, WCPL)

13. Correspondence about the difficult economic situation of a Jew and a request for assistance, 1830s; excerpt from a letter about Jews seizing advantageous plots in Warsaw [R], 1858; correspondence about the exile of Jewish preacher, I. Kramsztyk [R], 1862.

(GARF, Moscow, Tret'e otdelenie…)

14. A request for a residence permit [R], 1844; A request by a Jew of Warsaw for a passport to live in St. Petersburg [R], 1844–51; a request for honorary citizenship of Warsaw, 1852–58; requests concerning *arenda* [R], 1858–60; request for permission to trade with England [R], 1859; a request to an insurance company regarding goods rescued from a fire, 1864.

(AGAD, Warszawa, SSKP)

15. Files on the Rabbinical Seminary: statutes, syllabus, employees, a list of graduates, reports and correspondence, 1858–61.

(AP Lublin, Rząd Gubernialny, Lublin)

16. Certificates and photographs of candidates for the rabbinate [R], 1886–1913; a petition by Jews requesting exemptions from the community tax [R], 1914; correspondence about a request of payment for building materials [R], 1914–15.

(AP Białystok, Rząd Gubernialny, Łomża)

17. An official form for Jews arriving in Warsaw, 1880's.

(AP Wrocław, Ossolineum)

18. A file on authorization for Abraham Piórko to publish a Hebrew children's periodical, *Gan Sha'ashuim L'yaldei Yisrael* [R], 1890; a file on secret Jewish organizations, including lists of suspects and arrested persons and a brochure about the 4th conference of the *Bund* [R, Y], 1900–03; a file on violence between Jews and Christians [R], 1903–04; correspondence about measures to end or prevent pogroms [R], 1906.

(GARF, Moscow, Departament politsii…)

19. Report about an index of books forbidden for publication [R], 1894; a file on prohibition of plays in Yiddish, and plays with biblical motifs [R], 1899–1907.

(RGIA, St. Petersburg, Peterburgskii tsenzurnyi komitet)

20. Newspapers and proclamations of the *Bund* and handwritten translations into Russian (issues of *Varshever Arbeter, Der Klassen Kampf, Arbeter Shtyme)* [R, Y], 1898–1901.

(GARF, Moscow, TSEVAAD)

21. A file on a donation by a Warsaw Jew to the synagogue in Łódź [R], 1902–03.

(AP Łódź, Rząd Gubernialny, WA, Piotrków)

22. Donations for the poor [R], 1904–05.

(AP Łódź, Rząd Gubernialny, RO, Piotrków)

23. A file on Jews accused of possessing illegal literature [R], 1904; a file on Jews inciting workers against the regime [R], 1905; an investigation against members of the *Bund* [R], 1913.

(AP Łódź, GZŻ, Piotrków)

24. Correspondence of the Warsaw branch of the Society for the Attainment of Full Rights for the Jewish People in Russia, including a letter by Vladimir Jabotinsky [R], 1905–06.

(RGIA, St. Petersburg, Obshchestvo polnopraviia...)

25. Files on Jewish cultural societies [R], 1907–09.

(AP Łódź, Rząd Gubernialny, KP, Piotrków)

26. A file on a "Jewish national club" of electors [R], 1907; a file on a Jewish information bureau for Jewish emigrants, 1909.

(AP Łódź, Rząd Gubernialny, KP, Piotrków)

27. Files on persecution by Poles of Jews in military zones [R], 1914–15.

(GARF, Moscow, Katsenel'son)

28. A report on the activity of *Bnai Brith* in Warsaw, 1928, 1930.

(DAIFO, Ivano-Frankivs'k, *Achduth Bnai Brith* in Stanisławów)

29. Minutes of the section for the study of revolutionary movements among Jews and documentation on Jewish political activists [R], 1931; testimonies on workers' movements during 1909–14 [R], 1934; testimonies about the *Bund* in 1899 [R], 1934; testimonies concerning events of 1905 in Warsaw [R], 1935.

(GARF, Moscow, Vsesoiuznoe obshchestvo...)

30. An issue of the newspaper *Hajtige Najes*, No 159 (Warszawa, July 12, 1934) [Y], 1934; a decision of the Polish government to liquidate the *Centralny Związek Rzemieślników Żydów w Polsce*, 1938.

(DATO, Ternopil', UW, Tarnopol)

31. Statutes of the Jewish sports club, *Shomriya* (*Warta*), 1935–39.

(DARO, Rivne, Starostwo Powiatowe, Równe)

32. Circular letter published by the Self-Defence Committee in Warsaw [R, Y], n.d.

(GARF, Moscow, Kollektsiia nelegal'nykh izdanii...)

WARSZAWA, surroundings, 1818–1917
Microfilms:

1. Files concerning setting up *eruvim* and the ensuing litigation with Christians about them, 1818–71; files on *shechita*, on corruption concerning the sale of kosher meat in the area and on supervising the sale of kosher meat to poor Jews [P, R], 1848–64;

(AGAD, Warszawa, CWW)

2. A report following the inspection by Leon Mandelshtam of Jewish schools including information about teachers, rabbis, patrons and the Jewish community in Warsaw [F, H, P, R], 1856–62.

(RGIA, St. Petersburg, Departament narodnogo prosveshcheniia)

3. Lists and addresses of Zionist organizations in the Warsaw *guberniia* [R], 1907–16.

(TsGAU, Tashkent, Turkestanskoe okhrannoe otdelenie)

4. A report about synagogues and rabbis in the Warsaw *guberniia* [R], 1908.

(RGIA, St. Petersburg, Departament dukhovnykh del...)

5. Correspondence about the investigation of activities and persecution of Jewish businessmen accused of fraud and speculation [R], 1914–17.

(RGVIA, Moscow, Kantseliariia nachal'nika shtaba)

WARTA (pow. Sieradz, woj. łódzkie) 1765–1914
Microfilms:

1. Confirmation by King Stanisław August Poniatowski of the charter granted to Jews [L, P], 1765.

(AGAD, Warszawa, Księgi Kanclerskie)

2. Files on Jewish ownership of real estate, 1815–60; a description of the town, 1818–26.

(AGAD, Warszawa, Komisja Województwa Kaliskiego)
3. Records on the cancellation of certificates granted to Jewish craftsmen living outside the Pale of Settlement [R], 1912–14.
(AP Łódź, Rząd Gubernialny, WA, Kalisz)

WASILKÓW (pow. Białystok, woj. białostockie) 1930–1931
Original:
Death records, 1930–31.

WĄGROWIEC (woj. poznańskie) 1801–1897
Originals:
Pinkas of the burial society [H], 1801–44; community accounts [G], 1847, 1848, 1861, 1869; a file on the construction of two buildings in the cemetery [G], 1897.

WĄSOSZ (pow. Szczuczyn, woj. białostockie) 1840–65
Microfilms:
Birth, marriage and death records (fragmentary), 1840–65.
(AP Ełk)

WĄWOLNICA (pow. Puławy, woj. lubelskie) 1820–1859
Microfilms:
1. A statistical description of the town, 1820–59.
(AP Lublin, Rząd Gubernialny, Lublin)
2. Reports and correspondence concerning the appointments of rabbis and their relationships with the communities, including a list of rabbis, 1853–56.
(AGAD, Warszawa, CWW)

WEŁDZIRZ (pow. Dolina, woj. stanisławowskie) 1930–1936
Microfilms:
Lists of members of the *Opieka nad Żydowską Młodzieżą, Gordonia*, association 1930–1936.
(DAIFO, Ivano-Frankivs'k, UW, Stanisławów)

WERBIŻ (pow. Lwów, woj. lwowskie) 1425
Microfilms:
A charter to found villages on unsettled land in the area of Werbiż, granted by King Władysław II to a Jew [L], 1425.
(TsDIAU, L'viv, Collection of documents on parchment)

WĘGRÓW (woj. lubelskie) 17th cent.–1915
Microfilms:
1. Records of a loan taken by the community to erect community buildings, 17th cent.
(AGAD, Warszawa, DP)
2. Files on *arendas*, 1772–97.
(AP Kraków, IT)
3. Reports and correspondence concerning appointments of rabbis, 1853–56.
(AGAD, Warszawa, CWW)
4. A file on *arenda* contracts [R], 1910–13; a request for exemption from the community tax [R], 1914; a decision of the community council to renovate the *mikve* and slaughter house [R], 1914–15; file on the

arrest of a Jewish surgeon's assistant, suspected of issuing false exemptions from military service [R], 1914–15.
(AP Białystok, Rząd Gubernialny, Łomża)

WIDAWA (pow. Łask, woj. łódzkie) 1787–1913
Microfilms:
1. An agreement between the *kahal* in Łask and the Jews of Widawa [H, P], 1787.
(AGAD, Warszawa, Arch. Lubomirskich z Małej Wsi)
2. Records concerning the community, 1837–50.
(AP Łódź. Anterioria Rządu Gubernialnego, Piotrków)
3. Ratification of community elections and accounts [R], 1899–1913.
(AP Łódź, Rząd Gubernialny, WA, Piotrków)
4. Fines for evading conscription [R], 1901–02.
(AP Łódź, Rząd Gubernialny, WP, Piotrków)

WIELEŃ nad Notecią (pow. Czarnków, woj. poznańskie) 1642–1891
Originals:
Pinkas of the burial society [H], 1724–1838; *pinkas* of the "new" cemetery, including a list of the deceased [H], 1829–38; files on Jews joining the community [G], 1835–53; *pinkas* of the *Rashi* study society [H], 1838–51; financial records [G], 1844.
Microfilms:
1. Confirmation of the town constitution (incl. references to Jewish rights) by the owner, 1642.
(AP Poznań, Akta miast, woj. poznańskie)
2. Correspondence with the authorities, legal matters, taxes, construction of the school building [G], 1829, 1872–91.
(Centrum Judaicum, Berlin)

WIELICZKA (woj. krakowskie, pow. Kraków) 1749–1916
Originals:
Copies of two antisemitic letters written by Piotr Krokiewicz to Rabbi Dr. Osias Thon, 1915–16.
Microfilms:
Extracts from municipal records concerning Jews, 1749–68.
(AP Kraków, IT)

WIELKIE OCZY (pow. Jaworów woj. lwowskie,) 1763–1933
Microfilms:
1. A *suplika* by the Jewish community, 1763–66
(TsDIAU, Kyiv, Arch. Potockich z Tulczyna)
2. Circulars, reports and correspondence concerning elections to the community council, 1928–29, and ratification of the community budget, including a list of tax payers, 1932–35; correspondence and complaints against the community council because of an illegal raise of community taxes, 1932–33.
(DALO, L'viv, UW, Lwów)

WIELKIE SOLECZNIKI (pow. Wilno–Troki, woj. wileńskie) 1697–1765
Microfilms:
Contract for the *arenda* of a tavern; records of the construction of an inn, 1697–1765.
(AP Kraków, Arch. Młynowskie Chodkiewiczów)

WIELOPOLE (pow. Ropczyce, woj. krakowskie) 1895–1896
Microfilms:
Correspondence with the district authorities about the Jewish community and ratification of its statutes, 1895–96.
(TsDIAU, L'viv, Namiestnictwo Galicyjskie)

WIELUŃ (woj. łódzkie) 1731–1903
Microfilms:
1. Records of a financial dispute between a burgher and a Jew, 1731.
(AP Kraków, IT)
2. Extracts from municipal records concerning Jews, 1777–97.
(AGAD, Warszawa, Księgi Miejskie, Wieluń)
3. Records concerning a request to the burial society [R], 1903.
(AP Łódź, Rząd Gubernialny, WA, Kalisz)

WIELUŃ, surroundings, 1765–1914
Microfilms:
1. *Lustracja* of the royal estates, 1765.
(AGAD, Warszawa, Wieluńskie Akta Grodzkie i Ziemskie)
2. Records of the Civil and Military Commission for the Wieluń and Ostrzeszów districts, and a census of the inhabitants, 1790–92.
(AGAD)
3. A list of rabbis in the district, 1821–71.
(AGAD, Warszawa, CWW)
4. Files on the settlement of Jews in agricultural districts [R], 1883–1914.
(AP Łódź, Komisja Włościańska, pow. wieluński)
5. Ratification of the accounts and elections of various communities in the district [R], 1895–1914.
(AP Łódź, Rząd Gubernialny, WA, Kalisz)

WIENIAWA (pow. Lublin, woj. lubelskie, today a quarter of Lublin) 1652–1864
Microfilms:
1. Requests, reports and complaints concerning estates of the Sieniawski and Czartoryski families [H, L, P], 1652–1766.
(Bibl. Czartoryskich, Kraków)
2. Reports and correspondence concerning appointment of rabbis, their education and salaries, 1856–64.
(AGAD, Warszawa, CWW)
3. Description and statistical data, 1860–61.
(AP Lublin, Rząd Gubernialny, Lublin)

WIERUSZÓW (pow. Wieluń, woj. łódzkie) 1820–1919
Microfilms:
1. A description of the town, 1820.
(AGAD, Warszawa, Komisja Województwa Kaliskiego)
2. A file on the rabbi of the community, 1919.
(AP Łódź, Gmina Żydowska, Łódź)

WIKTORÓW (pow. Stanisławów, woj. stanisławowskie) 1937
Microfilms:

Reports and correspondence about anti-Jewish activities, 1937.
(DAIFO, Ivano-Frankivs'k, Sąd Okręgowy, Stanisławów)

WILAMOWO (pow. Łomża, woj. białostockie) 1773–1777
Microfilms:
Arenda contracts of inns in Wilamowo estates [L, P], 1773–77.
(AGAD, Warszawa, Arch. Lubomirskich z Małej Wsi)

WILANÓW (pow. Warszawa, woj. warszawskie) 1723–1729
Microfilms:
Requests and letters from Wilanów to Princess E. Sieniawska, 1723–29.
(Bibl. Czartoryskich, Kraków)

WILKOWYJA (pow. Rzeszów, woj. lwowskie) 1819–1881
Microfilms:
Correspondence, *arenda* contracts and legal proceedings concerning the *arenda* [G, P], 1819–45, 1865–81; complaints by a Jewish creditor [G, L, P], 1872–80.
(AGAD, Warszawa, Arch. Ostrowskich z Ujazdu)

WILNO (woj. wileńskie) 1632–1946
Originals:
Authorized copies from municipal records concerning the community and individual Jews [L, P, Y], 1633–1758; a license granted by the bishop to the community to build a synagogue, 1745; excerpts from municipal books concerning charters for Jews, debts and conflicts with the local population, 1749–56; copy of a letter from 1714 from the *shtadlan* to the Lithuanian chancellor concerning Jewish rights in the city, 1755; copy of a royal decree from 1788 on a dispute between the community and its rabbi, 1799; declaration by the Butchers' Guild concerning a dispute with the community over *shechita*, 1800; a letter from the Lithuanian Hospital Commission to the community, 1800;
a letter by the Council for Hospitals to the *Kahal* about funds for the poor, 1803; five deeds of sale for synagogue seats [H], 1810–78; Polish translation of a community regulation concerning income from marriage ceremonies, 1812; declaration of funds collected for charitable purposes, 1814; correspondence of the community with the community in Berlin [G, H, Y], 1818; copy of a charter granted to Aharon Gordon and his descendants in 1713, 1834; copies of correspondence on Jewish charity funds [R], 1841; announcement about the collection of community taxes [R, Y], 1841; a document concerning the construction of a building for the community [R], 1842; a document on community finances [R], 1845; a circumcision register [H], 1854–84; the Jewish oath, forms, and a proclamation urging the maintaining of clean houses [H, R, Y], 1861;an order to the Jews to keep the exterior of their houses in good condition [R, Y], n.d.; letter from Sir Moses Montefiore to the heads of the community [H], 1864; two printed copies of the *Vilna Gaon's cherem* against the *chasidim* [H], n.d.;
documents and excerpts from the state archives and the community minute book concerning *chasidim* in Lithuania (1880), the statutes and accounts of charitable societies [H, R], 1903–15; various documents concerning technical education for Jews [P, Y], 1905; a Zionist proclamation following the pogroms [Y], 1905; certificates of the Hebrew Gymansium and of the Committee for Jewish Education, 1923–24; receipts of the Council of Yeshivot, 1924–39; announcements of the ORT school, 1924–39; a list of the deceased registered by the Beit Yaacov burial society [H], 1926; announcements of YIVO [Y], 1926, 1928; a proclamation by Rabbi Chaim Ozer Grodzienski forbidding the participation of women in the elections in Jerusalem [H], 1928; a report about the activities of the Jewish community [Y], 1928–1933; statutes and

a proclamation of the Hebrew Scientific Society [H], 1920s–30s; list of members of the Leather Merchants' Religious Association [H], 1926; printed documents of a workers' association [Y], 1930s; a report about *aliya* between July 1940 – January 1941 [H], 1940–1941; declarations of the association of Jews from Wilno in Poland [Y], 1946; the Israel Klausner collection, containing various documents and notes about the Jews in Wilno.

Photocopies:

1. A file about a conflict between *chasidim* and *misnagdim* in Wilno [R], 1800.
(RGIA, St. Petersburg, Tretii departament Senata)
2. A file about a prize granted to a Jewish merchant for his charitable activity during the cholera epidemic in 1831 [R], 1832; a file about disorders caused by Jews during recruitment activities [R], 1839–40; a file on an investigation against Leon Mandelshtam for distributing unauthorized textbooks to Jewish schools [R], 1849–51.
(GARF, Moscow, Tret'e otdelenie…)
3. A file concerning a Jew from Jerusalem in Wilno [R], 1833.
(LCVIA, Vilnius, Vilniaus civilinio gubernatoriaus kanceliarija)
4. A file on the organization of Jewish schools [R], 1840–44.
(RGIA, St. Petersburg, Departament narodnogo prosveshcheniia)
5. Reports on the synagogues, *Taharos ha-Kodesh* and *Tzedaka Gedola* [H, R], 1886–1906.
(RNB, St. Petersburg)
6. Proposed statutes of the Jewish Polytechnical Institute [R], 1890–1914.
(TsGIAP, St. Petersburg, Sheftel)

Photographs:

Album of photographs with images of the Jewish cemetery [G], WW I; a postcard of the Jewish cemetery, n.d.; two negatives of the Great Synagogue.

Microfilms:

1. Charter regarding tribunals and town council in Wilno, granted by King Zygmunt III [L, P], 1632; various documents concerning Jews, 1668–1817; confirmation by King Jan III Sobieski of charters for the Jews, 1669; petitions by the *kahal* to the king concerning a conflict with the Jews, 1786; requests of the Jews living in the Wilno and Snipiski *jurydyki* to the Radziwiłł Commission, 1804–21; detailed records of sales of real estate [R] 1807–87; records of the inhabitants on the Wilno *jurydyka* of the Radziwiłł family, 1811–16; agreements and contracts, 1811–94.
(AGAD, Warszawa, Arch. Radziwiłłów)
2. A file on a request by a converted Jew from Wilno for permission to live in Moscow [Rt], 1657.
(RGADA, Moscow, Prikaz Velikogo kniazhestva Litovskogo)
3. Decrees for the Jews of Wilno, 1668.
(AGAD, Warszawa)
4. Records of a financial dispute between the *starosta* of Grodno and the Jews of Wilno [Byelorussian, H, Rt], 1674–86.
(Bibl. PAN, Kraków)
5. File on litigation between J. S. Szukszta and the Jews of Wilno [Rt], 1678.
(AGAD, Warszawa, Arch. Zabiełłów)
6. Letters by the *kahal* about infringements on the Jewish school's land by the Piarist order, 1775.
(RGADA, Moscow, KFE)
7. *Pinkas Chevras Mishnayos* in the *kloiz* of Leib Ben Eliezer [G, H, Y], 1776–1889; anonymous handwritten plays in Yiddish, n.d.

(GARF, Moscow, TSEVAAD)

8. Records concerning litigation between a Jew and the community [H], 1780s.

(Bibl. Jagiellońska, Kraków)

9. Correspondence about transgressions during elections to the city council, prohibitions for Jews to be candidates and rules regarding testimony by Jews in cases concerning Russians [R], 1792, 1824–26.

(RGIA, St. Petersburg, Documenty iz unichtozhennykh del...)

10. *Pinkas* of the *Vilna Gaon's* study house [H], 1798–1916.

(YIVO, New York)

11. A *lustracja* of Lithuania containing details on Jews in Wilno, 18th cent.

(Biblioteka Narodowa, Warszawa)

12. A letter by the mayor of Wilno about the suspension of a senate decision from 1802, permitting Jews to be elected to the city council, a description of the situation of the Jews and rights granted the Jews by Polish and Lithuanian authorities [R], 1803.

(RGADA, Moscow, Vorontsovy)

13. Files about conversions of Jews to Christianity and their return to Judaism [R], 1804–05.

(RGIA, St. Petersburg, Rimsko-katolicheskaia duchovna kolegia MVD)

14. Regulations, orders, requests and correspondence about the employment of educated Jews at the offices of governor-generals in various tasks [R], 1816–84; decrees, reports, requests and correspondence about elections of a rabbi and community council [R], 1883–89.

(RGIA, St. Petersburg, Departament dukhovnykh del...)

15. A file on the appointment of Wolf Tugendhold as censor [R], 1828; a file about closing the Committee for Censorship and about Jewish printing houses publishing books without permission of the censorship [R], 1830–32.

(RGIA, St. Petersburg, Glavnoe upravlenie tsenzury)

16. Files on collecting funds among the Jews of Wilno to enable Jewish deputies in St. Petersburg to campaign for the exemption of Jews from conscription, including lists of names, 1828–29; files on exemption of Jews from conscription [R], 1835–37; files on closing Jewish printing houses and documents about abuses of power by censors of Jewish books [R], 1836–38; file on a prize to a merchant for handing over of an emissary [R], 1840–41; files about measures by the authorities to transform Jewish social and economic life in the Russian Empire, documents on the emergence of *Chasidism* and correspondence about exempting Karaites from prohibitions relating to Jews in the civil service [R], 1850–63; information by two Jews from Wilno about Poles preparing a rebellion [R], 1858; a letter about student demonstrations [F], 1860; information from a student at the surgeon's assistants' school [R], 1878; documents on student disturbances at the Jewish Institute [R], 1878.

(GARF, Moscow, Tret'e otdelenie)

17. Files on resettling Jewish families from Wilno to a colony in the Kherson *guberniia* [R], 1840–41.

(DAOdO, Odessa, Kantseliariia Novorossiiskogo i Bessarabskogo general-gubernatora)

18. File on economic aid for Jewish families transferred to the Kherson *guberniia* [R], 1840–42.

(TsDIAU, Kyiv, Kantseliariia... general-gubernatora)

19. Notes in the journal of a committee for censorship of Jewish books [R], 1852.

(RGIA, St. Petersburg, Buturlinskii komitet po delam pechati)

20. Circulars, correspondence and lists of the School Inspectorate about Jewish Schools and about a home for poor Jewish students at the Rabbinical Seminary [R], 1853–1909; minutes of *Chovevei Zion* [H], 1891; notes of an anonymous author about inspections of Jewish vocational schools [R], 1900.

(GARF, Moscow, Marek)

21. Files about changes in teaching Jewish subjects and minutes from a meeting of the school pedagogical council [R], 1862–1865.
(DAZhO, Zhytomyr, Zhitomirskoe ravvinskoe uchilishche)
22. File about construction of Jewish hospitals and shelters [R], 1863–64.
(RGIA, St.-Petersburg, Khoziaistvennyi departament MVD)
23. Correspondence about the activity of the Rabbinical Seminaries in Zhitomir and Wilno and about the closing of the Rabbinical Seminary in Wilno [R], 1865–67.
(TsDIAU, Kyiv, Upravlenie Kievskogo uchebnogo okruga)
24. Records on the blood libel against David Blondes [R], 1900; records about setting up Jewish charitable institutions [R], 1900; records about a conference in Wilno of the Society for Attainment of Full Rights for the Jewish People [R], 1905; Society correspondence about elections to the *Duma*, including letters by Simon Dubnov [H, R, Y], 1905–07.
(RGIA, St. Petersburg, Obshchestvo polnopraviia...)
25. File about clandestine Jewish organizations, including lists of those arrested or under surveillance [R], 1900–04.
(GARF, Moscow, Moskovskoe okhrannoe otdelenie)
26. Records about the Association for Aid to Workers [R], 1902–03; files on measures taken by the authorities to prevent pogroms [R], 1906; a file on the Jewish Socialist Workers' Party, its literature and foreign committee [R], 1910–14; files on the local branch of the Society for the Attainment of Full Rights for the Jewish People in Russia [R], 1914.
(GARF, Moscow, Departament politsii...)
27. Circulars, instructions and reports about the Jewish Socialist Workers' Party and Zionist youth groups in Wilno [R], 1907–16.
(TsGAU, Tashkent, Turkestanskoe okhrannoe otdelenie)
28. File on the activity of the local branch of OPE [R], 1911–16; records about registration of a Society for Support of Jewish Education (excerpts from the statutes of the *Talmud Tora* in Wilno) [R], 1914.
(TsGIAPb, St. Petersburg, Kantseliariia peterburgskogo gradonachal'nika)
29. Requests for permission to sell currant wine [R], 1914–15.
(RGIA, St. Petersburg, Glavnoe upravlenie neokladnykh sborov...)
30. Requests to abolish the "Pale of Settlement", addressed to the city council [R], 1915.
(TsGIAPb, St. Petersburg, Evreiskoe literaturno-khudozhestvennoe obshchestvo)
31. Testimonies and excerpts from newspapers about the attitude of the German occupation authorities to the Jewish population in Wilno [R], 1915.
(TsDIAU, Kyiv, Fridman)
32. Notes about antagonism between Poles and Jews in the pharmaceutical association in Wilno [R], 1917.
(GARF, Moscow, Katsenel'son)
33. Correspondence about evacuation of the P. Kohan Gymnasium from Wilno to Ekaterinoslav, including a list of teachers [R], 1918.
(DAOdO, Odessa, Kantseliariia popechitelia...)
34. Minutes of the Section for the Study of the Revolutionary Movement among the Jews, including memoirs about revolutionary circles at the Institute for Jewish Teachers in Wilno in 1870–90 [R], 1931; material about the revolutionary movement among the Jews at the end of the 1880's and the beginning of the 1890's [R], 1931, 1934; testimonies concerning Jewish members of revolutionary movements [R], 1931; testimonies about the activity of the Russian Social-Democratic Worker's Party among Jewish

workers in Wilno at the beginning of the 20th cent. [R], 1933; testimonies about the *Bund* in Wilno during the revolution of 1905 [R], 1934.
(GARF, Moscow, Vsesoiuznoe obshchestvo…)

WILNO, surroundings, 1853–1916
Microfilms:
1. A file on the liquidation of the Committee for Censorship of Jewish books [R], 1828; an *ukase* by the Tsar concerning censorship of Jewish books and the closing of all printing houses except Wilno and Kiev [R], 1836–37; reports by censors from Wilno and other towns about books not approved for publication [P, R], 1894; letters by Jewish authors to censorship committees requesting to publish their works [R], 1896.
(RGIA, St. Petersburg, Peterburgskii tsenzurnyi komitet)
2. Correspondence with the chancellery of the Wilno *guberniia* about preparing lists of former inhabitants of the Wilno *guberniia*, living in the Kherson and Ekaterinoslav *guberniias*, inncluding lists [R], 1853–55.
(DAOdO, Odessa, Popechitel'skii komitet…)
3. A file about the appointment of Jewish referents (*Uchenyi evrei*) in government offices [R], 1856; a file on the inspection of Jewish schools in the western *guberniias* of Russia and the Polish Kingdom by Leon Mandelshtam, information about schools, teachers, rabbis and benefactors in various Jewish communities and documents concerning Mandelshtam's publishing activity [F, H, R, P], 1856–62.
(RGIA, St. Petersburg, Departament narodnogo prosveshcheniia)
4. A file about support for rabbis from the *korobka* tax [R], 1877–81; statistical data about synagogues and rabbis in various towns of the Wilno *guberniia* [R], 1908.
(RGIA, St. Petersburg, Departament dukhovnykh del…)
5. Distribution of the candle tax among Jews in different *guberniias* [R], 1879–80.
(TsDIAU, Kyiv, Chancery of the general governor of Kiev, Podolia and Volhynia)
6. A file about measures by the authorities to prevent anti-Jewish disturbances [R], 1881–82.
(GARF, Moscow, Val')
7. Reports about Jewish charitable institutions in various towns of the *guberniia* [R], 1886.
(RGIA, St. Petersburg, Khoziaistvennyi departament MVD)
8. Files on funds from taxes destined for education in the Wilno *guberniia* [R], 1891–1903; files about the legal situation of Jews in Russia, about participation of Jews in self government in towns and about participation of Jews in revolutionary movements [R], 1882–1906; a report of the Jewish Colonization Association (JCA) about the situation of the Jews in Russia [R], 1900;
(RGIA, St. Petersburg, Obshchestvo polnopraviia...)
9. Lists and addresses of Zionist associations and groups in various *guberniias* [R], 1907–16.
(TsGAU, Tashkent, Turkestanskoe okhrannoe otdelenie)
10. Correspondence about the displacement of suspected Jews from military zones, a prohibition to sell alcoholic beverages and requests by Jews to modify repressive measures [R], 1914–16; correspondence about Jews suspected of buyng up copper and gold coins, of political disloyalty and of espionage [R], 1915.
(RGVIA, Moscow, Shtab Dvinskogo voennogo okruga)

WINIARY (pow. Myślenice, woj. krakowskie) 1729
Microfilms:
Asekuracja (charter) given to a Jew, 1729.
(AP Kraków, Arch. Sanguszków, teki tzw. arabskie)

WINNIKI (pow. Lwów, woj. lwowskie) 1789–1938
Microfilms:

1. Correspondence with the district administration about aid for Jews settled in colonies, including a list of names [G], 1789.
(TsDIAU, L'viv, Namiestnictwo Galicyjskie)
2. A report on teaching religion in public schools [G, P], 1882–89.
(TsDIAU, L'viv, Krajowa Rada Szkolna)
3. A list of tax payers, 1930s.
(DALO, L'viv, Magistrat, Żółkiew)
4. Correspondence about community matters, 1938.
(DALO, L'viv, UW, Lwów)

WIŚNICZ (pow. Bochnia, woj. krakowskie) 1719–1896
Microfilms:
1. Community accounts, 1719.
(AP Kraków, Arch. Sanguszków, teki tzw. arabskie)
2. A document issued by the mayor concerning an agreement between a Jewish tobacco merchant and a Christian merchant from Kraków, 1739; investigation of a Jew accused of stealing from a tavernkeeper, 1793.
(AP Kraków)
3. Correspondence about the vacant rabbinate in Wiśnicz [G, Hung., P], 1896.
(TsDIAU, L'viv, Namiestnictwo Galicyjskie)

WIŚNICZ NOWY (pow. Bochnia, woj. krakowskie) 1896–1904
Microfilms:
Reports from inspections of Baron Hirsch Foundation (JCA) schools [P, G], 1896–1904.
(TsDIAU, L'viv, Krajowa Rada Szkolna)

WIŚNIOWIEC (pow. Krzemieniec, woj. wołyńskie) 1837–1939
Microfilms:
1. A file on prosecution of a Jew for printing books without permission from the censorship and on uncensored prayer books found in the possession of the rabbi [R], 1837–39.
(TsDIAU, Kyiv, Kantseliariia... general-gubernatora)
2. Requests, reports and correspondence about clandestine fundraising by the community, including a list of inhabitants [H, R], 1837–41; a list of conscripted Jews [H, R], 1840–41; requests, accounts and correspondence by the Jewish community about payment of debts to the Church in Stary Wiśniowiec, including lists [P, R], 1841–51.
(DATO, Ternopil', Magistrat, Krzemieniec)
3. Minutes and reports on the establishment and activities of the Zionist Organization in Wiśnowiec, including a list of founding members, 1921–34; reports and correspondence about activity of *Tarbut*, including a list of board members, 1922–34; reports and correspondence on the registration and activity of a branch of *Palestyńskie Towarzystwo Emigracyjne w Łucku* in Wiśniowiec, including a list of founding members, board members and statutes, 1925–34; a report on the foundation of *Poalei Zion* in Wiśniowiec, including a list of board members, 1926–34; a list of children under the care of the society for the care of poor orphans, *Towarzystwo Opieki nad Żydowskimi Sierotami*, 1928, as well as reports on its activity, 1931-38; correspondence of *WIZO* in Warsaw about establishing a branch in Wiśniowiec, 1928–35; reports and correspondence concerning registration, activity and liquidation of the local branch of the *Zjednoczenie Szkół Żydowskich* association, including lists and statutes, 1928–34; reports and correspondence concerning registration and activity of *Gmilus Chasodim* and a list of board members, 1930–38; reports about election

of the board members of *Brit Hatzohar*, including lists, 1933–37; reports and correspondence concerning community elections, including a list of council members, 1935; a file on introducing taxes on *shechita* and kosher meat consumption, 1936; materials on ratification of the community budget and a list of tax payers, 1936–37.
(DATO, Ternopil', Starostwo Powiatowe, Krzemieniec)
4. Reports, syllabus and correspondence on the opening of a *Talmud Tora*, 1926–32; statistical reports on the activities of the *Tarbut* and *Talmud Tora* schools, 1930–31; government instructions about improving the organization of private Jewish schools, inspection reports of the *Talmud Tora* and *Tarbut* schools and a list of teachers, 1931–35; a statistical report and correspondence with the authorities concerning appointments of teachers in the *Tarbut* school, 1937–39.
(DATO, Ternopil', Inspektorat Szkolny, Krzemieniec)

WITKÓW (pow. Radziechów, woj. tarnopolskie) 1711–1898
Microfilms:
1. Real estate contracts, testimonies before the rabbinical court, obligations, etc. [H, Y], 1711–1845.
(TsDIAU, Kyiv, Arch. Potockich z Tulczyna)
2. Promissory notes [G, P], 1749–58.
(NBANU, L'viv, Zb. Goldsteina)
3. *Pinkas* of the burial society [H], 1820–68.
(ŻIH, Warszawa)
3. Correspondence regarding communal matters, 1898.
(TsDIAU, L'viv, Namiestnictwo Galicyjskie)

WITKÓW NOWY (pow. Radziechów, woj. tarnopolskie) 1928–1939
Microfilms:
Questionnaires containing names of community council members, 1928, 1932–33; reports and correspondence concerning community elections and lists of community members, 1932–35; community budget for 1936; community tax payers for 1939.
(DATO, Ternopil', UW, Tarnopol)

WIZNA (pow. Łomża, woj. białostockie) 1566–1913
Microfilms:
1. *Lustracje* of the *województwo*, 1566.
(AGAD, Warszawa, ASK)
2. Birth, marriage and death records (fragmentary), 1828–65.
(AP Łomża)
3. Certificates and photographs of candidates for the rabbinate [R], 1886–1913; files about the arrest of Jews suspected of assisting clandestine border crossings [R], 1912–13.
(AP Białystok, Rząd Gubernialny, Łomża)

WIŻAJNY (pow. Suwałki, woj. białostockie) 1936–1937
Photocopies:
Correspondence with the authorities regarding the community budget, 1936–37.
(AP Suwałki, Starostwo Powiatowe Suwalskie)

WŁOCŁAWEK (woj. warszawskie) 1818–1871
Microfilms:
Files concerning permission to set up an *eruv* in the Jewish quarter and the ensuing conflicts with Christian neighbors, 1818–71; a project to distribute kosher meat to poor Jews and support sick Jewish hospital patients [P, R], 1848–56; correspondence about exemption from conscription for graduates of the Rabbinical Seminary in Warsaw and a list of rabbis, 1865–71.
(AGAD, Warszawa, CWW)

WŁOCŁAWEK, surroundings, 1821–1871
Microfilms:
Decrees, minutes and correspondence concerning religious observance – participation in prayers in recognized synagogues, a prohibition of marriage not in the place of residence, payment for burial services and a list of rabbis in the Włocławek district, 1821–71.
(AGAD, Warszawa, CWW)

WŁODAWA (woj. lubelskie) 1853–1910
Microfilms:
1. Government reports and correspondence concerning appointments of rabbis and conflicts between them and the communities, including a list of rabbis, 1853–56.
(AGAD, Warszawa, CWW)
2. Records of *arendas*, 1867–1910.
(AP Lublin, Arch. Zamoyskich z Włodawy)

WŁODZIMIERZ (woj. wołyńskie) 1558–1906
Originals:
A report of the regional administration about settling Jews in the Novorossiysk area [R], 1807; a report of the administration about *propinacja* [R], 1809.
Microfilms:
1. Royal charters exempting the Jews of Włodzimierz from taxes and customs [R], 1558–61.
(RGADA, Moscow, ML)
2. Documents concerning Jews in files of the Castle Court [Rt], 1566–1607.
(TsDIAU, Kyiv, Vladimirskii grodskii sud)
3. Copies of documents concerning a blood libel accusation [R], 1569; a request for material assistance for the Jewish community, following a pogrom [R], 1883.
(TsDIAU, Kyiv, Dokumenty, sobrannye…)
4. Lustracja of the *starostwo* and its inhabitants, 1663.
(AP Wrocław, Ossolineum)
5. Complaints by the *kahal* about assaults and damages to the synagogue and private homes, 1728–37.
(TsDIAU, Kyiv, Arch. Zamoyskich)
6. Requests by the *kahal* regarding debt payments, 1779–81.
(RGADA, Moscow, KFE)
7. Decrees, instructions, requests and correspondence concerning the employment and salaries of educated Jews in government offices, and the salaries of Jewish translators and teachers [R], 1816–84; correspondence on a request by the Jewish community to prevent the election of a certain Jew to the city council [R], 1833–34.
(RGIA, St. Petersburg, Departament dukhovnykh del…)

8. Records about high payments for burial services [R], 1833; a file on opposition by Jews to the magistrate and the community leadership [R], 1834–35; file on collection of funds to construct a synagogue in Jerusalem [R], 1837–38; correspondence, reports, and court verdicts concerning debts of the community to monasteries [R], 1845–47; a report on threats to the Jewish community official responsible for conscription [R], 1847–48; a complaint by a Jew due to oppressions by the town governor [R], 1851–53; a report by the district police superintendent about antisemitic disturbances, expulsion of a Jewish family from the town [R], 1882–84.
(TsDIAU, Kyiv, Kantseliariia... general-gubernatora)
9. A report on Jewish schools [R], 1852–58.
(DAKhO, Kamianets'-Podil's'kyi, Direktsiia narodnykh uchilishch...)
10. A report on the construction of Jewish hospitals and shelters [R], 1863–64.
(RGIA, St. Petersburg, Khoziaistvennyi departament MVD)
11. Correspondence of the Society for the Attainment of full Rights for the Jewish People in Russia about elections to the *Duma* [R], 1906.
(RGIA, St. Petersburg, Obshchestvo polnopraviia...)
12. Correspondence about measures to end and/or prevent pogroms [R], 1906.
(GARF, Moscow, Departament politsii...)

WŁODZIMIERZ, surroundings, 1834–1871
Microfilms:
1. Reports about the number of communities, synagogues, Jewish schools, functionaries, and inhabitants in the *guberniia* of Volhynia and *uezd* of Włodzimierz [R], 1834, 1842, 1850; a file about *propinacja* rights for Jewish inhabitants [R], 1849–52.
(TsDIAU, Kyiv, Kantseliariia... general-gubernatora)
2. Report and statistics on towns in the district [R], 1871.
(RGIA, St. Petersburg, Khoziaistvennyi departament MVD)

WŁODZIMIERZEC (pow. Sarny, woj. wołyńskie) 1834–1876
Microfilms:
Copies of documents concerning *chasidic tzadikim* [R], 1834–76.
(TsDIAU, Kyiv, Dokumenty, sobrannye...)

WŁOSZCZOWA (woj. kieleckie) 1835–1915
Microfilms:
1. Correspondence aboput a request for tax exemption, 1835–39.
(AGAD, Warszawa, KRzPiS)
2. An investigation of Jews suspected of espionage [R], 1914–15.
(AP Białystok, Rząd Gubernialny, Łomża)

WODZISŁAW (pow. Jędrzejów, woj. kieleckie) 1680–1835
Microfilms:
1. A file about a loan from a priest to the Jewish community, 1680.
(AP Kraków, IT)
2. An *arenda* contract for *propinacja* of alcoholic beverages [H, P], 1791–1802, 1811; an inventory of damages made by Russian soldiers to properties in Wodzisław, 1792.
(TsDIAU, L'viv, Arch. Lanckorońskich)

3. Files on leasing of community taxes, accounts and reports, requests for tax exemptions, 1811–35; documents on community debts, 1820–31.
(AGAD, Warszawa, KRzPiS)

WOHYŃ (pow. Radzyń, woj. lubelskie) 1853–1856
Microfilms:
Reports and correspondence regarding appointments of rabbis, 1853–56.
(AGAD, Warszawa, CWW)

WOJNICZ (pow. Brzesko, woj. krakowskie) 1878
Microfilms:
Reports about the reorganization of elementary schools attended by Jews [G, P], 1878.
(TsDIAU, L'viv, Krajowa Rada Szkolna)

WOJNIŁÓW (pow. Kałusz, woj. stanisławowskie) 1778–1939
Microfilms:
1. *Summariusz* of town revenues, 1778.
(NBANU, L'viv, Zb. Czołowskiego)
2. Statutes, minutes and correspondence concerning Jewish associations [G, P], 1894, 1899, 1924–39; a list of board members of *Hatzofim Brit Trumpeldor*, 1930–37; reports and correspondence on salaries of rabbis and *dayanim* and on the community council elections 1932–36; correspondence with the district authorities on setting up a local branch of *Makabi*, 1932–37; lists of board members of: *Liga Pomocy Pracującym w Palestynie 'Hitachdut'*, 1933–37, and *Związek Opieki nad Sierotami i Młodzieżą Żydowską*, 1937–38; material on the ratification of the community budget and religious tax, 1938.
(DAIFO, Ivano-Frankivs'k, UW, Stanisławów)
3. Correspondence between the community and the district authorities regarding the statutes, 1897; complaints by the community against religious taxes, 1904–06; complaints about corruption, 1907.
(TsDIAU, L'viv, Namiestnictwo Galicyjskie)
4. Reports on anti-Jewish actions by Ukrainian nationalists, 1936–37.
(DAIFO, Ivano-Frankivs'k, Komenda Wojewódzka PP, Stanisławów)

WOJSŁAWICE (pow. Chełm, woj. lubelskie) 1749–1867
Microfilms:
1. An inventory of Wojsławice, containing lists of Jewish and Christian inhabitants, 1749.
(NBANU, L'viv, Zb. Czołowskiego)
2. A charter for the Jews, granted by M. Kurdwanowska, 1780.
(AP Lublin, Księgi Grodzkie Chełmskie)
3. A file on conversion to Christianity [R], 1867.
(AP Lublin, Rząd Gubernialny, Lublin)

WOLA MICHOWA (pow. Lesko, woj. lwowskie) 1895–1935
Microfilms:
1. Correspondence concerning vacant rabbinical positions, 1895.
(TsDIAU, L'viv, Namiestnictwo Galicyjskie)
2. Correspondence about the community budget and a list of tax payers, 1932–35.
(DALO, L'viv, UW, Lwów)

WOLA RANIŻOWSKA (pow. Kolbuszowa, woj. lwowskie) 1928–1930
Microfilms:
Authorization by the district authorities to collect money for the Polish–Galician community in Palestine, including a list of donors, 1928–30.
(DALO, L'viv, UW, Lwów)

WOLANKA (TUSTANOWICE, pow. Drohobycz, woj. lwowskie) 1913–1930
Microfilms:
1. Statutes of the *Chevra Kedosha* society, 1913–20.
(TsDIAU, L'viv, Namiestnictwo Galicyjskie)
2. Correspondence about the registration of *Agudas Yisroel*, 1925–30.
(DALO, L'viv, Magistrat, Lwów)

WOLBÓRZ (pow. Piotrków, woj. łódzkie) 1906–1915
Microfilms:
The establishment of a community in the town [R], 1906–08; ratification of community accounts and elections [R], 1908–15.
(AP Łódź, Rząd Gubernialny, WA, Piotrków)

WOLBROM (pow. Olkusz, woj. kieleckie) 1822–1910
Microfilms:
1. Reports and complaints concerning burial societies, 1822–50.
(AGAD, Warszawa, CWW)
2. Birth, marriage and death records, 1826–70.
(AP Chrzanów)
3. A file on the conversion of a Jewish woman to Christianity [R], 1910.
(AP Łódź, Rząd Gubernialny, WA, Piotrków)

WOLSZTYN (woj. poznańskie) 1698–1867
Microfilms:
Files (incl. charters, regulations and correspondence) concerning Jews [G, P], 1698–1833; *pinkas hakahal* [H], 1721–1834; files on government taxes paid by Jews [G, H], 1739–1817; files on the community [G], 1739–1838; *pinkassim* of the synagogue [H], 18th cent.; community accounts [G, H], 18th–19th cent.; a will of Mordechai Schiff [H], 1830–67; files on Jewish education [G], 1833–38; a register of *aliyot la-Tora* [H], early 19th cent.
(AP Poznań, Gmina Żydowska, Wolsztyn)

WOŁKOWYSK (woj. białostockie) 1803–1923
Originals:
Divorce certificates, 1928.
Microfilms:
1. Reports about tanneries [R], 1803.
(RGADA, Moscow, Manufaktur-kollegiia)
2. A file on the construction of a Jewish hospital and shelters [R], 1863–64.
(RGIA, St. Petersburg, Khoziaistvennyi departament MVD)
3. Correspondence of the Society for the Attainment of full Rights for the Jewish People in Russia about elections to the *Duma* [R], 1906.
(RGIA, St. Petersburg, Obshchestvo polnopraviia...)

4. A file on setting up a home for the elderly and statutes of a charitable society [R], 1909–11.
(AP Białystok, Rząd Gubernialny, Łomża)
5. A list of people exiled from the district, 1923.
(DATO, Ternopil', Komenda Powiatowa PP, Trembowla)

WOŁOŻYN (woj. wileńskie) 1714–1892
Originals:
3 personal documents of a *yeshiva* student [H], 1888–92.
Microfilms:
Correspondence, accounts, *arenda* contracts and requests to Prince A. Czartoryski, 1714–45; orders of payments, accounts, contracts, reports and other documents concerning estates of the Sieniawski family, 1720–28; inventories and accounts containing a list of Jewish and Christian inhabitants (1740), 1740, 1771.
(Bibl. Czartoryskich, Kraków)

WOŁPA (pow. Grodno, woj. białostockie)
Drawing of a wooden synagouge, n.d.
(IKG Wien - Juedisches Museum)

WOROCHTA (pow. Nadwórna, woj. stanisławowskie) 1932–1939
Microfilms:
Files on Jewish associations and founding members of the *Gmilus Chasodim* society, 1932–39.
(DAIFO, Ivano-Frankivs'k, UW, Stanisławów)

WÓJCIN (woj. łódzkie, pow. Wieluń) 1534–1615
Microfilms:
Inventory, 1534–1615.
(AGAD, Warszawa, ASK)

WRONKI (pow. Szamotuły, woj. poznańskie) 1633–1911
Originals:
Copies of charters granted to the Jews, 1633, 1714, 1742, 1758; a file on seats in the women's section of the synagogue [H], 1791; files on taxes paid by Jews and requests for refunds [G], 1822–84; litigation between the community and two local parishes [G], 1833–36; files on corruption among community members [G], 1831–69; minutes of community meetings [G], 1834–50; records of community finances [G], 1835–55; files on Jewish education and the Education Fund [G], 1835–53; *pinkas* of the burial society [H], 1840–1911; file on a member leaving the community [G], 1881; a letter by a rabbi from Poznań to the community in Wronki [G], 1882; a *memorbuch* [H], n.d.
Microfilms:
Naturalization of a Jew from Wronki [G], first half of 19th cent.
(AP Poznań, Akta miast, woj. poznańskiego)

WRZEŚNIA (woj. poznańskie)
Originals:
Community minutes [G], 1859

WYBRANÓWKA (pow. Bóbrka, woj. lwowskie) 1882–1889
Microfilms:
Reports on teaching Jewish religion in elementary schools [G, P], 1882–89.
(TsDIAU, L'viv, Krajowa Rada Szkolna)

WYGODA (pow. Dolina, woj. stanisławowskie) 1895–1939
Microfilms:
Files on ratifying the statutes of: the *Talmud Tora, Agudas Achim* and the *Mizrachi* [G, P, U], 1895, 1920–27; statutes, minutes and correspondence concerning Jewish associations, 1921–39; a list of *Hatikva* board members, 1932–36.
(DAIFO, Ivano-Frankivs'k, UW, Stanisławów)

WYK (pow. Ostrołęka, woj. białostockie) 1915
Microfilms:
A file on the arrest of a Jew suspected of espionage and his expulsion to the eastern *guberniias* of Russia [R], 1915.
(AP Białystok, Rząd Gubernialny, Łomża)

WYKNO STARE (pow. Wysokie Mazowieckie, woj. białostockie) 1905
Microfilms:
Fines for evading conscription [R], 1905.
(AP Białystok, Rząd Gubernialny, Łomża)

WYSOCK (pow. Równe, woj. wołyńskie) 1663–1860
Microfilms:
1. Circulars, accounts, decrees, *uniwersały* concerning inhabitants and estates of M. Sapieha, St. Siemieński and A. Czartoryski, 1663–1765.
(Bibl. Czartoryskich, Kraków)
2. Litigation regarding real estate, 1744.
(RGADA, Moscow, KFE)
3. *Revizskie skazki* [R], 1858–60.
(DARO, Rivne, Rovenskoe uezdnoe kaznacheistvo)

WYSOKA (pow. Wyrzysk, woj. poznańskie) 1936
Microfilms:
Monographs containing demographic and statistical data on Jews, 1936.
(AP Wrocław, Ossolineum, WKNZNP, Lwów)

WYSOKIE LITEWSKIE (pow. Brześć, woj. poleskie) 1927
Originals:
Certificates of bachelorhood, 1927.

WYSOKIE MAZOWIECKIE (MAZOWIECK, woj. białostockie) 1833–1939
Originals:
Birth, marriage and death records (fragmentary) [P, R], 1842–1939.
Drawing of a wooden synagouge, n.d.
(IKG Wien - Juedisches Museum)
Microfilms:
1. Birth, marriage and death records, 1833–65.
(AP Łomża)
2. Files on the acquisition of a pharmacy by a Jew [R], 1889–1912; a file on the opening of a dentist's surgery [R], 1906–12; a complaint by a Jew from Wysokie against the *wójt* of Zambrów [R], 1913–14; registration of a Jew as a citizen of the town [R], 1914; a file on the arrest of people suspected of illegal

political activity and evading conscription [R], 1914; regulations concerning dispatch of parcels between the communities of the *guberniia* [R], 1914–15.
(AP Białystok, Rząd Gubernialny, Łomża)
3. Reports and correspondence by government offices about appointments of rabbis and their relations with the leadership of the communities, 1853–56.
(AGAD, Warszawa, CWW)

WYSZANÓW (pow. Kępno, woj. poznańskie) 1534–1615
Microfilms:
Inventories and accounts containing data on Wyszanów, 1534–1615.
(AGAD, Warszawa, ASK)

WYSZOGRÓD (pow. Płock, woj. warszawskie) 1566–1845
Microfilms:
1. *Lustracje*, 1566.
(AGAD, Warszawa, ASK)
2. Confirmation of the rights of the Jews by King Zygmunt III (1588), 1589; the conditions for Jewish settlement in the town, 1766.
(AGAD, Warszawa, Księgi Grodzkie Wyszogrodzkie)
3. A file concerning the *lustracja* of the town, 1766.
(AP Wrocław, Ossolineum)
4. Records of litigation between the community and the Treasury over tax payments, 1842–45.
(AGAD, Warszawa, KRzSW)

WYSZOGRÓDEK (pow. Krzemieniec, woj. wołyńskie) 1840–1936
Microfilms:
1. Correspondence and reports on the incrimination of employees of the local recruiting board for irregularities regarding Jewish conscripts and a list of Jewish conscripts [H, R], 1840–41; census of the Jews for tax purposes [R], 1847–48; an investigation file of community officials suspected of forging signatures in community tax registers [R], 1855–59.
(DATO, Ternopil', Magistrat, Krzemieniec)
2. Budget of *Towarzystwo Opieki nad Żydowskimi Sierotami i Opuszczonymi Dziećmi na Wołyniu* for the support of orphans, and a list of the children supported, 1928; a list of *Tarbut* board members, 1932; a report about the activity of the Zionist Organization's local board and a list of founding members, 1933; correspondence with the district authorities on registering the *Histadrut Hanoar Hatziyoni* and a list of founding members, 1933; a list of Zionist Organization board members, 1935–36.
(DATO, Ternopil', Starostwo Powiatowe, Krzemieniec)

WYŻWA (pow. Kowel, woj. wołyńskie) 1604–1664
Microfilms:
Files on litigation between Jews and Christians [Rt], 1604–64.
(TsDIAU, Kyiv, Magistrat, Wyżwa)

ZABŁOCIE (pow. Żywiec, woj. krakowskie) 1895–1896
Microfilms:
Correspondence with the district authorities concerning ratification of statutes, 1895–96.
(TsDIAU, L'viv, Namiestnictwo Galicyjskie)

ZABŁOTÓW (pow. Śniatyn, woj. stanisławowskie) 1780–1939
Microfilms:
1. Documents concerning debts of the Jewish community [G, L], 1780.
(TsDIAU, L'viv, Kolektsiia dokumentuv…)
2. Inventory of the estate and surrounding villages containing a list of Jewish inhabitants [L, P], 1810.
(NBANU, L'viv, Zb. Czołowskiego)
3. Files on the ratification of Jewish community statutes, 1846–96; correspondence with the district authorities regarding *chadorim,* including lists of teachers in the district [G, P], 1875–1908; correspondence with the district authorities and the Ministry of Religion regarding the elections [G, P], 1883–89.
(TsDIAU, L'viv, Namiestnictwo Galicyjskie)
4. Documents on the statutes of the *Mizrachi, Agudas Yisroel* and other Jewish organizations, including lists of *Agudas Yisroel* and *Mizrachi* members, 1893, 1920–30; reports and correspondence concerning the registration, statutes and activities of Jewish libraries, 1921–30; files on registration of an association for Jewish war victims, 1921–30; a file on the founding of the Jewish women's association, *Lev Tov,* 1922–30; reports and correspondence concerning ratification of statutes and registration of Jewish charity associations, 1923–28; minutes, reports and correspondence concerning community board elections and complaints about the results and increases in salaries of community functionaries [H, P], 1928–38; lists of board members of: a society for aid to orphans (1930), *Gmilas Chesed* (1930–31), *Achva* (1930–37), *Hatzofim Brit Trumpeldor* (1930–37), Jewish sports associations (1931–36), *Hashomer Hatzair* (1931–37), *Hatchiya* (1932–38), *Yad Charutzim* (1933–35), *Tarbut* (1934–38) and other Jewish associations, 1930–39; files on an organization of Jewish schools, 1933–37; files on Jewish agricultural associations, 1933–38.
(DAIFO, Ivano-Frankivs'k, UW, Stanisławów)
5. Circulars of the authorities concerning elections and inspection of Jewish communities and a report about the community board elections, 1928–32, 1939; index of the register of Jewish marriages and deaths, 1937; reports and correspondence concerning ratification of the community budget and a list of taxpayers, 1938–39.
(DAIFO, Ivano-Frankivs'k, Starostwo Powiatowe, Śniatyn)
6. A report on the activity of OŻPP and a list of board members, 1933; reports about the activities of: Revisionist Zionists, *Poalei Zion Lewica, Hitachdut Poalei Zion, Hechalutz, Hakoach* and *Yad Charutzim,* 1935.
(DAIFO, Ivano-Frankivs'k, Posterunek PP, Śniatyn)
7. Community budget (1933, 1934) and lists of community tax payers, 1934, 1939.
(DAIFO, Ivano-Frankivs'k, Gmina Żydowska, Zabłotów)
8. Statistics regarding the population, 1938.
(DAIFO, Ivano-Frankivs'k, UW, Stanisławów)

ZABŁUDÓW (pow. Białystok, woj. białostockie) 1622–1750
Originals:
Drawing of a wooden synagogue, n.d.
(IKG Wien - Juedisches Museum)
Photocopies:
Inventories of estates, containing lists of Jews, 1622.
(NIAB Minsk, Arch. Radziwiłłów)
Microfilms:
Excerpts from municipal books, relating to the prosecution of Christians accused of insulting or assaulting Jews, 1750.

(AGAD, Warszawa, Arch. Radziwiłłów)

ZAGÓRÓW (pow. Konin, woj. łódzkie) 1902–1907
Microfilms:
A file on the enlargement of the Jewish cemetery [R], 1902; a file on the construction of a ritual slaughter house [R], 1907.
(AP Łódź, Rząd Gubernialny, WA, Kalisz)

ZAGÓRZ (pow. Sanok, woj. lwowskie) 1895–1908
Microfilms:
Correspondence with the district authorities about the Jewish community and ratification of statutes, 1895–96; correspondence about the *Osei Tov* and *Dorshei Tov* societies[G, P], 1908.
(TsDIAU, L'viv, Namiestnictwo Galicyjskie)

ZAKLICZYN (pow. Brzesko, woj. krakowskie) 1878
Microfilms:
Reports on the reorganization of elementary schools attended by Jewish children [G, P], 1878.
(TsDIAU, L'viv, Krajowa Rada Szkolna)

ZAKLIKÓW (pow. Janów, woj. lubelskie) 1835–1919
Original:
An identity card, 1919.
Microfilms:
Statistical data on the town, 1835–61.
(AP Lublin, Rząd Gubernialny, Lublin)

ZAKOPANE (pow. Nowy Targ, woj. krakowskie) 1877–1908
Microfilms:
Correspondence with the district authorities about *chadorim*, and a list of teachers, 1877–1908.
(TsDIAU, L'viv, Namiestnictwo Galicyjskie)

ZAKRAKÓWKA (pow. Miechów, woj. kieleckie) 1847–1851
Microfilms:
A file on a Jewish colony, 1847–51.
(AP Kielce)

ZAKROCZYM (pow. Warszawa, woj. warszawskie) 1566–1866
Microfilms:
1. *Lustracje*, 1566.
(AGAD, Warszawa, ASK)
2. Birth, marriage and death records, 1825–63.
(AP Warszawa)
3. Records concerning the community, 1864–66.
(AGAD, Warszawa, KRzSW)
4. *Pinkas* of the burial society [H], 19th cent.
(Private Collection)

ZALESIE (pow. Limanowa, woj. krakowskie) 1643–1767
Microfilms:

1. Contract for the *arenda* of flour mills, 1643.
(AP Kraków, Teki sanguszkowskie, tzw. rzymskie)
2. Contract for the *arenda* of a tavern, 1767.
(AP Kraków)

ZALESZCZYKI (woj. tarnopolskie) 1793–1939
Originals:
A poster on the registration of children for a school [H, Y], 1931.
Microfilms:
1. Correspondence with the provincial authorities about financial matters of the community, the *krupka* tax, *arenda*, real estate and petitions concerning residence rights [G, P], 1793–95, 1819–22, 1834–37; tables concerning taxes [G], 1842–59; correspondence about *chadorim* and a list of *melamdim*, 1874–1908; correspondence about supporting Jewish schools [G, P], 1880; correspondence with the police about pogroms and lists of emigrants to America, 1882; reports and correspondence on the reorganization of the Jewish community file on slaughter houses, complaints by community members against high taxes and inappropriate community administration and the vacant post of the rabbi [G, P], 1890–97; correspondence with the *Ahavas Zion society* about emigration to *Eretz Yisroel* [G, P], 1898; correspondence with the Ministry of Religion about antisemitic incidents [G, P], 1898; construction of the Baron Hirsch Foundation (JCA) school, 1902.
(TsDIAU, L'viv, Namiestnictwo Galicyjskie)
2. Files on the activity and financial standing of the *kahal* and a list of Jewish inhabitants [G, H, P], 1797–1851; a file on the theft of a horse from a Jew, 1798.
(TsDIAU, L'viv, Arch. Lanckorońskich)
3. Reports containing lists of *chadorim* and teachers [G, P], 1875–77; reports about teaching Jewish religion in elementary schools [G, P], 1882–89; reports folowing inspections of Baron Hirsch Foundation (JCA) schools, including the personal files of the teachers, S. Jaffe and D. Feldman [G, P], 1896–1904.
(TsDIAU, L'viv, Krajowa Rada Szkolna)
4. Correspondence on ratifying the statutes and activity of *Hatchiya*, 1922; reports on the participation of Orthodox Jews in parliamentary elections, 1928; questionnaires containing names of Jewish community council members, 1928; a list of political parties containing numbers of members, names and short descriptions of their activities, 1929; correspondence on the activity and liquidation of *Agudas Yisroel*, including a list of board members, 1930–36; reports and correspondence concerning community elections, 1932–35; correspondence with the Ministry of Interior and the local authorities about emigration to Palestine, including a list of Jews leaving for Palestine, 1933–34; community budget, 1935–36; reports on the election of rabbis, 1937–38; documents on the rabbi's salary, 1937–38; a community financial report, 1939.
(DATO, Ternopil', UW, Tarnopol)

ZALESZCZYKI, surroundings, 1877–1934
Microfilms:
1. A report about *chadorim* in the district and a list of *chadorim*, 1877–1908.
(TsDIAU, L'viv, Namiestnictwo Galicyjskie)
2. Report of the local authorities on the expulsion of Jews living within 10 mile of the Dniester river [R], 1915.
(DATO, Ternopil', Kantseliariia Tarnopol'skogo gubernatora)

3. Lists of Jewish and Greek-Catholic inhabitants of the district, 1923–24; reports about community elections in the district, 1928; statistical report concerning conversions in the district, 1918–33; a register of periodicals distributed in the district, 1934.
(DATO, Ternopil', UW, Tarnopol)

ZAŁOŹCE (pow. Zborów, woj. tarnopolskie) 1842–1939
Microfilms:
1. Minutes and inventories regarding the sale of Jewish real estate, 1842.
(TsDIAU, L'viv, Kolektsiia dokumentiv…)
2. Correspondence between the community and the authorities regarding *chadorim* and a list of *melamdim* in the area [G, P], 1877–1908; reports about the Jewish community [G, P], 1890.
(TsDIAU, L'viv, Namiestnictwo Galicyjskie)
3. Reports and correspondence on the activity and liquidation of *Agudas Yisroel*, including a list of board members, and material on courses in religion for girls from *Beis Yaakov* (1936), 1927–1937; questionnaires containing names of Jewish community board members, 1928; a list of political parties containing names of members and short descriptions of their activity, 1929; minutes, reports and correspondence on elections, the community council, budget, taxes and the elections of rabbis, including lists of tax payers, rabbis and *dayanim*, 1932–39.
(DATO, Ternopil', UW, Tarnopol)

ZAŁUCZE (pow. Śniatyn, woj. stanisławowskie) 1933–1938
Microfilms:
Files on Jewish agricultural associations, 1933–38.
(DAIFO, Ivano-Frankivs'k, UW, Stanisławów)

ZAMARSTYNÓW (part of Lwów since 1934) 1918–1919
Microfilms:
Reports of robberies and assaults on Jews, commited by inhabitants and soldiers, 1918–19.
(DALO, L'viv, Dyrekcja Policji, Lwów)

ZAMBRÓW (pow. Łomża, woj. białostockie) 1842–1913
Microfilms:
1. Birth, marriage and death records [P, R], 1842–73.
(AP Łomża)
2. Certificates and photos of candidates for the rabbinate [R], 1886–1913; permission to produce and distribute soda water [R], 1890, 1911–13; a file on illegal medical practice [R], 1906–07; permission to open a dentist's office [R], 1908–09.
(AP Białystok, Rząd Gubernialny, Łomża)

ZAMBRÓW, surroundings, 1842–1867
Microfilms:
Birth, marriage and death records for Jews living in the district, 1842–67.
(AP Białystok)

ZAMOŚĆ (woj. lubelskie) 1604–1907
Microfilms:
1. Charters for the Jews, 1604–80; complaints by Catholic merchants against Jewish spice merchants, 1770; files on contracts of a Persian merchant for delivery of silk belts, and his complaints against Jewish merchants, 1772.
(TsDIAU, Kyiv, Arch. Zamojskich)
2. Records of the community's debts to the Church, 1658–1824.
(AP Lublin, Kolegiata w Zamościu)
3. Charters granted to Jews by the Zamoyski family; settlement of a dispute between the community of Zamość and those of Bełz and Chełm over the allocation of the poll tax, 1684–1745.
(AP Lublin, Księgi Grodzkie Krasnostawskie)
4. Documents on financial matters, testimonies from the rabbinical court, etc. [H, Y], 1711–1845.
(TsDIAU, Kyiv, Arch. Potockich z Tulczyna)
5. Files on Jewish inhabitants and taxes, 1705–08; *supliki* by Jews from Zamość, 1716–18.
(Bibl. Czartoryskich, Kraków)
6. A letter concerning a dispute between the communities of Zamość and Opatów, 1725.
(AGAD, Warszawa, Arch. Zamoyskich)
7. Court files [P,L], 1741–78.
(AP Lublin, Księgi Miejskie, Zamość)
8. Correspondence about Karaites, 1775–80.
(TsDIAU, L'viv, Namiestnictwo Galicyjskie)
9. Files on synagogues, 1818–60; reports about burial societies, 1822–50; a project to distribute kosher meat to poor Jews and support sick Jewish hospital patients [P, R], 1848–56; records concerning the community, reports and financial matters, 1829–65.
(AGAD, Warszawa, CWW)
10. A file about confiscation of smuggled goods from Jews [R], 1826–41.
(AGAD, Warszawa, SSKP)
11. Records on the conversion of a Jew to Christianity [R], 1842–43; a statistical description of Zamość, 1821–61; files on the Jewish hospital, 1843–66.
(AP Lublin, Rząd Gubernialny, Lublin)
12. A complaint by a surgeon's assistant's wife, asking for the return of her husband to Judaism [R], 1866.
(AP Lublin, Kancelaria Gubernatora Lubelskiego)
13. Correspondence of the Society for the Attainment of full Rights for the Jewish People of Russia about elections to the *Duma* [R], 1905–07.
(RGIA, St. Petersburg, Obshchestvo polnopraviia…)

ZAMOŚĆ, surroundings, 1860–1871
Microfilms:
1. Statistical descriptions of towns in the district, 1860–61.
(AP Lublin, Rząd Gubernialny, Lublin)
2. Correspondence about exemptions from conscription for graduates of the Rabbinical Seminary in Warsaw and a list of rabbis, 1865–71.
(AGAD, Warszawa, CWW)

ZANIEMYŚL (pow. Środa, woj. poznańskie) 1815–1881
Originals:

A receipt, 1815; varia [G], 1820–81; records of payments for synagogue seats [G], 1827, 1837; litigation between the community and the Department of Education in the Grand Duchy of Posen [G], 1833; files on the reorganization of the community [G], 1834–37; records of community elections, 1834–81; community resolutions, 1834–81; community accounts, 1835; paving the Jewish quarter, 1835, police documents [G], 1835; tax records, 1837; a file on the tenure of a temporary rabbi, 1843–54; records concerning the Jewish law of 1847, 1847–53; community statutes [G], 1863.

Microfilms:
Minutes of the community board (fragmentary) [G], 1834–58.
(Centrum Judaicum, Berlin)

ZARĘBY KOŚCIELNE (pow. Ostrów, woj. białostockie) 1818–1915
Originals:
Marriage records, 1858–70.
Microfilms:
1. Files on synagogues, 1818–60.
(AGAD, Warszawa, CWW)
2. Certificates and photos of candidates for the rabbinate [R], 1886–1913; a file on the closing of a bakery belonging to a Jew [R], 1909; permission to produce and distribute soda water [R], 1909; a file on the arrest of Jews suspected of illegal political activity [R], 1912–15.
(AP Białystok, Rząd Gubernialny, Łomża)

ZARSZYN (pow. Sanok, woj. lwowskie) 1928–1933
Microfilms:
1. Authorization by the district authorities to collect money for the Polish–Galician community in Palestine, including a list of donors, 1928–30.
(DALO, L'viv, UW, Lwów)
2. Correspondence about the registration of *Agudas Yisroel*, 1933.
(DALO, L'viv, Magistrat, Lwów)

ZARZECZE (pow. Nadwórna, woj. stanisławowskie) 1926–1928
Microfilms:
A file on construction of a school [P, U], 1926–28.
(DAIFO, Ivano-Frankivs'k, Wydział Powiatowy Samorządu, Bohorodczany)

ZASZKÓW (pow. Złoczów, woj. tarnopolskie) 1733–1734
Microfilms:
Arenda contract of Jesuit properties, 1733–34.
(TsDIAU, L'viv, Kolektsiia dokumentiv pro katolyts'ki monastyri…)

ZATOR (pow. Wadowice, woj. krakowskie) 1570–1703
Microfilms:
Extracts from records of the municipal court concerning Jews, 1570–1703.
(AP Wrocław, Ossolineum)

ZAWAŁÓW (pow. Podhajce, woj. tarnopolskie) 1778–1938
Microfilms:
1. A court verdict regarding a complaint by the Basilian monastery against Jews [L], 1778.
(NBANU, L'viv, Klasztor Bazylianów)

2. Reports and correspondence about community elections, including names of council and community members, 1922–35; material on uniting the Jewish communities of Zawałów and Podhajce, 1933; an inspection report of the Jewish community, 1934–37; a list of rabbis and *dayanim*, 1937–38.
(DATO, Ternopil', UW, Tarnopol)

ZAWICHOST (pow. Sandomierz, woj. kieleckie) 1782
Microfilms:
A verdict in a court case between the community and a Christian, 1782.
(Bibl. im. Łopacińskiego, Lublin)

ZAWIERCIE (woj. kieleckie) 1891–1910
Microfilms:
1. Fines for evading conscription [R], 1891–1901.
(AP Łódź, Rząd Gubernialny, WP, Piotrków)
2. A file on the establishment of a charitable society [R], 1901–06.
(AP Łódź, Rząd Gubernialny, RO, Piotrków)
3. A file on Jews accused of possessing illegal literature and organizing illegal meetings, 1905–06.
(AP Łódź, GZŻ, Piotrków)
4. A request to register a charitable society [R], 1908–10.
(AP Łódź, Rząd Gubernialny, KP, Piotrków)

ZBARAŻ (woj. tarnopolskie) 1648–1939
Microfilms:
1. Documents concerning Chmielnicki's troops and the anti-Jewish riots in Zbaraż, 1648–49.
(NBANU, L'viv, Arch. Ossolińskich)
2. Excerpts from minutes of the tribunal (*sąd ławniczy*) in Zbaraż concerning the sale of houses, mills and land to Jews, the participation of the *kahal* in the election of town councillors and a decree by Prince Potocki permitting Jews to trade in the inns of the town, 1714–21.
(NBANU, L'viv, Zb. Czołowskiego)
3. Correspondence with the provincial authorities about taxes [G], 1820–41; tax registers [G], 1842–59; statutes of the Jewish community [G], 1882; correspondence with the police about pogroms in Russia and a list of Russian Jewish emigrants to America, 1882; correspondence with the *Starostwo* about complaints by community members regarding elections to the community council, 1905–06.
(TsDIAU, L'viv, Namiestnictwo Galicyjskie)
4. Accounts and financial reports of the community [R], 1914–16.
(DATO, Ternopil', Upravlenie nachal'nika Zbarazhskogo uezda)
5. Correspondence with the district authorities about community board elections, 1922–25; questionnaires containing names of community council members, 1928; reports about the participation of Orthodox Jews in elections to the *Sejm*, 1928; A register of political parties, lists of members and short descriptions of their activities, 1929; material on the registration of *Bnei Akiva*, including statutes, 1932–33; material on the election of the community council, including lists of community members, 1932–36; circulars, reports and correspondence concerning the activity of the OŻPP [P, Y], 1934; community budget, 1934–35; a list of community tax payers, 1934–37; a list of debtors, pensioners and widows, 1935–38; financial and economic reports of the community, 1936–39; a register of rabbis and *dayanim*, 1937–38.
(DATO, Ternopil', UW, Tarnopol)
6. Material about an increase in community taxes, 1938.
(DATO, Ternopil', Starostwo Powiatowe, Zbaraż)

ZBARAŻ, surroundings, 1883–1939
Microfilms:
1. A report about *chadorim* in the district, including a list of *chadorim*, 1883–1908.
(TsDIAU, L'viv, Namiestnictwo Galicyjskie)
2. A report about Jewish farmers in Nowe Sioło [R], 1914; correspondence with the governor of Tarnopol about Jewish migration to the district [R], 1915.
(DATO, Ternopil', Pomoshchnik nachal'nika Zbarazhskogo uezda v Novom Sele)
3. Reports on Jewish farmers [R], 1914.
(DATO, Ternopil', Upravlenie nachal'nika Zbarazhskogo uezda)
4. A description of the district and its economic development, 1928; correspondence concerning OŻPP in the district, 1933; correspondence about the *Bund*, 1938; reports about elections of Jewish community councils in the district, 1938–39.
(DATO, Ternopil', Starostwo Powiatowe, Zbaraż)
5. Statistics concerning Jewish inhabitants in the district, 1923–24; reports of the district authorities about community elections and statistics of Jewish communities in the district, 1928; reports by the district authorities about meetings organized by Zionist parties and elections of delegates to the Zionist Congress, 1929; a list of periodicals distributed in the district, 1934.
(DATO, Ternopil', UW, Tarnopol)
6. General characteristics and a plan of the area, 1933; reports about pre-election activities of political parties and associations in the district, 1935–36.
(DATO, Ternopil', Komenda Powiatowa PP, Zbaraż)

ZBORÓW (woj. tarnopolskie) 1661–1939
Photocopies:
Inventories, 1661–1779;
(NIAB Minsk, Arch. Radziwiłłów)
Microfilms:
1. Correspondence about *chadorim* and a list of *melamdim*, 1906–08.
(TsDIAU, L'viv, Namiestnictwo Galicyjskie)
2. Data on Jewish inhabitants of the town, 1923–24; records on the registration of the *Chevra Kadisha*, 1924, 1936–37; questionnaires with names of community council members, 1928; a list of political parties, names of members and short descriptions of their activities, 1929; a report on the activity of *Agudas Yisroel* and a list of members, 1929–39; reports about community elections and lists of community members, 1932–35; reports and correspondence about the OŻPP [P, Y], 1934; the community budget and a list of tax payers, 1935–37; applications for the rabbinate, 1936–37; a file on an examinationy in Polish for Jacob Schalit, a candidate for the rabbinate, 1937; a list of rabbis and *dayanim* and information on their education and background, 1937–38; correspondence regarding the salaries of rabbis, 1937–38; an inspection report on the community's economic and financial activity, 1939; reports on the elections and appointments of rabbis and *dayanim*, 1939.
(DATO, Ternopil', UW, Tarnopol)

ZBORÓW, surroundings, 1928–1934
Microfilms:
Reports of the district authorities about elections and statistics of Jewish communities in the district, 1928; reports by the district authorities about meetings organized by Zionist parties and elections of delegates to the Zionist Congress, 1929; a list of periodicals distributed in the district, 1934.

(DATO, Ternopil', UW, Tarnopol)

ZDUŃSKA WOLA (pow. Sieradz, woj. łódzkie) 1828–1912
Microfilms:
1. A file on Jewish settlement in the town, 1828–62.
(AGAD, Warszawa, Komisja Województwa Kaliskiego)
2. Files on illegal political activities by Jews [R], 1895, 1911–12; fines for wearing traditional Jewish dress [R], 1901; records on the expulsion of a Jew during the Russo–Japanese war [R], 1905–06.
(AP Łódź, Kancelaria Gubernatora Kaliskiego)
3. The appointment of Leizer Lipshitz from Lublin as rabbi [R], 1907–09; a complaint by a community member against the community budget [R], 1908; records on the purchase of land by the community [R], 1908.
(AP Łódź, Rząd Gubernialny, WA, Kalisz)
4. A police file on the arrest of a Jew [R], 1910.
(AP Łódź, GZŻ, Piotrków)

ZDUNY (pow. Krotoszyn, woj. poznańskie) 1840-1875
Originals:
Duplicate of a will [G], 1840–43; records of the community accounts [G], 1865–75; accounts of the Educational Society [G], 1865–75; a copy of the *memorbuch* [H], 19th cent.

ZEMBRÓW (pow. Sokołów, woj. lubelskie) 1566
Microfilms:
1. *Lustracja* of the region, 1566.
(AGAD, Warszawa, ASK)

ZEMBRZYCE (pow. Wadowice, woj. krakowskie) 1898
Originals:
School certificate, 1898.

ZERKÓW (pow. Jarocin, woj. poznańskie) 1849–1894
Originals:
Pinkas of a tailors' society [H], 1849–94; *pinkas* of the study-house [H], 1868–93; membership list of the burial society [G], 1888.

ZGIERZ (woj. łódzkie) 1825–1930
Microfilms:
1. Records concerning the Jewish community, 1825–64.
(AP Łódź, Anterioria Rządu Gubernialnego, Piotrków)
2. A file on the construction of a factory by a Jew [R], 1878; files on the construction and *arenda* of a *mikve* [R], 1879–80. 1893–1902; the enlarging of the cemetery [R], 1884–85; ratification of the community elections [R], 1893–94, 1900–10; community accounts [R], 1899–1913; a file on election of a cantor [R], 1900–01; renovation of the synagogue and of the rabbi's apartment [R], 1900–06; donations for the synagogue [R], 1907.
(AP Łódź, Pząnd Gubernialny, WA, Piotrków)
3. Files and correspondence about Jewish schools [P, R], 1885–1913.
(AP Łódź, Dyrekcja Szkolna, Łódź)
4. Fines for evading conscription [R], 1890–1902.

(AP Łódź, Rząd Gubernialny, WP, Piotrków)

5. Records concerning the establishment and registration of charitable and professional societies [R], 1899–1902.

(AP Łódź, Rząd Gubernialny, RO, Piotrków)

6. A file on demonstrations with the participation of students from the commercial school [R], 1905; records on the possession and distribution of illegal literature, files on Jews suspected of illegal political activity [R], 1905–06.

(AP Łódź, GZŻ, Piotrków)

7. The private papers of Lejzer Sirkis, representative of *Agudas Yisroel* in the Sejm and the municipality [P, Y], 1917–30.

(Private collection)

8. Records on the expulsion of Jews [R], 1908.

(AP Łódź, Kancelaria Gubernatora Kaliskiego)

9. Records concerning the establishment and registration of cultural, charitable and professional societies: *Hazamir*, *Yagdil Tora* etc. [R], 1909–13.

(AP Łódź, Rząd Gubernialny, KP, Piotrków)

10. Minutes of community meetings [G, H, Y], 1915–30.

(Private collection)

ZIELÓW (pow. Łask, woj. łódzkie) 1878–1913

Microfilms:

1. Files on the establishment of the Jewish community [R], 1878–79, 1904–06; ratification of community elections [R], 1910–13; community budget [R], 1907–10.

(AP Łódz, Rząd Gubernialny, WA, Piotrków)

2. Fines for evading conscription [R], 1893–94.

(AP Łódz, Rząd Gubernialny, WP, Piotrków)

ZŁOCZÓW (woj. tarnopolskie) 1661–1939

Originals:

An invitation of a Jewish sport club, 1926.

Photocopies:

Inventories, 1661–1724; tax register, 1745.

(NIAB, Minsk, Arch. Radziwiłłów)

Microfilms:

1. Letters concerning robbery and assault on a Jew, 1694.

(TsDIAU, L'viv, Kolektsiia lystiv…)

2. Promissory notes given by the *kahal* of Złoczów to a Dominican monastery in Żółkiew [L], 1738, 1771; a letter by the secretary of the Piarist Order, concerning a promissory note given by the *kahal* [H, L, P], 1782.

(TsDIAU, L'viv, Kolektsiia dokumentiv pro katolyts'ki monastyri…)

3. Copies of decrees by Prince M. K. Radziwiłł regarding economic and legal matters, *arenda* contracts with Jews, 1746–47.

(AGAD, Warszawa, Arch. Radziwiłłów)

4. *Arenda* contract with a Jew for a brewery in Strykowce, 1785–87, 1799.

(TsDIAU, L'viv, Arch. Lanckorońskich)

5. Correspondence with the district authorities about assistance for Jews willing to settle in new areas, including a list of names [G], 1789; complaints by Jews against restrictions of residence [G], 1819–20; correspondence regarding litigation between Menashe Rapp of Zborów and the Jewish community in Złoczów [G], 1849–69; correspondence with the district authorities about citation of citizenship in civil registers, 1891–92; files on ritual slaughter houses, 1894–97; correspondence between the community, the district authorities and the Ministry of Religions about problems regarding *shechita*, including complaints by *Machzikei Hadas* [G, P], 1897–1900; correspondence about the statutes [G, P], 1897–1906; correspondence about the *Ahavas Zion* society, 1899–1910; correspondence about the community elections [G, P], 1901–04; statutes of a tailors' society [G, P, Y], 1901–06; correspondence between the community, the district authorities and the Ministry of Religions about qualifications of candidates for rabbinical positions [G, P], 1904–06; correspondence about the *Kaufmannischen Verein - Osei Tov* and *Dorshei Tov* societies [G, P], 1908.
(TsDIAU, L'viv, Namiestnictwo Galicyjskie)
6. Circular letters for the *kahal*, 1809–15; a register of Jewish homeowners required to pay taxes for quartering Russian soldiers [G, P], 1812–14; marriage permits for Jews [G, P], 1812–14; inventory of the town, containing a list of Jewish inhabitants, 1816; answers to a questionnaire regarding the Jews, 1922.
(NBANU, L'viv, Zb. Czołowskiego)
7. Reports about robberies and assaults on Jews by soldiers and inhabitants of the town, 1918–19; reports and correspondence about the confiscation of a book, "Die Zukunft des juedischen Volkes" [G, P], 1919–20.
(DATO, Ternopil', Dyrekcja Policji, Lwów)
8. Material on the registration and activities of *Ezras Yisroel* and *Agudas Yisroel*, including lists of board members [G, P], 1918–25, 1936–37; reports concerning pre-election meetings, 1924–27; reports, requests and correspondence on the ratification of the statutes and the elections of *Beis Strzeliska* (1906), 1925; records regarding the statutes and subsequent liquidation of the *Towarzystwo Szkoły Żydowskiej*, 1925, 1936–37; police reports about the foundation of the *Jugendverein Zukunft* and *Poalei Zion*, 1926; questionnaires containing names of community board members, 1928; reports about the participation of Orthodox Jews in elections to the *Sejm* and Senate, 1928; records on the registration of *Histadrut Hanoar Hatziyoni*, 1928–34; a list of political parties, their memberships and information about their activities, 1929; records about the foundation of the *Gmilus Chesed* society, 1929; reports and correspondence concerning the foundation and elections of *Ahavas Zion*, including statutes and lists of members, 1929–39; records on the foundation and activity of the *"Herzliyah"* Zionist club, including a list of members, 1931–35; reports and correspondence about registering the *Chevra Kadisha*, 1932–33; records concerning the registration of *Toras Chayim*, including a list of founding members, 1934; reports and correspondence about OŻPP [P, Y], 1934; a list of community tax payers, minutes and correspondence regarding financial and economic activities of the Jewish community [H, P], 1934–39; records about elections of rabbis, 1935–39; community budgets, 1936–37, 1939; records about the registration of a butchers' association, *Samopomoc*, including a list of founding members, 1936–37; records about the liquidation of: *Poalei Zion* and the *Safa Berura* association, 1936–37; correspondence about revenues from ritual slaughter of poultry, 1937; reports by the district authorities about anti-Jewish incidents and a Jewish protest strike, 1937; names and personal information about rabbis and *dayanim*, 1937–38.
(DATO, Ternopil', UW, Tarnopol)

ZŁOCZÓW, surroundings, 1793–1938
Microfilms:

1. Correspondence with the provincial authorities about taxes, financial matters of Jewish communities, elections of rabbis, community board elections, and complaints against results of the elections [G, P], 1793–95, 1819–41; tables of taxes [G], 1842–59; files concerning ratification of statutes of Jewish communities, 1846–96; reports about *chadorim* in the district and a list of them, 1877–1908; reports and correspondence about reorganization of the Jewish communities in the district, 1890.
(TsDIAU, L'viv, Namiestnictwo Galicyjskie)
2. Reports about taxes paid by Jews, 1809–15.
(NBANU, L'viv, Zb. Czołowskiego)
3. Reports about organization of community board elections and composition of the board, 1928; a list of periodicals distributed in the district, 1934; reports and correspondence concerning financial inspections of various Jewish communities, 1935–38.
(DATO, Ternopil', UW, Tarnopol)

ZŁOTNIKI (pow. Podhajce, woj. tarnopolskie) 1928–1938
Microfilms:
Questionnaires containing names of community council members, 1928; records concerning the community elections and finances, including lists of community members and tax payers, 1932–37; names and personal information about rabbis and *dayanim*, 1937–38.
(DATO, Ternopil', UW, Tarnopol)

ZŁOTY POTOK (pow. Częstochowa, woj. kieleckie) 1898
Microfilms:
Fines for evading conscription [R], 1898.
(AP Łódź, Rząd Gubernialny, WP, Piotrków)

ZWOLEŃ (pow. Kozienice, woj. kieleckie) 1765
Microfilms:
Confirmation by King Stanisław August of rights and charters given to the Jews of Zwoleń by Kings Michał Korybut, Jan III Sobieski and August III [L, P], 1765.
(AGAD, Warszawa, Księgi Kanclerskie)

ŻABIE (pow. Kosów, woj. stanisławowskie) 1893–1938
Photocopies:
Records concerning registration of the Zionist Organization, 1927–38.
(DALO, L'viv, Lwowskie Starostwo Miejskie)
Microfilms:
Records concerning the *Mizrachi, Achva* and other Jewish associations [G, P], 1893, 1920–37; records of Jewish agricultural associations, 1933–38.
(DAIFO, Ivano-Frankivs'k, UW, Stanisławów)

ŻABNO (pow. Dąbrowa, woj. krakowskie) 1877–1908
Microfilms:
Correspondence with the authorities about *chadorim* and names of teachers, 1877–1908.
(TsDIAU, L'viv, Namiestnictwo Galicyjskie)

ŻARKI (pow. Zawiercie, woj. kieleckie) 1780–1914
Microfilms:
1. Extracts from official court records concerning Jews, 1780–82.

(AP Kraków, IT)

2. Records on the community, 1849–66.

(AP Łódź, Anterioria Rządu Gubernialnego, Piotrków)

3. Reports and correspondence about the appointment of rabbis, 1853–56.

(AGAD, Warszawa, CWW)

4. Fines for evading conscription [R], 1891–1902.

(AP Łódź, Rząd Gubernialny, WP, Piotrków)

5. Community accounts [P, R], 1899–1908; ratification of community elections [R], 1900–08; records concerning the enlargement of the cemetery [R], 1901–06; the *arenda* of the mikve [R], 1901–14; the liquidation of community debts [R], 1902–04; a request to open a kerosene store [R], 1907; the appointment of a new rabbi [R], 1908.

(AP Łódź, Rzand Gubernialny, WA, Piotrków)

ŻARNOWIEC (pow. Olkusz, woj. kieleckie) 1790–1868
Microfilms:

1. Reply of the Military Commission to the memorandum of a Jew concerning compulsory payments, 1790; an investigation in the burglary of a Jew's house, 1791.

(AP Kraków, IT)

2. Exemption of the *kahal* from the recruitment tax due to damages during a fire, 1818.

(AGAD, Warszawa, KRzPiS)

3. Birth, marriage and death records (fragmentary) [P, R], 1826–68.

(AP Kraków)

4. Reports and correspondence about appointment of rabbis, 1853–56.

(AGAD, Warszawa, CWW)

ŻELECHÓW (pow. Garwolin, woj. lubelskie) 1755–1860
Microfilms:

1. Agreements and contracts with Jews, 1755–60.

(AP Wrocław, Ossolineum)

2. Reports and correspondence concerning appointments of rabbis, their educations and salaries and a list of members of the commission examining candidates for positions of rabbi or *dayan*, 1856–64.

(AGAD, Warszawa, CWW)

3. Files concerning community accounts and distribution of taxes among the inhabitants, 1860.

(AP Lublin, Rząd Gubernialny, Lublin)

ŻELECHÓW WIELKI (pow. Kamionka Strumiłowa, woj. tarnopolskie) 1934–1935
Microfilms:

Reports on the establishment of a branch of *Chaklaim Zionim*, including lists of board members, 1934–35.

(DATO, Ternopil', UW, Tarnopol)

ŻERNICA NIŻNA (pow. Lesko, woj. lwowskie) 1935–1938
Originals:

3 letters from a local family to relatives in the United States [P, Y], 1935–38.

ŻMIGRÓD (pow. Jasło, woj. krakowskie) 1685–1818
Photocopies:

Inventories estates, 1685.

(NIAB, Minsk, Arch. Radziwiłłów)

Microfilms:
1. Consent for the appointment of a rabbi [L, P], 1753.
(AGAD, Warszawa, Arch. Radziwiłłów)
2. A request by Jews of Gorlice to separate their community from that of Żmigród and the response of the authorities [G, H, L, P], 18th cent.
(AP Kraków, Teki Schneidra)
3. Inventory of the town [L, P], 1776.
(LNBANU, Zb. Czołowskiego)

ŻMIGRÓD NOWY (pow. Jasło, woj. krakowskie) 1846–1896
Microfilms:
Files on ratification of community statutes, 1846–96.
(TsDIAU, L'viv, Namiestnictwo Galicyjskie)

ŻOŁYNIA (pow. Łańcut, woj. lwowskie) 1933–1939
Microfilms:
Correspondence about various community matters, among them the budget, including a list of taxpayers, 1933–39.
(DALO, L'viv, UW, Lwów)

ŻORY (pow. Rybnik, woj. śląskie) 1812–1861
Originals:
Death register [G], 1812–36; *pinkas* of the *Bikur Cholim* society [H], 1829–41; records on the sale and mortgage of community properties [G], 1845–47; records on the tax on kosher meat and other taxes [G], 1846–50; files on Jewish education [G], 1859–61.

ŻÓŁKIEW (woj. lwowskie) 1613–1938
Original:
Copy of the burial society *pinkas* (fragmentary) [H], 1930s.
Microfilms:
1. Extracts from municipal records concerning Jews [L], 1613–71; regulations of the butchers' guild (incl. references to Jewish butchers), 1636.
(AGAD, Warszawa, Zb. Czołowskiego)
2. A document issued by King Jan Sobieski concerning the rights of Jews, 1678; copies of decrees by Prince M. K. Radziwiłł and *arenda* contract with Jews [H, L, P], 1746–53; confirmation of an agreement between the *kahals* in Brody and Żółkiew [L, P], 1752.
(AGAD, Warszawa, Arch. Radziwiłłów)
3 Minutes of legal proceedings in litigation between M. Lejbowicz, a Jew from Żółkiew, and U. Krasicka from Siczyn, accused of raping Lejbowicz's child and sending him to a monastery, including a letter from King Jan III Sobieski, requesting the return of the child to Lejbowicz, 1688–1691.
(AP Lublin, Arch. Woronieckich z Huszlewa)
4. Letters to Princess E. Sieniawska regarding Żółkiew, 1707–09, 1716–22.
(Bibl. Czartoryskich, Kraków)
5. Declarations of merchants about taxes from trade in Radziwiłł estates, 1781–86; correspondence with the district authorities about *propinacja* and a list of holders of *propinacja* rights, 1844–1909; a list of families, citing addresses and professions of heads of families, 1899; copies of birth, marriage and death records, 1901–33; a list of candidates for community elections, 1933; a list of tax payers, n.d.

(DALO, L'viv, Magistrat, Żółkiew)

6. A request to open a printing house [G], 1803; complaints by Jews against restrictions on places of residence [G], 1819–22, 1829–35; correspondence and tax tables [G], 1819–59; correspondence with the authorities about the rabbinate, statutes, taxes, community elections and complaints against election results [G, P], 1819–23, 1897–1905; correspondence about *chadorim* and a list of *melamdim* in the area, 1874–1908.

(TsDIAU, L'viv, Namiestnictwo Galicyjskie)

7. Orders, reports and correspondence about closing *chadorim* [G, P], 1868–74; reports on teaching Jewish religion in elementary schools [G, P], 1882–89.

(TsDIAU, L'viv, Krajowa Rada Szkolna)

8. Correspondence regarding various incidents involving Jews, Ruthenians and Poles [G, P], 1873.

(TsDIAU, L'viv, Prokuratura, Lwów)

9. Statutes of the Jewish community, 1897.

(TsDIAU, L'viv, Gmina Żydowska, Lwów)

10. Lists of voters to city council by neighbourhoods and professions, 1905–33; correspondence about celebrations honoring the inauguration of the Hebrew University in Jerusalem, 1924–25; correspondence about the *Kultur Liga*, 1926; correspondence about the registration of the local branch of *Małopolski Związek Pszczelarski*, including a list of members, 1928; documents concerning community elections, budget and election of a rabbi, 1928–36; report and complaints against community council elections, 1935–36; reports containing the names of community council members, rabbis and *dayanim*, 1937.

(DALO, L'viv, UW, Lwów)

11. Records about the registration of associations among them *Tarbut*, 1922–26, *Agudas Achim*, 1932–33, *Machzikei Hadas*, 1934, *Poalei Agudas Yisroel* including a list of board members, 1937–38.

(DALO, L'viv, Magistrat, Lwów)

ŻÓŁKIEWKA (pow. Krasnystaw, woj. lubelskie) 1775–1869
Microfilms:
1. Accusations by the *kahal* of Żółkiewka against the *kahal* in Turobin for conducting a *lustracja* in the former community's territory, 1775; a receipt to the *kahal* for money paid to the General Education Commission, 1785.

(AP Lublin, Księgi Grodzkie Krasnostawskie)

2. A report by the district administrator about the return to Judaism of a soldier who completed his military service [R], 1869.

(AP Lublin, Rząd Gubernialny, Lublin)

ŻUCHOWICZE (pow. Stołpce, woj. nowogródzkie) 1696–1711
Microfilms:
Inventory of the Żuchowicze *klucz*, 1696–1711.

(Bibl. Czartoryskich, Kraków)

ŻUKÓW (pow. Równe, woj. wołyńskie) 1696–1711
Microfilms:
Inventory of the Żuków estate 1696–1711.

(Bibl. Czartoryskich, Kraków)

ŻURAKI (pow. Nadwórna, woj. stanisławowskie) 1936–1937
Microfilms:

Reports and correspondence concerning anti-Jewish actions by Ukrainian nationalists, 1936–37.
(DAIFO, Ivano-Frankivs'k, Komenda Powiatowa PP, Stanisławów)

ŻURAWNO (pow. Żydaczów, woj. stanisławowskie) 1853–1939
Microfilms:
1. Correspondence with the district authorities about inns on land belonging to Christians [G], 1853; correspondence about *chadorim* and a list of *melamdim*, 1877–1908; correspondence with the district authorities about the election of a rabbi, 1888–1908; correspondence regarding communal taxes, statutes and elections [G, P], 1895–98; correspondence with *Juedische Nationalverein in Oesterreich* concerning persecution of Jews, including descriptions of several cases [G, P], 1915.
(TsDIAU, L'viv, Namiestnictwo Galicyjskie)
2. Statutes, minutes and correspondence about Jewish associations and charitable societies, 1921–38; a list of Jewish civil registers, 1923–24; a file on changes in the statutes and community elections, 1923–25; files on the election of a rabbi, 1925–39; correspondence about inspection of Jewish communities, 1926–35; files on ratification of statutes and liquidation of *Gmilus* Ch*esed* [G, P], 1904, 1912–13, 1928–30; lists of community council members, 1930–37; files on registration, activity and subsequent liquidation of *Hashomer Hatzair* and the *Juedischer Kulturverein-J. L. Perec*, including lists of board members, 1931–35; reports and correspondence concerning elections to the community council; reports about the activities of: *OŻPP, Histadrut Hanoar Haivri, Hashomer Hatzair* and *Tsofe*, 1933; correspondence about elections and appointments of rabbis and *dayanim*, 1934–37; a file on ratification of the budget and a list of taxpayers, 1938.
(DAIFO, Ivano-Frankivs'k, UW, Stanisławów)
3. Reports and correspondence on the legalization of *chadorim* and other Jewish religious and secular schools, including a list of *chadorim* and names of teachers, 1934–36.
(DAIFO, Ivano-Frankivs'k, Inspektorat Szkolny, Stanisławów)

ŻYDACZÓW (woj. stanisławowskie) 1701–1955
Photocopies:
Reports about the activity of the Jewish community [R], 1949, 1951, 1955;
(DALO, L'viv, Drogobyts'kyi obkom…)
Microfilms:
1. Excerpts from official court records concerning Jews, 1701–66.
(AP Wrocław, Ossolineum)
2. Inventory of a Jew's house, 1768.
(TsDIAU, L'viv, Arch. Lanckorońskich)
3. Correspondence with the district authorities regarding *chadorim,* and a list of *melamdim*, 1877–1908; correspondence about the community statutes, 1898–1906; correspondence with the *Juedische Nationalverein in Oesterreich* concerning persecutions of Jews and descriptions of several cases [G, P], 1915.
(TsDIAU, L'viv, Namiestnictwo Galicyjskie)
4. Records concerning the registration of the *Merkaz Ruchani*, 1920–27; statutes, minutes and correspondence about Zionist associations, 1921–30; lists of *Yad Charutzim* board members, 1925, 1933–37; file on *Gmilus Chesed*, 1922–30; reports and correspondence concerning registration of Jewish charitable associations aiding children and youth, 1923–28; records regarding ratification of the statutes and the registration of *Żydowski Dom Ludowy, "Beth Am"*, including a list of founding members, 1925–30; reports about collecting funds for Jews in Palestine, 1926; reports about the activity of Revisionist Zionists,

1927; reports about the activity of *Hashomer Hatzair* and other Jewish youth organizations, 1929–30; results of the second general census, 1931; files on registration, activity and subsequent liquidation of *Hashomer Hatzair* and the *Juedischer Kulturverein-Y. L. Peretz,* including board lists, 1931–35; reports and correspondence about elections to the community council, 1932–36; reports about the activities of: *OŻPP, Histadrut Hanoar Haivri, Hashomer Hatzair* and *Cofe,* 1933; orders, reports and correspondence concerning the activity of *Hitachdut Poalei Zion* and meetings organized by other Zionist associations, 1935; statistical data on the population, 1938.
(DAIFO, Ivano-Frankivs'k, UW, Stanisławów)
5. Monthly reports of the district headquarters about the activities of political parties and associations, 1930–32; reports concerning the activities of Zionist associations, 1935–36; reports and correspondence concerning anti-Jewish actions by Ukrainian nationalists, 1936–37.
(DAIFO, Ivano-Frankivs'k, Komenda Wojewódzka PP, Stanisławów)

ŻYDACZÓW, surroundings, 1922–1936
Microfilms:
1. Descriptions of political and social conditions in the district, 1935.
(DAIFO, Ivano-Frankivs'k, Komenda Wojewódzka PP, Stanisławów)
2. A register of associations in the district [P, U], 1922–25; data on the Jewish population in the district, 1923–24; a statistical description of the district, 1935; information about the distribution of anti-Jewish brochures, 1936.
(DAIFO, Ivano-Frankivs'k, UW, Stanisławów)

ŻYRARDÓW (pow. Błonie, woj. warszawskie) 1914–1916
Microfilms:
Correspondence about a request by the Jews of Żyrardów to free a local surgeon's assistant from the military front [R], 1914–16.
(RGVIA, Moscow, Kantseliariia glavnogo nachal'nika snabzheniia…)

ŻYWIEC (woj. krakowskie) 1871–1898
Microfilms:
1. Reports about anti-Jewish incidents, 1871.
(TsDIAU, L'viv, Namiestnictwo Galicyjskie)
2. Proclamations, reports and correspondence about *chadorim* and Jewish private schools [G, P], 1878–81; correspondence with the district authorities about citation of citizenship in civil registers, 1891–92; correspondence with *Ahavas Zion* about emigration to Palestine, 1898.
(TsDIAU, L'viv, Krajowa Rada Szkolna)

Breinigsville, PA USA
19 November 2010
249583BV00004B/7/A